Bohdan Lewicki was born in 1921 and earned his D.Sc. in 1951. From 1956 to 1960, he was Professor of Building Construction at the Silesian Polytechnic. In 1960 he was appointed Head of the Concrete Structures and Industrialized Building Section of the Institute of Building Research, and Secretary to the Civil Engineering Committee of the Polish Academy of Sciences.

For the past fifteen years Professor Lewicki has been dealing with the problems of industrialized building. This means he has been involved in this field since the beginning of this branch of science in Poland. He has made a number of visits abroad to study building construction of large size precast elements. He takes an active part in the work of several international organizations, including the CIB. He developed an original method for calculating factors related to loadbearing walls as well as a new approach to statistical analysis for buildings under action of horizontal loads.

Professor Lewicki is presently Chairman of the Polish Standards Committee in the field of industrialized building.

BUILDING WITH LARGE PREFABRICATES

Original title

Budynki mieszkalne z prefabrykatów wielkowymiarowych
Wydawnictwo "ARKADY", Warszawa 1964
© 1966 by Arkady

Translated by
EXPRESS TRANSLATION SERVICE, LONDON

BUILDING WITH LARGE PREFABRICATES

by

BOHDAN LEWICKI

Institute for Building Research, Warsaw

ELSEVIER PUBLISHING COMPANY
AMSTERDAM — LONDON — NEW YORK
1966

ELSEVIER PUBLISHING COMPANY
335, JAN VAN GALENSTRAAT, P. O. BOX 211, AMSTERDAM

AMERICAN ELSEVIER PUBLISHING COMPANY, INC.
52, VANDERBILT AVENUE, NEW YORK, N. Y. 10017

ELSEVIER PUBLISHING COMPANY LIMITED
RIPPLESIDE COMMERCIAL ESTATE, BARKING, ESSEX

CONTENTS

7

Chapter 1

PRINCIPAL IDEAS AND DEFINITIONS

1.1. INDUSTRIALISED BUILDING AND LARGE UNIT CONSTRUCTION

The use of large prefabricated units is the basis of an industrialised building industry. The essential features of industrialised building are the mechanisation of labour, rhythm of production — as evinced by continuity and evenness of output, and mass production. The division of labour into separate, distinct phases facilitates the demarcation of labour and trade specialisation.

Industrialisation results in a smaller labour outlay, more efficient use of materials, and a marked shortening of the constructional cycle. Moreover, it makes the building industry much less seasonal.

The ratio of work carried out in the factory to the total constructional work is a measure of the level of industrialisation reached.

The respective levels of industrialisation reached by various building methods are shown in Fig. 1.1.1.

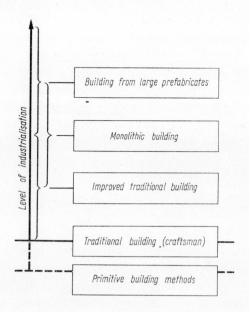

Fig. 1.1.1. The ladder of industrialisation in the building industry

The *industrialised building* is said to be the antonym of the *traditional building*.

The term "traditional building" describes the methods prevailing in Poland around 1950. These were characterised by a prolonged cycle of operations with a large outlay of manual labour, as a rule upwards of 8 hours for every cubic metre of the building. All basic operations were carried out on the building site, resulting in a pronouncedly seasonal industry.

The so-called "improved traditional building" represents a first step in the direction of industrialisation. The masonry is still hand-laid, but many elements of the building, such as lintels, floor and roof slabs, stair flights and landings, are made away from the site in the form of prefabricates and erected as the masonry work progresses. The use of prefabricates, especially those which are mass-produced, shortens construction time and normally introduces some mechanisation of labour. This also applies to finishes, although the volume of the finishing work remains undiminished. There is still no rhythm in construction, but there is a noticeable drop in the volume of manual labour, compared with the traditional craftsman methods.

In skeleton structures at this stage of industrialisation, prefabricated floor, roof and stair components are used and some reinforcement may be assembled into cages away from the site. Standardisation and the repeated use of formwork is also aimed at (climbing, shuttering).

Monolithic structures are those in which the masonry walls are replaced by in-situ concrete, multiple use of formwork being easily achieved. The floors may be laid in-situ or precast. Nearly all operations can be partly mechanised, especially on larger housing estates.

In technical literature, three distinct steps are sometimes quoted as being the successive rungs in the ladder of progress, namely:

(1) the use of large prefabricated floor, roof and stair components with the traditional loadbearing masonry walls;

(2) the masonry walls are replaced by prefabricated wall blocks or panels suitably finished or textured on the external faces; large prefabricated floor units; all internal finishes, including plastering, are carried out by traditional methods;

(3) erection of buildings with the prefabricates fully finished on both faces; the work outstanding after erection being limited to the laying of floor finishes and painting.

It is evident that this gradation is based on the industrialisation only of those activities which are directly concerned with the erection of the building and neglects progress in the manufacture of the prefabricates. Therefore, the real level of industrialisation of a particular building may differ greatly from the position it occupies in our "ladder of progress". For example, if a prefabricated wall panel is given a coat of plaster by the traditional manual method in the factory, then the level of industrialisation remains very low, even though the panel is erected completely finished on both sides. Conversely, industrialisation may be well advanced in a build-

10

ing in which the inner panels of a two-leaf wall (section 7.1) are erected by hand, together with the partitions, in the second phase of construction.

Thus, real technological progress is achieved only when industrialisation embraces the whole process of construction, comprising both the manufacture of the components and their erection.

The choice of a level of industrialisation best suited to the type and size of the project and to the actual ratio of the factory costs to the cost of labour, is the basic consideration in building economics.

1.2. PREFABRICATION AND PREFABRICATES

Prefabrication means the production away from the building site of components traditionally constructed on the site. The components thus prepared are known as prefabricates.

The factory-made units are classified as:
— small prefabricates, when their plan areas do not exceed 2 m², and
— large prefabricates, with plan areas over 2 m².

Prefabricates are also grouped into:
— light, not exceeding 30 kg in weight and meant to be erected by one man,
— medium weight, up to 500 kg, to be handled with simple mechanical equipment,
— heavy, upwards of 500 kg, the erection of which requires the use of heavy handling plant.

Depending on the shape of the prefabricates they are known as blocks, panels, frames, etc. There is no need to state a precise definition, but for guidance:

"blocks" are wall units with the proportions shown in Fig. 1.2.1a, as a rule very stable during erection (section 4.1.3),

"panels" — wall or slab units as in Fig. 1.2.1b,

"beams and columns" — where the cross-sectional area is very small compared with the length of the unit (Fig. 1.2.1c).

The division of the wall units into blocks and panels is not very distinct and is not subject to universal agreement. In some systems the term "panel" is applied only to "room-sized" units, all smaller ones being referred to as blocks. In this second group, however, there is a marked difference between construction using storey-height units and construction using smaller-sized units. For this reason, storey-height blocks are sometimes known as panel-blocks.

From the points of view of erection technique (temporary shoring) and design, panel-block walls bear a closer resemblance to the large-panel types of walls.

The terminology accepted by the International Council for Building (C.I.B.) defines all walls made of storey-height prefabricates as "panel-walls", limiting the term "block-walls" to those made of units less than one storey high.

The above division results from the influence of the horizontal joints on the strength of the wall. The presence of these joints causes the block-wall to be weaker than

11

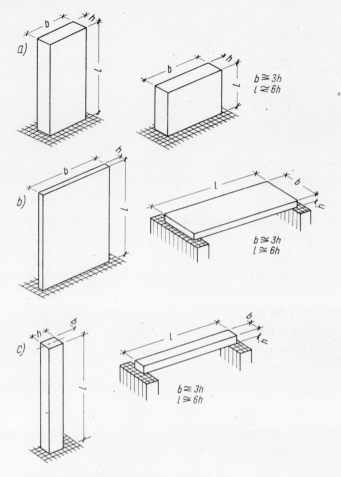

Fig. 1.2.1. Flat prefabricates:
(a) block, (b) panel, (c) post or beam

a similar panel-wall, given identical dimensions and concrete mix (section 7.5.4).

Blocks, panels and also beams and columns are all used to construct the mono-planar members of the building (walls and slabs). They are therefore known as plane prefabricates.

As distinct from the plane prefabricates, components forming parts of space-enclosing members in two or more planes are called three-dimensional or space prefabricates. In all such units one can distinguish components situated in several planes.

The simplest example of a space prefabricate is shown in Fig. 1.2.2a. This consists of two blocks (or panels), forming a monolithic unit. Tray panels or hollow slabs, however, are not space units, since, because of their role in the structure, they may be classified as plane prefabricates.

12

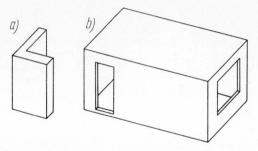

Fig. 1.2.2. Space prefabricates:
(a) two blocks forming a monolithic unit, (b) box prefabricate

In a group of their own are box units (Fig. 1.2.2b). These are large space prefabricates enclosing whole rooms or even suites of rooms.

In projects using box prefabricates the level of industrialisation can be extremely high, the work on site being reduced to the assembly of completely decorated and fitted units and to the connecting of services.

Prefabricates may be classified as homogeneous or composite, according to the number of different materials used in their fabrication.

Homogeneous units, consisting of only one material, may be solid, hollow, ribbed, etc. (Fig. 1.2.3).

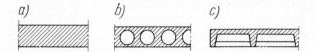

Fig. 1.2.3. Homogeneous prefabricates:
(a) solid cross-section, (b) hollow or cored unit, (c) ribbed panel

Composite prefabricates usually take the form of sandwich units (Fig. 1.2.4). The individual layers of these units may again take various forms of construction.

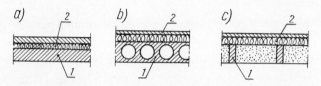

Fig. 1.2.4. Composite prefabricates:
(a) with solid cross-section, (b) cored, (c) ribbed
(1) structural layer, (2) non-structural layers (e.g. insulation, finishing layer)

13

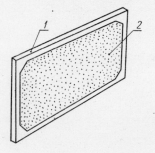

Fig. 1.2.5. Skeletal prefabricate:
(*1*) framework, (*2*) filler

Another type of composite prefabricate, in which one material forms a framework filled with another, usually lighter or weaker material, is shown in Fig. 1.2.5.

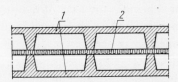

Fig. 1.2.6. A typical compound prefabricate:
(*1*) ribbed panels, (*2*) insulating layer

Some composite units are built-up of separately prepared units which may be of the same or of different materials (Fig. 1.2.6).

Chapter 2

USE OF PREFABRICATES IN THE CONSTRUCTION OF HOUSES

2.1. THE STRUCTURE OF BUILDINGS

In essence, a building is made up of foundations, structural walls (or frames) and a set of floors. The structure is designed to distribute loads and to resist external forces.

Structural walls are those which in addition to their own weight, carry or distribute external loads, vertical or horizontal, and the loads from other elements of the structure.

Depending on their function, structural walls may be:
— loadbearing walls — the main task of which is to distribute vertical loading from slabs and from the upper storey walls;
— non-loadbearing walls, which do not support floors but only the dead weight of the walls above;
— stiffening walls, whose function is to provide three-dimensional stiffness.

The term "structural" is often wrongly thought to be synonymous with "loadbearing" when applied to walls. Although every loadbearing wall is structural, not all structural walls are loadbearing.

Some walls are non-structural. Such are partition walls, which transfer their own weight only (one storey-height), and external panel walls, which also resist direct wind pressure.

In addition to the main structure, there also exist separate components connected with the former by expansion joints, e.g. chimney stacks or covered ways between buildings.

Non-structural walls are provided to create barriers (visual, thermal or acoustic). It is normally inadvisable to attach these walls rigidly to the structure, since they are then protected from stresses induced by the deformation of the latter.

Some walls, which are here referred to as supported walls, do not possess foundations of their own, but are either carried by slabs or beams, or are directly attached to the loadbearing walls. The supported walls can form an integral part of the structure (stiffening walls), or remain non-structural, depending on their stiffness and the method of their attachment to the main structural components.

Depending on the structural system of load distribution, prefabricated buildings fall into the following general groups:

— buildings with loadbearing walls of large blocks or panels;
— buildings based on a system of skeleton construction;
— buildings formed from prefabricated box units.

The above classification is somewhat complicated by the fact that external walls are often constructed from prefabricates other than those used for the internal structure. Thus, in a skeleton structure the outside walls may consist of panels or blocks.

The type of a prefabricated building is, however, best described by the arrangement of the loadbearing structural units. Depending on the orientation of the main beams or loadbearing walls relative to the long axis of the building, we have:
— long-wall system, where the main beams or loadbearing walls are placed longitudinally, or parallel, to the main axis of the building (Fig. 2.1.1a);

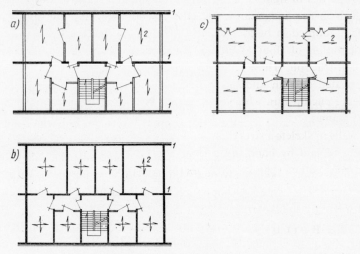

Fig. 2.1.1. Arrangement of loadbearing walls in buildings:
(a) long-wall system, (b) two-way span system, (c) cross-wall system
(1) loadbearing walls, (2) direction of floor span

— cross-wall system, where the main beams or loadbearing walls run at right angles to the long axis of the building (Fig. 2.1.1c);
— ring or two-way span system, where the supporting members run both longitudinally and transversely (Fig. 2.1.1b).

In buildings with the ring system of support, the floors are normally supported on all four edges, and span two directions. In skeleton constructions based on this system the slab units may rest directly on columns, completely eliminating beams as structural components.

The long-wall system applied to a building with large prefabricates has much in common with traditional brickwork techniques. Longitudinal external walls,

16

which carry floor loads, must possess not only suitable thermal properties, but also sufficient loadbearing capacity. Thus the structural requirements influence the ratio of the widths of windows to the widths of the load-carrying bands.

In buildings based on the ring system only part of the floor load is carried by the outside walls.

In the cross-wall system the external long walls do not distribute floor loads. If these walls are required to carry their own weight down to the foundations, the elevational treatment will not differ much from that of a long-wall building. However, when normal non-structural facade walls are supported at each level, the width of windows is unrestricted.

In cross-wall buildings there is a clear distinction between the structural and the thermal insulation functions of walls, which permits the full utilisation of the structural properties of ordinary concrete in the internal loadbearing walls, and of the thermal properties of light concrete in the outside walls. Because of this, and of the ease with which new insulating materials can be introduced, the cross-wall system is very often adopted in buildings with prefabricated loadbearing wall components.

The orientation of floor slabs, i.e. the structural system, is less significant in skeleton construction. These may be classified as:
— prefabricated column and beam structures,
— beamless structures, in which floor panels bear directly on columns, and
— precast frames.

All the walls in skeleton structures may consist of large prefabricated units, or may alternatively be laid by hand using smaller precast units. It may be advantageous to use materials other than concrete in the construction of light external walls in skeleton structures.

2.2. Buildings with loadbearing walls

2.2.1. The Long-Wall System

The long-wall system of construction is typical of the "classic" large-block buildings, which were the first large precast-component buildings to be erected in Poland. A diagrammatic view of such a building is shown in Fig. 2.2.1.

The special pier blocks between windows, which carry loads from lintels and from the walls above, are characteristic here. The horizontal sill blocks are not loaded. When the crane used in erection is of small capacity, the pier consists of two or three smaller blocks laid one upon the other.

In some designs, the space between the piers is filled by a prefabricated unit consisting of a r.c. window frame complete with window.

The internal wall blocks are normally of full storey height, subject to the limitations imposed by the lifting equipment available.

Both internal and external wall blocks are usually made of the same material,

17

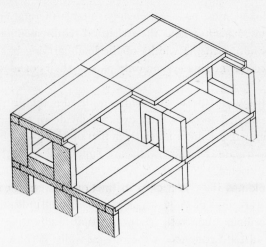

Fig. 2.2.1. Diagrammatic view of a "classic" long wall construction in a prefabricated building

generally clinker concrete (density 1.4–1.8 t/m³), or cellular concrete (density 0.9–1.3 t/m³). For thermal reasons the thickness of the external blocks is 40–45 cm.

Fig. 2.2.2 shows an example of a large-block building.

The weight of this type of building is around 380–430 kg/m³ of the cubic capacity; the reinforcement used in the earlier designs was upwards of 6.0 kg/m³, now it is about 4.5 kg m³.

Two variants of the long-wall system are shown in Fig. 2.2.3.

The arrangement shown in Fig. 2.2.3a differs from the classic system in that the floors are not supported directly on the loadbearing long walls, but on cross beams normally coincident with the lines of partitions.

The spans of the floor panels resting on the floor beams are considerably shorter here than in the previous scheme, and a saving in thickness is made possible. A further economy of steel is achieved if the beams are made as deep as possible. Good results are also obtained by the use of prestressed beams.

The system shown in Fig. 2.2.3a has been adopted in many buildings in Moscow; it is sometimes referred to as the "Moscow system" as distinct from the basic scheme shown in Fig. 2.2.1, which is known as the "Leningrad system".

The use of the Moscow system is particularly justified in buildings with large cross-spans, over 6.0 m long. The total weight of the floor construction, including the weight of beams, could be much less than in the classic system. A flaw in this system is that it is difficult to obtain a satisfactory beam seating on the wall blocks. The only true solution, when dealing with clinker concrete outside walls, is to use rather thicker wall blocks, as in the U.S.S.R., where this is necessary for climatic reasons.

The structural arrangement shown in Fig. 2.2.3b is a development of the Moscow system. Here, the central loadbearing wall has been replaced by a row of pier blocks.

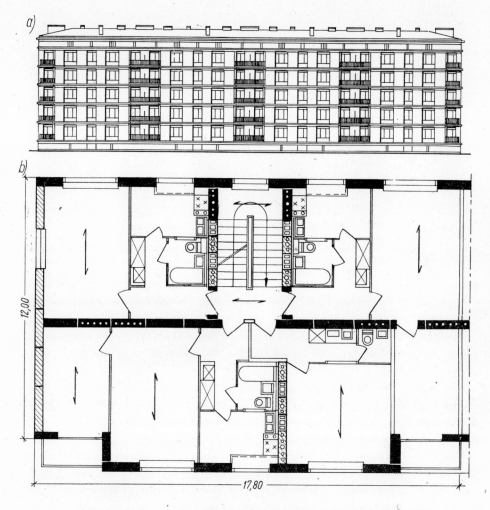

Fig. 2.2.2. A large-block long-wall building on the Wierzbno estate in Warsaw:
(a) elevation, (b) typical floor plan

In this arrangement of beams and piers, the application of skeleton construction is evident.

This last system could be labelled Czechoslovakian, as it has found wide use in Czechoslovakia. The material used in the wall blocks, however, was not concrete but brick.

The brick blocks, built on site or preferably in the brickyard, need to be rendered on both faces after erection. The degree of prefabrication of this type of building, therefore, is not very high. A considerable reduction in handling costs is possible, however, and so is some mechanisation of the brick laying. The strength of the brickwork may also be improved by vibrating.

Fig. 2.2.4 shows the standard Czechoslovakian building T-16-S. The external walls

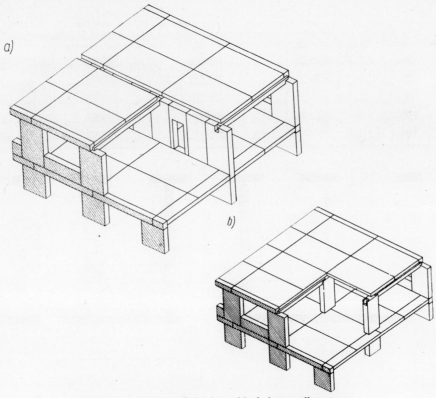

Fig. 2.2.3. Variants of the large-block long-wall system:
(a) Moscow system, (b) Czechoslovakian system

Fig. 2.2.4. Standard Czechoslovakian building T-16-S during erection

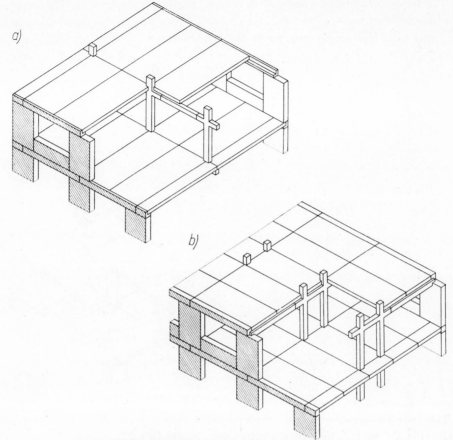

Fig. 2.2.5. Mixed block and frame structures:
(a) long-wall system, (b) cross-wall system

consist of load-carrying pier blocks separated by window panels. The conception of separate window panels is worth stressing as an example of specialised production.

The schemes in Fig. 2.2.5 are clear examples of mixed block and skeleton structures. Both arrangements have been used in the Soviet building industry.

The construction shown in Fig. 2.2.5a is a counterpart of the basic system of Fig. 2.2.1, the long loadbearing wall giving way to a prefabricated reinforced concrete structure. This system is seldom used in two-bay buildings; in three-bay or corridor buildings the middle precast beam and column structure is replaced by two similar rows, the character of the building remaining unchanged.

The example in Fig. 2.2.5b is, in turn, a development of the Moscow system. The framed units are in this case orientated transversely. The building shown is a three-bay structure; as the middle span is very short, the central beam and the columns were combined to form a single precast unit.

21

This type of construction was used in housing projects in the Ukraine. The external wall blocks were made of two materials: ordinary concrete in the loadbearing skin, and slag wool lightweight concrete in the insulation.

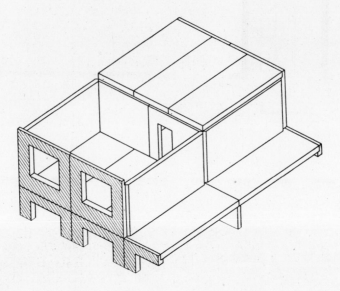

Fig. 2.2.6. Diagrammatic view of a large-panel long-wall structure

The long-wall system is seldom employed in housing designs with large-panel walls (Fig. 2.2.6). It is best known from some desings by a French firm, "Constructions Edmund Coignet", whose founder built a prefabricated structure (a casino) in Biarritz as long ago as 1892.

A plan and a general erection view of a housing project built on the Coignet system are shown in Fig. 2.2.7.

The long-wall system is more common in the building of schools, hospitals or offices. Structurally speaking, the external wall panels with large glazed areas are an approach to precast skeleton systems.

2.2.2. The Two-Way Span System in Building

Because of the close cooperation of all walls in load distribution, it is said that the ring system of walls, with the floors spanning in two directions (Fig. 2.2.8), is ideal for large-panel buildings. This system allows the best utilisation of the structural materials, and the finished buildings are very rigid in both directions. The greatest economy of steel is obtained when the floor panels are nearly square.

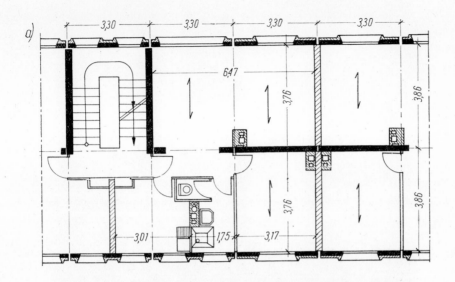

Fig. 2.2.7. A "Coignet" building:
(a) typical floor plan, (b) view of erection

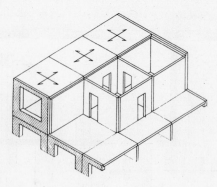

Fig. 2.2.8. Diagram of the "classic" arrangement in a large-panel two-way span system building

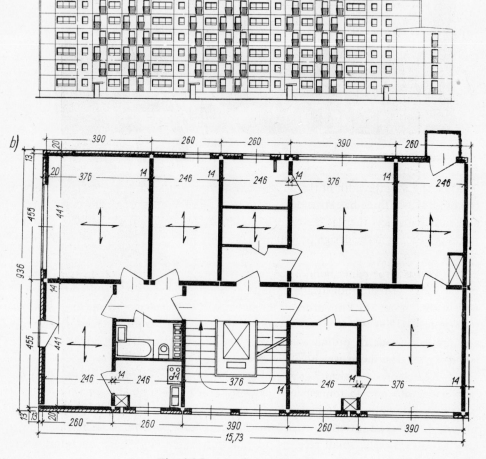

Fig. 2.2.9. (see also next page)

Fig. 2.2.9. Standard PBU building:
(a) elevation, (b) typical floor plan, (c) view during construction

When the overall width of the building is more than 10 m it is normally necessary to design it as a three-bay structure, which increases the number of wall components and rather restricts the flat layout. The load-carrying function of the external wall restricts freedom in the design of wall prefabricates, just as in the case of the long-wall system.

The Polish large-panel building industry of the early nineteen sixties is typified by the PBU system (Industrialised Building Undertaking). PBU construct houses with walls 14 cm thick in ordinary concrete Mk. 170 (blocks of up to 7 storeys high), or Mk. 250 (up to 11 storeys). 9 cm thick floor slabs are cross-reinforced, and are also made of ordinary concrete. The approximate weight of the building is 340 kg/m³, the mean weight of the reinforcement being 3.6 kg/m³.

Fig. 2.2.9 shows a typical 7-storey PBU building. These buildings are designed to be erected with one 45 tonnemetres capacity crane, the heaviest units, having the full structural width of 9.36 m, must not weigh more than 4200 kg. To reduce their weight, the largest external wall panels incorporate additional light insulation inserts. Alternatively, small recesses are cast into them, and these are bricked up after erection.

25

A large-panel building, the scheme of which is shown in Fig. 2.2.10, illustrates the method used to reduce the unit weight of the structure.

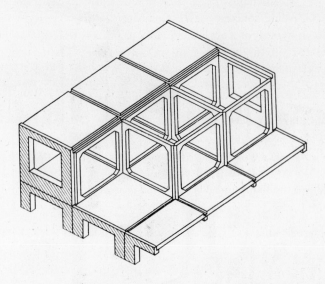

Fig. 2.2.10. Schematic view of a ring-frame construction

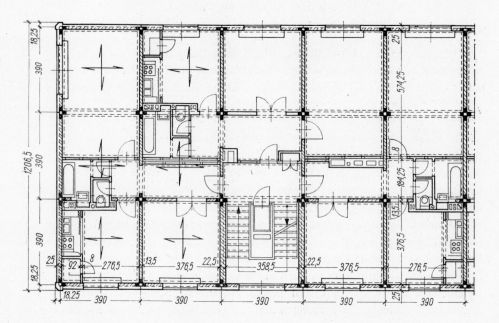

Fig. 2.2.11. Typical floor plan of a Czechoslovakian building type BA

For structural purposes the wall panels are limited to reinforced concrete ring frames, which are filled with any suitable material. This system, originated in Moscow by W. W. Michajlov, was used in Czechoslovakia in BA type buildings (Fig. 2.2.11). Gravelite concrete was used as the infilling material.

In practice, the idea of composite walls, especially internal walls, was rather difficult to realise; in the new variants of BA buildings, battery-moulded, homogeneous concrete panels are used instead.

2.2.3. Cross-Wall System Buildings

In the present stage of development, the dominant system in prefabricated construction is the cross-wall system.

The use of ordinary concrete Mk. 170–250 in the internal loadbearing walls, and of lightweight concretes in the external walls results in an appreciable reduction in the unit weight of the building. As a rule, this type of building should not be heavier than 300 kg/m³.

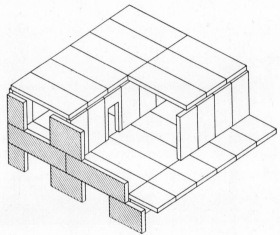

Fig. 2.2.12. Structural diagram of a large-block cross-wall building with self-supporting external wall

A diagrammatic view of a large-block cross-wall construction with self-supporting external walls is shown in Fig. 2.2.12. The external walls consist of two basic block units: pier block and sill block. Both blocks are of similar weights, which is of advantage both in transport and during erection.

A building built to this scheme at Berezhniki, in U.S.S,R., is shown in Fig. 2.2.13; here, the structural walls are constructed of foamed concrete blocks.

The elevation of the building is rather modest. The introduction of balconies and French windows involves the use of smaller blocks and an increase in the number of types employed. Some difficulties are also encountered here in designing a satisfactory connection between the load-carrying cross-walls and self-supporting external walls.

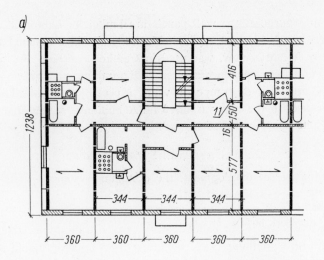

Fig. 2.2.13. Foamed concrete block building in Berezhniki (U.S.S.R.):
(a) typical floor plan, (b) general view

For these reasons, the blocks in the self-supporting walls are often arranged in the same manner as the loadbearing walls in Figs. 2.2.1 and 2.2.3. An example of this "classic" arrangement of blocks in outside walls is shown in Fig. 2.2.14. Very similar block arrangements were adopted in the large-block buildings on a new housing estate at Golonóg in Silesia. The external walls are of aerated silicate blocks, Mk. 07, laid on precast lintels.

A schematic view of a building with self-supporting external panel walls is given in Fig. 2.2.15, the lay-out of panels, however, being non-typical. A more common arrangement is shown in Fig. 2.2.16, which is analogous to the other structural systems (Fig. 2.2.6 or 2.2.8).

Fig. 2.2.14. A large-block building in Riga, with self-supporting foamed concrete external walls

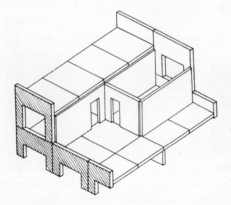

Fig. 2.2.15. Schematic diagram of a building with a large-panel external wall

A further example of an arrangement similar to Fig. 2.2.16 is the Czechoslovakian large-panel building, first erected in 1954 at Gottwaldov, and shown in Fig. 2.2.17. The floor panels embody central-heating coils. Vertical joints in the external walls (always a very troublesome detail), are hidden from the outside. The outside walls take part in the spatial work of the building and are considered to be structural units.

A different and increasingly popular trend is to buildings with non-structural external walls. The principles of two variants of such construction are illustrated by Fig. 2.2.18.

In the first example (Fig. 2.2.18a), the facade blocks laid on the floor panels are flush with the edges of the cross-wall blocks visible from the outside. For visual effect, the edges of the cross-wall blocks are sometimes designed to protrude somewhat beyond the line of the facade blocks.

29

Fig. 2.2.16. Typical arrangement of panels in an external wall. Elevation of a Dutch "Dura-Coignet" building

In the second scheme (Fig. 2.2.18b), the external wall blocks (or panels) cover the outside edges of the structural cross-walls.

In the first example, the arrangement of wall blocks is a development of the basic system shown in Fig. 2.2.1. The edge of the floor panel is the counterpart of the lintel; the pier block is divided in two by the edge of the cross-wall block; the sill block remains unchanged.

To avoid heat losses from room corners, suitable thermal insulation should be applied to the edges of the external walls and floor panels. As this is always troublesome, exposure of the edges of the internal structural units, although architecturally effective, is not recommended in climates similar to that of Poland.

In the large-panel T-3 building, erected at Nowe Tychy, Silesia (Fig. 2.2.19), the reinforced aerated silicate blocks in the outside walls are arranged as in Fig. 2.2.18a.

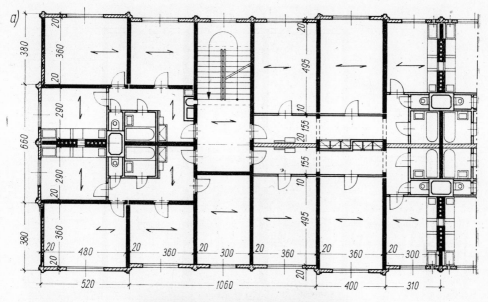

Fig. 2.2.17. Czechoslovakian type C building:
(a) typical floor plan, (b) view during erection

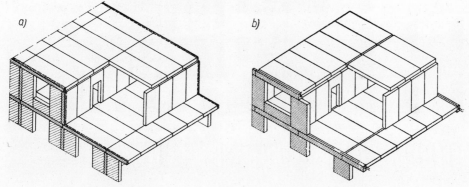

Fig. 2.2.18. Diagrams of buildings with non-loadbearing external walls:
(a) wall erected on floor panels, (b) wall erected on a ring beam

31

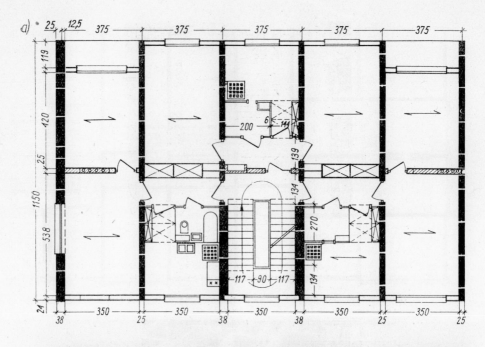

Fig. 2.2.19. T-3 type building at Nowe Tychy:
(a) typical floor plan, (b) general erection view

32

Fig. 2.2.20. A Swedish building with non-structural external walls rested on the floor slabs

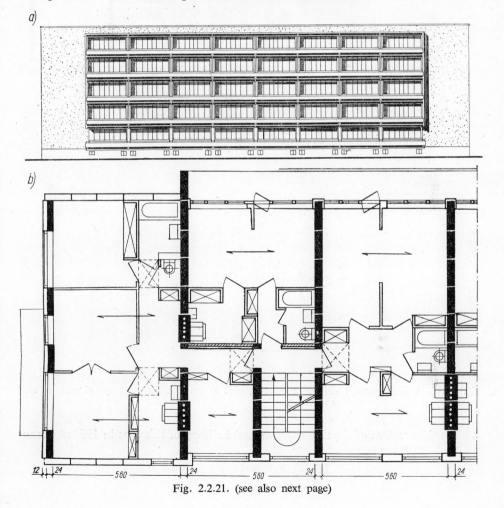

a)

b)

Fig. 2.2.21. (see also next page)

33

Fig. 2.2.21. The prototype of a building made of cored blocks:
(a) elevation, (b) typical floor plan, (c) view of the unfinished building during construction

Fig. 2.2.20 shows a Swedish building in which relatively narrow external wall panels are supported on monolithic floors; the exposed edges of the floor panels are thermally insulated by a cast-iron skin of gas concrete Mk. 0.4.

The arrangement of 2.2.18b has been adopted in Polish buildings in which all wall and floor prefabricates are of oridinary concrete possessing a uniform hollow cross-section of 24 cm.

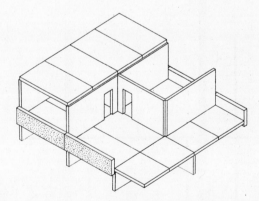

Fig. 2.2.22. A diagrammatic view of a building with a non-structural large-panel external wall

Since the erection of the first experimental building of this type in 1959 at Żeran, a suburb of Warsaw, many similar blocks, and even whole estates, have been built in all parts of Poland (Fig. 2.2.21). External walls are mostly constructed from small gas concrete blocks and require rendering.

34

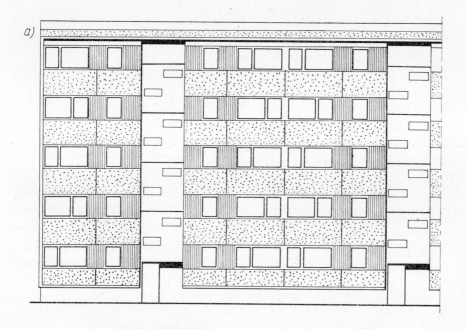

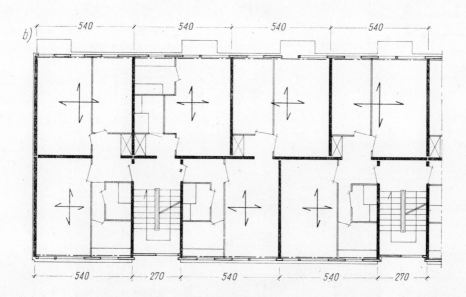

Fig. 2.2.23. Large-panel building type OW-1700:
(a) elevation, (b) typical floor plan

35

In similar buildings erected in Czechoslovakia, the external walls consist of large, light concrete blocks or panels, which markedly raises the level of industrialization.

A scheme of a building whose external walls consist solely of sill panels is shown in Fig. 2.2.22. Besides this type of panel, room-size panels as in Figs. 2.2.6 and 2.2.8 are often used.

Fig. 2.2.23 shows a Polish building with a sill panel external wall. The weight of this building, known as OW-1700, is 250 kg/m³; the weight of reinforcement is 3.5 kg/m³. Compared with the PBU type building, much larger prefabricates were used, as the capacity of the erecting crane was 80 metric tonnes.

French buildings of the "Tracoba" system at Meaux (Fig. 2.2.24) are original in design in that the external walls consist of inverted T panels weighing 6 tons, erected with a 120 metric tonne crane. Interesting plastic effects were obtained by varying the surface texture of individual panels.

To exemplify the use of room-size external wall panels, Fig. 2.2.25 shows one of the buildings erected by a French firm, R. Camus. From 1950 to 1962 this firm built

Fig. 2.2.24. One solution of the external wall problem. "Tracoba" building during erection

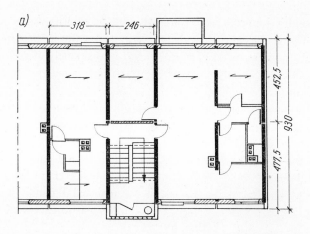

Fig. 2.2.25. Building at Nanterre constructed by Messrs. R. Camus:
(a) typical floor plan, (b) general view of the building

over 40 thousand flats (approx. 150,000 rooms), in prefabricated large-panel buildings, mostly on the cross-wall system.

R. Camus have established a large factory at Baku, U.S.S.R., with a yearly
production capacity of over 3000 rooms, and another plant in Tashkent.

A Danish firm, Larsen-Nielsen, produces similar buildings, shown in Fig. 2.2.26.

In a class of their own are buildings where the external cladding panels are made
of materials other than concrete. The use of light cladding panels is not exclusive

37

Fig. 2.2.26. A view of a Danish building constructed by Messrs. Larsen-Nielsen

to prefabricated buildings, but is also encountered in monolithic and even traditional buildings. An example is shown in Fig. 2.2.27.

Besides the basic structural systems discussed above, some individualistic solutions have been successfully employed.

Fig. 2.2.28 shows an arrangement where the internal loadbearing walls act as girder walls. This arrangement has been adopted by W. P. Lagutienko for a series

Fig. 2.2.27. A Swedish building with non-concrete curtain walls

of prefabricated panel buildings in Moscow (Fig. 2.2.29). Vertical loads from upper storeys are distributed only by the end parts of girder walls, each of which carries, in bending, only its own weight plus a single floor load. The separation between the walls, obtained by means of a recessed upper edge, increases the acoustic barriers between flats.

A cross-wall system, in which the internal walls consist of L-shaped panels, is

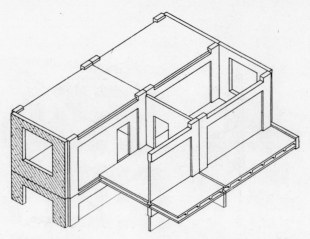

Fig. 2.2.28. Diagrammatic view of a structure in which the internal loadbearing walls act as girder walls

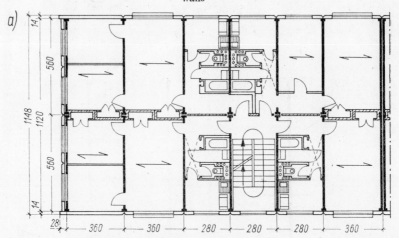

Fig. 2.2.29. A building in Moscow designed by W. P. Lagutienko:
(a) typical floor plan, (b) elevation of the finished building

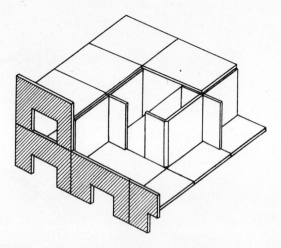

Fig. 2.2.30. Diagram of a building with L-shaped loadbearing wall panels

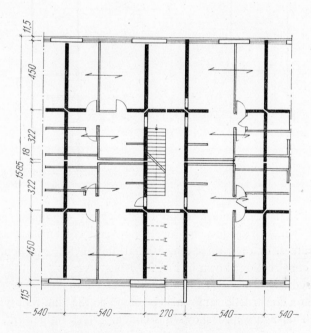

Fig. 2.2.31. Building type WUF-62, typical floor plan

shown in Fig. 2.2.30. Such panels are very stable and do not require temporary propping during erection. Building WUF-62 (Fig. 2.2.31) is an example of this type of construction.

41

2.3. SKELETON CONSTRUCTION

2.3.1. Prefabricated Columns and Beams

A diagrammatic view of a skeleton structure consisting of prefabricated columns and beams is shown in Fig. 2.3.1. This scheme employs the same structural elements as are used in a monolithic in-situ cross-frame building. One essential difference is that there are no longitudinal edge beams to support the external walls. These walls are fixed directly to the column members.

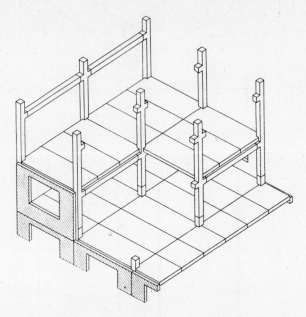

Fig. 2.3.1. Diagram of a skeleton structure consisting of prefabricated columns and beams

Prefabricated skeleton members as in Fig. 2.3.1 are of simple shape and easy to transport. Often, to expedite erection, beams and columns are assembled into larger units, frames, or even three-dimensional units before erection.

The type of construction shown in Fig. 2.3.1 has been applied to many buildings erected in Moscow and other towns of the Soviet Union.

Precast skeleton constructions may also be based on the long-wall system as shown in Fig. 2.3.2. This figure also shows a secondary steel framework, the function of which is to ensure that the precast columns are plumb.

Another example of skeleton construction from prefabricated columns and beams is taken from the Bulgarian building industry, Fig. 2.3.3. Spun concrete circular columns go the full height of the building. As the external walls are in traditional brickwork, longitudinal edge beams are provided in addition to the floor-supporting cross-beams.

42

Fig. 2.3.2. An erection view of a Moscow skeleton building

Fig. 2.3.3. A Bulgarian skeleton building with one-piece precast spun concrete columns, views
of the building in various stages of erection

Fig. 2.3.4 shows a Czechoslovakian skeleton construction which is an evolution
from the T-16-S design discussed in section 2.2.1. The rather squat, pier-like columns,
are only one storey high. The external line of columns is set back from the wall face.
The main cross-beams sit in swallow-tail pockets formed at the top of the columns
and project outwards, providing supports for the external wall panels.

43

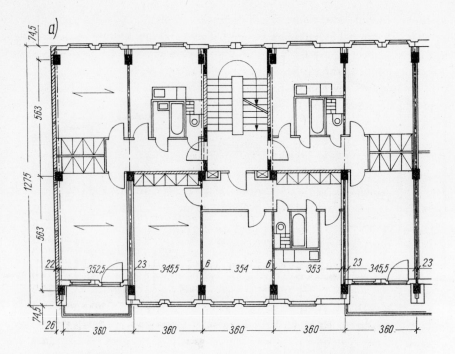

Fig. 2.3.4. A Czechoslovakian two-bay skeleton construction:
(a) typical floor plan, (b) a view during erection

The shape of the main beam is rather complex and the beam-column joints resemble connections used in timber constructions. Fig. 2.3.4b also shows the secondary framework used during erection to ensure rigidity in the system until the cross-wall panels are connected (by welding).

44

A similar, though rather simpler, solution was adopted in a development involving a number of large-panel buildings at Nowe Tychy, Silesia. During the design stage, the original conception was changed: the precast block columns were replaced by in-situ columns in the casting of which the vacuum process was used (Fig. 2.3.5).

It is the author's opinion that skeleton construction, consisting of precast beams and in-situ columns, is particularly worthy of recommendation.

2.3.2. Beamless Skeleton Construction

Two arrangements of a beamless skeleton construction are shown in Fig. 2.3.6.

The floor panels are normally cross-reinforced to span in two directions. From the standpoint of economy of steel, it is less advantageous to design the floor units to span in one direction, with cross-beams hidden within the thickness of the panel.

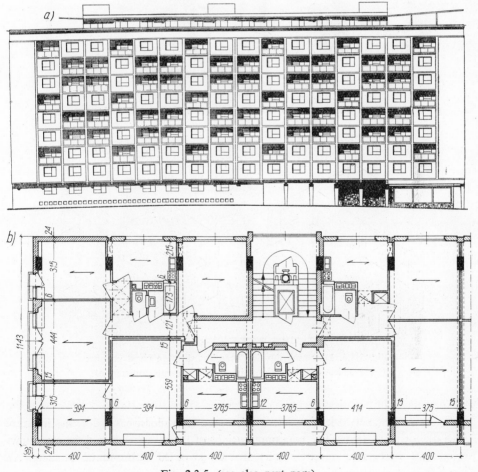

Fig. 2.3.5. (see also next page)

Fig. 2.3.5. A skeleton construction at Nowe Tychy:
(a) elevation, (b) typical floor plan, (c) a view during erection

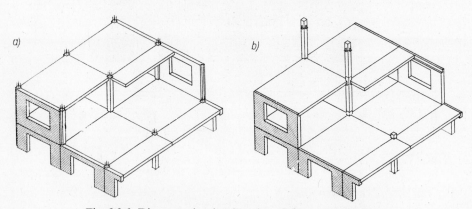

Fig. 2.3.6. Diagrams showing beamless skeleton constructions:
(a) skeleton construction, (b) skeleton-panel construction

An example of beamless skeleton construction taken from Polish practice is shown in Fig. 2.3.7. The network of columns is comparatively close, but it does not interfere with the interior design. The maximum weight of the precast units, 1.5 tons, allows erection to be carried out by means of a crane of 20 metric-tonne capacity. An ingenious detail at the joint, shown in Fig. 2.3.7b provides a flat soffit.

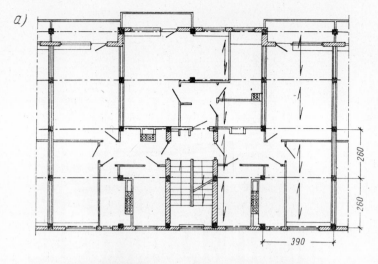

Fig. 2.3.7. A Polish beamless skeleton construction on the Wierzbno estate (Warsaw):
(a) typical floor plan, (b) a detail of the erection

Of great interest are beamless skeleton constructions erected by the American "lift-slab" method, Fig. 2.3.8.

The essence of this method is that, in the first stage, steel stanchions are erected to the full height of the building, after which whole floor-slabs are cast in succession for all storeys. When the concrete has reached the requisite strength, the floors are lifted one-by-one by means of hydraulic jacks to their proper levels, where they are welded to the steel stanchions.

Buildings of similar construction are also found in the Soviet Union.

An example of a Russian building with two-way spanning floor panels supported by columns and panel walls is shown in Fig. 2.3.9. Of particular interest is the method used to connect the slabs to the columns.

Fig. 2.3.8. An American "lift-slab" construction

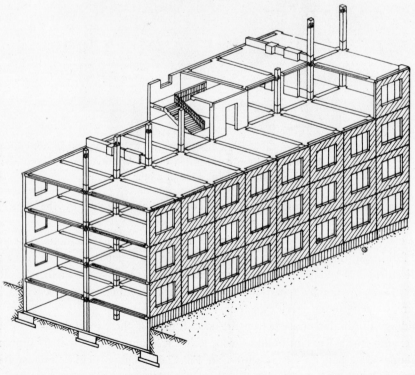

Fig. 2.3.9. A building using the skeleton-panel construction principle, designed in the U.S.S.R.

A Czechoslovakian C-58 building, shown in Fig. 2.3.10, is a variant of the original T-16 design, previously discussed. The external wall is little changed: the piers, which consisted of several small masonry blocks, are replaced here by single large gravelite concrete blocks. The spaces between the pier blocks are filled with light window panels, similar to curtain walling.

The essential change, however, has occurred in the internal construction. In place of a masonry pier block with swallow-tail pockets to house main beams with small floor panels, there is now a steel stanchion loaded directly by large, diagonally-reinforced floor panels (Fig. 2.3.11).

It is difficult to classify building C-58 as a block, panel or skeleton construction. There are blocks in the external walls, panels in the loadbearing party walls and columns inside the flats. Similar difficulties in definition are quite often encountered when dealing with buildings made of large prefabricated components.

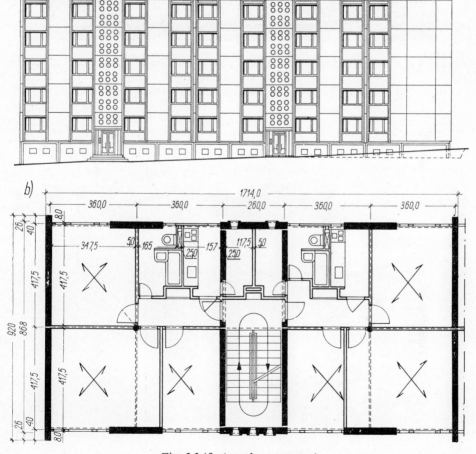

Fig. 2.3.10. (see also next page)

Fig. 2.3.10. A Czechoslovakian building with diagonally spanning floors, a mixture of skeleton and block construction:
(a) elevation, (b) typical floor plan, (c) view of the finished building

Fig. 2.3.11. Internal steel stanchion

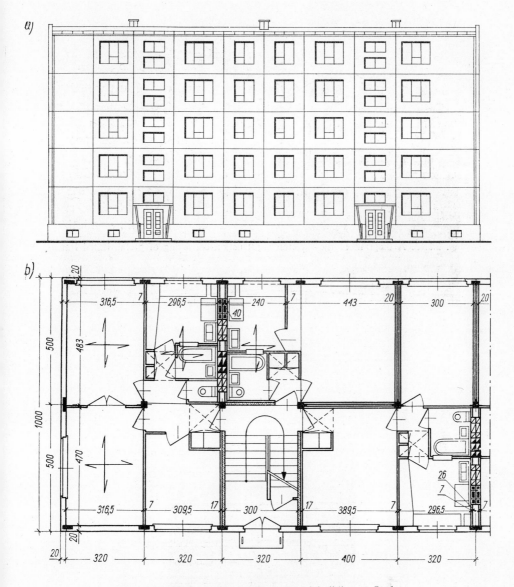

Fig. 2.3.12. The prototype skeleton panel building at Lodz:
(a) elevation, (b) ground floor plan

A Polish mixed panel and column building erected in 1960 in Lodz is shown in Fig. 2.3.12. In this case, unlike the Czechoslovakian project just described, column units occur in the external walls. Following the experience gained from this prototype, several similar blocks are now being built on another estate in Lodz.

51

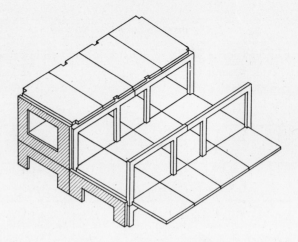

Fig. 2.3.13. A diagram of the skeleton construction consisting of prefabricated frames

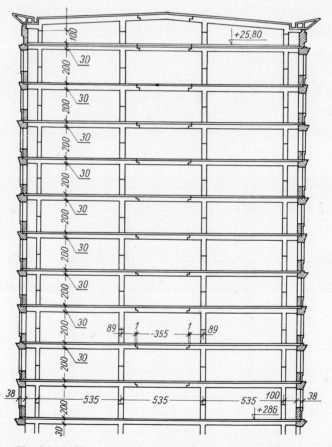

Fig. 2.3.14. The structural scheme of the university library at Lodz

52

2.3.3. Precast Skeleton Structure

A diagrammatic view of a structure consisting of prefabricated portal frames is given in Fig. 2.3.13. Several versions of this type of construction have been widely used in many countries.

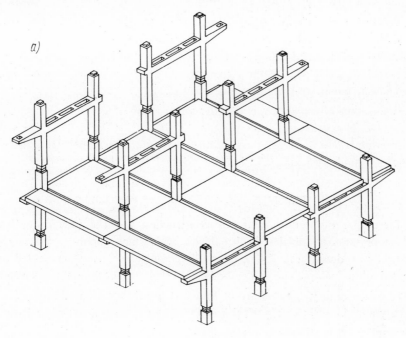

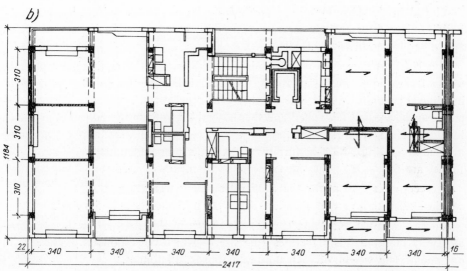

Fig. 2.3.15. A skeleton construction on the Muranów estate in Warsaw:
(a) the principle of construction, (b) typical floor plan

One of the Soviet examples has been described in section 2.2.1, in connection with large-block construction. It must be stressed, however, that buildings featuring prefabricated portal frames are not typical for the Soviet building industry. Panels in conjunction with precast beams and columns are much more often used, as they are more suitable for industrialised production and long-distance transport.

A prefabricated skeleton construction was used in Poland in the erection of the new 11-storey university library in Lodz. The structural skeleton (Fig. 2.3.14) consists of prefabricated double-cantilever H-frames and hinge-connected beams in the central span. The legs of the frames are welded together to form columns. The external wall panels rest on frame cantilevers.

A similar type of frame was used in the construction of a series of housing projects in Warsaw. The structural principles are illustrated in Fig. 2.3.15. The weight of the structure is 210 kg/m³, the expenditure of reinforcement per cubic metre being 5.6 kg of round steel and 0.72 kg of deformed steel.

2.4. Building from box prefabricates

The forerunner of prefabricated box construction was the practice of installing ready-made sanitary cubicles. Such cubicles, which have for many years now been industrially produced (Fig. 2.4.1), internally completely finished and fitted out, are delivered to the building site and embodied in otherwise traditional types of building.

As a rule, sanitary cubicles are of little structural importance. More often than not, they are placed in one vertical line and, at best, form a self-supporting tower.

As applied to the living quarters, the idea of box prefabricates has only been developed in the last few years, particularly in the Soviet Union. Experimental buildings have been erected on several estates in Moscow, Leningrad, Minsk, Kiev, and other towns in the U.S.S.R.

In a block of flats at Nowe Kuzminki near Moscow, the prefabricates take the form of two-room units (Fig. 2.4.2), their length being equal to the width of the building. Flat units, in this case consisting of roller-pressed ribbed reinforced concrete panels, are first fabricated and then assembled to form the box unit, as shown in Fig 2.4.3. Later, still in the factory, all necessary finishes are applied, including all sanitary fittings, built-in furniture, etc. Thus prepared units weighing 12—16 tonnes are delivered to the site and erected by means of a 35 tonne gantry crane.

The economic factors for the 6735 m³ building were:
weight — 286 kg/m³, reinforcement — 10.7 kg/m³, cement — 70.5 kg/m³.

Another example of a "box" building is shown in Fig. 2.4.4. Here the prefabricates were made as in-situ "crates" the size of which corresponded to the size of one room. The weight of each unit was approx. 14 tonnes.

Building with prefabricated boxes is still an experimental process. Studies and tests are continuing in many countries, Poland included, and it is too early yet

Fig. 2.4.1. Prefabricated W. C. cubicles:
(a) preparation for despatch, (b) during erection on site

55

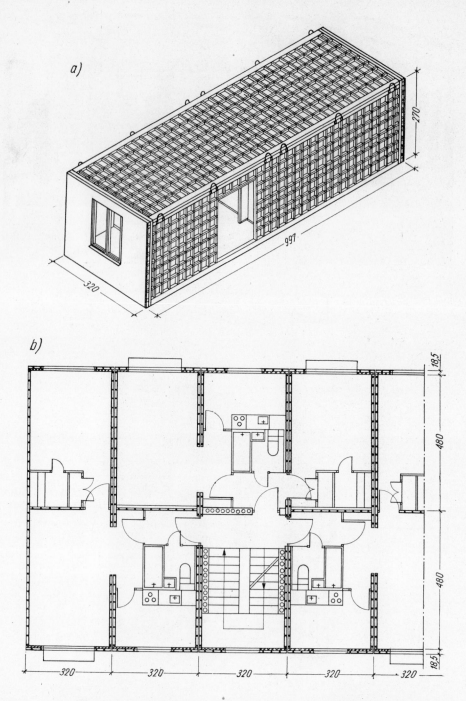

Fig. 2.4.2. A block of flats composed of box-prefabricates:
(a) two-room box unit consisting of reinforced panel units, (b) part of the typical floor plan.

56

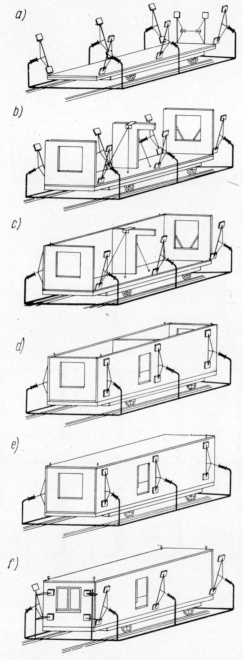

Fig. 2.4.3. Box-unit assembly procedure:
(a) floor panel laid on travelling bogey, (b) cross-walls inserted, (c), (d) longitudinal box wall (cross-walls of the building) erected, (e) ceiling panel fixed, (f) additional end panels (outer skins of the external walls) erected

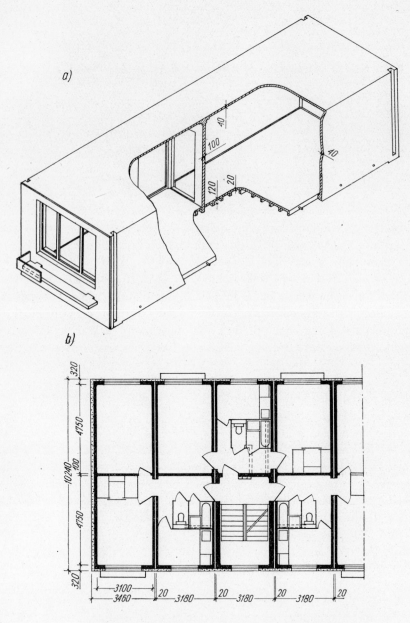

Fig. 2.4.4. A block of flats made of box prefabricates:
(a) monolithic box element, (b) part of typical floor plan

to voice a final opinion as to their future. Noting, however, that the highest level of industrialisation is attainable in areas of intensive housing development, we may expect wide use of this new technique.

Chapter 3

PRINCIPLES OF PREFABRICATED BUILDING DESIGN

3.1. THE COMPLEXITY OF THE PROBLEM

The planning of a prefabricated building is a complex task, in which architect, engineer and technologist all work together. The leadership of the team is taken by the man who, besides his own speciality, is best versed in the other two fields.

In the design of new types of buildings, structural questions and the problems of production technology and of erection are indivisible. It would be ideal if the author of the structural conception of the building were equally competent in both of the other fields of technology. It is also most desirable that the future training of engineers should take this into account instead of tending, as at present, towards a definite division of the interests of constructors and technologists.

Both the construction and the production technology of the project should lie within the capabilities of those who will carry it out.

This recommendation applies particularly to the choice of materials, the method of production of the components, and the type of erection plant used. Although progress in the building industry is dependent on research into new types of buildings and new methods of construction, the desirable economic benefits are only obtained when already known and proven designs and techniques are exploited to the full.

Thus, the adoption and adaptation of standard designs and mass-produced prefabricates are fundamental to the principle of design.

3.2. DIMENSIONAL COORDINATION AND STANDARDISATION

3.2.1. Dimensioning of Prefabricates

There are three commonly recognised basic types of unit dimensions (Fig. 3.2.1):
(a) the design (or erection) dimension, l_M, governing the dimensional coordination of prefabricates;
(b) the theoretical dimension, l, the planned dimension of a prefabricate;
(c) the actual dimension, l_w, the actual size of the element when delivered.

The design dimension should be a multiple of a basic module nM, or of a project module nM_p. In this case, the design dimension is also called the modular dimension.

59

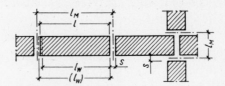

Fig. 3.2.1. The basic dimensions in prefabricates:
l_M — erection dimension, l — theoretical dimension, l_w — actual dimension, s — width of the joint

Non-modular design dimensions result in an increase in the number of types of units used.

The theoretical dimension is obtained by subtracting the size of the joint from the design dimension, i.e.:

$$l = nM - s \quad \text{or} \quad l = nM_p - s \qquad [3.2.1]$$

where s is the width of the joint.

The space between two adjacent elements is termed a joint, whether the gap is filled with additional jointing material or not.

The actual dimension of an element differs from its theoretical dimension by the value of the production discrepancy. When $l < l_w$, the discrepancy is positive, and when $l > l_w$ it is negative.

On working drawings, one should give the theoretical dimensions of the units and of the joints between them (in centimetres).

The width of the joint must not be less than the settled limiting value of positive discrepancy, or (if the discrepancy has not been settled) not less than 3/4 of the value of the tolerance (section 3.4.4). Those dimensions of units which have a bearing on their position in relation to the neighbouring units are subject to dimensional coordination. Prefabricates may be coordinated:

(a) three-dimensionally, if the unit is connected to its neighbours in three directions (length, width and thickness, or depth);

(b) superficially, if the unit is jointed to others in two directions (e.g. length and width of a roof panel), or if the use of a modular dimension in the third direction is impossible or unwarranted (e.g. the thickness of a roof panel);

(c) linearly, when the unit is connected to other units in one direction only (e.g. length of a beam), or if the use of modular dimensions in the other two directions is impossible or unwarranted (e.g. the cross-sectional dimensions of a beam of a column).

3.2.2. Modular Coordination

By modular coordination we mean the interdependent arrangement of dimensions, based on a primary value accepted as a module. Strict observance of the rules of modular coordinations facilitates the assembly of single components into larger combinations, the fewest possible different types of component and a minimum of wasteful cutting being needed. In this context, modular coordination is the basis of all attempts at a standardisation of mass produced components.

In Polish building practice the obligatory basic module is $M = 10$ cm.

A larger modular unit is the project module M_p.

In the prefabricated housing industry, essential practice includes:
— Horizontal coordination, based on the project module $M_p = 30$ cm;
— Vertical coordination, on the basic module $M = 10$ cm.

The storey-height in flats, measured between finished floor levels, is fixed at 2.80 m, except that in buildings with floors less than 15 cm thick, the storey-height may be reduced to 2.70 m.

Centre-to-centre distances (L) between the loadbearing walls are chosen from the following:
$nM_p = 2.70, 3.00, 3.30, 3.60, 3.90, 4.50, 5.10, 5.40, 5.70$ and 6.00 m.

The width of the staircase, measured between the centre lines of walls is fixed at 2.70 m.

The use of other dimensions is only allowed on large multiple projects, backed by a particular supply organisation. Here the condition is imposed that the dimensions used should be multiples of the project module $M_p = 30$ cm.

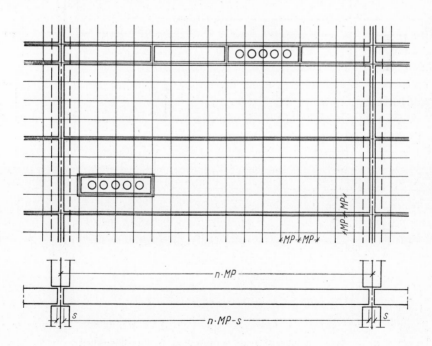

Fig. 3.2.2. Typical layout of the modular grid with ductless loadbearing walls

61

3.2.3. Location of Prefabricates in the Building

In the design of a building, use must be made of a modular (project) grid, consisting of parallel lines spaced at the value of the module M or M_p. A grid line, chosen as the base for setting out a given part of the building, becomes its modular axis.

In prefabricated projects, the internal walls are so placed that their centre lines coincide with the modular axes.

A typical modular grid is shown in Fig. 3.2.2. The flues and ventilation ducts are located inside walls running parallel to the span of the floor components. The design dimensions of wall and floor components are modular dimensions.

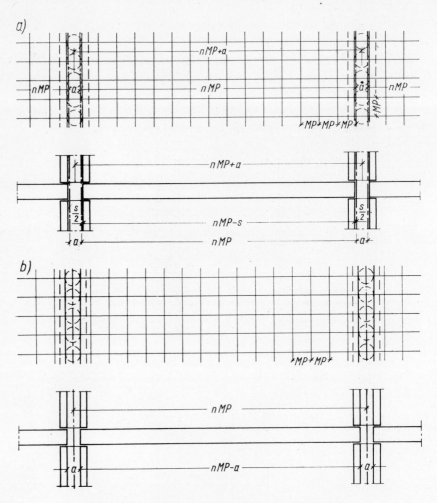

Fig. 3.2.3. Modular grids for hollow loadbearing walls:
(a) for floor length $l = a \cdot M_p - a - s$, (b) for $l = n \cdot M_p - s$

When dealing with loadbearing walls incorporating hollow ducts, one can either
— retain a modular axis coinciding with the geometrical axis of the wall, and
introduce floor panels with the length $l = nM_p - a - s$, as in Fig. 3.2.3a, or
— correct the grid, introducing, for each wall, two modular grid lines spaced at
a distance a, as in Fig. 3.2.3b.

The first arrangement does not interfere with the modular coordination of the
wall components, and is thus more convenient for prefabricated buildings.

In the second arrangement, the modular dimensions of the floor components
remain intact, and this is therefore more often used in buildings with loadbearing
masonry walls and large-panel floors. A similar procedure may be adopted in order
to reduce the area over which floor panels are directly supported, when the loadbearing walls are thicker than 30 cm.

In external walls, the modular axis does not generally coincide with the centre
line of the wall.

In a loadbearing external wall, the modular axis lies at a distance from the inside
face of the wall equal to the width of the floor-supporting area, plus half the thickness of the joint (Fig. 3.2.4).

Self-supporting walls are placed in the so-called "zero position" relative to the
modular axis (Fig. 3.2.5). The axis lies at the mid-point of the joint.

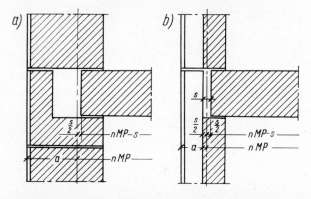

Fig. 3.2.4. Position of the modular axis in external loadbearing walls:
(a) with "in-situ" r.c. ring beam, (b) without ring beam

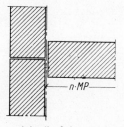

Fig. 3.2.5. "Zero position" of the non-loadbearing wall

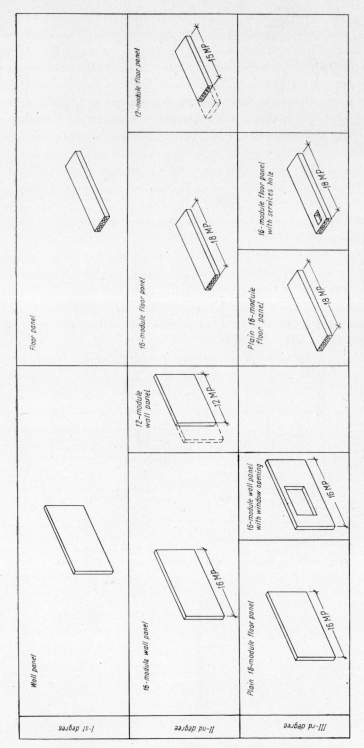

Fig. 3.2.6. The three degrees of diversity of prefabricates

3.2.4. Diversity of Prefabricates

Large prefabricated units may be of three degrees of diversity (Fig. 3.2.6).

(I) — the units differ from each other in basic shape, cross-section of material, and their production demands separate formwork and different technology;

(II) — the units are of varying length or width, but can be cast by the same methods and using the same formwork, suitably adapted by means of inserts or separators;

(III) — the difference between the units is in the internal details and does not affect the basic sizes or production methods (incorporation of window openings, surface treatment, etc.).

An example of the diversification of prefabricates is shown in Table 3.2.1.

The Ist and IInd degrees of diversity essentially affect the capital expenditure while the IIIrd degree dictates the organisation of production and erection.

In industrialised building the obvious tendency is to employ the largest possible units. The larger the units, the less work remains to be done on site and the less joints there are to fill and waterproof. On the other hand, the adoption of large-sized prefabricates of a few basic types, greatly curtails the freedom of architectural design.

The relationship between the architectural, structural and productional aspects is shown in Table 3.2.2, after Z. Kleyff.

With a restricted range of large prefabricates, architectural design becomes rather stereotyped (column 1), whilst if an attempt is to be made to retain a degree of freedom in design, while dealing with large precast units, the number of types of the latter must be multiplied (column 2). A restricted number of types of prefabricates combined with full architectural freedom precludes the use of large units (column 3). This in fact describes traditional building, in which the smallest unit, a brick, allows almost complete freedom of design.

The above argument is summarised by Fig. 3.2.7, which illustrates the relationship between the size of the prefabricates and their numerical variety.

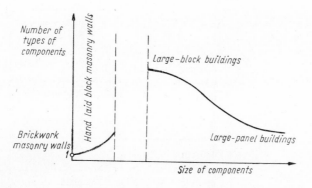

Fig. 3.2.7. The relationship between the size of the unit and the number of types of prefabricates

65

TABLE 3.2.1.

EXAMPLE OF THE DIVERSIFICATION OF PREFABRICATES

Ist degree			IInd degree			IIIrd degree			
Diversity marking	Description	No.	Diversity marking	Description	No.	Diversity marking	Description	No.	Full marking of the unit
1	External wall panel	126	1	180 cm wide (6-module)	18	1	plain	10	1.1.1
						2	window	8	1.1.2
			2	300 cm wide (10-module)	20	1	plain	16	1.2.1
						2	window	4	1.2.2
			3	360 cm wide (12-module)	88	1	plain	8	1.3.1
						2	window panel (2-light window)	60	1.3.2
						3	window panel (3-light window)	20	1.3.3
2	Internal wall panel	220	1	300 cm wide (10-module)	80	1	plain	16	2.1.1
						2	door panel (central doors)	24	2.1.2
						3	door panel (doors at one edge)	40	2.1.3
			2	420 cm wide (14-module)	128	1	plain	58	2.2.1
						2	door panel (doors at one edge)	70	2.2.2
			3	480 cm wide (16-module)	12	1	plain	12	2.3.1

TABLE 3.2.1. (continued)

Ist degree			IInd degree			IIIrd degree		
Diversity marking	Description	No.	Diversity marking	Description	No.	Diversity marking	Description	No.	Full marking of the unit
3	Floor panel	112	1	300×420 (10×14 module)	16	1	normal reinforcement	4	3.1.1
						2	extra reinforcement for partitions	4	3.1.2
						3	normal reinforcement, service opening provided	8	3.1.3
			2	300×480 (10×16 module)	24	1	normal reinforcement	12	3.2.1
						2	extra reinforcement for partitions	12	3.2.2
			3	360×420 (12×14 module)	72	1	normal reinforcement	28	3.3.1
						2	normal reinforcement, service opening provided	44	3.3.2
	3 types of the Ist degree	458		9 types of the IInd degree	458		20 types of the IIIrd degree	458	

TABLE 3.2.2.

INTERRELATION OF CONSTRUCTION, ARCHITECTURE AND PRODUCTION
IN LARGE-PREFABRICATE DESIGN

Criteria	Compatibility		
	1	2	3
Large size components	yes	yes	no
Small number of types of components	yes	no	yes
Freedom of architectural design	no	yes	yes

Two factors, then, decide the number of different types of prefabricates to be employed: the technique of construction and the architectural conception of the project.

A real achievement in restricting the number of types of components used is exemplified by the construction, in France, of a number of houses by E. Coignet—only six forms were necessary to cast all the prefabricates used.

A similar success may be claimed for the Polish Żeran buildings, in which the internal loadbearing walls and the floor panels are all hollow multiduct slabs produced in the same basic mould.

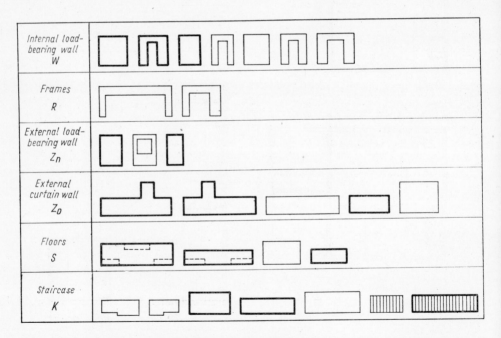

Fig. 3.2.8. A typical list of standard prefabricates prepared for a large-panel housing estate. Prefabricates applicable to the particular block are shown in heavy outline

68

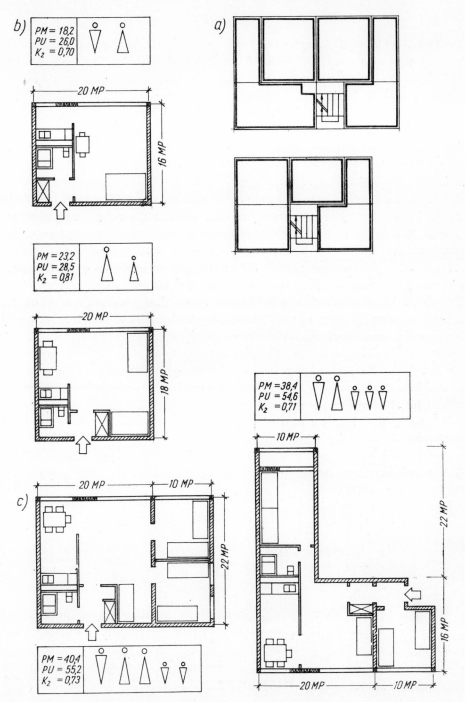

Fig. 3.2.9. Sample pages from the catalogue of prefabricated houses such as shown in Fig. 3.2.8: (a) layout of flats, (b) two-person flat type M2, (c) family flat type M5

69

3.2.5. Standardisation of Components

The term "component" of a building may mean either a single prefabricate used in construction, or a series of prefabricates assembled into a complete residential or functional unit forming part of the building. Both these types are subject to standardisation in industrialised building.

Standardisation may be on a national scale, obligatory over the whole country, provided that the competent authorities publish catalogues of standard prefabricates and standard housing units, or even of whole buildings.

Sometimes standardisation may be purely local, entailing a particular architectural and constructional conception. This is found useful in the design of a coordinated set of buildings, a housing estate or an urban district. Catalogues or lists of standard prefabricates and of whole apartment units are compiled, and these are of great help in design work, and in planning the production and erection of the prefabricates.

Fig. 3.2.8. gives an example of a list of standard prefabricates of various sizes and functions, compiled for a series of large-panel buildings. On the basis of an analysis of the architectural, structural and technological problems, it was possible to design a complete range of prefabricates representing all the prefabricates necessary for the building of all the blocks on programme.

The specifications of all prefabricates are contained in a separate document. The number and types of components to be used in a particular building are indicated in a catalogue, such as described above, which is enclosed with the specifications for the building.

Using the same list of standard prefabricates, a catalogue of apartment units was prepared, containing many variants of the most rational arrangement of living space, based on the size of the family, regulations in force, etc. Buildings of varying sizes, positions on the site, compass aspects and uses, may then all be designed on the basis of the catalogue.

Fig. 3.2.9 shows typical pages from the catalogue of apartment units.

3.3. Principles of design

3.3.1. The Structure

In a prefabricated building the structure must be sufficiently rigid in all directions and the loadbearing system must be simple and clear-cut. Solutions, in which the fixity conditions of units are doubtful, where the loadbearing functions of individual elements are difficult to define, or where the points of application of loads are uncertain, should be avoided (Fig. 3.3.1).

In particular, precast and in-situ work forming parts of the loadbearing walls of a single storey should not be mixed. If for any functional or practical reasons

70

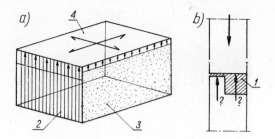

Fig. 3.3.1. Examples of poorly-defined support conditions:
(a) floor panel resting on walls of different elasticity, (b) wall element partly resting on old and partly on new concrete
(1) fresh concrete, (2), (3) loadbearing walls of two different materials, (4) two-way reinforced floor panel

some walls or columns must be constructed in-situ, due consideration must be given in the design to the differential rheological deformations which will take place in the wet and dry work.

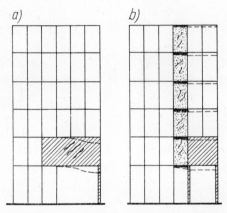

Fig. 3.3.2. Examples of partly prefabricated and partly in-situ loadbearing wall:
(a) original design, (b) improved solution

Fig. 3.3.2 shows a loadbearing wall, part of which had to be cast in-situ for structural reasons.

In the improved design (Fig. 3.3.2b), the part of the wall composed solely of precast panels is distinctly separated from the other half, in which in-situ columns and wall occur. Slender beams joining the two halves of the wall make allowance for a small difference in the vertical deformations.

The spaces between these floor-level beams are filled with panels built of small gas concrete blocks. Should the relative movements of the two parts of the wall be of any appreciable magnitude, cracks will form in the infill panels, but they will not affect the loadbearing capacity of the structure. In the original design

71

Fig. 3.3.3. A building in which an in-situ core is erected first

(Fig. 3.3.2a) cracks in the in-situ girder wall would lower the strength of the whole wall.

The solution shown in Fig. 3.3.2b, although correct in structural detail, is nevertheless basically faulty. When the lower storeys of a building must differ from the upper standard storeys, all the non-standard storeys should be of monolithic design, and prefabricated construction should be limited to the upper storeys.

Because of the shrinkage of fresh concrete, with the consequent formation of cracks, it is also inadvisable to introduce in-situ stiffening walls into an otherwise prefabricated building. It is perfectly in order, however, to construct in-situ the stiffening "core" of the building to which, in the second stage of erection, the remainder of the building, made of prefabricated units, is connected.

This solution was adopted in a Swedish system shown in Fig. 3.3.3.

There are no structural objections to part-precast and part in-situ floor construction. The differential shrinkage movements in fresh and mature concrete need only be considered in design calculations concerning large span beams, prefabricated parts of which are joined together with in-situ concrete. This type of construction, however, is seldom used in housing projects.

Equally acceptable are monolithic floors on prefabricated panel walls, or precast floors supported on in-situ walls, provided all walls of a given storey are in-situ.

The spatial rigidity of a building made of prefabricated units is achieved by means of rigid longitudinal and transverse walls, which extend the full height of the building (Fig. 3.3.4a). These walls distribute over the foundations two kinds of horizontal load, namely, forces due to direct wind pressure on the external walls, and horizontal forces resulting from the non-vertical or non-symmetrical layout of the loadbearing walls.

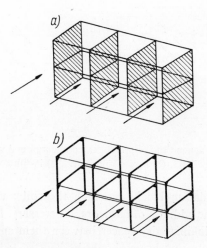

Fig. 3.3.4. Transverse stiffening of the building by means of:
(a) cross-walls, (b) frames

73

Because of the presence of the stiffening walls, only vertical loads need be considered in the design of the loadbearing elements in a building (loadbearing walls or columns).

From the structural point of view, it is possible to provide the necessary lateral stiffness by means of beams and columns rigidly connected at the joints (Fig. 3.3.4b). This results, however, in an increased consumption of reinforcement and additional production difficulties, and is therefore admissible only when economically justified.

3.3.2. Foundations

The foundations of a building may be cast in-situ, or may consist of large prefabricates. In either case, the underground structure must be very rigid and must ensure an even distribution of loads over the plan area of the building. Buildings assembled from prefabricates are very prone to the formation of cracks in construction joints; the designer must make certain that the whole building will settle evenly, acting as a three-dimensionally rigid body.

As a rule, in-situ construction below ground level adequately ensures an even distribution of loads over the plan area. This method is commonly used in Polish practice, and rightly so, in the author's opinion.

In soils of low compressibility, large prefabricates can provide a satisfactory foundation structure. Attention must be paid, however, to the rigidity of connections. One way of ensuring this is to block-bond the units, as in masonry walls (Fig. 3.3.5).

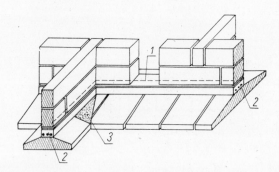

Fig. 3.3.5. Fragment of the prefabricated underground structure of a building: (1) cellar floor level, (2) in-situ ring beam, (3) in-situ concrete infilling

Before precast foundation blocks are laid, the soil must be carefully levelled and compacted, with the addition of hardcore, if necessary. Blocks should be bedded in cement mortar to eliminate dry spaces between them and the ground. A monolithic reinforced concrete ring beam should be constructed immediately above the foundation blocks. A similar ring beam should encircle the building at ground floor slab level. All lintel blocks below ground must be given generous bearings to ensure the monolithic behaviour of the foundation walls.

When considerable ground movements are anticipated, the design of the underground structure should be in-situ monolithic, with suitably small expansion joints. The span of the foundation walls should not be more than three times, and the thickness not less than 1/20, of their height.

3.3.3. Correlation of Structure and Architecture

The structure of a building must reflect the architectural concept.

In designing buildings with loadbearing walls, the normal practice is to utilise the latter to separate individual apartments. Loadbearing walls as a rule make adequate acoustic barriers.

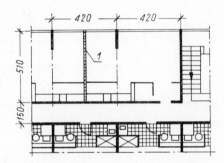

Fig. 3.3.6. An example of improper positioning of non-loadbearing party walls between flats:
(1) wall located at mid-span of the floor panel

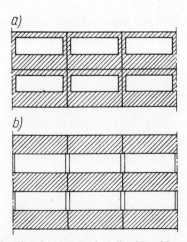

Fig. 3.3.7. Division of loadbearing external wall with wide windows into components:
(a) incorrect, (b) correct

75

Dividing walls should not be located in the middle of floor panels (Fig. 3.3.6), because of the ensuing loss of useful space (thickness of the wall) and the increased consumption of steel (concentrated load at mid-span).

In skeleton constructions, the walls dividing the total space into individual apartments should also be placed over the beams, and not on floor panels.

When the architectural concept calls for a building with very wide windows, external walls should be designed as nonstructural walls, e.g. curtain walling.

Although sometimes practised in long-wall and ring-wall buildings, it is not strictly correct to design external walls as loadbearing (or even self-supporting) if panels with large window openings are required (Fig. 3.3.7a). It is advisable in such cases to alter the structural arrangement and to employ simpler panels, as in Fig. 3.3.7b.

All chimney flues and ventilation ducts should be grouped in walls running parallel to the span of the floor panels.

The walls housing these ducts should be self-supporting. When it is possible to cap them efficiently to the structural walls of the building, the chimney walls may be assumed to have a stiffening effect on the structure.

3.4. TECHNOLOGICAL PROBLEMS OF PREFABRICATION

3.4.1. Location of Production

The level of industrialisation of building with large prefabricates depends mainly on the industrialisation of production and the degree to which the products are finished in the course of their manufacture.

The highest level of industrialisation is reached in permanent stationary plants. It must be added, however, that full industrialisation of production, with consequent economic benefits, can only be achieved when large numbers of given prefabricates are produced for stock, to no specific order. This in turn is dependent on the degree to which prefabricates are standardised, and on how extensive is their use in building projects.

A plan of a permanent prefabricates factory, based on the actual plant of "Faelbet" at Żeran, Warsaw, is shown in Fig. 3.4.1. In this factory are to be found the following basic production shops, each responsible for a particular range of products: large panel floors (1), panel walls (2), prestressed units (3), gas concrete (4), and specialised prefabricates, such as lintels, cornices, stair flights, roof panels, etc. (5). Equally important are the auxiliary production units: reinforcement shop (6), mechanical workshops (7), transport base (8), testing laboratory (9), boilerhouse (10), and the recreation and administrative block (11). The basic production shops, in addition to the machinery necessary to make their specialised products, all have their own concrete plants together with raw materials storage yards (12) (cement silos, bunkers

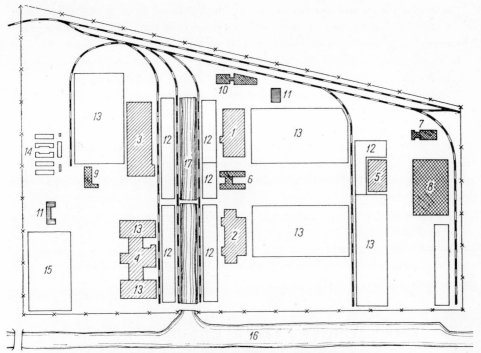

Fig. 3.4.1. Schematic layout of a permanent prefabricates factory:
(1) to (5) basic production units, (6) to (10) auxiliary works, (11) social and administrative buildings, (12) raw material stores, (13) finished products stores, (14) living quarters, (15) sports ground, (16) navigable canal, (17) loading dock

for sand, gravel and other aggregates), maintenance workshops, staff rooms and storage sheds for the finished products (13).

The raw materials are delivered by rail (special sidings) or water (own river-barge dock). Next to the factory are the living quarters (14) and sports ground (15). The daily output of this factory is approx. 1000 m³ of concrete and reinforced concrete products.

Permanent prefabricates factories can also be of smaller proportions, with correspondingly smaller output capacities (e.g. 100 m³ daily). Common characteristics are long term investment (amortisation spread over decades), and the permanency of labour.

Prefabricates may also be produced in temporary field factories, serving the immediate neighbourhood (e.g. a new town). These plants are of seasonal character and most of the work is done by craftsman methods, the degree of mechanisation being lower than in the permanent factories. Only specific units are produced, to meet delivery dates requested by the customer. The rhythm and the volume of production are dependent on the needs of the projects served.

An example of a field factory, organised to serve a specific housing estate is shown diagrammatically in Fig. 3.4.2. Prefabricates are made in the open air (whence the

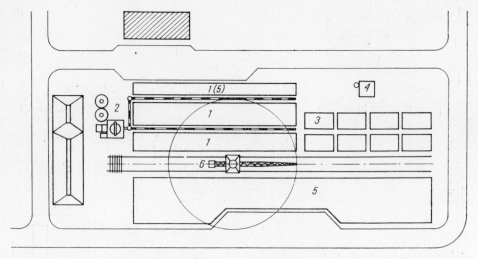

Fig. 3.4.2. Layout of a field precasting factory (explanation in text)

name field factory), on specially prepared production beds (*1*). Concrete is supplied from a central mixing plant (*2*) by means of narrow-gauge dumpers. Accelerated steam curing of the prefabricates is carried out in collapsible autoclaves (*3*), with

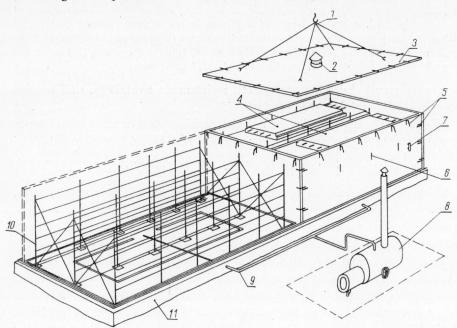

Fig. 3.4.3. A portable box autoclave:
(1) crane hook, (2) vent cowl, (3) roof panel, (4) prefabricates, (5) clamps, (6) handling lugs, (7) thermometers, (8) steam-producing boiler, (9) steam pipes, (10) tubular, stands, (11) base

the steam fed from a small boiler (*4*). Both the production and the storage ground (*5*) are served by a tower crane (*6*) with 45 metric tonnes capacity. Supply of raw materials to the works and delivery of prefabricates to the building site is by means of motor lorries and trucks.

A collapsible autoclave is illustrated in Fig. 3.4.3.

When the prefabricated units are easy to produce and difficult to handle or transport, a casting yard can be prepared on the building site, within reach of the erection crane (Fig. 3.4.4.)

Fig. 3.4.4. A view of an on-site precasting yard

In deciding where the precast components will be made, one must also choose the proper production technology.

As a general principle, it must be accepted that the separation of production from the building site must be accompanied by technological progress, i.e. reduction of manual labour in favour of machines. If, for any reason, mechanisation of the production of a particular prefabricate is not possible, there is no point in transferring the production to a factory far away from the building site.

It may sometimes be advantageous to divide the production of prefabricates for one project between two or more factories. Thus a permanent, highly mechanised factory may produce only floors and internal walls, of which there may be only a few types with IIIrd degree diversification in the whole building. External wall components of much greater diversity may then be made in a field or on-site plant.

Fig. 3.4.5. Examples of the stand system of production:
(a) movable bed, tilting form, (b) fixed bed, picture frame form

According to O. H. Ledderboge, mass production only pays when at least 90% of the total volume of walls built consist of only four types of components with Ist degree diversification. The remainder of the components can be produced by less highly mechanised methods.

3.4.2. Production Techniques

The term "production technique" describes a series of operations directly concerned in the process of making, or, more aptly, of moulding precast units. On the face of it, there are very many techniques, since almost every type of prefabricate requires a specific series of operations in its production. These techniques, however, may be grouped into three basic methods of production. These are:

— the stand system;
— the conveyor belt or production line system;
— the aggregate system.

In the stand system, the prefabricates mature at the point where they were moulded, while the production team moves to successive stands. The bed on which prefabricates are cast may be fixed or movable; tilting forms are often used (Fig. 3.4.5a). The use of a fixed bed is exemplified by the production of precast units in frame forms laid directly on the polished concrete floor of the steam curing chamber (Fig. 3.4.5b).

In a variant of the stand system of production, panels are cast in vertical multi-compartment forms, known as battery moulds (Fig. 3.4.6).

Fig. 3.4.6. Vertical battery moulds for the production of large panels

The conveyor belt system of production splits the whole production process into a series of operations carried out at separate, successive and permanent points, served by specialised teams. The movement of the mould or prefabricate from one point to the next may be by means of a conveyor belt, trolleys, cranes, etc.

As an example of the conveyor belt system, let us take the production of prestressed floor panels, schematically shown in Fig. 3.4.7. Rigid steel forms are assembled

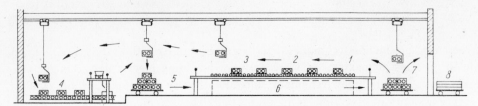

Fig. 3.4.7. A scheme for the conveyor belt production of prestressed floor panels (Explanation in text)

at station 1, where they are cleaned and treated with mould oil to reduce the adhesion of the concrete. The conveyor moves the form to station (2) where the prestressing wires are fixed, the stressing and anchoring being carried out at the next station.

Fig. 3.4.8. An example of the "aggregate" production of hollow floor panels

82

The prepared form is then moved to the casting station (4), where it is filled with concrete and vibrated, and then shifted to station (5), where it remains during the setting time. In turn, forms are loaded on trolleys and introduced into a tunnel autoclave (6). On completion of the steam curing cycle, the trolleys are taken to the de-moulding station (7), whence the finished prefabricates (8) are removed to storage. The forms return to the starting station (1).

The word "aggregate" describes a large, complex, permanently installed set of machines and mechanical appliances, which carry out most of the separate operations involved in casting concrete components (Fig. 3.4.8). The stand is operated by a permanent team. The only move the prefabricate makes is to its maturing point.

Aggregates are used in the production of multiduct hollow floor panels at the Faelbet plant in Warsaw. At the production point, the reinforcement is fixed in the form, and the remote-controlled aggregate then inserts duct formers, casts and vibrates the concrete, floats the top face of the panel and removes the formers. The prepared prefabricate then goes directly to an autoclave chamber, in which the hardening of the concrete is accelerated.

In many factories, combined techniques are employed. Thus, when a particularly complex prefabricate is required, several aggregates are used in succession. This in fact amounts to a production line of aggregates.

The stand technique is the most flexible one. It is used, in varying degrees of mechanisation, in all kinds of precasting factories, though the most common application is in field factories, on account of the simplicity of the operations involved, and of the relatively low capital outlay needed.

On the other hand, large permanent factories often install expensive, but very efficient, aggregates for the mass-production of standardised prefabricates. The same applies to the conveyor-belt system, which is particularly advantageous when the total production process can be easily divided into distinct phases, each demanding special machinery and specialised labour.

3.4.3. Shape and Structure of Prefabricates

The methods of fabrication are greatly influenced by the shape of the products and their structural composition.

Easiest to make are orthogonal prismatic shapes with flat faces. Any variations from the basic shape of the component consisting of small projections, not only complicate manufacture, but are very often damaged in transit. For the same reason, sharp edges should be rounded-off wherever possible.

Any deviation from a simple rectangular shape normally means primitive, and often expensive, production methods. The designer should always judge whether the increased production costs will be balanced by the benefits obtained from the complicated shape.

For example, long hollow ducts, built into floor and wall panels to reduce their weight, are only financially justified when the area of the section of the voids exceeds 30 % of the gross cross-sectional area of the panel.

When prefabricates are cast in tilting forms, or in forms with openable sides, care must be taken to ensure that the proposed shape will allow easy striking (Fig. 3.4.9). More elaborate edges can be achieved by the use of intermittent horizontal inserts.

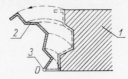

Fig. 3.4.9. An example of the shape of a prefabricate designed to facilitate de-moulding: (1) prefabricate, (2) side view, (0) axis of rotation of the profile

The technology of production is also affected by the material of which the prefabricate is composed.

Generally speaking, we distinguish (section 1.2):
— homogeneous prefabricates, made of a single material, which may be solid or hollow;
— composite, sandwich prefabricates;
— ribbed or grid construction with filler blocks.

The production of homogeneous components is the easiest to mechanise.

Sandwich panels must be made in horizontal forms.

As a rule, the production of ribbed or grid panels with hollow pot or light concrete fillers demands more manual labour than the production of the other two types.

Not only is the production technology, but also its organisation, affected by the composition of the prefabricates.

Since the fabrication of ribbed units requires manual work in laying out filler blocks, and cannot therefore be mechanised, there is no point in transferring their production to a distant specialised factory. They are best made on the building site, within reach of the erection crane, or even directly on a floor already laid.

Sandwich units are made both in permanent factories and in the field casting-yards. In Poland, the technology of sandwich component production is rather primitive in both cases, so there is no point in discussing the relative superiority of factory production over field work. However, the rhythm of field production is less rigid and IIIrd degree diversification of elements is a lesser problem. Further, plant-site contact is much easier in the case of a field factory situated in the vicinity of the building project.

The Russians, and particularly the French, however, have shown that the fabrication of sandwich units can be highly industrialised (E. Coignet).

Homogeneous prefabricates can also be made in the factory or in the field. In this case, however, production technology can vary enormously.

The industrialisation of production necessarily restricts considerably the number of types of prefabricates which can be produced. Only large series are financially worth while.

3.4.4. Tolerances

Tolerance is the limiting value of the admissible deviation in the size or shape of the finished prefabricate from the design requirements (see Fig. 3.4.10).

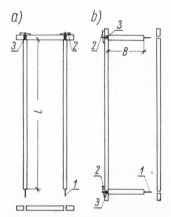

Fig. 3.4.10. Effect of the method of construction on the dimensional accuracy of the finished product: (a) smaller errors in length, (b) more accurate width (1) dowel, (2) wedge, (3) oversize hole for dowel

In practice, it is impossible to make products which will have the exact design dimensions. In fact, extreme precision is pointless, as inaccuracies are unavoidable during erection. Remembering this, the designer should however be able to forecast, or even to dictate, the maximum tolerance values which will guarantee the correct assembly and the efficient functioning of the individual prefabricates. As a decrease in tolerances leads directly to increased costs of production, optimum values of admissible deviations must be established. It must also be noted that large admissible deviations, which are normally made positive as a safety factor, lead to a waste of materials, especially in mass production.

It was discovered, in an establishment making large-block prefabricates, that as a result of working on positive margins the average volume of concrete in their products was increased by 1.5% (the thickness of blocks was on the average 0.5 cm greater). With the production running to 3000 m³ of concrete per month, the excessive monthly use of cement amounted to nearly 15 metric tonnes.

Deviations in the dimensions of prefabricates are attributable in the main to production equipment, but above all to formwork. The crucial factors are the material used in formwork and the manner in which the parts of the forms are joined together.

Because of their deformability and their tendency to warp with moisture, timber

85

forms cannot ensure as close margins of accuracy as can steel or concrete forms. Bolted connections are not recommended for formwork because of the difficulty of threadcleaning. The best accuracy is obtained with self-locking or wedged forms.

As in the machine-tool industry, the notion of the "degree of precision" has been introduced into the prefabricates building industry. This is a conventional scale, defining (in relation to the theoretical dimension of a prefabricate) the maximum permissible tolerance. The scale of precision and the corresponding tolerances are summarised in Table 3.4.1.

TABLE 3.4.1.

DEGREE OF PRECISION AND BASIC TOLERANCES
(DIMENSIONS AND TOLERANCES IN MM)

Degree of precision required	Dimensions of prefabricates (approximate mean dimensions)				
	2 m		15 m		60 m
	up to 100	100 to 300	300 to 3000	3000 to 9000	above 9000
3	0.5	1	2	3	4
4	1	2	3	4	6
5	2	3	4	6	10
6	3	4	6	10	16
7	4	6	10	16	25
8	6	10	16	25	40

Precision in the production of precast components should be higher than the design accuracy of the components themselves. It is advisable to design:
— frame units with an assumed 3rd or 4th degree of precision;
— large panels or blocks, assuming a precision not worse than the 5th degree.

A 6th degree precision may be adequate for non-structural components, provided that their dimensional coordination with other units in not adversely affected.

To determine the overall nominal degree of precision of a prefabricate, we adopt the following rules:
— when only one dimension is critical, the degree of precision corresponding to this dimension is calculated,
— when more than one dimension of the component are allowed tolerances, the degree of precision corresponding to the most vital dimension is computed.

The required degree of precision must be shown on working drawings. This gives the manufacturer a pointer as to what type of formwork he must use in production. It may be accepted that certain specific ranges of precision may be assigned to given types of formwork, namely:
— steel or cast iron moulds   4–5
— concrete moulds   4–6

— vertical battery moulds, steel   5–8
— vertical battery moulds, concrete 6–8
— collapsible steel forms   5–8
— timber forms, bolted or wedged 7–8.

In order to adhere to the design tolerances, the fabrication of the formwork must be more accurate by at least one degree.

The admissible dimensional deviations of the prefabricated components, in accordance with current Polish regulations, are:

(a) blocks,

		(b) panels,	
thickness	−0 +5 mm	thickness	−0 +5 mm
width	−5 +8 mm	width	−5 +10 mm
length (height)	−15 +10 mm	length (height)	−5 +10 mm

(c) beams and columns,

thickness	−3 +5 mm
width	−5 +5 mm
length (height)	−15 +15 mm.

In order to establish the manufacturing tolerances accepted in the production of prefabricates, several branches of the Research Station of the Institute of Building Technology carried out a series over measurements, covering over 2500 prefabricates used in housing construction.

The survey showed that the maximum tolerances were in the following ranges:

(a) with timber forms,		(b) with steel forms,	
thicknesss	7.5–14.0 mm	thickness	3.0–20.0 mm
width	6.5–24.0 mm	width	11.0–22.0 mm
length (height)	10.0–30.0 mm	length (height)	8.0–28.0 mm.

The majority of the results (80%) were grouped near the lower end of the scale of errors. Nevertheless, all the results obtained show deviations larger than the tolerances demanded by the regulations mentioned above.

Of the many regulations governing the permissible discrepancies in components prefabricated abroad, the most interesting is the Hungarian approach. The limiting values of tolerances (in cm) (Fig. 3.4.10) are calculated from the following formulae:

$$\delta_1 = +6 \cdot \frac{l+0.6}{l+6} \; ; \quad \delta_2 = -3 \cdot \frac{l+0.6}{l+6}$$

$$\delta_3 = \pm \frac{5l}{l+6} \; ; \quad \delta_4 = \pm 5 \cdot \frac{l+0.6}{l+6}$$

where $l =$ the length of the edge for which the tolerance is being calculated, in metres.

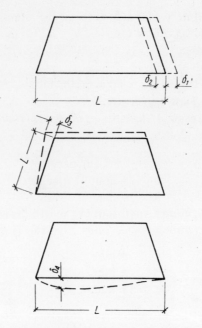

Fig. 3.4.11. Types of deviations in prefabricate recognised by the Hungarian specifications

TABLE 3.4.2.

PREFABRICATE TOLERANCES IN ACCORDANCE WITH
SOVIET STANDARD SPECIFICATIONS

Type of prefabricate	Tolerances, mm		
	Length	Width of cross section	Thickness or height of cross section
Floor panels	±10	±5	±5
Roof panels	+10−5	+5−10	±5
Wall panels	±10	±5	±5
Foundation blocks in housing and in industrial buildings			
— o/a dimensions	±15	±15	±10
— inside dimensions of pockets	+15	+15	+20
Columns			
— o/a dimensions	±10	±5	±5
— from base to top of bracket	−5	—	—
Gantry girders	±10	±5	±5
Beams and trusses up to 18 m span	±10	±5	±5
over 18 m span	±20	±5	±5
Main beams	+10−5	±5	±5
Stair flights	±5	±5	±5
Stair landing slabs	+8−5	±5	+5−3

88

Thus, for a block 2.20 m × 1.20 m × 0.24 m, the admissible deviations are:
For the height (2.20 m): $\delta_1 = 1.9$ cm $\delta_2 = -1.0$ cm
for the width: $\delta_1 = 1.5$ cm $\delta_2 = -0.75$ cm
for the thickness: $\delta_1 = 0.75$ cm $\delta_2 = -0.4$ cm.

These values are thus slightly higher than those set by the Polish authorities.
The tolerances operating in the Soviet Union are given in Table 3.4.2.

3.5. PROBLEMS OF ERECTION

3.5.1. Transport and Erection Equipment

In addition to the conventional motor trucks and railway wagons, special transporters are used to carry prefabricated units from the factory to the building site

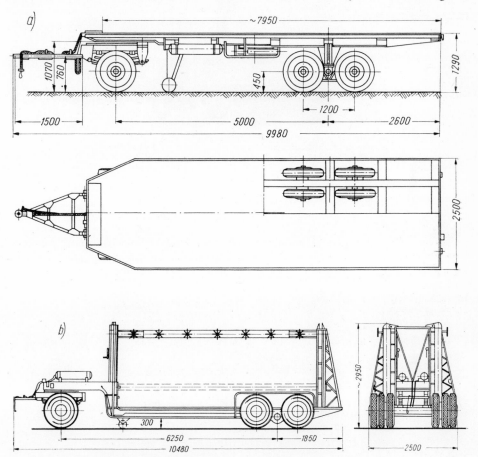

Fig. 3.5.1. Transport trailers for carrying large prefabricates:
(a) in horizontal position, (b) in upright position

89

These are designed to suit prefabricate dimensions and weights, and take into account the most convenient method of loading (Fig. 3.5.1).

In Scandinavia, the lorries used to transport large prefabricates are equipped with power-operated unloading derricks (Fig. 3.5.2). This small investment simplifies enormously the organisation of the site, and also lowers its cost.

Fig. 3.5.2. Prefabricates delivery truck equiped with unloading crane

Tower cranes are most commonly used for the vertical transportation of prefabricates. Their main use is in erection, but they are also used to unload delivery vehicles and to serve the field casting-yards.

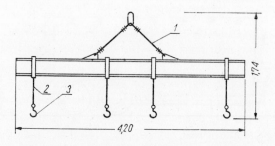

Fig. 3.5.3. Lifting tackle used on Warsaw sites:
(1) 22 mm dia. steel rope, (2) 20 mm dia. steel rope, (3) hooks, each of at least 2.0 tonnes capacity

90

Buildings may also be erected with gantry cranes or truck-mounted cranes.

The tackle used to lift prefabricates consists of steel ropes and beams (Fig. 3.5.3). The beams reduce or completely eliminate the horizontal forces which would otherwise act on the lifting lugs provided in the precast units. The angle of inclination of the ropes in the tackle should not be greater than 30° to the vertical, otherwise the stresses in the lifting lugs may cause them to fail.

Fig. 3.5.4. Erection stays

To facilitate positioning and to steady individual units until their connections are made fast, erection stays are used (Fig. 3.5.4). These stays are attached to the prefabricates after their erection but before the lifting tackle is uncoupled.

3.5.2. Erection of Buildings

Before commencing erection, the setting-out at the level concerned must be carefully checked with surveying instruments. At the same time, the working of the crane and the correct layout of the crane track must be checked.

Any unevenness of the ground often makes it difficult to lay a horizontal crane track. With fairly steep slopes, a rather high embankment is required, and this is both costly and technically difficult. In Czechoslovakia, in such cases, dry staging is built out of large prefabricated blocks specially made for this purpose.

Prefabricated buildings are erected in convenient sections, which, when correctly fixed, should be sufficiently rigid in all directions.

91

The normal sequence of erection is:

(a) structural wall units;

(b) non-structural wall units (partitions, etc.);

(c) floor panels, balconies, stair units;

(d) specialised prefabricates (chimney flues, ventilation ducts, sanitary installations).

If the external walls are hand-laid from small blocks or bricks, all necessary materials should be hoisted by crane and stacked on the floor near to their ultimate position. The masonry work is begun after the floor immediately above is laid.

The erection schedules of two prefabricated buildings in Warsaw are shown in Fig. 3.5.5 and 3.5.6.

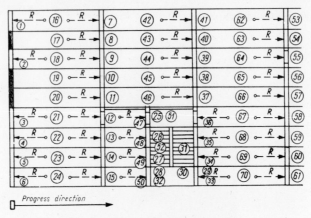

Fig. 3.5.5. Erection schedule of a large-block "Żerań" type building, numbers in circles give the sequence of prefabricate erection, R = stays

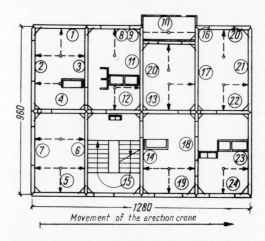

Fig. 3.5.6. Erection schedule of a PBU type large-panel building, numbers in circles denote the sequence of assembly, R = stays

In the large-block building (Fig. 3.5.5), the longitudinal external walls are not shown in the schedule, since these were put up by hand from lightweight curtain-walling units.

In large-panel buildings, as in Fig. 3.5.6, where two external and one internal wall panels come to a common joint, the external panels are erected first and the joint between them is then sealed, before the internal panel is placed.

The progress of erection is largely dependent on the atmospheric conditions.

In accordance with Polish regulations, normal erection work may proceed in winds of up to 10 m/sec (force 5 on the Beaufort scale). In winds of 14 m/sec (force 7), the maximum load of the erection crane must be reduced by 25 %; in winds of 17 m/sec (force 8) by 50 %. When the wind reaches 20 m/sec (force 9), all work must stop and the power supply to the crane must be cut off.

TABLE 3.5.1.

MAXIMUM ERECTION TOLERANCES, MM

Measurements	Types of construction		
	Large-block buildings with walls thicker than 24 cm	Large-block buildings with walls up to 24 cm	Large panel buildings
Displacement of the axes of structural walls	± 5	± 3	± 3
Displacement of the axes of partitions	±10	± 5	± 5
Displacement from the vertical of walls over the height of one storey	±10	± 5	± 5
Displacement from the vertical of walls over the whole height of the building	±30	±20	±20
Deviation of wall from the plane within one apartment	± 5	± 5	± 2.5
Deviation of wall from the plane over the whole length or width of the building	±15	±15	±10
Deviation from the horizontal of the top surface of the wall (per metre)	± 1	± 1	± 1
Deviation from the horizontal of the top surface of the wall (in one apartment)	±10	±10	± 6
Deviation from the horizontal of the top surfaces of the wall (over the whole length of the building)	±30	±30	±25
Deviation of floors, landings and stair steps (per metre)	± 1	± 1	± 1
Thickness of the horizontal joints between prefabricates	+10 −5	+ 5 − 2	+ 5 − 2
Thickness of the vertical joints between prefabricates	+10 −5	+ 5 − 2	+ 5 − 2
Deviation from the design height of the height of each storey height	±30	±20	±20
Deviation from the design height of the total height of the building	±50	±40	±40

When erecting large precast units it is advisable to cease work even sooner, at wind speeds of 17 m/sec. German regulations, on the other hand, forbid work in wind speeds of over 10 m/sec.

For work in artificial light, the intensity of illumination, according to the Polish regulations, must be:

in storage areas   20–50 lux (2–5 foot-candles);
in assembly areas   50–200 lux (5–20 foot-candles).

It is prohibited to proceed with erection during fog, rain or snow, which causes bad visibility and reduce the alertness of the erection crew.

Particular precautions must be taken in the event of erection in cold weather, below freezing point. Only connections similar to those used in structural steelwork (bolting or welding) may be carried out without taking special steps to protect the work from the frost. All cement grouting, however, must be avoided or postponed.

In wintry weather, additions of calcium chloride are very beneficial to the concrete. It can be taken that the addition of 2% by weight of $CaCl_2$ will lower the freezing point of the concrete to $-3\ °C$ (27 °F), and 5% of $CaCl_2$ to $-8\ °C$ (18 °F).

The use of calcium chloride is particularly advisable when ground frost is expected during the night, as it will protect the concrete or the mortar from freezing, and will speed up the hardening process.

In large-panel buildings, electrical heating of concrete in the joints may be well worth the cost.

3.5.3. Erection Tolerances. Completion Checks

The obligatory Polish erection tolerances are given in Table 3.5.1. These tolerances are comparatively strict, but they are normally easily complied with by a skilled erection gang, the final positioning of prefabricates being effected with the aid of adjustable props and stays.

Each horizontal unit should be checked with a spirit level and each vertical unit with a plummet and a spirit level. The distance between the walls is measured with a steel tape, and the thickness of joints with a rule having a millimetre scale.

The accuracy of erection of each completed section of the building is verified by means of surveying instruments after all joints are concreted or grouted.

Chapter 4

GENERAL DESIGN ASSUMPTIONS AND STRUCTURAL REQUIREMENTS

4.1. LOADING CONDITIONS AT VARIOUS STAGES OF THE WORK

4.1.1. General Observations

In the design of a large-prefabricate building, three stages of work, each with their own sets of loading conditions, must be taken into consideration. These are:

Stage A — de-moulding and transport of components;

Stage B — erection;

Stage C — function of individual components in a finished building, and service conditions of the building as a whole.

The service conditions prevailing during Stage C dictate the construction of individual units and the structural concept of the building as a whole, and are therefore the basis of design calculations. If, in later chapters of this work, reference is made to the loading conditions without specifically naming the stage referred to, Stage C conditions are implied.

4.1.2. Stage A

Stage A calculations must check the adequacy of the lifting eyes and the strength of the precast unit, taking into account the adhesion of concrete to the formwork and the dynamic effects of lifting.

In the case of panels cast in the horizontal position, the designer must also check the safety factor allowed against cracks developing on the face of the prefabricate.

The designer should visualize all conditions of support to which a unit is likely to be subjected during the handling stage.

(a) *Loading.* The forces created by the adhesion of a concrete filling to the formwork should be taken at their true value. Where no real estimate of this factor can be made, Polish regulations recommend the assumption of a value:

$$q_A = 300 \text{ kg/m}^2. \qquad [4.1.1]$$

Dynamic effects are guarded against by the condition

$$q_A \geqslant 1.5 \text{ g} \qquad [4.1.2]$$

where *g* is the weight of the unit itself.

95

Following experiments designed to determine the adhesive forces which hold rather complicated ribbed panels in their steel moulds, R. N. Maselnickij found that values of q_A as high as 820 kg/m² occurred only in new, not sufficiently smooth forms, when no mould oil was used. The use of properly oiled forms, ground smooth by prolonged use, reduced the value of q_A to 100–200 kg/m². The strength of the concrete at the moment of de-moulding was 30–100 kg/cm². In other cases, when the strength of the concrete was lower, q_A was correspondingly reduced.

The smoothness of the formwork is the most important factor in deciding the magnitude of q_A. The use of mould oil can only be regarded as an additional measure.

Due allowance must be made in design calculations for the true weight of the wet prefabricate.

The difference in the weight of a component, Δg, when the concrete of which it is made is wet and dry, may be taken for calculation purposes as:

for ordinary concrete · 50 kg/m³
for breeze concretes and cellular concretes 150 kg/m³.

Block units and wall panels should be transported in the vertical position. Floor panels can however be carried vertically, and laid horizontally. Prefabricates are considered to be stacked vertically if they are not inclined more than 2–3° from the vertical.

If, for practical reasons, wall units cannot be transported in the vertical position, the stresses induced in them by the actual conditions of support must be ascertained. Furthermore, the possibility of causing cracks on the exposed faces, both while demoulding and during transport, must be investigated and prevented.

(b) *Lifting devices*. Lifting lugs are made of mild steel in bar form. To avoid internal structural deformations, the lugs should be bent cold when shaped.

The lugs should be so arranged in relation to the centre of gravity of the unit, that each of them carries an equal share of the total load.

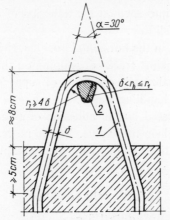

Fig. 4.1.1. Shape and dimensions of a lifting device:
(1) lifting eye, (2) hook in section

96

The lugs may be anchored in the concrete, when the lifting function relies on the bond between the steel and the concrete, or they may be welded to the reinforcement. The latter method is more positive and is to be recommended.

Lifting lugs are normally formed from bars with diameters $\delta = 8-14$ mm, or, in exceptional cases, $\delta = 16$ mm.

The internal radius of the bend r_1 should not be less than 4 δ.

The recommended relationship between the curvature of the bearing surface of the crane hook r_h and the lug dimensions r_1 and δ is given by

$$\delta < r_h \leqslant r_1. \qquad [4.1.3]$$

The most commonly used types of lifting lugs are shown in Figs. 4.1.2 and 4.1.3.

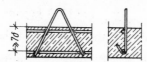

Fig. 4.1.2. Lifting lug welded to prefabricate reinforcement

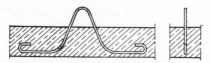

Fig. 4.1.3. Lifting lug embedded in the concrete

The reinforcing bar, to which the lifting eye is welded (Fig. 4.1.2), must be at least 7 δ away from the top surface of the unit.

No welding is involved in the arrangement shown in Fig. 4.1.3. The anchorage length of the bar l_z should be not less than 15 δ in ordinary concrete and 25 δ in lightweight concretes.

Lifting lugs in prefabricates made of cellular concretes must be attached to the reinforcement by welding.

A different provision for lifting is shown in Fig. 4.1.4. Here, one of the main reinforcing bars is exposed over a short length near the edge of the panel. This type of lifting eye is advantageous in production, but is relatively weak.

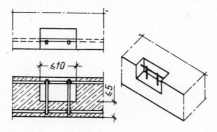

Fig. 4.1.4. Lifting device formed by exposing one bar of the main reinforcement

The required cross-sectional area of a lifting lug is given by the equation:

$$F_z \geqslant \frac{P}{\sigma_z} \qquad\qquad [4.1.4]$$

where P is the tensile strength of the rope attached to the lug, σ_z is the admissible shear stress in the lug, considered to be in single shear.

The force P is obtained from the general equilibrium conditions of the forces acting on the lifting tackle, taking into account adhesion to the formwork, and dynamic effects of hoisting. When a unit is hoisted by means of three or more lugs the calculated value of force P should be increased by 30%.

The admissible shear stress is given by:

$$\sigma_z = m \cdot 1300 \text{ kg/cm}^2$$

where m is a factor dependent on the diameter of the bar, δ:

$$
\begin{array}{lll}
\text{for } \delta = 8 \text{ mm} & m = 1.1 \\
\text{for } \delta = 10 \text{ or } 12 \text{ mm} & m = 1.0 \\
\text{for } \delta = 14 \text{ mm} & m = 0.95 \\
\text{for } \delta = 16 \text{ mm} & m = 0.85
\end{array}
$$

4.1.3. Stage B

It is necessary to check that the units possess adequate strength to resist the working loads encountered during Stage B (the erection stage), and that individual fragments of the structure are stable during assembly.

The working load comprises the weight of the materials stored, scaffolding, men and their implements. As a rule, the maximum permissible value of the working load per unit area is calculated for Stage B, on the basis of the behaviour of the units, with their reinforcement, under Stage C conditions.

In some cases, e.g. roof slabs with an upper layer of lightweight concrete originally containing a large quantity of water, it may be the case that the weight of materials during the erection stage may be much greater than its final weight, estimated during Stage C. This condition must be taken into account in Stage B calculations.

When the prefabricated components are joined by in-situ infills, an estimate has to be made of the strength of the concrete required to support the load of the upper levels after the latter are erected.

The stability of any part of the structure is ensured when all prefabricated components in that part are either stable of themselves, or are connected into a space system which is stable.

Components are stable when they meet the following conditions (Fig. 4.1.5):

$$G(z - e_t) \geqslant 0.6 \ w \cdot b \cdot l^2 \qquad\qquad [4.1.5]$$

where G is the weight of the component, and $z \leqslant \dfrac{h}{2}$ is the smallest distance between

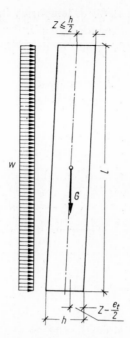

Fig. 4.1.5. Diagram showing the self-equilibrium of a prefabricate

the centre of gravity and the edge of the component, e_t is the eccentricity resulting from unavoidable errors in the production and erection of the component; this is given by:

$$e_t = \left[0.03 + \frac{l/h - 3}{300} \right] h = 0.02 h + \frac{l}{300}$$

where l is the height of the unit, w the wind pressure per unit area, and b the width of the unit.

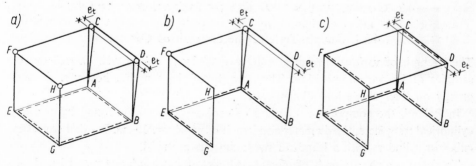

Fig. 4.1.6. Stability of a set of prefabricates:
(a) unstable, (b), (c) stable

99

When condition [4.1.5] is not fulfilled, temporary bracing must be provided and maintained until the components are connected in three dimensions. The conditions describing the spatial stability of a group of prefabricates are shown in Fig. 4.1.6.

4.1.4. Stage C

Stage C calculations deal with the ability of the completed structure to withstand the working loads for which it was designed, taking atmospheric factors into account.

The loads acting during Stage C may be of permanent, long-term nature, or they may be temporary or of short duration.

Concrete is subject to additional rheological deformations when under long-term stress. Thus, it is essential to remember the time characteristics of a system of loads when calculating the deflections of the horizontal components (floors, roofs, stairs), and the loadbearing capacity of eccentrically loaded slender components.

The effect of long-term loading on the strength of eccentrically loaded slender components manifests itself in an increase in the eccentricity due to long-term bending deformations. With greater eccentricity of the loading, the permissible load decreases.

Although prolonged loading increases the deflection of flexural components, it does not essentially affect their strength, and no distinction is made between long and short-term loads in strength calculations pertaining thereto.

Polish regulations recognise the following as long-term loads:
— the weight of the structure itself and of other built-in portions of the buildings;
— the weight of any soil supported, or the pressure of soil retained by the structure;
— the full superimposed load in buildings or parts of buildings of warehouse class (libraries, archives, etc.);
— the superimposed floor load in workshops, less 150 kg/m².

The short-term loads are:
— the full superimposed floor load in housing construction;
— snow and wind loads.

4.2. CONCRETE AS A STRUCTURAL MATERIAL

4.2.1. Sample Tests of the Strength of Concrete

The strength of various concretes is determined by means of tests carried out on samples of known composition. The strength of the samples, however, depends greatly on their shape and dimensions.

In Poland, the compression strength of ordinary concrete is found by crushing cylindrical test pieces, the diameter and length of which are 16 cm. In other countries, cubes or cylinders with a length of two diameters are used.

To determine the strength of mortar, cylinders 8 cm in diameter and length are used in Poland, while for cellular concretes, 10 cm cubes are standard.

When utilising the research results of others, it is extremely important to allow for the size and shape of the test pieces used in the research.

TABLE 4.2.1.

CONVERSION FACTORS FOR STANDARDISING THE RESULTS OF THE COMPRESSION TESTS CARRIED OUT ON SAMPLES OF VARIOUS SHAPES

Shape of sample	Conversion factors A for several strength groups (R_c, kg/cm^2)				
	$\leqslant 150$	151–250	251–350	351–450	$\geqslant 451$
20 cm cube	1.15	1.21	1.24	2.27	1.31
15 cm cube	1.30	1.35	1.38	1.40	1.47
10 cm cube	1.34	1.37	1.41	1.44	1.50
7 cm cube	1.36	1.40	1.44	1.47	1.53
5 cm cube	1.38	1.43	1.50	1.50	1.56
20×20×60 cm prism	0.92	0.97	0.99	1.02	1.05
Cylinder, 20 cm dia. × 20 cm	1.00	1.00	1.00	1.00	1.00
,, 16 cm dia. × 16 cm	1.09	1.10	1.11	1.12	1.13
,, 8 cm dia. × 8 cm	1.25	1.27	1.28	1.28	1.29
,, 15 cm dia. × 30 cm	1.00	1.00	1.00	1.00	1.00

Table 4.2.1 gives the values of a coefficient A, which is the ratio of the crushing strengths R_d of test samples of various shapes to the standard value R_c.

$$A = \frac{R_d}{R_c}.$$ [4.2.1]

The coefficients A shown in Table 4.2.1 are the mean values for carefully compacted samples with a w/c ratio varying between 0.3 and 0.6. Ordinary concrete, the cement content of which varied from 280 kg/m^3 to 400 kg/m^3, was used.

The value of A is considerably affected by the modulus of elasticity of the concrete used. For this reason, the values of A for lightweight concrete are really somewhat lower than those given in Table 4.2.1.

4.2.2. The Basic Strength and the Required Strength of Concrete

The basic strength of concrete is the strength of a standard sample after 28 days of hardening under fixed conditions of temperature (18 °C) and relative air humidity (60 %). The strengths of samples provide no real basis for comparison.

In design, and particularly in the design of prefabricated components, the concrete strength required for a particular loading condition need not necessarily be the basic, 28 day strength. Indeed, it is important that the desired strength should be

101

attained at a much earlier stage, and to this end steps are very often taken to accelerate the hardening of the concrete.

The strength of the concrete required for Stage A work is denoted by $R(A)$, for Stage B by $R(B)$, and for Stage C by $R(C) = R$.

4.2.3. Strength of Concrete as used in Structural Calculations

It is common knowledge that the crushing strength of a test piece is not identical to the strength of the same concrete in the mathematical sense, i.e. the stresses obtained in tests do not strictly correspond to the failure strains in axial compression. The discrepancies are due, firstly, to friction occurring between the surfaces of the sample and the pressure plates of the testing machine, and secondly, to eccentricity of loading. Consequently, the sample is subjected to a stress system more complex than the purely compressive stress and the distribution of stresses over the tested cross-section is not uniform. To determine the true mathematical strength of concrete in compression, one would have to ensure (at the cross-section at which the failure is to occur), an ideally uniform distribution of stresses, so that failure would occur simultaneously at all points of the section. Only then would the value of the failure load, divided by the area of the destroyed cross-section, give the true mathematical compressive strength of the concrete, R.

It is possible, by simply increasing the height of the test piece, to eliminate the effect of friction at the contact surfaces. Much more difficult is to ensure strict concentricity of loading. Axial compression could be guaranteed if the testing machine could be adjusted during the test to give equal (measured) strains on all four side faces of the sample, at all times until failure occurs.

Such test presses, which allow for the adjustment of the loading axis during the test (without release of pressure), are at present in the possession of very few laboratories, and it will be some time yet before an exact relationship between the crushing strength of a sample and the true compressive strength of the concrete can be determined.

The discrepancy between the failure loads obtained when testing various concrete and reinforced concrete components to destruction, and the theoretical values of the loads estimated from the strength of the concrete as shown by sample tests, was discovered long ago. Attempts to account for this along empirical lines did not immediately disclose all the reasons for this discrepancy, and as a result, two separate concepts were introduced into the standard specifications: the strength of the concrete under direct compression R_s, and its strength under compression due to bending R_m. The first of these appears in formulae for structural components loaded "axially" or with a small eccentricity, and the latter in formulae for components compressed non-axially or in bending. The values quoted in current Soviet standard specifications are shown in Table 4.2.2.

The strength under direct compression is determined by testing rectangular

TABLE 4.2.2.

STRENGTH OF CONCRETE USED IN STRUCTURAL CALCULATIONS CURRENT IN SOVIET STANDARD SNiP II-W 1-62

Kind of strength	Designations	Strength of concrete $R_{□20}$ as measured on cubic samples 20×20×20 cm										
		35	50	75	100	150	200	250	300	400	500	600
Strength of concrete under direct compression	R_s	28	40	60	80	115	145	175	210	280	350	420
Strength of concrete under compression due to bending	R_m	35	50	75	100	140	180	215	260	350	440	520
Strength of concrete under tension R_r		5	6	8	10	13	16	18	21	25	28	30

prisms, whose height is usually three times the width of the base, say 20×20×60 cm. These proportions permit the assumption that the friction at the ends of the test piece has no effect on the result. The pressure on the sample, however, is still inadvertently eccentric to some extent. In effect, then, that factor, which in a short sample increases its strength, is eliminated, while the eccentricity of loading will still cause failure at stresses less than the theoretical. The distribution of stress is not uniform and failure does not occur simultaneously over the whole cross-section. In consequence, as is evident from Table 4.2.2, the direct compression strength R_s is smaller than the strength $R_{□20}$ obtained with short test samples. Because of the eccentricity, it is also lower than the true calculated compression strength R. On the average, it can be taken that:

$$R_s = 0.8 \ R. \tag{4.2.2}$$

The strength under direct compression, R_s, has been incorporated in standard specifications because the results of tests carried out on axially-loaded structural components are thereby brought into agreement with the calculated values. However, this conformity of results is deceptive. When testing full-size structural components under compression, a degree of eccentricity of loading is unavoidable, just as when prismoidal specimens are tested to determine R_s. Thus, an underestimated value of R_s is apparently confirmed by full-scale tests. When the eccentricity of load acting on the structural components under test can be accurately estimated, the experimentally determined strength of the component will be considerably higher than its theoretical strength calculated on the basis of the given value R_s.

There is little chance that similar errors of appreciation of the test conditions will occur when dealing with flexural components. For this reason, the value of R_m specified for the strength of concrete under bending compression is higher than R_s.

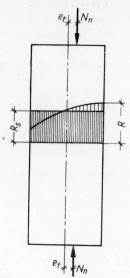

Fig. 4.2.1. The distribution of stresses over the cross-section of a sample used to determine the strength R_s

The value R_m is determined by loading to destruction test beams which are very strongly reinforced in the tensile zone and unreinforced in the compression zone. A rectangular distribution of the stresses in the compression zone is assumed. This is in fact a simplification of the true distribution at the instant of failure, which is closer to parabolic. The result obtained is, nevertheless, so close to the true value of R, that for practical purposes it may be accepted that

$$R_m = R. \qquad [4.2.3]$$

Table 4.2.2 shows that for low strength concretes $(R < 100 \text{ kg/cm}^2)$, $R = R_{\square 20}$, but for stronger concretes $(R > 300 \text{ kg/cm}^2)$, $R \approx 0.85\ R_{\square 20}$.

An appreciation of the true strength of a concrete under compression R is particularly important in the design of slender wall components, generally unreinforced, in which all the stresses are carried by the concrete. In view of the small thickness of the components and the presence of an appreciable degree of incidental eccentricity of loading (relative to this thickness), it is imperative to allow for this eccentricity in design calculations. In this situation, the use of the value R_s would lead to unnecessary over-design.

By allowing for the incidental eccentricity of loading one can also replace R_s, in empirical formulae, by the value $R = R_m$.

The tensile strength of concrete, R_r, given in standard specifications, is also lower than the true tensile strength, as in the case of the compression strength. However, as this property is of lesser importance in the design of walls and is greatly influenced

104

by incidental factors (shrinkage, curing conditions), the discrepancy may be over-looked and the standard value R_r used.

An approximate value of R_r for lightweight concretes having $R < 100$ kg/cm^2 may be obtained from the expression:

$$R_r = 0.5 \sqrt[3]{R^2}. \qquad [4.2.4]$$

For stronger lightweight concretes, the ratio R_r/R is similar to that for normal concretes.

4.2.4. Reduced Concrete Strength

It is occasionally necessary to take into account the conditions in which a concrete is expected to serve when determining its design strength.

Normally, the strength assumed in design is the strength of the concrete in the air-dry condition, i.e. with a moisture content equal to its natural absorption capacity from air of 60 % relative humidity at 18 °C. If the actual conditions are expected to be more humid, the strength of lightweight concrete should be suitably adjusted for design purposes.

The reduction of strength due to wetting is particularly sharp in cellular concretes. Table 4.2.3 (after Makarichev), gives the mean values of the ratio of wet strength $R(w)$ to oven-dry strength, for concretes with varying moisture contents; the latter are quoted as percentages of the total weight.

TABLE 4.2.3.

REDUCTION OF THE STRENGTH OF CELLULAR CONCRETE WHEN DAMP

Water content as % of dry weight	0	5	8	10	15	20	25
$\dfrac{R_{(w)}}{R_{\mathrm{dry}}}$	1	0.90	0.84	0.80	0.75	0.70	0.65

In concretes made from lightweight aggregates, the effect of moisture content on the strength is somewhat lesser. Nevertheless, if the moisture content rises from 5 % to 20 %, a 10–15 % decrease in strength must be allowed for in calculations.

A fall in the strength of a concrete may also result from the action of high temperatures. For this reason it is necessary to manufacture components which contain smoke flues from special concretes (section 7.1.4).

The strength of the concrete used for such units should, for design purposes, be taken to be

$$R' = 0.5 \, R$$

and not higher than $R' = 75$ kg/cm^2.

105

4.2.5. Frost Resistance and Minimum Strength

The concrete in a prefabricated component should be resistant to the action of frost.

Lightweight concretes are considered to be frost-resistant if, after 10 cycles of freezing to −15 °C and thawing at +15 °C, the strength of the test samples is not less than 90 % of the untreated samples. As an additional condition respecting the use of light concrete components, is the stipulation of 2–3 cm external render.

The requirements for ordinary concretes are stricter. Polish regulations require that concretes of Mk. 90 and below, exposed constantly to frost and damp, be subjected to 25 test cycles of freezing to −15 °C and thawing. The resulting reduction in strength should not be more than 20 %. There is no prescription for testing the resistance of concretes stronger than Mk. 110, since these may be considered resistant to the action of frost.

Concretes used as non-structural elements need not be highly resistant to the action of frost, provided that they are protected from damp in the finished building, and that steps are taken to prevent their freezing when wet during transportation, storage and erection. In several instances, when cellular concrete blocks used in ribbed floor units were damaged by frost during storage, plaster ceilings subsequently fell off over large areas.

The minimum strength of the concrete used to build prefabricated components must also be related to the resistance of the latter to damage during transportation.

Polish regulations demand that structural walls should consist of components made from ordinary concretes not weaker than 140 kg/cm², or light concretes not weaker than 30 kg/cm².

Prefabricates made of light concrete with a crushing strength of 30 kg/cm² may be used only in non-loadbearing walls, or in loadbearing walls in buildings of not more than two storeys. In taller buildings, the concretes used for loadbearing wall components must not be weaker than 50 kg/cm².

4.2.6. Strength of Concrete during Stage A

The strength of the concrete required at the time of demoulding and during transportation must be stipulated in the design.

The commonly used criterion

$$R_A \geqslant 0.5 R \qquad [4.2.5]$$

where R is the Stage C design strength, is, in the author's opinion, inadequately substantiated. Production conditions and the likelihood of cracks forming on the face of the prefabricate should be borne in mind when deciding the required value of R_A.

According to Soviet recommendations, the strength R_A of ordinary concrete should not be less than:

— for components with $h/l > \dfrac{1}{15}$, $\quad R_A = 80$ kg/cm²;

— for components with $h/l \leqslant \dfrac{1}{15}$, or with a surface area of more than 10 m²,

$R_A = 100$ kg/cm²,
where h is the thickness of the component and l the length.

When these conditions are fulfilled, there is no need to check the safety factor s_A under normal conditions of transportation.

4.2.7. Elasticity of Concrete

Normal structural calculations utilise the concept of the modulus of elasticity. This is a constant, giving the ratio of stresses σ to strains ε for a given material,

$$E = \frac{\sigma}{\varepsilon} \qquad [4.2.6]$$

In reality, concrete deforms under load in a plastic manner in addition to the elastic strains, and the function $\varepsilon(\sigma)$ is consequently non-linear. Over a narrow range of stresses, however, the modulus of elasticity is given by the expression:

$$E = \frac{\sigma_2 - \sigma_1}{\varepsilon(\sigma_2) - \varepsilon(\sigma_1)} \qquad [4.2.7]$$

where $\varepsilon(\sigma_1)$ and $\varepsilon(\sigma_2)$ are the strains corresponding to stresses σ_1 and σ_2 respectively.

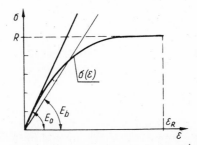

Fig. 4.2.2. Relationship between stresses σ and strains ε in concrete

In theoretical considerations, two values are used (Fig. 4.2.2):
E_0, the initial modulus of elasticity of the concrete, defined by the slope of the tangent to the function $\varepsilon(\sigma)$ at the point $\sigma = 0$;
E_b, accepted as the modulus of elasticity of the concrete, and defined by the slope of the secant to the function $\varepsilon(\sigma)$ through the points $\sigma_1 = 0$ and $\sigma_2 = 0.50 \ R$.

The term E_0 occurs in formulae based on the non-linearity of function $\varepsilon(\sigma)$, and is most often used in calculating the strength of unreinforced concrete walls (section 7.5).

The relationship of E_0 to the ultimate compression strength of the concrete R, may be written:

$$E_0 = a \cdot R \qquad\qquad [4.2.8]$$

where a is the elasticity characteristic of the concrete.

The term E_b is employed in calculations based on the assumption of a linear variation of $\sigma(\varepsilon)$.

In the stress range $0 < \sigma < 0.3R$, and occasionally for stronger concretes, up to $0 < \sigma < 0.5R$, the variation of $\varepsilon(\sigma)$ is very nearly linear. This range of stresses is therefore considered to be the elasticity range of the concrete, and E_b is known as its modulus of elasticity.

Values of E_b, related to the quality of the concrete, are given in various specifications governing the design characteristics of reinforced concrete.

On the average, it may be taken that

$$E_b = 0.85 \, E_0. \qquad\qquad [4.2.9]$$

Sometimes, in addition to E_b, reinforced concrete design specifications also mention a term E_{br}, the modulus of elasticity of concrete in tension, or more accurately, in bending. An approximate value for E_{br} is given by:

$$E_{br} = 0.6 \, E_b. \qquad\qquad [4.2.10]$$

This term is used in deflection calculations involving methods of serial approximation, for example, when solving statically indeterminate systems. By decreasing the value of the modulus of elasticity of the concrete, allowance is made for the decrease in the flexural rigidity of the members, occurring due to the formation of cracks in the tensile zone.

E_{br} must not be identified with the tensile modulus of elasticity of the concrete, E_r, which is analogous to E_b. These factors are related approximately by the formula:

$$E_r = 0.9 \, E_b. \qquad\qquad [4.2.11]$$

The technical literature quotes a wide range of values of E in respect of concrete of various qualities. Comparison of the values quoted in the standards specifications of various countries may reveal disparities as high as 20 %. This is because such values are obtained on the basis of tests of samples involving a wide variety of aggregates and methods of compacting. Moreover, as E is in any case a conventional value, the character of the research and the assumptions made when evaluating the results must have an appreciable effect.

Table 4.2.4 and Fig. 4.2.3. give values of the initial modulus of elasticity E_0, in accordance with Soviet specifications. The caption of the original table states that these figures were obtained for stresses $\sigma = 0.2 \, R_s$. They are, however, rather low and should be considered nearer to the corresponding values of E_b.

Table 4.2.5 shows the values of E_b and E_{br} given in the Polish specifications.

TABLE 4.2.4.

INITIAL MODULUS OF ELASTICITY E_0
(from SNiP II-A 10-62)

Initial modulus of elasticity E_0, kg/cm²

Mark of concrete	Ordinary concrete (except no-fines concrete)			Lightweight aggregate concrete (except no-fines)				Cellular concrete		No-fines concrete	
	Cement-bound		Silica concrete	Artificial aggregate with unit weight, kg/m³		Natural aggregates with unit weight, kg/m³		Cement-bound	Silicate	Normal	Light-weight
	Ordinary aggregates	Sand aggregates		$\geqslant 700$	< 700	$\geqslant 700$	< 700				
1	2	3	4	5	6	7	8	9	10	11	12
25	—	—	—	—	—	—	—	17000	14000	—	14000
35	—	—	—	50000	35000	30000	25000	20000	50000	20000
50	110000	85000	—	70000	50000	40000	38000	30000	70000	30000
75	155000	115000	—	95000	65000	50000	50000	40000	100000	50000
100	190000	140000	—	110000	80000	65000	75000	60000	130000	—
150	230000	170000	110000	130000	100000	80000	100000	80000	—	—
200	265000	200000	135000	150000	115000	95000	—	—	—	—
250	290000	220000	160000	165000	125000	—	—	—	—	—
300	315000	235000	185000	180000	135000	—	—	—	—	—
400	350000	255000	210000	—	—	—	—	—	—	—
500	380000	285000	—	—	—	—	—	—	—	—
600	400000	300000	—	—	—	—	—	—	—	—

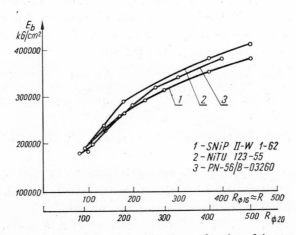

1 – SNiP II-W 1-62
2 – NiTU 123-55
3 – PN-56/B-03260

Fig. 4.2.3. Graph of the modulus of elasticity E_b as a function of the strength $R_{\square 20}$

109

TABLE 4.2.5.

ELASTICITY MODULI OF CONCRETE, E_b AND E_{br}, IN TONNES/cm²
(Polish standards)

Elasticity modulus	Type of concrete	Strength of concrete $R_{\phi 16}$, kg/cm²									
		50	70	90	110	140	170	200	250	300	400
E_b	ordinary	—	—	180	200	230	260	290	320	340	380
	lightweight	70	90	103	120	—	—	—	—	—	—
E_{br}	ordinary	—	—	110	125	140	160	180	200	210	240
	lightweight	44	56	64	75	—	—	—	—	—	—

For purposes of comparison, the values of E quoted in the British Code of Practice CP 115 for ordinary concrete, are shown below in both British and metric units.

28-day strength of 6 inch cubes		Modulus of elasticity	
lbs/in²	kg/cm²	lbs/in² $\times 10^6$	T/cm²
3000	211	3	211
4000	281	4	281
5000	352	4.5	316
6000	422	5	352
8000	565	6	422
10,000	703	6.5	457

4.2.8. The Use of Parameters R, R_r and a in Structural Calculations

Tables 4.2.6 and 4.2.7 present a series of values of the basic parameters R, R_r and a, which are, in the author's opinion, applicable to strength calculations.

The elasticity characteristic a was obtained, in the case of ordinary concretes, by taking the ratio E_b/E_0, according to Eq. [4.2.9]:

$$a = \frac{E_b}{0.85} \cdot \frac{1}{R} = \frac{1,180,000}{\left(1.7 + \dfrac{375}{R}\right) R}. \qquad [4.2.12]$$

The value of E_b for sand concrete was accepted as seven tenths of that of ordinary concrete.

The values of a quoted for light aggregate concretes in Table 4.2.6 apply when the concrete is close-textured. Where the structure is cellular, the value of a is reduced by 20–60 %, depending on the porosity of the concrete.

The values quoted in Table 4.2.7 for the parameters R, R_r and a of aerated concretes apply when the moisture content of the air-dry material contributes not more

TABLE 4.2.6.

Strength of concrete				Elasticity characteristic α						
$R_{\phi 16}$	$R_{\square 20}$	R	R_r	ordinary concrete	sand concrete	clinker concrete with clinker sand	clinker concrete with natural sand	expanded clay concrete	concrete with expanded shale aggregate	
	kg/cm²									
30	32	30	4.5	—	—	1200	—	1400	—
50	53	30	6.5	—	—	1200	1500	1200	—
70	74	70	8	—	—	1000	1400	1100	1450
90	95	90	10	2250	1500	—	1300	1000	1400
110	116	110	11.5	2100	1400	—	1200	950	1300
140	151	140	13.5	1900	1300	—	—	900	1200
170	187	170	15.5	1750	1200	—	—	800	1100
200	220	200	17.5	1650	1100	—	—	—	1000
250	280	250	20	1500	1000	—	—	—	—
300	340	300	24	1350	900	—	—	—	—
400	450	400	28	1100	—	—	—	—	—

TABLE 4.2.7.

Type	Class	$R_{\square 10}^{dry}$	R	R_r	α
			kg/cm²		
09	I	75	60	6.0	600
07	extra	60	40	4.5	600
	I	50	35	3.5	650
05	I	30	20	2.5	600

than 10 % of its unit weight. Should the dampness of the concrete be greater, they must be adjusted proportionally to $R(w)/R(s)$.

4.3. THE SAFETY FACTOR

4.3.1. The Basic Value of the Safety Factor

The aim of structural calculations is, amongst others, to check that the safety factor of the structure or its components is at least equal to a so-called global safety factor s, given in the relevant regulations.

The value of this factor is given by the product

$$s = s_0 \cdot m \qquad [4.3.1]$$

where s_0 is the basic safety factor, and m the correction factor designed to take into account the conditions of service.

Values of s_0, taken from the Polish "Regulations for the Design of Buildings made of Large Prefabricates", are as follows:

— *for prefabricated structures classified for design purposes as being of plain concrete*
— ordinary concrete, at least Mk 140 $\qquad s_0 = 2.5$
— lightweight close-textured concretes
 and autoclaved cellular concretes $\qquad s_0 = 3.0$
— open-textured concretes (no-fines) $\qquad s_0 = 3.5$
— *for reinforced concrete structures and for welded connections*, values of s_0 to be taken from appropriate standards.

The above s_0 values for plain concrete structures apply when failure is due to the fact that the concrete had reached its ultimate compression strength.

When tension is critical, an adjustment to the basic factors is made; a new value $s_1 > s_0$ is used, where:
— for ordinary concretes $\qquad s_1 = 3.0$
— for close-textured lightweight concretes $\qquad s_1 = 3.5$
— for autoclaved cellular concretes $\qquad s_1 = 4.5$
— for open-textured concretes (no-fines) $\qquad s_1 = 4.0$.

Values of s_1 are also used in checking the principal stresses in reinforced lightweight concrete components.

When designing joints and considering the possibility of crack formation, the basic factors should be adjusted as follows:
— when cracks would alter the structural system assumed in the design (sections 5.2.4; 6.2): $\qquad s_1 = 4.5$
— when the formation of cracks does not affect the strength of the structure (section 7.2): $\qquad s_1 = 1.5$.

The basic safety factors s_0 and s_1, as specified by Polish standards, were obtained from the formula

$$s_0 = \frac{\nu}{\mu} \qquad [4.3.2]$$

where ν is the load-increase factor, μ is the product of μ_1 — the strength-reduction factor — and μ_2, a coefficient allowing for the specific characteristics of the component.

The load-increase factor ν is the ratio of the maximum load q_{ex} which could occur during construction and while the building is in service, to the load q taken in the design.

The value of q_{ex} is determined by the probability of the occurrence of extremes

112

of load, in such a way that v becomes greater for superimposed loads than for dead loads.

The term μ_1 is calculated as the ratio of the lowest possible strength of the material, within defined limits of probability, to the mean strength accepted in design calculations.

The coefficient μ_2 represents the effect on the safety of the structure of such factors as evenness of compacting, degree of reinforcement (particularly with respect to the not-so-well compacted parts of the component), etc.

Greater economy in the design is achieved when the basic safety factor s_0 is replaced in calculations by the terms v and μ.

The Soviet standard SNiP II-A 10-62 gives the following values for the load-increase factors:

— for dead loads (except the weight of retaining walls and the weight of thermal insulation) $\qquad v = 1.1$
— for the weight of retaining walls themselves $\qquad v = 0.8$
— for the weight of thermal insulation material $\qquad v = 1.2$
— for superimposed floor loads (in apartments) $\qquad v = 1.4$.

Assuming that, in the loadbearing walls of a block of flats, 25 % of the total load consists of superimposed floor loads, the value of v may be determined as follows:

$$v = 0.75 \times 1.1 + 0.25 \times 1.4 = 1.18.$$

Values of v, μ_1, and μ_2, calculated on the basis of the Soviet standard mentioned above by similar methods, together with the resulting basic safety factors s_0 for buildings made of unreinforced large prefabricates, are given in Table 4.3.1.

The reduction in μ_2 for components cast in vertical battery moulds is necessitated by the fact, confirmed in tests, that the strength of the upper parts of such components is reduced.

The values of s_0 given in Table 4.3.1 compare well with those quoted in the Polish Guiding Regulations mentioned earlier.

Granted that stringent quality control of the concrete has been maintained, and if the results of tests provide good reason, the value of μ_1 may be increased by 0.05. This results in a decrease in the safety factor s_0 by some 10 %.

For reinforced prefabricates, the values of μ_2 are increased by 10 %, which also lowers s_0 by approx. 10 %.

4.3.2. The Correction Factor

A factor m is used to correct the value of the basic safety factor s_0 according to the degree to which the working conditions have been allowed for in the design. The discrepancy between the theoretical and actual cross-sectional dimensions, and also the various types of loads considered in the calculations are of primary concern.

113

TABLE 4.3.1.

THE SAFETY FACTOR s_0, CALCULATED ACCORDING TO SOVIET
STANDARD SPECIFICATIONS

Type of concrete		Component factors			
		over-load	unifor-mity of mate-rial	specific character-istics	Safety factor
		v	μ_1	μ_2	s_0
Ordinary concrete $R_{\square 20} \leqslant 200$ kg/cm²	Horizontal forms	1.18	0.55	0.90	2.38
and lightweight concrete $R_{\square 20} \geqslant 150$ kg/cm²	Vertical battery moulds (wall units)	1.18	0.55	0.77	2.79
Ordinary concrete $R_{\square 20} \geqslant 250$ kg/cm²	Horizontal forms	1.18	0.60	0.90	2.18
	Vertical battery moulds (wall units)	1.18	0.60	0.77	2.55
Lightweight concrete, $R_{\square 20} \leqslant 100$ kg/cm²		1.18	0.50	0.90	2.62
Autoclaved cellular concrete		1.18	0.45	0.90	2.91
Vibrated brickwork prefabricates		1.18	0.40	0.90	3.28
No-fines concretes in monolithic walls		1.18	0.40	0.90	3.28

The Polish "Guiding Regulations" treat m as a product of several factors, namely:

$m_1 = 0.9$, if the external forces used in calculations include the wind load and the horizontal forces present in walls which are not vertical;

$m_2 = 1.20$ (for wall components), if the cross-sectional area is less than the critical value, which is:

$F = 0.06$ m² for concretes Mk. 140 or stronger,

$F = 0.10$ m² for other concretes;

$m_3 = m_{d1}$ in Table 7.5.1, for wall components, when no distinction is made between permanent and short-term loads (section 7.5.2);

$m_4 = 0.9$, for wall components the strength of which is calculated according to the basic method given in section 7.5.6.

In most countries, provision is made in practice for modifying the required safety factor relating to the cross-sectional area of the component. Thus, for wall prefabricates with $F < 0.1$ m², the Soviet standard SNiP II-W I-62 recommends a modifying factor

$$m_2 = \frac{1}{0.80} = 1.25.$$

Particularly stringent are the Czechoslovak regulations, in accordance with which the value of m_2 is related to the smallest lateral dimension, h, of the component. For columns and walls with h less than 30 cm,

$$m_2 = 1 + 0.05(30 - h). \qquad [4.3.3]$$

It must be explained, however, that the high values of m_2 thus obtained are justified by the fact that calculations based on this standard disregard the question of initial eccentricity (section 7.5).

4.3.3. Safety Factors for Stages A and B

The failure of a prefabricate during Stages A and B would cause less damage than if it occurred during Stage C, and in view of this, the values of the safety factors s corresponding to the early stages may be reduced.

Polish "Guiding Regulations" authorise the following reductions in the value of s in these stages:

$$\text{for Stage A} \qquad s(A) = 0.75 \ s$$

$$\text{for Stage B} \qquad s(B) = 0.85 \ s.$$

In the case of wall panels cast in the horizontal position, the safety factor allowed against cracking during Stage A should not be less than

$$s(A) = 1.3.$$

Generally speaking, prefabricates should be so designed that they are not likely to require more reinforcement during Stages A and B than is needed for Stage C.

4.4. EXPANSION JOINTS

4.4.1. Maximum Spacing of Expansion Joints

The maximum spacing L_{max} of expansion joints in a prefabricated building depends on the type of construction under consideration, the materials used in the external walls, and local temperature variations.

Values of L_{max} suggested in the "Guiding Regulations" are shown in Table 4.4.1.

The recommendations of various standards in this matter are based mainly on practical observations and often vary widely.

TABLE 4.4.1.

MAXIMUM SPACING OF EXPANSION JOINTS

Type of external wall	Maximum spacing of expansion joints, or maximum length of the building, metres
Large-block	35
Large-panel, homogeneous	45
Large-panel, sandwich	60
Curtain walls	80

One method of calculating the spacing of expansion joints is given by A. Emelianov.

After a series of investigations, he decided that concrete external walls, whose thermal conductivity $U = 0.7$ to 1.1 kcal/m²h °C, are affected only by variations in the mean daily temperature, and, because of their considerable thermal inertia, are not deformed by temperature changes occurring in 24-hour cycles.

The thermal deformations of the walls are directly proportional to changes in the mean daily temperature (Fig. 4.4.1).

The relationship between thermal deformation ΔL_t and change in temperature Δt (mean daily) is expressed by

$$\Delta L_t = k \cdot a_t \cdot L \cdot \Delta t \qquad [4.4.1]$$

where k is a coefficient defining the horizontal stiffness of the structure in the plane

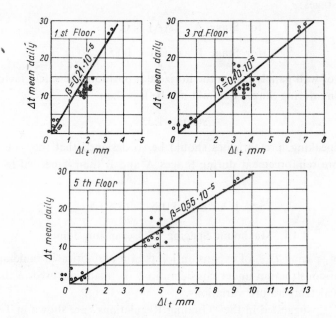

Fig. 4.4.1. Thermal deformation of external walls in large-panel buildings in relation to mean daily temperature variations

of the external wall, a_t is the coefficient of thermal expansion of the wall material, and L the length of the building.

The greatest total deformations occur in the uppermost storeys, whereas the greatest deformation differences take place in the lowest storey (Fig. 4.4.2).

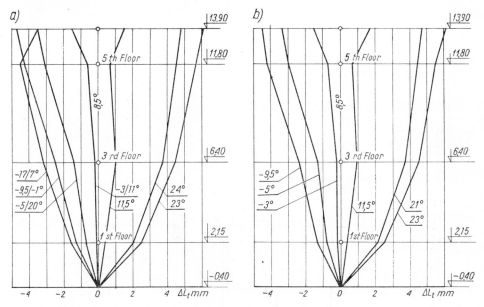

Fig. 4.4.2. Variation in thermal deformation with the height of the building:
(a) building with external walls made of concrete panels, (b) building with brick panel walls

The end panel of the lowest storey is the most affected (Fig. 4.4.3). Its relative deformation γh is

$$\gamma h = 1/2 \cdot \Delta L_t \qquad [4.4.2]$$

where γ is the angle of deformation, and h the height of the storey.

If the angle γ is limited to a maximum value γ_{max}, and taking the yearly range of the mean daily temperature Δt_r in place of Δt, then the maximum spacing of the expansion joints may be obtained from

$$L_{max} = \frac{2 \cdot \gamma \cdot h}{k \cdot a_t \cdot \Delta t_r}. \qquad [4.4.3]$$

Values of k and γ are given in Table 4.4.2.

Emelianov assumes that welded joints between panels permit some initial rotation of the latter which does not, however, affect their shape. The value used for γ in formula [4.4.3] may therefore be somewhat higher for welded joints than for reinforced concrete joints, which are more rigid.

117

TABLE 4.4.2.

COEFFICIENTS γ AND k

(after Emelianov)

Structural system	Type of joint			
	welded		concrete or r.c.	
	$\gamma \cdot 10^{-3}$	k	$\gamma \cdot 10^{-3}$	k
Longitudinal loadbearing walls:				
(a) floors resting directly on walls		0.40		0.40
	0.75		0.50	
(b) floors supported by beams		0.35		0.35
Loadbearing cross-walls:				
(a) floors connected to external walls		0.35		0.40
	0.75		0.50	
(b) floors not connected to external walls		0.30		0.35

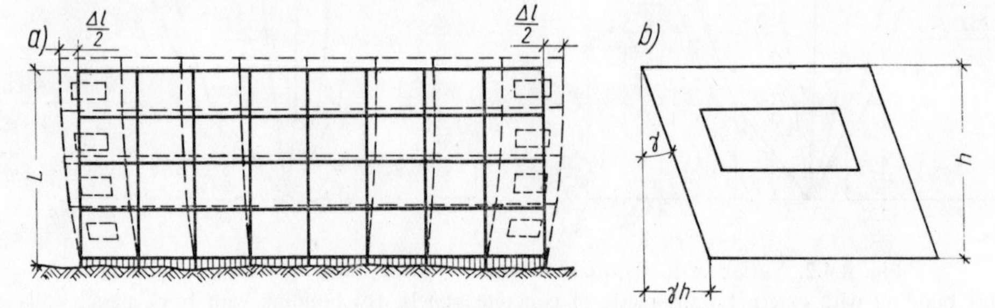

Fig. 4.4.3. Diagram showing the thermal deformations in a building:
a) deformations in a long external wall, (b) deformations in an end panel of the first storey above) ground level

For sandwich panels, the layers of which are rigidly interconnected, a value of the coefficient a should be chosen which will allow for the individual moduli of elasticity of the layers:

$$a_t = \frac{\sum a_{ti} \cdot E_i \cdot d_i}{\sum E_i \cdot d_i}$$ [4.4.4]

where E_i, d_i are respectively the elasticity modulus and thickness of the individual layers.

The temperature range Δt_r should theoretically be related to the temperature at which the rigid joints in the building are made. Emelianov does not, however, consider this temperature to be of prime importance, on account of the considerable initial settling of the building, and the inevitable shrinkage and creep of the concrete. Instead, he proposes a value given by the formula:

$$\Delta t_r = \frac{t_{max} - t_z}{2}$$ [4.4.5]

118

where t_{max} is the maximum mean daily temperature over several years, t_z the assumed minimum temperature; t_z is found as follows:

for unheated buildings:

$t_z = t_{min}$, the minimum mean daily temperature over several years;

for heated buildings:

$t_z = \dfrac{t_{min} + t_w}{2}$ where t_w is the temperature inside the building.

When the external walls consist of two skins, and the outside skin is free to deform independently of the structural skin, the temperature at the outer face of the latter should be taken as t_{min}.

Emelianov's method of calculating the spacing of expansion joints is of great value in its approach to the problem and its analysis of the role of various factors. The numerical values of the parameters involved, however, should be more accurately determined.

In curtain-wall buildings, the angle of deformation of the outside wall is not critical, as a rather high limiting value of γ can be assumed, in view of the manner in which the curtain walling is attached to the structure, and due to the construction of the wall panels. However, longitudinal deformations in the building are restricted by the internal stiffening walls, which are normally located in the end bays.

Assuming that the temperature inside the building is between 10 and 24 °C, we obtain from formula [4.4.5]

$$\Delta t_r = \frac{24° - 10°}{2} = 7\,°C.$$

TABLE 4.4.3.

LINEAR COEFFICIENTS OF THERMAL EXPANSION α_t FOR VARIOUS TYPES OF CONCRETE

Type of aggregate	Coefficient $\alpha_t \cdot 10^{-6}$, per °C	
	Range	Recommended design value
Gravel	9.5–15.0	13.0
Furnace clinker	4.5–6.0	6.0
Blast-furnace slag	8.3–13.1	11.0
Expanded clay	7.7–14.1	10.0
Limestone	8.2–10.9	10.0
Expanded shale	7.7–11.3	10.0
Perlite	8.9–11.3	11.0
Vermiculite	9.8–16.8	14.0
Cellular concretes	–	8.0
Brick	–	5.0

This value must be considered to be the minimum temperature range to be used in calculating L_{max} for buildings with concrete stiffening walls.

In Polish climatic conditions, the value of $\varDelta t_r$ in buildings with concrete external walls should be taken:
— for homogeneous walls as $\varDelta t_r = 13\ °C$,
— for composite walls, in which the external skin may move independently of the structural skin, as $\varDelta t_r = 9\ °C$.

The linear coefficients of thermal expansion a_t for various types of concrete are shown in Table 4.4.3.

In the case of walls made of large blocks, arranged as in Fig. 2.2.1, cracks form easily when horizontal forces are present in the plane of the wall. In the author's opinion, a much smaller maximum value of the angle of deformation should be allowed in such walls than in the case of "room-size" wall panels, say $\gamma = 0.25 \times 10^{-3}$.

The value of k should usually be taken as $k = 0.4$, except in the case of buildings with curtain walling, being allowed complete freedom of deformation relative to the internal structure, when $k = 0.35$.

TABLE 4.4.4.

MAXIMUM SPACING OF EXPANSION JOINTS, CALCULATED FOR POLISH CLIMATIC CONDITIONS BY EMELIANOV'S METHOD

Type of external wall	Material	$\varDelta t_r$ in °C	a_t	γ	k	L_{max}
Large-block	foamed slag concrete	13	11	0.25	0.40	25
	clinker concrete	13	6	0.25	0.40	45
	cellular concrete	13	8	0.25	0.40	34
Large-panel, homogeneous	foamed slag concrete	9	11	0.50	0.40	50
	expanded clay concrete	9	10	0.50	0.40	55
Large-panel, sandwich	ordinary concrete in the structural leaf	9	13	0.50	0.40	61
Curtain walling	ordinary concrete in the internal stiffening walls	7	13	0.50	0.35	90

The spacing of the expansion joints, L_{max}, calculated from Eq. [4.4.3] for several types of prefabricated buildings, is shown in Table 4.4.4. These values are close to those given in Table 4.4.1 (Guiding Regulations). Emelianov's method, however, makes greater allowance for the methods of construction of the building and for the materials used.

4.4.2. Roof Expansion Joints

Roof slabs are particularly exposed to wide temperature differences, which may lead to correspondingly large thermal deformations.

Especially large deformations take place in ventilated composite roofs (section 6.1.10). In view of the low thermal inertia of the ventilated space, the upper roof panels reach the ambient temperature in a relatively short time (1.5–2 hours).

Unlike external walls (section 4.4.1), which deform in accordance with the mean daily temperatures, significant movements of the upper slabs of ventilated roofs occur even within 24-hour periods (Fig. 4.4.4).

Emelianov has found that in several observed cases (buildings with brick panel walls and expanded clay concrete panels), the thermal deformation in roof panels was four times greater than in the external walls of the top storey.

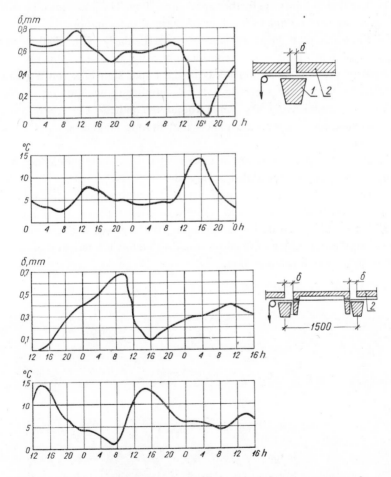

Fig. 4.4.4. Thermal deformation in prefabricated reinforced concrete roofs:
(1) r.c. beam, (2) roof panel

121

When the roof panels are rigidly attached to the structure of the top storey, such differential thermal deformations also cause cracks to appear on the external face of the building (Fig. 4.4.5).

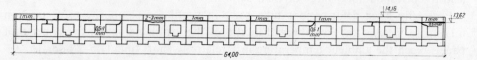

Fig. 4.4.5. Crazing and cracks in the external wall panels of the top storey of a building, caused by thermal deformations in the roof structure

To avoid the formation of cracks the roof should be divided by suitably closely-spaced expansion joints.

Polish standards specify that roof structures not insulated on the upper surface must have expansion joints not further apart than 20 m. The joints must be sufficiently deep to give the roof complete freedom of thermal deformation.

In buildings made of large prefabricates, particularly with shallow ventilated roofs, the fulfilment of the above requirements could be rather difficult.

The need to provide expansion joints in the upper skin of a roof structure may be obviated by laying the panels loosely on supporting walls or on the beams of the main roof, and leaving dry joints round the panels. Emelianov asserts that thermal deformations in separate panels laid in this manner do not damage the waterproofing skin.

The spacing of expansion joints in unventilated roof slabs should not be greater than 40 m, according to the Polish standards.

Experience has shown that, in prefabricated buildings with unventilated roofs, the expansion joints should be spaced even more closely (approx. 30 m). Alternatively, the roof slab should be so designed that along the edges of the building, the upper skin of the roof has a degree of freedom which will allow it a measure of deformation relative to the lower insulating skin.

Chapter 5

THREE-DIMENSIONAL STIFFNESS OF BUILDINGS CONSTRUCTED FROM PREFABRICATED COMPONENTS

5.1. PRINCIPLES OF THREE-DIMENSIONAL STIFFENING OF BUILDINGS AND STATIC CALCULATIONS

5.1.1. Three-Dimensional Stiffness of Buildings

Three-dimensional stiffness is imparted to a building by full-length lateral and longitudinal stiffening walls, acting in conjunction with the floor slabs (Section 3.3.1).

The stiffening walls may be:

— loadbearing walls,
— non-loadbearing, self-supporting walls, rigidly connected to other structural units,
— panel walls, provided they are sufficiently rigidly attached to the structural components, and provided that the flexural rigidity in their own plane is not less than the rigidity of a 24 cm thick gas concrete block wall.

The total area of openings in the stiffening walls must not exceed 50 % of the wall area.

The stiffening walls resist horizontal forces by acting as cantilevers rigidly fixed in the monolithic basement structure, or, less frequently, in the ground. In the latter case, elastic fixity of the walls is assumed.

With regard to the participation of the walls in the three-dimensional stiffening of the structure, buildings may be said to be built on the open or closed systems.

In closed system buildings (Fig. 5.1.1), both longitudinal and lateral external walls are rigid enough in their own planes to be considered as stiffening walls (Section 5.1.3). These walls counteract any twisting of the structure during the bending of the whole three-dimensional system, and it is not vital in this case that they should be fully symmetrical.

Buildings with loadbearing external walls, i.e. long-wall and two-way span system buildings, constitute the majority of closed system structures. Cross-wall and skeleton structures may, however, also be considered to belong to this category, provided their external walls are sufficiently stiff.

When calculating deformations in the stiffening walls in closed system structures, the contribution of lateral walls may be taken into account. The stiffening walls are then built in the shape of a T or I.

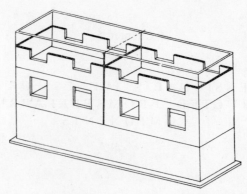

Fig. 5.1.1. Diagrammatic view of a closed system building

The underground structure of closed system buildings generally forms a rigid box. As all wall deflections are nil at the upper surface of this box, the stiffening walls may be treated as cantilevers fixed at this level.

The sum of all moments of the horizontal forces, equal to the sum of all wall fixing moments, is further distributed through the basement structure. In calculating ground pressures and horizontal deflections of walls due to the external forces, we should really consider the distribution of stresses under each segment of the foundations. Because of the small magnitude of the quantities involved, however, the fact that the ground on which the building stands settles unevenly is normally neglected, and the top surface of the rigid basement box is taken as the reference level.

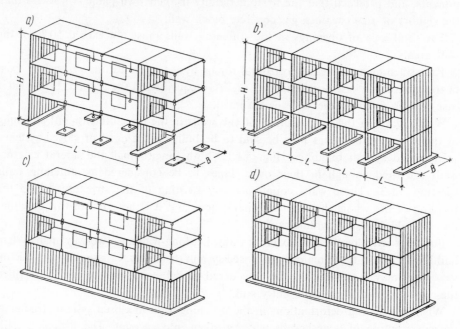

Fig. 5.1.2. Diagrams of open system buildings:
(a), (b) first type, (c), (d) second type

124

In open system buildings (Fig. 5.1.2), the external walls are either very slender, or are so constructed that they can deform independently of the structure (curtain walls). The role of such walls is purely passive, since they merely transfer wind loads to the floors.

In this system, the stiffening walls act as vertical slabs held together only by the floor slabs. In this case, a torsional deformation of the whole structure will be produced if these walls are unsymmetrically spaced and then subjected to horizontal loading.

Depending on the design of the basement part of the structure, two types of open-system buildings can be distinguished. These differ greatly with respect to the functions of the stiffening walls.

The first type comprises buildings in which the general structural scheme is carried into the basement and down to the foundations (Fig. 5.1.2a, b). In this case, under horizontal loading, the stiffening walls deflect, after the manner of cantilevers elastically fixed in the ground. Thus, in calculating the deflections of the building, elastic settling of the wall foundations must be taken into consideration.

In the second type of building, the basement forms a rigid box, as in the case of closed system buildings. The walls are considered to be rigidly fixed at the top of the basement box, and the effect of ground settling is neglected in deflection calculations.

In skeleton construction the effective span of a floor slab is, in this context, the distance between the stiffening walls. This is very often extremely large, and particular attention must be paid to the monolithic characteristics of the functioning of the horizontal slabs.

In buildings with loadbearing walls, the effective spans of the horizontal slabs are much smaller, and the problem of their slenderness is of lesser importance.

All buildings designed on the open system necessitate very careful analysis of their three-dimensional stiffness.

It is advisable, in order to stiffen the whole structure, to make the external walls situated in the extreme bays of the building stiffer than those situated elsewhere. A framework of closed structural units should then be formed by these and the internal walls.

5.1.2. The Scope of Design Calculations

In static calculations the three-dimensional stiffness of the structure must be checked in both the longitudinal and the transverse directions.

Calculations are carried out to determine the maximum deflection of the stiffening walls, f_{max}, measured at the level of the slab above the top storey, and to evaluate the internal forces in the walls resulting from the action of horizontal loading.

When stiffening walls are designed as non-loadbearing walls, the manner in which horizontal forces are transferred from the floor slabs to the stiffening walls must be checked by calculation. If the ratio of the width of a floor slab, B, to its effective span L (i.e. the distance between the stiffening walls) is less than $B/L = 1/3$, then the floor slab must be checked against the possibility of cracking.

There is normally no need to check the deflection of horizontal slabs in the planes of the horizontal forces acting on them.

All floor panels should be interconnected to form a rigid slab, which for all practical purposes will not deflect in its own plane (Section 5.2.1). The fulfilment of this condition, and of the need to join all wall components into monolithic slabs (Section 5.3.1) are the assumptions on which all further rigidity calculations are based.

A building is considered to be sufficiently rigid if the maximum deflection of the stiffening walls, f_{max}, is not greater than

$$f_{max} = \frac{H}{2000} \qquad [5.1.1]$$

where H is the height of the building measured between the top of the basement box and the top of the roof slab.

The value of f_{max} is a function of the geometric properties of the wall, the size of the load, and the elasticity modulus of the concrete used, E. When the stiffening wall is constructed *in situ*,

$E = E_b$ (elasticity modulus under compression; Section 4.2.7).

In the case of walls built of large prefabricates, however, a lower value of E is assumed, to allow for the tendency of the joints between wall components to yield. In this case,

$E = E_{br}$ (elasticity modulus in bending, Section 4.2.7).

In buildings without rigid basement structures, where the stiffening walls are considered to be cantilevers elastically fixed in the ground (Section 5.1.1), due allowance must be made for the elastic deformations of the ground when calculating the value of the maximum deflection f_{max} due to horizontal forces.

The strength of a wall should be checked over the most unfavourable sections, according to the normal procedure for concrete and reinforced-concrete structures. When, in calculating the deflections of a stiffening wall, the cooperation of walls at right angles to it has been admitted, the adequacy of the joints between these walls must also be checked.

It is just as important to check the safety factor applying to the strength of the most critical sections of the wall, as it is to determine its maximum deflection at these points. But, whereas the strength of the wall over any section can easily be improved by suitable reinforcement measures, when excessive deflections are produced, then either the cross-sectional plan area of the wall must be increased (thickening), or additional stiffening walls must be introduced.

Polish Guiding Regulations stipulate that the three-dimensional stiffness of prefabricated buildings need not be checked if they possess:

(a) *in the short direction* — stiffening walls not shorter than 0.25 of the height of the building, and spaced not further than 6.0 m apart; or walls not shorter than 0.33 of the height of the building, spaced not further than 15.0 m apart, and
(b) *in the long direction* — symmetrically spaced stiffening walls, not shorter than 0.33 of the height of the building.

The stiffening walls should rise the whole height of the building. The horizontal cross-section must not be broken up by openings to the extent of more than 40%, and no opening should extend beyond 1.20 m from the end of the wall.

5.1.3, Horizontal Loads

In the design of stiffening walls, two types of horizontal loading are considered: wind pressure and the horizontal forces occurring when the structural component supporting a vertical load are not, themselves, mounted vertically.

Wind pressure: Suitable figures are quoted in national standards specifications. In the Polish standards, these values vary stepwise with the height of the building (Fig. 5.1.3).

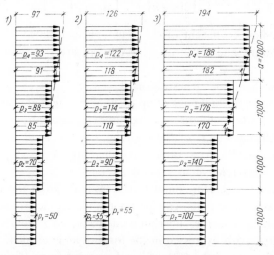

Fig. 5.1.3. Wind loading on buildings in accordance with Polish regulations. Graphs of the basic wind pressure p, depending on the height of the building and the climatic zone: (1) zone I (plains), (2) zone II (maritime), (3) zone III (mountains)

In structural calculations dealing with stiffening walls, it is more convenient to substitute an equivalent uniformly distributed wind pressure. Some national Codes, e.g. the British ones, give the values of wind pressure in a form representing uniform distribution.

When calculating the internal stresses in the walls, the equivalent wind pressure w_σ should be such that it would create the same bending moment at the support

127

as the stepped wind pressure quoted in the standards. In deflection calculations, a different value for the equivalent wind pressure w_t is used, giving the correct value of the maximum deflection.

To simplify such calculations, the value w_t can also be adopted in strength calculations without unduly affecting the results.

Values w_σ and w_t are functions of the height of the building, H. For the basic wind pressures shown in Fig. 5.1.3 and provided $30 < H < 40$ m, the equivalent wind pressures will be:

$$w_\sigma = k \left[p_1 + \frac{a(p_4 - p_1)(60 + a)\,10 + 500\,(p_3 - p_1) + 300\,(p_2 - p_1)}{(30 + a)^2} \right] \qquad [5.1.2]$$

$$w_t = k \left\{ p_1 + \frac{1}{3}(p_2 - p_1)\left[8\left(\frac{20 + a}{30 + a}\right) - 6\left(\frac{20 + a}{30 + a}\right)^2 + \left(\frac{20 + a}{30 + a}\right)^4 \right] + \right.$$

$$+ \frac{1}{3}(p_3 - p_2)\left[8\left(\frac{10 + a}{30 + a}\right) - 6\left(\frac{10 + a}{30 + a}\right)^2 + \left(\frac{10 + a}{30 + a}\right)^4 \right] +$$

$$\left. + \frac{1}{3}(p_4 - p_3)\left[8\left(\frac{a}{30 + a}\right) - 6\left(\frac{a}{30 + a}\right)^2 + \left(\frac{a}{30 + a}\right)^4 \right] \right\} \qquad [5.1.3]$$

where k is the air-flow coefficient of the structures, calculated without distinguishing between windward and leeward, p_1, p_2, p_3, p_4 are the wind pressures at the respective levels.

For buildings with normal fenestration, $k = 1.3$.

Graphs of w_σ and w_t for buildings of up to 40 m in height are shown in Fig. 5.1.4.

The equivalent loading should only be used in calculations dealing with the stiffening walls. All other units of the building, e.g. the bending of external panel walls, should be designed to resist direct wind pressures consistent with the elevation of the individual units relative to ground level.

Values of horizontal forces. Horizontal forces resulting from the non-verticality of vertically loaded structural units, can be approximately determined from the unit weight of the building and the superimposed loads. To simplify the calculations, the effect of this loading is expressed in the form of an equivalent uniformly distributed load w_p acting, as in the case of wind pressure, over the entire area of the external walls.

In average erection conditions, up to 1.0 cm error of plumbing is allowed per storey and w_p may therefore be obtained from

$$w_p = \frac{B}{450}\left(G + \frac{0.5\,p}{h} \right) \qquad [5.1.4]$$

where B is the width of the building in m, G the weight of 1 m^3 of the structure, including partitions, in kg/m^3, p the superimposed load on a typical floor in kg/m^2, and h the storey height in metres.

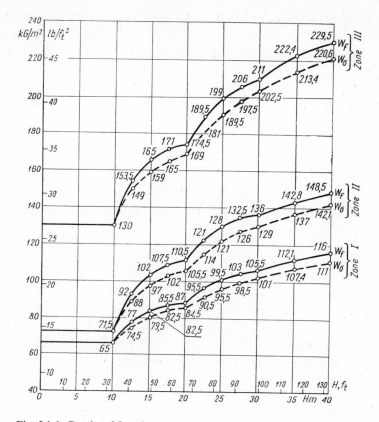

Fig. 5.1.4. Graphs of functions w_σ and w_f for buildings up to 40 m high

When checking the stiffness of the building along its length, the value of B used in the above formula is taken to be the spacing of the expansion joints.

The following approximate values for the weight of the structure, G, can be used in evaluating w_p:

"long-wall" buildings made of large clinker concrete $G = 450 \text{ kg/m}^3$

"cross-wall" buildings, large-block loadbearing walls, and external walls lighter than 250 kg/m² $G = 250\text{–}300 \text{ kg/m}^3$

large-panel buildings $G = 200\text{–}300 \text{ kg/m}^3$

skeleton structures depending on the weight of the external walls $G = 200\text{–}300 \text{ kg/m}^3$

In calculations, the total horizontal load transferred to the stiffening walls, is:

$$w = w_w + w_p. \qquad\qquad [5.1.5]$$

This represents the wind load and the horizontal forces due to non-verticality of the walls.

129

5.1.4. Distribution of Horizontal Loads between Stiffening Walls

5.1.4.1. Horizontal forces. Because of the introduction of the equivalent horizontal load w, the three-dimensional structure of the building may be considered to be uniformly loaded.

The loading is transferred to the stiffening walls through the floor slabs in the form of concentrated forces acting at the floor levels.

The total horizontal load transferred by one floor slab to all the stiffening walls is the product of the equivalent unit load w, the storey height h, and the length of the building L,

$$W = w \cdot h \cdot L. \tag{5.1.6}$$

Each total load W is resolved into the forces P_i acting on individual walls

$$W = \sum P_i. \tag{5.1.7}$$

The distribution of the total load W among individual walls is determined:
— in closed-system buildings, by assuming that f_{max} are equal for all walls;
— in open-system structures, by taking into account the torsional deformations of the building.

In both cases, the share of the total load W accepted by any individual load i is a function of the unit deflection $f_i(P = 1)$ of this wall, when acted upon by a force $P = 1$. The value of $f_i(P = 1)$ is given by:

$$f_i(P = 1) = a_i \cdot 1 \tag{5.1.8}$$

where the coefficient a_i depends on the dimensions of the wall, the elasticity modulus of the wall material, and on how firmly the wall is fixed in the ground.

5.1.4.2. Closed-system buildings. From the conditions of equality of the deflections (Fig. 5.1.5)

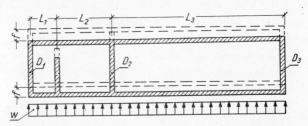

Fig. 5.1.5. Horizontal dislocation of a floor under horizontal loading (Closed system building)

$$f = a_i \cdot P_i = a_{i+1} \cdot P_{i+1} = \ldots = a_n \cdot P_n \tag{5.1.9}$$

we obtain

$$P_i = \frac{f}{a_i}, \ P_{i+1} = \frac{f}{a_{i+1}}, \ldots P_n = \frac{f}{a_n}. \tag{5.1.10}$$

Putting these values into formula [5.1.7] we obtain

$$f = \frac{W}{\displaystyle\sum_{j=1}^{j=n} \frac{1}{a_j}}$$

[5.1.11]

whence

$$P_i = \frac{W}{a \displaystyle\sum_{j=1}^{j=n} \frac{1}{a_j}}.$$

[5.1.12]

In the building shown in Fig. 5.1.5, wall D_1 is acted upon by a force

$$P_1 = W \frac{\dfrac{1}{a_1}}{\dfrac{1}{a_1} + \dfrac{1}{a_2} + \dfrac{1}{a_3}}$$

and wall D_2 by a force

$$P_2 = W \frac{\dfrac{1}{a_2}}{\dfrac{1}{a_1} + \dfrac{1}{a_2} + \dfrac{1}{a_3}} \text{ etc.}$$

In the case of walls with identical unit deflections, i.e. similar walls identically fixed at their footings,

$$P_i = P_{i+1} = \ldots = \frac{W}{n}$$

[5.1.13]

where n is the number of stiffening walls.

5.1.4.3. *Open-system buildings.* In open-system buildings with stiffening walls arranged asymmetrically (Fig. 5.1.6), the share of any wall i in supporting the horizontal force W is expressed by the algebraic sum of
— the force $P_{z,i}$ caused by parallel translation of the floor slabs, as in the case of closed system buildings, and
— the force $P_{s,i}$ caused by the rotation of the floor slabs about the centre of rotation of the building.

The centre of rotation is the point of application of the resultant of the forces causing unit deflections in the stiffening walls.

The abscissa of the centre of rotation (x_0) is given by:

131

$$x_0 = \frac{\displaystyle\sum_{j=1}^{j=n} \frac{1}{a_j} \cdot x_j}{\displaystyle\sum_{j=1}^{j=n} \frac{1}{a_j}}$$ [5.1.14]

where x_j is the distance of wall j from the y-axis, a_j, as in Eq. [5.1.8], is a coefficient defining the magnitude of the deflection of wall j due to a force $P = 1$ parallel to the y-axis.

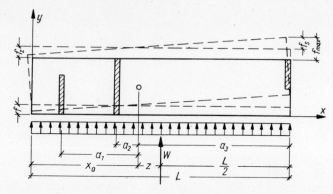

Fig. 5.1.6. Dislocation of a floor under horizontal loading in an open system building

By analogy, substituting y for x and using suitable values of a_j, the ordinate y_0 for the deflection of wall j due to a force $P = 1$, parallel to the x-axis, may be determined from

$$y_0 = \frac{\displaystyle\sum_{j=1}^{j=n} \frac{1}{a_j} \cdot y_j}{\displaystyle\sum_{j=1}^{j=n} \frac{1}{a_j}}$$ [5.1.15]

The resultant of all the external forces, W, acts through a point a distance z from the centre of rotation. The twisting moment

$$M = W \cdot z$$ [5.1.16]

is balanced by the sum of the moment of forces in individual walls, given by:

$$\sum M_i = \sum P_{s,i} \cdot a_i$$ [5.1.17]

where a_i is the distance of wall i from the axes $x = x_0$ or $y = y_0$.

The forces $P_{s,i}$ are inversely proportional to the distances a_1 and to the unit deflections due to the force $P = 1$.

132

Introducing the term

$$\bar{a}_i = \frac{a_{max}}{a_i} \geqslant 1 \qquad [5.1.18]$$

where a_{max} is the unit deflection of the least stiff of the walls under consideration, we obtain

$$P_{s,i} = W \cdot z \frac{\bar{a}_i \cdot a_i}{\sum\limits_{j=1}^{j=n} \bar{a}_j \cdot a_j^2} \cdot \qquad [5.1.19]$$

$$(j = \text{number of walls})$$

The deflection in a wall, f_s, caused by the rotation of the building, is then given by

$$f_s = a_i \cdot P_{s,i} \qquad [5.1.20]$$

where $P_{s,i}$ is taken from formula [5.1.19].

The total deflection f_{max} of any stiffening wall in the open system structure is given by

$$f_{max} = f_z + f_s \qquad [5.1.21]$$

where f_z is taken from formula [5.1.11], and f_s from formula [5.1.20].

The assumptions made in the foregoing rather oversimplify the case of open-system structures, but the results may be deemed sufficiently accurate for most housing structures. Only in the case of very tall tower blocks (over 70 m) is a more precise analysis needed. In such cases, analysis of a model is often resorted to.

5.2. FLOOR SLABS

5.2.1. Function of Floor Slabs

Floor slabs resist horizontal loading by bending in their own planes in the manner of girder walls. In all future calculations, when dealing with the transfer of horizontal loads to the stiffening walls, slabs will be treated as infinitely rigid plates.

To verify the validity of this assumption in floors consisting of prefabricated units, the Polish Building Institute investigated the behaviour of three types of floor slabs (Fig. 5.2.1):

A — solid *in situ* slabs;

B — slabs consisting of prefabricated panels attached to a reinforced concrete ring beam, with all joints between the panels filled with cement mortar;

C — as type B, but with the gaps between the panels left open.

The deflections of the three slabs under two concentrated loads are shown in Fig. 5.2.2.

133

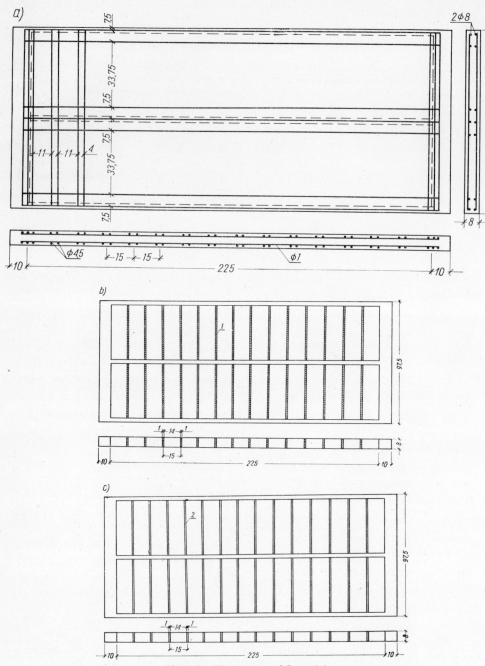

Fig. 5.2.1. Three types of floor slabs:
(a) monolithic, type A, (b) precast planks with filled joints, type B, (c) precast planks with joints
left open, type C
(1) joints filled with cement mortar, (2) open joints

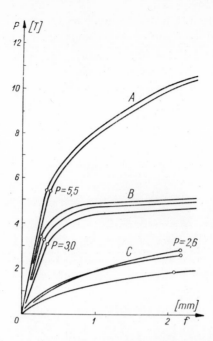

Fig. 5.2.2. Graphs of the deformation of floor slabs,
P — force causing cracking

The deflection of the *in situ* slab under a load of 0.9 tonnes equivalent — after allowing for the scale of the model — to 100 kg/m² on the external wall, was 1/43000 of the effective span of the slab ($L_s = 20$ m), or 1/6500 of the storey height ($h = 3.0$ m). This may be considered negligible. In practice, slab deflections are smaller still, as the slabs normally extend over several bays, and their deflections are further reduced by intermediate supports (walls, columns), the stiffness of which is neglected in three-dimensional stiffness calculations.

The deflection of slab B was also small, from a practical point of view, until cracks formed in the ring beam. After cracking had occurred, a rapid increase in the deflection was observed.

The bending moment at the instant of cracking was

$$M_r = \frac{1}{k} \cdot g \cdot B^2 \cdot R_r \qquad [5.2.1]$$

where $k = 2.5$ to 3.4 (aver. 3.0), g, B = thickness and width of slab, R_r = tensile strength of the reinforced concrete ring beam.

It may therefore be concluded that, until cracking occurs in the ring beam, slabs made from prefabricated panels with the joints filled in with mortar, effect as good a horizontal stiffening of the structure as *in situ* slabs. The design assumption that such a slab is absolutely stiff is therefore completely justified.

135

The conditions change drastically as soon as the ring beam has cracked, and this point must therefore be regarded as the limiting state in which effective stiffening is provided by floor slabs resting on stiffening walls.

The deflections of slab C, which had open joints, were markedly larger than those of slabs A or B. This indicates the importance of good grouting of joints to the rigidity of the floor slabs.

Examples of typical failures of the slabs tested are shown in Fig. 5.2.3.

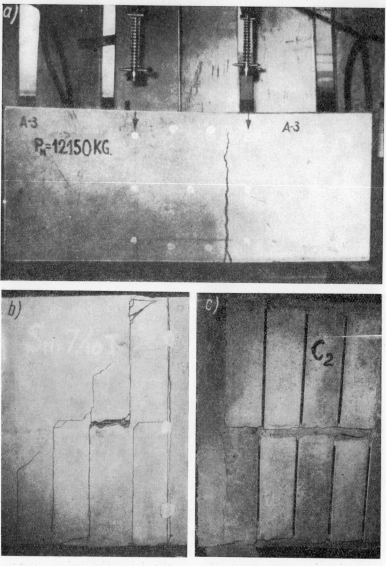

Fig. 5.2.3. The mode of failure of experimental floor slabs:
(a) monolithic, (b) with filled joints, (c) with open joints

136

5.2.2. Strength Calculations

The results of investigations into the circumstances of crack formation at the perimeters of floor slabs provide certain pointers with regard to static calculations. A floor slab loaded horizontally may to all intents and purposes be equated to a simply supported beam. Safety against cracking is ensured by satisfying the condition:

$$\frac{w_{st} \cdot L^2}{8} < \frac{1}{s} \cdot \frac{g \cdot B^2}{3} \cdot R_r \qquad [5.2.2]$$

where s is the safety factor, equal to at least 4.5 (see Section 4.3), g the thickness of the floor slab, measured at the centre of gravity of the ring beam, and R_r the tensile strength of the concrete.

For an average slab, with sides in the ratio $B/L = 1/3$, and thickness $g = 0.10$ m, supported on a reinforced concrete ring beam made from Mk. 140 concrete ($R_r = 136$ T/m²), and loaded to $w_{st} = 0.60$ T/m, the safety factor s is

$$s = \frac{8}{3} \left(\frac{B}{L}\right)^2 \frac{g \cdot R_r}{w_{st}} = 6.7 > 4.5.$$

It is then fairly easy to satisfy Eq. [5.2.2], but it is essential to fill all joints with mortar and to construct a reinforced ring beam of adequate cross-section at the perimeter of the slab, so that the floor structure may be considered monolithic.

When the stiffening walls are designed as non-loadbearing walls, the manner in which the horizontal forces are transferred by the floors to the walls must be investigated.

The components used to connect a floor slab to the stiffening wall are ring beams (joists in buildings of skeleton construction). These are laid at right angles to the walls in question (Fig. 5.2.4). The contact surface between the non-loadbearing wall and the adjoining floor panel is not taken into account in the calculations, since cracks frequently form in this joint. In fact, a gap is often purposely left between the floor panel and the wall.

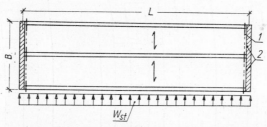

Fig. 5.2.4. Connection between floor slab and stiffening walls, designed as self-supporting only: (1) Centre line of a reinforced belt (ring beam), (2) Open joint between end floor panel and self-supporting wall

The strength of the connecting unit is determined by its shear capacity at the joint between slab and wall. The shear force, Q_{st}, acting on the cross-section under consideration is obtained from the expression:

$$Q_{st} = \frac{w_{st} \cdot L}{2} \cdot \frac{F_w}{\sum F_w}$$ [5.2.3]

where $w_{st} = (k_p + w_p)h$, k_p is the direct wind pressure, according to the effective height of the floor above ground level, w_p as in Section 5.1.3, h the storey height, L the spacing of stiffening walls, and F_w, $\sum F_w$ are respectively the cross-sectional area of the component considered, and the sum of the cross-sectional areas of all linking components.

If the investigated cross-section of the connecting component occurs at the junction of two unequally loaded walls, a shear force Q_{st} is added vectorially to the shear force due to the differential deformations of the walls (Section 7.6).

5.3. METHODS OF CALCULATING THE DEFLECTIONS OF STIFFENING WALLS

5.3.1. Mechanism of the Function of Stiffening Walls

Stiffening walls behave as cantilever slabs bent in their own planes by horizontal forces. If there are no openings in the walls, their behaviour and function are quite straightforward; in the case of stiffening walls with openings, the matter is somewhat complicated.

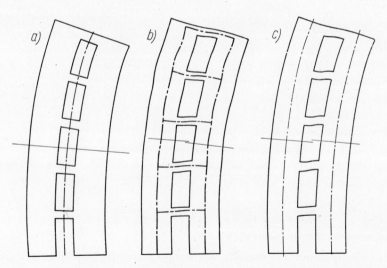

Fig. 5.3.1. Deformation of a wall with one row of openings, considered as:
(a) homogeneous cantilever slab with openings, (b) multi-storey frame, (c) two-band cantilever

138

Walls without openings are normally treated as uniform cantilever beams. The effect of shear forces on the deflection must be considered when the ratio of the width of the walls to its height, B/H, is greater than $1/5$.

Perforated walls are also treated sometimes as plain cantilevers, their true net areas and moments of inertia being used in the calculations. This is tantamount to saying that a cantilever wall weakened by perforations deforms exactly as would a solid, unperforated wall, i.e. that all points which are horizontally coplanar before deformation takes place, will remain so after deformation (Fig. 5.3.1a).

This assumption is however rather unrealistic. It neglects the effect of the connecting lintels on the internal stresses in the wall. A better approximation is to treat the wall as a multi-story frame (Fig. 5.3.1b), or as a cantilever consisting of several vertical bands, each of which is subjected to tangential forces representing the effect of the lintels (Fig. 5.3.1c). In both these schemes the assumption that the horizontally coplanar sections remain unaffected after deformation applies only within each individual vertical band.

The multi-storey frame approach is widely discussed in a work by A. Kacner and B. Lewicki, *Spatial Work of Prefabricated Buildings Acted upon by Horizontal Wind Forces*, in Vol. II of Building Studies, published by PWN, Warsaw, 1959. Deflection calculations allow for the effect of the axial and shearing forces in addition to that of the bending moments.

An exact solution of the problem in terms of multi-storey frames, which would need to allow for the effect of axial and shear forces, would be less laborious than a perforated plate approach, even if the latter were simplified; nevertheless it would still present difficulties. For practical purposes, an approximate method has been evolved in the work mentioned above. This treatment, given in Section 5.3.3, involves only three unknown quantities, irrespective of the number of storeys in the building.

Many researchers have worked with the banded cantilever approach, assuming that tangential forces act on the edges of individual bands. In contrast to the frame method, the external forces are here considered to be uniformly distributed, and not concentrated.

The various solutions differ among themselves in the expression for the equivalent tangential forces replacing the lintels. One author, A. S. Kalmanok, treats the vertical cantilever bands not as linear members, but as plates, abandoning the principle that all plane sections remain planar. The resulting formulae, however, are rather complicated.

A Yugoslav method due to R. Rosman is recommended for practical use, and is described further in Section 5.3.4.

The differences in f_{max} obtained by the frame and the banded cantilever methods are relatively insignificant. Their conformity with the results obtained by model analysis is also fully satisfactory, both with regard to the displacements and to the

139

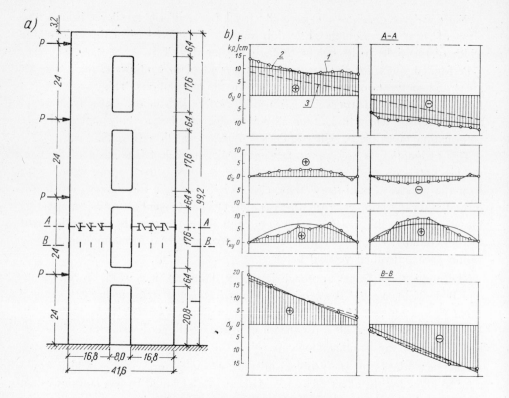

Fig. 5.3.2. One of the perspex models tested:
(a) distribution of strain gauges and deflection indicators, (b) stress diagrams for three sections in the model, showing σ_y, σ_x, and τ_{xy},
(1) stresses calculated from the actual strains measured on the model, (2) stresses calculated on the basis of the frame assumption, (3) stresses calculated for a two-band cantilever

magnitude of the internal stresses. The hypothesis concerning plane sections within vertical bands corresponds fairly well to the distribution of stresses over the cross-section (Fig. 5.3.2). However, the assumption that such sections remain planar over the whole width of the wall clearly disagrees with the measured results.

Table 5.3.1 gives a comparison of the deflection and stress results obtained by various methods.

Although the tests carried out on perspex models show that the results obtained by calculation, using the described methods, give a fairly accurate picture of the work of a perforated plate, it is necessary to verify the applicability of these solutions to structures made of concrete, a material in which the function $\varepsilon(\sigma)$ is linear over only a very short range.

The concrete models shown in Fig. 5.3.3 were built at the Warsaw Building Institute to the scale of 1/10.

TABLE 5.3.1

MAXIMUM DEFLECTION AND THE EXTREME FIBRE STRESSES AT THE
HEAVIEST STRESSED CROSS-SECTIONS OF THE STIFFENING WALL

			Extreme fibre stresses	
		Maximum deflection f_{max}	at the base of the wall I–I	in lintel under greatest stress II–II
	Method			
		in terms of $\dfrac{w}{E}$	in terms of w	
6-storey building	Kacner-Lewicki	1870 1870	− 570 + 155	+ 655 − 615
	R. Rosman	1820 1820	− 565 + 144	± 580
	H. Beck	1550 1550	− 545 + 109	± 540
	Baehre-Eriksson	1530 1530	− 488 + 16	± 540
18-storey building	Kacner-Lewicki	114000 114000	−3880 + 20	+1920 −1890
	R. Rosman	115000 115000	−4360 + 820	±1680
	H. Beck	102000 102000	−3520 + 520	±1930
	Baehre-Eriksson	101000 101000	−3520 + 520	±1730

The models were loaded with vertical forces, producing a compression stress of 2.9 kg/cm² on the wall cross-section, and with horizontal forces, increasing until failure occurred.

The deflections of the tested walls under the action of the horizontal force, and the calculated values for the deflection, are shown in Fig. 5.3.4. The E-value of concrete was used in the calculations.

The calculated deflections are within 10 % of the measured f_{mod} in the following ranges:

— the Baehre-Eriksson and Beck methods — in the range $f_{mod}/H = 1/8000$ to $1/2500$, (occasionally 1/2000);

— the Rosman method — in the range $f_{mod}/H = 1/2500$ to $1/1500$;

— the Kacner-Lewicki method — in the range $f_{mod}/H = 1/1700$ to $1/1200$.

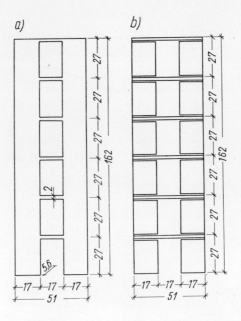

Fig. 5.3.3. Concrete models tested in Warsaw:
(a) model A — with monolithic walls, (b) model B — with walls built of precast components

It would not be advisable to deduce too much, as far as the proportions are concerned, from the results of the test on only one type of model. Nevertheless, these results seem to indicate that Rosman's method is the most applicable in practice.

In the Kacner-Lewicki method, the values of the deflection f are overestimated, but this method might be particularly useful in the case of walls with wide openings and relatively narrow column strips.

In Rosman's method, the shear forces (and bending moments) in the lintels reach the maximum value in a lintel located somewhere near 1/3 of the height of the wall from the base. This is a peculiarity which must be kept in mind when designing lintel reinforcements (Section 5.3.4).

When stiffening walls are monolithically connected to sufficiently rigid cross walls, the combined I or T-section wall should be considered as a whole for the purposes of calculation.

The joints of walls consisting of prefabricated components are as a rule less rigid than joints in monolithic walls, so that some circumspection is advised here.

The author believes that walls at right angles to each other should be considered to act together as stiffening units, provided that both walls are made of materials

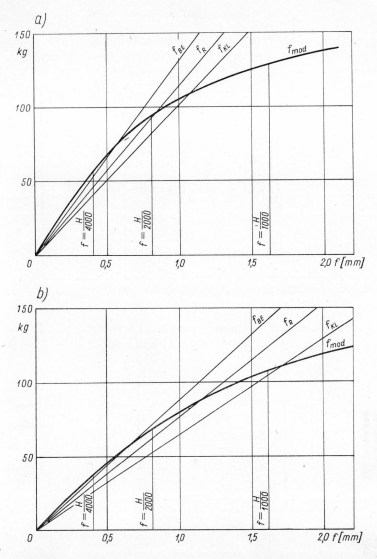

Fig. 5.3.4. Deflections f_{mod} measured on tested model walls and their theoretical values, calculated by the methods of f_{BE}— Baehre-Eriksson, f_{R} — Rosman, f_{KL} — Kacner-Lewicki: (a) model A, concrete strength $R_{\square 16} = 200 \ \mathrm{kg/cm^2}$, (b) model B, concrete strength $R_{\square 16} = 140 \ \mathrm{kg/cm^2}$

of similar elasticity and similar strength. The structure of the joint between the walls should prevent the formation of cracks.

In external walls weakened by window openings, only the width of the pier between the windows should be taken as contributing to the stiffness of the cross wall.

143

5.3.2. Unperforated Stiffening Walls

The deflection $f_{\max}$ of an unperforated stiffening wall loaded with n concentrated forces P as in Fig. 5.3.5, and treated as a cantilever beam, is given by:

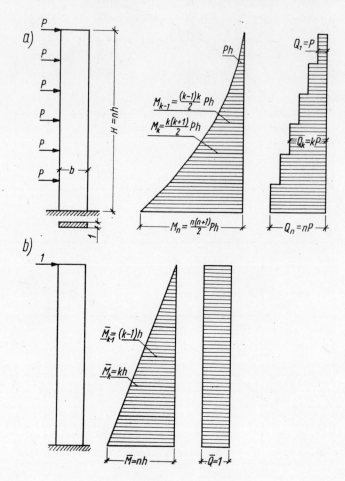

Fig. 5.3.5. Working diagrams for unperforated stiffening walls: (a) under actual external loading, (b) under a single unit load

$$f_{\max} = a \cdot P$$

$$a = \frac{h}{2}\, n^2 (n+1)(3n+1)\, U_M \left(1 + \frac{U_Q}{n(3n+1)\, U_M}\right) \quad\Biggr\} \qquad [5.3.1]$$

where

$$U_M = \frac{h^2}{12\, EJ}$$

and

$$U_Q = \frac{2(1+\mu)\lambda}{E \cdot F}.$$

Since for concrete, $\mu = 1/6$, and for a rectangular section $\lambda = 6/5$,

$$(1+\mu)\lambda = 1.4,$$

the value of the fraction in brackets in formula [5.3.1], for the case $h = \dfrac{H}{n}$ and

$\dfrac{B}{H} = \dfrac{1}{5}$, is

$$\frac{U_Q}{n(3n+1)\,U_M} = \frac{2.8}{3+\dfrac{1}{n}} \cdot \frac{B^2}{H^2} \qquad \frac{B^2}{H^2} = 0.04.$$

Thus, with $B/H < \dfrac{1}{5}$ the effect of shear forces on the deflection is negligible. Formula [5.3.1] then assumes the form

$$a = \frac{h^3}{24\,E \cdot J}\, n^2\,(n+1)\,(3n+1). \qquad [5.3.2]$$

For uniformly distributed loads, the deflection f_{max} will be

$$f_{max} = \frac{w \cdot H^4}{8E \cdot J}. \qquad [5.3.3]$$

5.3.3. Perforated Stiffening Walls Calculated according to the Multi-Storey Frame Method

5.3.3.1. *Wall with one vertical strip of openings, not necessarily central.* A diagrammatic sketch of an n-storey wall is given in Fig. 5.3.6, together with the cross-section areas of the members, F, and the moments of inertia, J.

In this basic, statically determinate system, the mid-points of the right hand columns are subject to redundant longitudinal forces N_k, lateral forces T_k and moments $\mathfrak{M}_k$.

The exact solution of the frame involves $3n$ unknowns, the values of N_k, T_k, and $\mathfrak{M}_k$. The conditions $\Sigma M = 0$, $\Sigma T = 0$, and $\Sigma N = 0$ allow the construction of $3n$ canonical equations.

In the method hereafter referred to as the simplified method, it has been assumed that N_k, T_k, and $\mathfrak{M}_k$ are related respectively to N_1, T_1 and $\mathfrak{M}_1$ in the following manner:

145

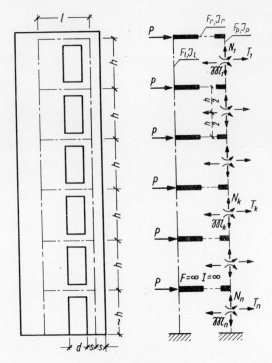

Fig. 5.3.6. Working diagram for a stiffening wall with a single row of openings treated as a multi-storey frame

$$N_k = k^2 \cdot N_1 \qquad \text{i.e. } N_1 = \frac{N_n}{n^2}$$

$$T_k = k \cdot T_1 \qquad \text{i.e. } T_1 = \frac{T_n}{n}$$

$$\mathfrak{M}_k = k^2 \cdot \mathfrak{M}_1 \qquad \text{i.e. } \mathfrak{M}_1 = \frac{\mathfrak{M}_n}{n^2}$$

[5.3.4]

Accepting the above relationships, the redundants may now be expressed as three groups of unknowns:

$$\sum_1^n N_k, \qquad \sum_1^n T_k, \qquad \sum_1^n \mathfrak{M}_k.$$

The basic frame and the diagrams of M^P, $\overline{M}^N$, $\overline{M}^T$, and $\overline{M}^{\mathfrak{M}}$, from which $f_{\max}$ and the internal forces can be determined, are shown in Fig. 5.3.7.

In place of a system of equations with $3n$ unknowns, we now find unknowns (N_1, T_1 and $\mathfrak{M}_1$) in three equations only, as shown in Table 5.3.2.

The numerical coefficients, occurring in the matrix, are

$$\overset{\circ}{A} = \frac{h \cdot l^2}{J} + h\left(\frac{1}{F_1} + \frac{1}{F_p}\right)$$

[5.3.5]

146

TABLE 5.3.2.

MATRIX OF THE SIMULTANEOUS EQUATIONS REQUIRED FOR THE
SOLUTION OF A STIFFENING WALL WITH A SINGLE ROW OF OPENINGS

N_1	T_1	$\mathfrak{M}_1$	
$\dot{A}\beta_n + \dot{B}$	$\dot{C}$	$\dot{D}\beta_n + \dot{E}$	$W^N\beta_n$
$\dot{C}$	$\dot{F}\gamma_n + G + \dfrac{6H}{(n+1)(2n+1)}$	$\dot{L}$	$W^T\gamma_n$
$\dot{D}\beta_n + \dot{E}$	$\dot{L}$	$\dot{R}\beta_n + \dot{S}$	$W^{\mathfrak{M}}\beta_n$

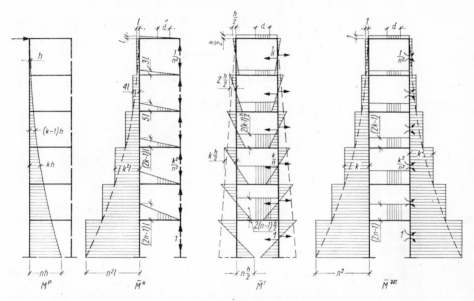

Fig. 5.3.7. Basic diagram and graphs of M^P, $\overline{M}^N$, $\overline{M}^T$, $\overline{M}\mathfrak{M}$ for determining the values N_1, T_1 and $\mathfrak{M}_1$ by the simplified method, allowing for the deformation of the lintels

$$\mathring{B} = \frac{d}{3J_r}\left[(d+s)^2 + (d+s)\,s + s^2\right] + 2.8\,\frac{d}{F_r} \qquad [5.3.6]$$

$$\mathring{C} = \frac{d}{J_r}\cdot\frac{d+2s}{2}\cdot\frac{h}{2} \qquad [5.3.7]$$

$$\mathring{D} = \frac{h\cdot l}{J} \qquad [5.3.8]$$

$$\mathring{E} = \frac{d}{J_r}\cdot\frac{d+2s}{2} \qquad [5.3.9]$$

$$W^N = -\,P\,\frac{l\cdot h^2}{2J} \qquad [5.3.10]$$

147

$$\mathring{F} = \frac{h^3}{12}\left(\frac{1}{J_1} + \frac{1}{J_p}\right) + 2.8h\left(\frac{1}{F_1} + \frac{1}{F_p}\right) \qquad [5.3.11]$$

$$\mathring{G} = \frac{d}{J_r} \cdot \frac{h^2}{4} \qquad [5.3.12]$$

$$\mathring{H} = \frac{d}{F_r} \qquad [5.3.13]$$

$$\mathring{L} = \frac{d}{J_r} \cdot \frac{h}{2} \qquad [5.3.14]$$

$$W^{\mathrm{T}} = P\left(\frac{h^2}{12J_1} + 2.8\frac{h}{F_1}\right) \qquad [5.3.15]$$

$$\mathring{R} = h\left(\frac{1}{J_1} + \frac{1}{J_p}\right) \qquad [5.3.16]$$

$$\mathring{S} = \frac{d}{J_r} \qquad [5.3.17]$$

$$W^{\mathfrak{M}} = -P\frac{h^2}{2J_1} \qquad [5.3.18]$$

$$\beta_n = \frac{1}{10} \cdot \frac{n+1}{2n-1}(3n^2 + 3n - 1) \qquad [5.3.19]$$

$$\gamma_n = \frac{1}{2} \cdot \frac{n+1}{2n-1}. \qquad [5.3.20]$$

After the redundant values for the topmost floor have been calculated, the bending moments, M, axial forces S, and shear forces Q at any section of the lower storeys may be easily obtained, and the value of the deflection f_{max} is then determinated.

The redundants N_k, T_k and $\mathfrak{M}_k$, for a lower storey k, counting from the top are given by the expressions [5.3.4].

The internal forces are calculated as in the case of statically determinate systems. At the base of the right hand column of the k-th storey, counting downwards,

$$\left.\begin{aligned} M &= -T_k \cdot \frac{h}{2} + \mathfrak{M}_k \\ S &= N_k \\ Q &= -T_k \end{aligned}\right\} \qquad [5.3.21]$$

At the base of the left hand column of the same storey,

$$M = \frac{1}{2} k (k + 1) P \cdot h - N_k \cdot l + T_k \cdot \frac{h}{2} - \mathfrak{M}_k$$

$$S = - N_k \text{ (tension)}$$

$$Q = k \cdot P + T_k$$

[5.3.22]

M, S and Q can be similarly obtained for other sections in the frame.

In the lintel of the k-th storey, at the face of the left hand column,

$$M = (N_k - N_{k-1}) (d + s) + (T + T_{k-1}) \frac{h}{2} + \mathfrak{M}_k - \mathfrak{M}_{k-1}$$

$$S = - (T_k - T_{k-1})$$

$$Q = N_k - N_{k-1}.$$

[5.3.23]

In the lowest storey, the internal forces predicted in accordance with the condition [5.3.4] are well within the safety limits. Values nearer to those obtained by an exact analysis can be chosen by considering the forces in the lintel of the 2nd storey from the bottom derived by the simplified method, to be at a maximum.

The deflection f_{max} is calculated from the general equation

$$f_{max} = \int_0^x \overline{M} \cdot M \cdot \frac{dx}{E \cdot J} + 2 \lambda (1 + \mu) \int_0^x \overline{Q} \cdot Q \cdot \frac{dx}{E \cdot F}$$

[5.3.24]

where μ is Poisson's ratio.

The relationship of N_k, T_k and $\mathfrak{M}_k$, which was defined by the expressions [5.3.24] can be simplified in a number of ways, as a result of which

$$f_{max} = a_1 P$$

$$a_1 = a - \frac{1}{P} \left[U_M (N_1 \cdot l + \mathfrak{M}_1) n (n + 1) (3 n^2 + n - 1) + \right.$$

$$\left. + (U_M + U_Q) \frac{T_1 \cdot h}{2} (n + 1) n \right]$$

[5.3.25]

where a is as defined by equation [5.3.1] with $J = J_1$, $F = F_1$.

5.3.3.2. *Walls with a single vertical row of openings near one edge.* When the openings are near one edge of a wall (Fig. 5.3.8), $b_p \leqslant b_1$, and the stresses generated in the narrow column by the forces N_k are much greater than those resulting from moments $M = \mathfrak{M}_k + T_k \frac{h}{2}$. The calculations can then be considerably simplified.

With $\mathfrak{M}_1 \approx 0$ and $T_1 \approx 0$, and using the system of equations presented in Table 5.3.2, we obtain directly

149

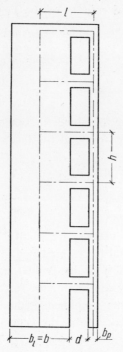

Fig. 5.3.8. Stiffening wall with one row of openings near one edge

$$N_1 = \frac{W^N \cdot \beta_n}{\mathring{A}\,\beta_n + \mathring{B}}, \quad N_k = k^2 \cdot N_1 \qquad\qquad [5.3.26]$$

where $\mathring{A}$, $\mathring{B}$, W^N can be determined from equations [5.3.5], [5.3.6], [5.3.7], and β_n from [5.3.19].

The expression for f_{max} is now:

$$f_{max} = a_2\,P$$

$$a_2 = a - \frac{U_M \cdot N_1 \cdot l}{P}\,n\,(n+1)\,(3\,n^2 + n - 1) \qquad\qquad [5.3.27]$$

where a and U_M have the values given by formulae [5.3.1] and [5.3.2].

5.3.3.3. *Walls with two symmetrical vertical rows of openings.* Fig. 5.3.9 is a schematic representation of a symmetrical wall with two vertical rows of openings.

Values of N_1, T_1 and $\mathfrak{M}_1$ are obtained from the series of equations given in the form of a matrix in Table 5.3.3.

The numerical coefficients used in the equations are:

$$\mathring{\mathring{A}} = 4\,\frac{h \cdot l^2}{J} + 2\,\frac{h}{F_p} \qquad\qquad [5.3.28]$$

$$\overset{\circ\circ}{F} = \frac{h^3}{6}\left(\frac{2}{J} + \frac{1}{J_p}\right) + 5.6\,h\left(\frac{2}{F} + \frac{1}{F_p}\right) \qquad [5.3.29]$$

$$\overset{\circ\circ}{R} = 2\,h\left(\frac{2}{J} + \frac{1}{J_p}\right) \qquad [5.3.30]$$

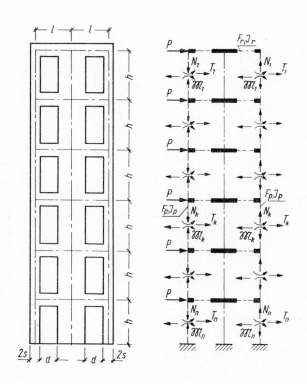

Fig. 5.3.9. Working diagram for a wall with two rows of openings

TABLE 5.3.3.

MATRIX OF THE SIMULTANEOUS EQUATIONS REQUIRED FOR THE
SOLUTION OF A STIFFENING WALL WITH TWO ROWS OF OPENINGS

N_1	T_1	$\mathfrak{M}_1$	
$\ddot{A}\beta_\mathrm{n}+2\dot{B}$	$2\dot{C}$	$4\dot{D}\beta_\mathrm{n}+2\dot{E}$	$2W^\mathrm{N}\beta_\mathrm{n}$
$2\dot{C}$	$\ddot{F}\gamma_\mathrm{n}+2(\dot{G}+\dot{K})$	$2\dot{L}$	$2W^\mathrm{T}\gamma_\mathrm{n}$
$4\dot{D}\beta_\mathrm{n}+2\dot{E}$	$2\dot{L}$	$\ddot{R}\beta_\mathrm{n}+2\dot{S}$	$2W^\mathfrak{M}\beta_\mathrm{n}$

151

The remaining values are:

$\mathring{B}, \mathring{C}, \mathring{D}, \mathring{E}, W^{N}, \mathring{G}, \mathring{H}, \mathring{L}, W^{T}, \mathring{S}, W^{\mathfrak{M}}$, which are obtained from formulae [5.3.6] to [5.3.18], and β_n and γ_n, given by [5.3.19] and [5.3.20].

After solving the matrix and obtaining the redundants, the values of the bending moments M, the axial forces S, and the shear forces Q in all members of the frame, and hence, of the deflection $f_{\max}$, can be calculated.

The relationships between the redundants in the k-th storey down remain as specified by Eq. [5.3.4], using appropriate values of N_1, T_1, and $\mathfrak{M}_1$.

The internal forces are calculated in accordance with the equivalent, statically determinate system shown in Fig. 5.3.8. In the outer columns of the k-th storey

$$
\left.
\begin{aligned}
M &= -T_{\mathrm{k}}\frac{h}{2}+\mathfrak{M}_{\mathrm{k}} \\[2mm]
S &= \pm N_{\mathrm{k}} \\[2mm]
Q &= -T_{\mathrm{k}}
\end{aligned}
\right\}
\qquad [5.3.31]
$$

In the central column:

$$
\left.
\begin{aligned}
M &= \frac{1}{2}k\,(k+1)\,P\cdot h - 2\,N_{\mathrm{k}}\,l + T_{\mathrm{k}}\cdot h - 2\,\mathfrak{M}_{\mathrm{k}} \\[2mm]
S &= 0 \\[2mm]
Q &= 2\,T_{\mathrm{k}}
\end{aligned}
\right\}
\qquad [5.3.32]
$$

The values of the internal forces in the lintel of the same storey, at the face of the central column, are obtained from equations [5.3.23].

As predicted by equation [5.3.4] for N_{k}, T_{k}, and $\mathfrak{M}_{\mathrm{k}}$, the expression giving the deflection $f_{\max}$ takes a form similar to [5.3.25], namely,

$$ f_{\max} = a_3\,P $$

$$ a_3 = a - \frac{2}{P}\left[U_{\mathrm{M}}\,(N_1\,l + \mathfrak{M}_1)\,n\,(n+1)\,(3\,n^2+n-1) - (U_{\mathrm{M}}+U_{\mathrm{Q}})\,\frac{T_1 h}{2}\,(n+1)\,n\right] $$

$$ [5.3.33] $$

where a can be determined from [5.3.1].

As was the case with walls possessing a single row of openings, when two rows of openings are situated symmetrically near the edges of the wall, the values of $\mathfrak{M}_{\mathrm{k}}$ and T_{k} may be neglected and the solution is thus greatly simplified.

Taking $\mathfrak{M}_1 \approx 0$ and $T_1 \approx 0$, and using the equations in the matrix of Table 5.3.2, we obtain

$$ N_1 = \frac{\overset{\circ}{W}{}^{N}\cdot\beta_n}{\overset{\infty}{A}\cdot\beta_n + 2\,\overset{\circ}{B}} \qquad [5.3.34] $$

whence, from [5.3.4]

$$N_k = k^2 \cdot N_1.$$

The formula for f_{max} now becomes:

$$f_{max} = a_4 P$$

$$a_4 = a - \frac{2 U_M N_1 l}{P} n (n+1)(3 n^2 + n - 1). \tag{5.3.35}$$

5.3.4. Perforated Stiffening Walls treated as Banded Cantilevers

5.3.4.1. *Wall with a single row of openings.* The equivalent diagram for a wall with a single row of openings, treated as a banded cantilever, is shown in Fig. 5.3.10.

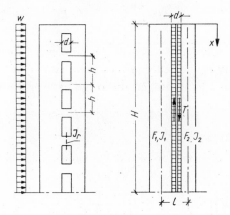

Fig. 5.3.10. Working diagram for a stiffening wall with one row of openings, treated as a two-band cantilever

The point load action of the lintels on the cantilever bands is replaced by continuous, uniformly distributed tangential forces. A unit force $\tau = 1$ causes a displacement δ at the midspan of a lintel (span d), equal to (Fig. 5.3.11)

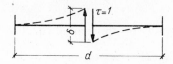

Fig. 5.3.11. Mid-span deflections in the lintels

$$\delta = 2 \times \frac{1}{3} h \frac{d}{2} \cdot \left(\frac{d}{2}\right)^2 \frac{1}{E \cdot J_r} = \frac{h \cdot d^3}{12 E \cdot J_r} \tag{5.3.36}$$

where h is the storey height, E, J_r are respectively the elasticity modulus and the moment of inertia of the lintel.

153

The sum of the tangential forces at any section a distance x from the top of the building is expressed by the integral

$$T = \int_0^x \tau \, dx \qquad\qquad [5.3.37]$$

The strain energy of deformation of all lintels in a wall of height H is given by

$$U_r = \frac{1}{2} \int_0^H \delta \cdot \tau^2 dx = \frac{1}{2E} \int_0^H \frac{h \cdot d^3}{12 J_r} (T')^2 \, dx \qquad\qquad [5.3.38]$$

The bending moment at section $x-x$ is

$$M = \frac{w \cdot x^2}{2} - T \cdot l \qquad\qquad [5.3.39]$$

where l is the distance between the axes of the cantilever bands.

Owing to the equality of the deflections of both bands, the moment M is divided into components M_1 and M_2 in proportion to the moments of inertia J_1 and J_2, i.e.

$$M_1 = \left(\frac{w \cdot x^2}{2} - T \cdot l \right) \frac{J_1}{J_1 + J_2}; \quad M_2 = \left(\frac{w \cdot x^2}{2} - T \cdot l \right) \frac{J_2}{J_1 + J_2}. \qquad [5.3.40]$$

The strain energy of deformation of the two bands is therefore expressed by

$$U_s = \frac{1}{2E} \int_0^H \left[\left(\frac{w \cdot x^2}{2} - T \cdot l \right)^2 \frac{1}{J_1 + J_2} + \left(\frac{1}{F_1} + \frac{1}{F_2} \right) T^2 \right] dx. \qquad [5.3.41]$$

The sum of [5.3.38] and [5.3.41] gives the total strain energy stored in the wall

$$U = \frac{1}{2E} \int_0^H \left[\frac{h \cdot b^3}{12 J_r} T'^2 + \frac{\left(\dfrac{w \cdot x^2}{2} - T \cdot l \right)^2}{J_1 + J_2} + \left(\frac{1}{F_1} + \frac{1}{F_2} \right) T^2 \right] dx. \qquad [5.3.42]$$

The variation in T is given by the differential equation

$$T'' - \lambda \cdot T + \mu \cdot x^2 = 0 \qquad\qquad [5.3.43]$$

where:

$$\lambda = \left[\frac{l^2}{J_1 + J_2} + \frac{1}{F_1} + \frac{1}{F_2} \right] \frac{12 J_r}{h \cdot d^3} \qquad\qquad [5.3.44]$$

$$\mu = \frac{1}{2} \cdot \frac{w \cdot l}{J_1 + J_2} \cdot \frac{12 J_r}{h \cdot d^3}. \qquad\qquad [5.3.45]$$

Rosman solved this equation by means of a rapidly converging trigonometric series

$$T = \sum a_i \sin \frac{i \cdot \pi \cdot x}{2H} \qquad [5.3.46]$$

$$a_i = \frac{\mu \left[-\dfrac{2}{\left(\dfrac{i \cdot \pi}{2H}\right)^3} \pm \dfrac{2H}{\left(\dfrac{i \cdot \pi}{2H}\right)^2} \right]}{\dfrac{1}{2} H \left[\left(\dfrac{i \cdot \pi}{2H}\right)^2 + \lambda \right]} \qquad (i = 1, 3, 5 \ldots) \qquad [5.3.47]$$

The positive sign $(+)$ is used for $i = 1, 5, 9 \ldots$
and the negative $(-)$ for $i = 3, 7 \ldots$
For practical purposes, the first three terms of this series, i.e. $i = 1, 3$ and 5, will provide values of sufficient accuracy.

The deflection f_{max} is calculated from the expression:

$$y'' = \frac{-\dfrac{w \cdot x^2}{2} + l \sum a_i \sin \dfrac{i \cdot \pi \cdot x}{2H}}{E\,(J_1 + J_2)} \qquad [5.3.48]$$

which, integrated twice, gives:

$$f_{max} = \frac{1}{E\,(J_1 + J_2)} \left[\frac{1}{8} w \cdot H^4 \mp l \sum a_i \left(\frac{2H}{i \cdot \pi}\right)^2 \right] \qquad [5.3.49]$$

The negative sign $(-)$ is used for $i = 1, 5, 9 \ldots$
and the positive $(+)$ for $i = 3, 7 \ldots$
The internal forces are obtained as follows:
for columns (Fig. 5.3.9):
— bending moment — from formula [5.3.40]
— axial force — from formula [5.3.46]

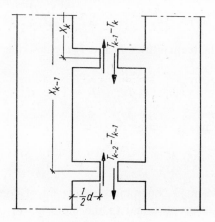

Fig. 5.3.12. Diagram of the internal forces

where x is the distance of the section considered from the upper edge of the wall; for the k-th lintel from the top (Fig. 5.3.12):

— bending moment — from the expression

$$M_k = \pm (T_{k-1} - T_k) \frac{1}{2} d \qquad [5.3.50]$$

where T_{k-1}, T_k are respectively the values of T obtained from the expression [5.3.46] for the storeys $k-1$ and k; d is the clear width of the opening.

5.3.4.2. *Walls with two rows of openings.* A method analogous to that described in Section 5.3.4.1 is used to solve the problem of a wall with two vertical rows of openings (Fig. 5.3.13).

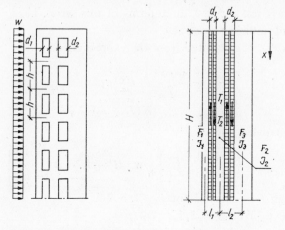

Fig. 5.3.13. Working diagram for a stiffening wall with two rows of openings, treated as a three-band cantilever

The deflections of the lintels, due to tangential forces in planes 1 and 2, are:

$$\delta_1 = \frac{h \cdot d_1^3}{12E \cdot J_{r1}}, \qquad \delta_2 = \frac{h \cdot d_2^3}{12E \cdot J_{r2}}. \qquad [5.3.51]$$

The statically indeterminate quantities T_1 and T_2 are described by expressions similar to [5.3.37]:

$$T_1 = \int_0^x \tau_1 \, dx; \qquad T_2 = \int_0^x \tau_2 \, dx. \qquad [5.3.52]$$

The bending moment at any section $x-x$ is

$$M = \frac{w \cdot x^2}{2} - T_1 l_1 - T_2 l_2. \qquad [5.3.53]$$

The total bending moment is, once more, made up of components M_1, M_2, M_3, the values of which are proportional to the moments of inertia J_1, J_2, J_3 of the cross-sections of bands 1, 2 and 3.

$$M_1 = \left(\frac{w \cdot x^2}{2} - T_1 \cdot l_1 - T_2 \cdot l_2\right) \cdot \frac{J_1}{J_1 + J_2 + J_3} \qquad [5.3.54]$$

$$M_2 = \left(\frac{w \cdot x^2}{2} - T_1 \cdot l_1 - T_2 \cdot l_2\right) \cdot \frac{J_2}{J_1 + J_2 + J_3} \qquad [5.3.55]$$

$$M_3 = \left(\frac{w \cdot x^2}{2} - T_1 \cdot l_1 - T_2 \cdot l_2\right) \cdot \frac{J_3}{J_1 + J_2 + J_3} \qquad [5.3.56]$$

The variables T_1 and T_2 are described by differential equations of the form

$$\left.\begin{aligned} - T_1'' + \lambda_{1,1} T_1 + \lambda_{1,2} T_2 + \mu_1 x^2 &= 0 \\ - T_2'' + \lambda_{2,1} T_1 + \lambda_{2,2} T_2 + \mu_2 x^2 &= 0 \end{aligned}\right\} \qquad [5.3.57]$$

where:

$$\left.\begin{aligned}
\lambda_{1,1} &= \left[\frac{l_1^2}{J_1 + J_2 + J_3} + \left(\frac{1}{F_1} + \frac{1}{F_2}\right)\right]\frac{12\,J_{r1}}{h \cdot d_1^3} \\
\lambda_{1,2} &= \left[\frac{l_1 \cdot l_2}{J_1 + J_2 + J_3} - \frac{1}{F_2}\right]\frac{12\,J_{r1}}{h \cdot d_1^3} \\
\lambda_{2,2} &= \left[\frac{l_2^2}{J_1 + J_2 + J_3} + \left(\frac{1}{F_2} + \frac{1}{F_3}\right)\right]\frac{12\,J_{r2}}{h \cdot d_2^3} \\
\lambda_{2,1} &= \left[\frac{l_1 \cdot l_2}{J_1 + J_2 + J_3} - \frac{1}{F_1}\right]\frac{12\,J_{r2}}{h \cdot d_2^3} \\
\mu_1 &= \frac{w \cdot l_1}{J_1 + J_2 + J_3} \cdot \frac{6\,J_{r2}}{h \cdot d_1^3} \\
\mu_2 &= \frac{w \cdot l_2}{J_1 + J_2 + J_3} \cdot \frac{6\,J_{r2}}{h \cdot d_2^3}
\end{aligned}\right\} \qquad [5.3.58]$$

and where: l_1 and l_2 are the distances between the centre lines of the cantilever bands, J_{r1}, J_{r2} are moments of inertia of lintels 1 and 2, d_1, d_2 are the widths of the openings.

The solution of equation [5.3.57] may be written in the form

$$\begin{aligned}
T_1 &= \sum a_{1,i} \sin \frac{i \cdot \pi \cdot x}{2H} \\
T_2 &= \sum a_{2,i} \sin \frac{i \cdot \pi \cdot x}{2H}
\end{aligned} \qquad (i = 1, 3, 5 \ldots n) \qquad [5.3.59]$$

where:

$$a_{1,i} = \frac{D_{1,i}}{D_i} \qquad a_{2,i} = \frac{D_{2,i}}{D_i} \qquad [5.3.60]$$

$$D_i = \frac{H^2}{4}\left(\frac{i \cdot \pi}{2H}\right)^4 + (\lambda_{1,1} + \lambda_{2,2})\left(\frac{i \cdot \pi}{2H}\right)^2 + \lambda_{1,1} \cdot \lambda_{2,2} - \lambda_{1,2} \cdot \lambda_{2,1}$$

$$D_{1,i} = -\frac{H}{2}\left(\frac{2H}{i \cdot \pi}\right)^3 \cdot (2 \mp i \cdot \pi) \cdot \left\{\mu_1\left[\left(\frac{i \cdot \pi}{2H}\right)^2 + \lambda_{2,2}\right] - \mu_2 \cdot \lambda_{1,2}\right\} \quad \Bigg\} \quad [5.3.61]$$

$$D_{2,i} = -\frac{H}{2}\left(\frac{2H}{i \cdot \pi}\right)^3 \cdot (2 \mp i \cdot \pi) \cdot \left\{\mu_2\left[\left(\frac{i \cdot \pi}{2H}\right)^2 + \lambda_{1,1}\right] - \mu_1 \cdot \lambda_{2,1}\right\}$$

(The positive sign is used when $i = 1, 5, 9 \dots$ and negative when $i = 3, 7 \dots$)

It is sufficient to use only the first three terms of the series ($i = 1, 3, 5$) when calculating the quantity T.

The deflection $f_{\max}$ is expressed by the formula

$$f_{\max} = \frac{1}{E(J_1 + J_2 + J_3)}\left[\frac{1}{8} w \cdot H^4 \mp \sum (a_{1,i} \cdot l_1 + a_{2,i} \cdot l_2)\left(\frac{2H}{i \cdot \pi}\right)^2\right]. \quad [5.3.62]$$

The summation is negative for $i = 1, 5$ and 9 and positive for $i = 3, 7$ etc.

5.3.4.3. *Walls with any number of vertical rows of openings.* In a wall with n rows of openings the bending moment at any section $x-x$ is

$$M = \frac{w \cdot x^2}{2} - \sum_{j=1}^{j=n} T_j \cdot l_j \quad [5.3.63]$$

and in proportion to the moments of inertia of the vertical bands, the total bending moment is divided into $j = n+1$ components.

$$M = \left(\frac{w \cdot x^2}{2} - \sum T_j \cdot l_j\right)_{j=n+1} \frac{J_j}{\sum\limits_{j=1} J_j} \quad [5.3.64]$$

The quantity T is determined from a system of equations of the form:

$$- T_j'' + \sum_{j=1}^{j=n} \lambda_{j,i} \cdot T_j + \mu_j \cdot x^2 \quad [5.3.65]$$

where

$$\lambda_{1,1} = \frac{\beta_1^2 + \gamma_1}{a_1}, \quad \lambda_{1,2} = \frac{\beta_1 \cdot \beta_2 + \delta_1}{a_1}, \quad \lambda_{1,3} = \frac{\beta_1 \cdot \beta_3}{a_1}, \qquad \lambda_{1,n} = \frac{\beta_1 \cdot \beta_j}{a_1}$$

$$\lambda_{1,2} = \frac{\beta_2 \cdot \beta_1 + \delta_1}{a_2}, \quad \lambda_{2,2} = \frac{\beta_2^2 + \gamma_2}{a_2}, \quad \lambda_{2,3} = \frac{\beta_2 \cdot \beta_3 + \delta_2}{a_2}, \qquad \lambda_{2,n} = \frac{\beta_2 \cdot \beta_j}{a_2}$$

$$\lambda_{1,3} = \frac{\beta_3 \cdot \beta_1}{a_3}, \quad \lambda_{2,3} = \frac{\beta_3 \cdot \beta_2}{a_3}, \quad \lambda_{3,3} = \frac{\beta_3^2 \cdot \gamma_3}{a_3}, \qquad \lambda_{3,n} = \frac{\beta_3 \cdot \beta_j}{\alpha_3} \qquad [5.3.66]$$

$$\lambda_{n,1} = \frac{\beta_n \cdot \beta_2}{a_n}, \quad \lambda_{n,2} = \frac{\beta_n \cdot \beta_2}{a_n}, \quad \lambda_{n,3} = \frac{\beta_n \cdot \beta_3}{a_n}, \qquad \lambda_{n,n} = \frac{\beta_n^2 + \gamma_j}{a_n};$$

$$\mu_j = \frac{\beta_0 \beta_j}{a_j}$$

$$a_j = \frac{h \cdot d_j^3}{12 J_{rj}}; \quad \beta_j = -\frac{l_j}{\sqrt{\sum J_j}}; \quad \gamma_j = \frac{1}{F_j} + \frac{1}{F_{j+1}}; \quad \delta_j = -\frac{1}{F_{j+1}}; \quad \beta_0 = \frac{1}{2} \cdot \frac{w}{\sqrt{\sum J_j}}$$

Following Rosman, we assume that the solution of equation [5.3.65] is a function of the form:

$$T_k = \sum a_{j,i} \sin \frac{i \cdot \pi \cdot x}{2 H}; \quad i = 1, 3, 5 \ldots \qquad [5.3.67]$$

where

$$a_{j,i} = \frac{D_{n,j}}{D_j},$$

$$D_n = \begin{vmatrix} \left(\dfrac{i \cdot \pi}{2H}\right)^2 + \lambda_{1,1} & \lambda_{1,2} & \lambda_{1,n} \\[2mm] \lambda_{2,1} & \left(\dfrac{i \cdot \pi}{2H}\right)^2 + \lambda_{2,2} & \lambda_{2,n} \\[2mm] \lambda_{n,1} & \lambda_{n,2} & \left(\dfrac{i \cdot \pi}{2H}\right)^2 + \lambda_{n,n} \end{vmatrix} \qquad [5.3.68]$$

$$D_{1,i} = \frac{2}{H}\left(\frac{2H}{i \cdot \pi}\right)^3 (2 \mp i \cdot \pi) \begin{vmatrix} \mu_1 & \lambda_{1,2} & \lambda_{1,n} \\[2mm] \mu_2 & \left(\dfrac{i\pi}{2H}\right)^2 + \lambda_{2,2} & \lambda_{2,n} \\[2mm] \mu_n & \lambda_{n,2} & \left(\dfrac{i \cdot \pi}{2H}\right)^2 + \lambda_{n,n} \end{vmatrix} \qquad [5.3.69]$$

$$D_{2,i} = \frac{2}{H}\left(\frac{2H}{i \cdot \pi}\right)^3 (2 \mp i \cdot \pi) \begin{vmatrix} \left(\dfrac{i \cdot \pi}{2H}\right)^2 + \lambda_{1,1} & \mu_1 & \lambda_{1,n} \\[2mm] \lambda_{2,1} & \mu_2 & \lambda_{2,n} \\[2mm] \lambda_{n,2} & \mu_n & \left(\dfrac{i \cdot \pi}{2H}\right)^2 + \lambda_{n,n} \end{vmatrix} \qquad [5.3.70]$$

$$D_{n,i} = \frac{2}{H}\left(\frac{2H}{i \cdot \pi}\right)^3 (2 \mp i \cdot \pi) \begin{vmatrix} \left(\dfrac{i \cdot \pi}{2H}\right)^2 + \lambda_{1,1} & \lambda_{1,2} & \mu_1 \\[2mm] \lambda_{2,1} & \dfrac{i \cdot \pi}{2H} + \lambda_{2,2} & \mu_2 \\[2mm] \lambda_{n,1} & \lambda_{n,2} & \mu_n \end{vmatrix} \qquad [5.3.71]$$

The positive sign $(+)$ is used for $i = 1, 5, 9 \ldots$ and the negative $(-)$ for $i = 3, 7 \ldots$

The deflection f_{max} is calculated from an equation analogous to [5.3.48], namely:

$$f_{max} = \frac{1}{E \sum J_j} \left[\frac{w \cdot H^4}{8} \pm \sum a_{n,i} \cdot l_i \left(\frac{2H}{n \cdot \pi} \right)^2 \right]$$ [5.3.72]

with $i = 1, 5, 9 \dots$ giving a negative, and $i = 3, 7 \dots$ positive summation term.

5.3.5. The Effect of Elastically Fixing the Stiffening Wall in the Ground

When a wall is semi-rigidly fixed in the ground (section 5.1.1), calculations of the deflection f_{max} must take into account the moment of inertia of the foundations, J_0, and the elastic deformability of the ground, C, according to Winkler's hypothesis.
The deflection f_{max} is then given by:

$$f_{max} = f_u + f_\varphi$$ [5.3.73]

where f_u is the wall deflection calculated from the formulae given for walls rigidly fixed at their bases, and f_φ the deflection caused by the rotation of the foundations through an angle φ, as in Fig. 5.3.14.

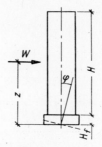

Fig. 5.3.14. Rotation of the wall through an angle φ due to the elastic deformation of the ground under the footing

The value of f_φ is given by an expression of the form:

$$f_\varphi = \frac{W \cdot z}{C \cdot J_0} (H + H_t)$$ [5.3.74]

where W is the resultant of the horizontal forces acting on the wall, z the height relative to the base of the foundations, at which W acts, and H, H_t are respectively the height of the wall and the thickness of the foundations.
The following values of C are given:

for weak soils	$C = 10$ to 30 kg/cm³
for medium soils	$C = 30$ to 70 kg/cm³
for compact soils	$C = 70$ to 150 kg/cm³
for rocks	$C = 150$ to 300 kg/cm³.

In each case, the larger of the values given above should be taken for narrow wall footings, and the smaller for very wide foundation bases.

5.3.6. Preliminary Check of the Deflections of Stiffening Walls

5.3.6.1. *General equations.* Approximate values of the deflections $f^*_{\max}$ of perforated stiffening walls may be determined in order to see if the more accurate, but laborious, calculations given previously need be carried out. The structure is treated as a solid cantilever beam, whose deflection under horizontal loading is equal to the deflection of the wall with its openings.

The equivalent moment of inertia of the solid cantilever, the shear force in the heaviest stressed lintel, and the force normal to the section at the base of the wall, can be calculated by mean of the numerical coefficients η, ϑ, and γ given in sections 5.3.6.2. and 5.3.6.3. These coefficients were obtained by solving a series of numerical examples by the Rosman method. The horizontal loading on the walls is thus considered to be uniformly distributed.

Formula [5.1.12] expressed the share of any wall in supporting the total horizontal loading, when the latter was due to concentrated forces. When, however, the horizontal loads are uniformly distributed,

$$w^*_i = \frac{w \cdot L}{2} \cdot \frac{E_i \cdot J^*_i}{\sum E_i \cdot J^*_i} \qquad [5.3.75]$$

where w^*_i is half the load exerted on a given wall, estimated by treating the latter as a cantilever, w the total horizontal load per unit area of the face of the building at right angles to that wall, L the length of the building, $E_i \cdot J^*_i$ the product of the elastic modulus and the equivalent moment of inertia of the wall under consideration, $\sum E_i J^*_i$ is the sum of the products of the elastic moduli and the moments of inertia of all stiffening walls in the building.

The deflection $f^*_{\max}$ is given by

$$f^*_{\max} = w^*_i \cdot \frac{H^2}{E} \left(\frac{H^2}{4 J^*_i} + \frac{2.8}{F_i} \right) \qquad [5.3.76]$$

where H is the height of the building.

If

$$f^*_{\max} \leqslant \frac{H}{2000} \qquad [5.3.77]$$

it may be accepted that the three-dimensional stiffness of the building is sufficient and no further calculations are required.

When

$$\frac{H}{2000} < f^*_{\max} < \frac{H}{1500} \qquad [5.3.78]$$

the three-dimensional stiffness of the building must be checked by more accurate methods, as given in Sections 5.3.3 and 5.3.4.

161

When

$$f^*_{max} \geqslant \frac{H}{1500} \qquad\qquad [5.3.79]$$

the three-dimensional stiffness of the building is definitely unsatisfactory, and additional stiffening must be introduced.

The coefficients η, ϑ, and γ were obtained for walls with door openings, i.e. the depth of the lintels was 2/9 of the storey-height. When these coefficients are used in the solution of walls with window openings, the deflections f^* are overestimated, and the shear forces Q in the lintels are underestimated. It is advisable to consider the depth of the lintels to be only 2/9 of the storey-height when checking the safety factor, although this depth may in fact be greater.

5.3.6.2. *Stiffening walls with one vertical row of openings.* The moment of inertia J^* of a cantilever beam equivalent to the wall with one row of openings, as in Fig. 5.3.15, is

$$J^* = \frac{1}{\eta} \cdot \frac{g \cdot b^3}{12} \qquad\qquad [5.3.80]$$

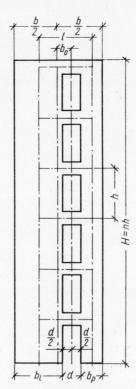

Fig. 5.3.15. Auxiliary diagram from which the equivalent inertia of a wall with one row of openings may be derived

where η is the numerical coefficient, g, b, are respectively the thickness and width of the wall.

Coefficients η are treated as functions of the ratios

$$K_1 = n^2 \left(\frac{b}{H}\right)^4; \quad K_2 = \frac{d}{b}; \quad K_3 = \frac{b_0}{b}$$

where n is the number of storeys, b the width of the wall, H the height of the wall, d the width of the openings, and b_0 the eccentricity of the openings relative to the centre line of the wall.

Coefficients η for $K_1 = 2$ and $K_1 = 8$ are given graphically in Fig. 5.3.16. The intermediate values of η should be obtained by linear interpolation.

The shear force in the lintel subject to the greatest stress (at $H/3$ from the base) and the corresponding bending moment are given by

$$Q = \frac{W^*}{\vartheta} \qquad\qquad [5.3.81]$$

$$M = Q \cdot \frac{d}{2} \qquad\qquad [5.3.82]$$

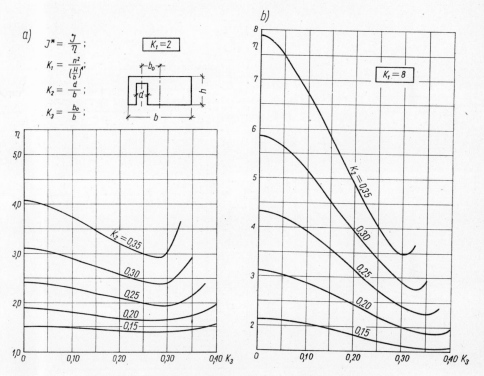

Fig. 5.3.16. Coefficients η for a wall with a single row of openings:
(a) for $K_1 = 2$, (b) for $K_1 = 8$

163

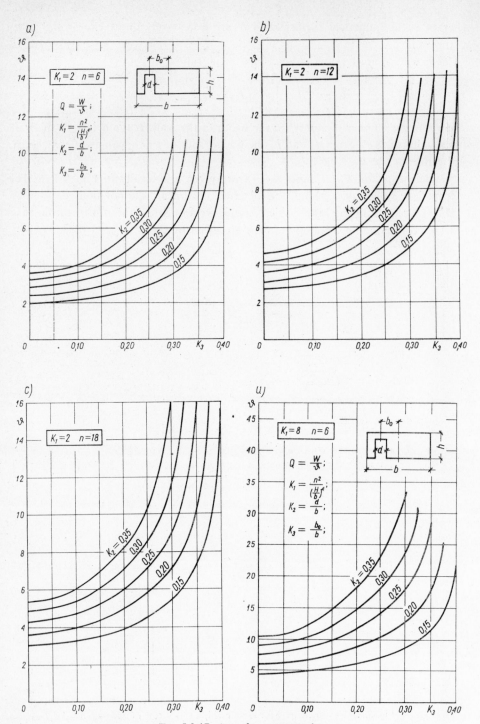

Eq. 5.3.17. (see also next page)

164

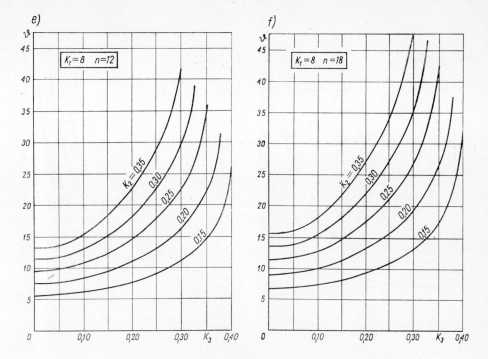

Fig. 5.3.17. Coefficients ϑ for a wall with a single row of perforations:
(a) $K_1 = 2$, $n = 6$, (b) $K_1 = 2$, $n = 12$, (c) $K_1 = 2$, $n = 18$, (d) $K_1 = 8$, $n = 6$, (e) $K_1 = 8$, $n = 12$,
(f) $K_1 = 8$, $n = 18$

where $W^* = w_i^* \cdot H$ is the total horizontal force, w_i^* is derived from formula [5.3.75], and ϑ is a numerical coefficient, given graphically in Fig. 5.3.17 as a function of the parameters K_1, K_2, and K_3 and the number of storeys n.

The normal forces N and the bending moments M_1 and M_2 at the base of the wall are given by

$$N = N_1 = - N_2 = \frac{W^* \cdot H}{\gamma \cdot b} \qquad [5.3.83]$$

$$\left. \begin{aligned} M_1 &= (w_i^* \cdot H^2 - N \cdot l) \frac{J_1}{J_1 + J_2} \\ M_2 &= (w_i^* \cdot H^2 - N \cdot l) \frac{J_2}{J_1 + J_2} \end{aligned} \right\} \qquad [5.3.84]$$

where γ is the numerical coefficient given in Fig. 5.3.18 as a function of the parameters K_1, K_2 and K_3, J_1 and J_2 are moments of inertia of the horizontal cross-sections through bands 1 and 2.

165

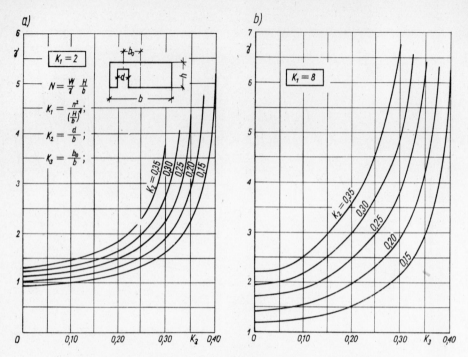

Fig. 5.3.18. Coefficients γ for a wall with a single row of openings:
(a) $K_1 = 2$, (b) $K_1 = 8$

5.3.6.3. *Walls with two rows of openings*. The moment of inertia of a solid cantilever beam, equivalent to the wall with two rows of openings (Fig. 5.3.19) is determined similarly to that for a wall with a single row of openings. Both openings were considered to be of the same width d and their height was taken to be $7/9h$. When the graphs are used in practice, due consideration must be given to the actual geometric conditions.

The coefficients η are shown graphically in Fig. 5.3.20 as functions of the parameters $K_1 = 2$ and 8; K_2, $K_4 = b_1/b$ and $K_5 = b_2/b$, where b_1 and b_2 are the eccentricities of the openings.

The values of the shear forces Q_1 and Q_2 occurring in the lintels under greatest stress are obtained from formulae

$$Q_1 = \frac{W^*}{\vartheta_1}; \qquad Q_2 = \frac{W^*}{\vartheta_2} \qquad\qquad [5.3.85]$$

Coefficients ϑ_1 and ϑ_2 are shown graphically in Fig. 5.3.21 as functions of K_1, K_2, n and K_4 or K_5. These graphs are prepared for the purpose of obtaining ϑ_1, but ϑ_2 is found by setting $K_4 = -K_5$ and $K_5 = -K_4$.

The bending moment in the lintel, caused by the shear force Q, is calculated from formula [5.3.82].

166

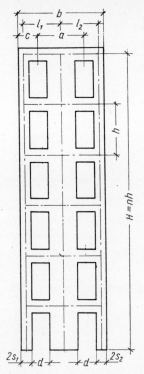

Fig. 5.3.19. Wall with two rows of openings

The axial forces N at the base of the wall are given by

$$N_1 = \frac{W^*}{\gamma_1} \cdot \frac{H}{b}; \quad N_2 = \frac{W^*}{\gamma_2} \cdot \frac{H}{b}. \tag{5.3.86}$$

The coefficients γ_1 and γ_2, as functions of K_1, K_2, K_4 and K_5, are found from the graphs in Fig. 5.3.22. To find γ_2, put $K_4 = -K_5$ and $K_5 = -K_4$.

The bending moments M at the base of the column bands are:

$$\left.\begin{aligned}
M_1 &= (w_i^* \cdot H^2 - N_1 \cdot l_1 - N_2 \cdot l_2) \frac{J_1}{J_1 + J_2 + J_3} \\[2mm]
M_2 &= (w_i^* \cdot H^2 - N_1 \cdot l_1 - N_2 \cdot l_2) \frac{J_2}{J_1 + J_2 + J_3} \\[2mm]
M_3 &= (w_i^* \cdot H^2 - N_1 \cdot l_1 - N_2 \cdot l_2) \frac{J_3}{J_1 + J_2 + J_3}
\end{aligned}\right\} \tag{5.3.87}$$

where H is the height of the building, J_1, J_2, J_3 are the moments of inertia of the cross-sections of the individual column bands, and w_i^* is taken from formula [5.3.75].

167

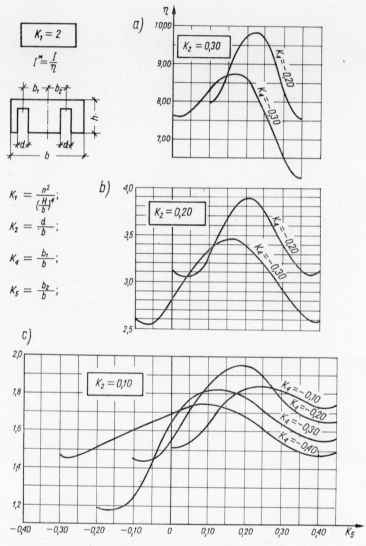

Fig. 5.3.20. Coefficients η for a wall with two rows of openings: (a) — (c) for $K_1 = 2$, (see also next page)

168

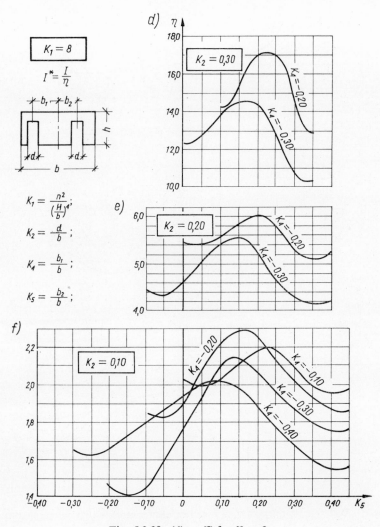

$K_1 = 8$

$I^* = \dfrac{I}{\eta}$

$K_1 = \dfrac{n^2}{\left(\dfrac{H}{b}\right)^4}$;

$K_2 = \dfrac{d}{b}$;

$K_4 = \dfrac{b_1}{b}$;

$K_5 = \dfrac{b_2}{b}$;

Fig. 5.3.20. (d) — (f) for $K_1 = 8$

169

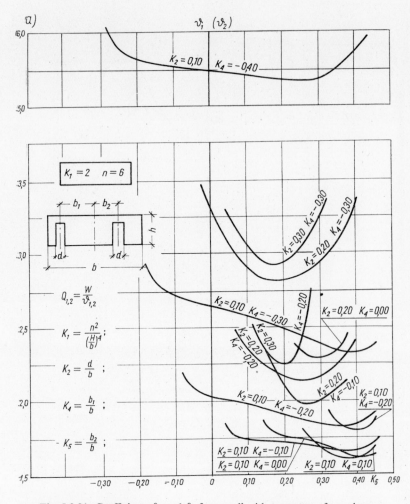

Fig. 5.3.21. Coefficients ϑ_1 and ϑ_2 for a wall with two rows of openings:
(a) $K_1 = 2$, $n = 6$, (see also pages 171-175)

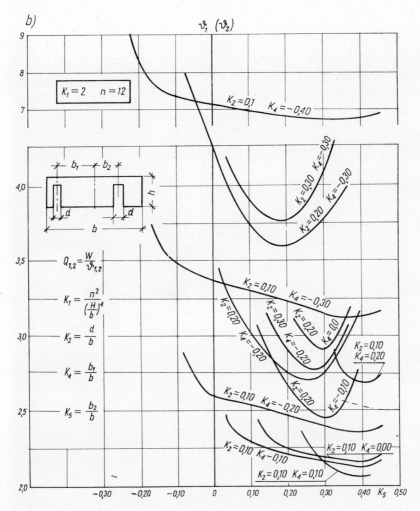

Fig. 5.3.21. (b) $K_1 = 2$, $n = 12$,

171

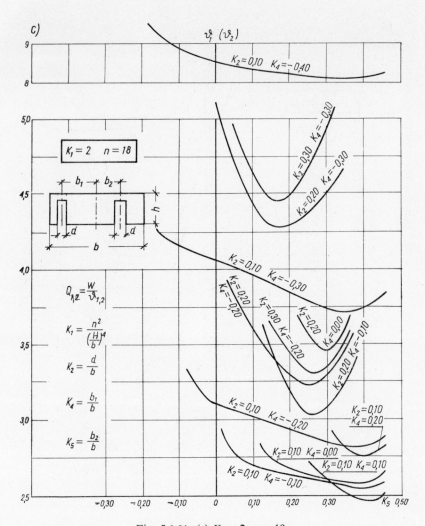

Fig. 5.3.21. (c) $K_1 = 2$, $n = 18$,

172

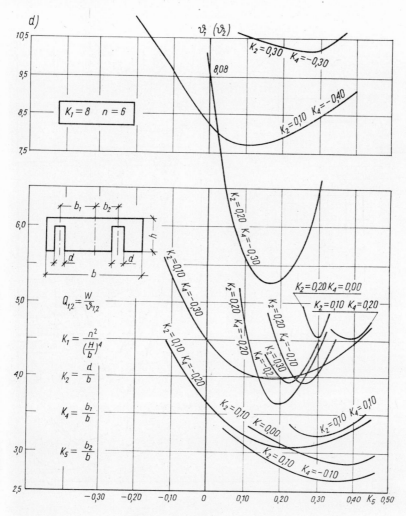

Fig. 5.3.21. (d) $K_1 = 8$, $n = 6$,

173

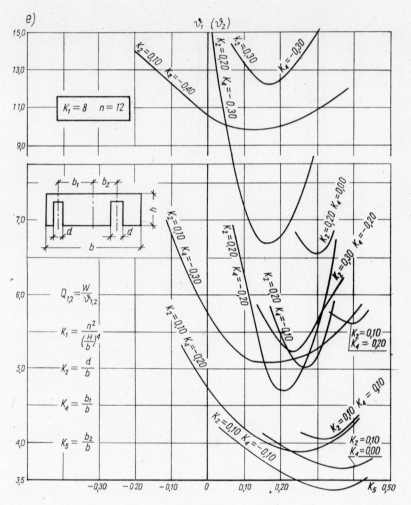

Fig. 5.3.21. (e) $K_1 = 8$, $n = 12$,

174

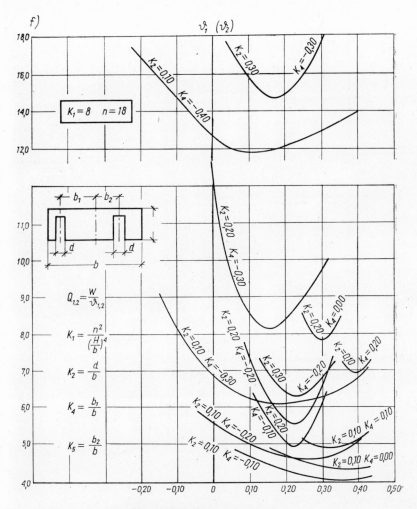

Fig. 5.3.21. (f) $K_1 = 8, n = 18$

175

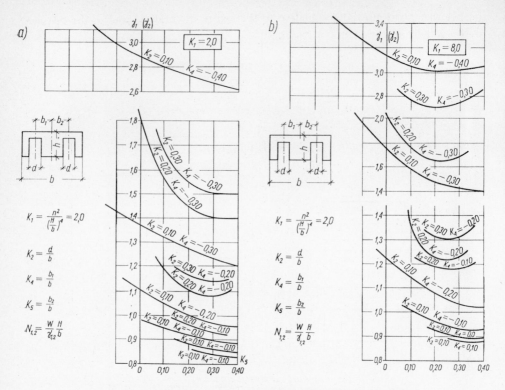

Fig. 5.3.22. Coefficients γ_1 and γ_2 for a wall with two rows of openings:
(a) $K_1 = 2$, (b) $K_1 = 8$

5.3.6.4. *Torsional deformation of open-system buildings.* To calculate the additional amount of wall deflection due to the rotation of the floor slabs (section 5.1.4.3) it is first necessary to determine the centre of rotation.

In equation [5.1.14], the abscissa x_0 is given by:

$$x_0 = \frac{\sum E_i \cdot J_i^* \cdot x_i}{\sum E_i \cdot J_i} \qquad [5.3.88]$$

where x_i is the distance between the y-axis and the axes of each wall (1 to n).

When the stiffening wall is subjected to uniformly distributed external loads, the value of the additional loading w_s, which balances the twisting moment, is expressed by

$$w_{s,i}^* = \frac{w \cdot L}{2} \cdot \frac{z \cdot a_i \cdot \beta_i^*}{\sum a_i^2 \cdot \beta_i^*} \qquad [5.3.89]$$

where w and L are as in formula [5.3.75], z is the eccentricity of the resultant of

176

the external horizontal loads relative to the centre of rotation, and a_i the distance of the wall from the centre of rotation,

$$\beta_i^* = \frac{E_i \cdot J_i^*}{E_0 \cdot J_0^*} \geqslant 1 \qquad [5.3.90]$$

where $E_i \cdot J_i^*$ is the rigidity of the wall under consideration, and $E_0 \cdot J_0^*$ the rigidity of the weakest of the walls.

After obtaining the values for the horizontal forces $w_{s,i}$, the additional deflections f_s are calculated from Eq. [5.3.76], substituting $w_{s,i}$ for w_i^*.

5.4. Procedure for calculating the three-dimensional stiffness of buildings

Three-dimensional stiffness calculations fall into two stages. The first stage consists in checking the stiffness of the building, first by an approximate method (Section 5.3.6), and then, if $f_{max}^* > H/2000$, by the accurate deflection formulae given in Sections 5.3.2 or 5.3.3.

For closed-system buildings, the procedure is as follows:
— from formula [5.1.5] we determine the load w, representing the joint effects of wind and the non-verticality of the wall components;
— from Eq. [5.3.80], using suitable graphs from Figs. 5.3.16 or 5.3.20, we obtain the equivalent inertias of the stiffening walls;
— from Eq. [5.3.75], we determine the distribution of the loads w_i^* between individual stiffening walls;
— from Eq. [5.3.76] we calculate the deflection f_{max}^*.

Depending on the ratio f_{max}^*/H, further calculations may be limited to obtaining the approximate values of the internal forces from formulae [5.3.81] to [5.3.87], or may involve a second stage, in the course of which more exact calculations are carried out.

The order of the calculations involved in the latter stage, when perforated walls are treated as frames, is:
— determination of the redundant quantities N_k, T_k and $\mathfrak{M}_k$ for unit forces $P = 1$, and hence of the distribution coefficients;
— distribution of the horizontal loading between individual walls, and determining the deflection f_{max} for one of the walls;
— determination of the internal forces.

If the wall is considered as a banded cantilever, we find:
— all auxiliary quantities and values of terms a_i;
— the deflection of the wall from formulae [5.3.49], [5.3.62] or [5.3.72];
— the internal forces.

For open-system buildings, the procedure is similar to that given above, but the

177

final deflection is the sum of the deflections f_z and f_s, due to the parallel translation of the floors and their rotation respectively.

Thus, after determining the equivalent moments of inertia from [5.3.80], we calculate:

— the distance x_0, from formula [5.3.88];
— the load $w_{s,i}$, from [5.3.89];
— the deflection f_s from [5.3.76] with $w_i^* = w_{s,i}$.

After finding the sum of f_z and f_s, we proceed as in the case of closed system buildings.

The values of the internal forces are then calculated, allowing for the joint action of forces $P_{z,i}$ and $P_{s,i}$ (Section 5.2.3.3).

5.5. NUMERICAL EXAMPLES OF STIFFNESS CALCULATIONS FOR A CLOSED SYSTEM BUILDING

5.5.1. Data

We shall consider the lateral stiffness of a six-storey long-wall building. The central segment of the building, which is bounded by expansion joints, is shown in Fig. 5.5.1.

The transverse stiffening consists of four walls constructed from large blocks. The widths of all walls, equal to the spacing of the loadbearing longitudinal walls, are $b = 5.20$ m.

Wall I is not perforated (Fig. 5.5.2a). Both walls II have doors near their interior edges (Fig. 5.5.2b); in wall III the door openings are on the centre line (Fig. 5.5.2c). Walls I and III are of clinker blocks Mk. 70, 20 cm thick, walls II are 12 cm thick and the blocks in them are of ordinary concrete Mk. 170.

In accordance with the Polish standards, we assume:

— for clinker concrete, Mk. 70 — $E_{br} = 56{,}000$ kg/cm^2
— for ordinary concrete, Mk. 170 — $E_{br} = 160{,}000$ kg/cm^2.

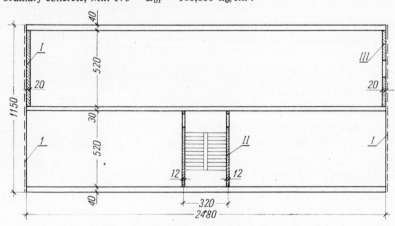

Fig. 5.5.1. Plan of the closed system building used in the example, illustrating the form of stiffness calculations:

(I), (II), (III) stiffening walls, (1) expansion joint

178

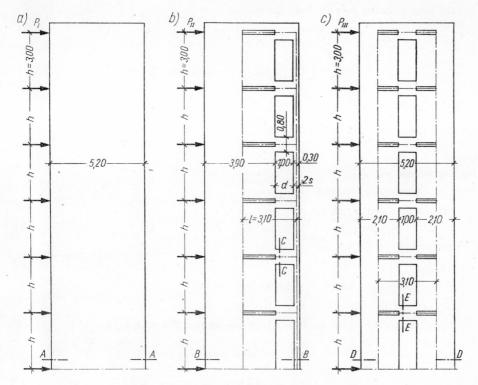

Fig. 5.5.2. Geometric dimensions of the stiffening walls:
(a) wall I, (b) wall II, (c) wall III

As the cross walls are only connected to the long walls by means of ring beams at floor level, the long walls are not considered to contribute to lateral stiffness.

5.5.2. Determination of the Horizontal Loads W

To find the magnitude of the force W, i.e. the horizontal force exerted by each floor slab on a the stiffening walls, we first ascertain the values of w_w and w_p, the unit horizontal loads due to wind pressure and the non-verticality of the walls, respectively.

The wind pressure w_w is found from the graph in Fig. 5.1.4. For a building 18.0 m high in exposure zone I,

$$w_w = 86 \text{ kg/m}^2$$

The load w_p is obtained from formula [5.1.4].

For $B = 11.50$ m, $h = 3.00$ m, $p = 150$ kg/m² and $G = 450$ kg/m³ (a large-block building in clinker concrete), we obtain:

$$w_p = \frac{11.50}{450} \cdot \left(450 + \frac{0.5 \times 150}{3.00}\right) = 12.1 \text{ kg/m}^2.$$

The total horizontal load is then

$$w = 86 + 12.1 = 98 \text{ kg/m}^2$$

179

and the force W acting on each floor slab is

$$W = 0.098 \times 3.00 \times 24.80 = 7.30 \text{ tonnes.}$$

5.5.3. Preliminary Stiffness Check

5.5.3.1. *Equivalent moment of inertia J^*.*

From the geometrical data in Figs. 5.5.2 it is possible to calculate the plan areas of the walls F and, with the help of the graphs shown in Fig. 5.3.16, the equivalent moments of inertia J^* of those areas.

(a) Unperforated wall I.

Data: $b = 5.20$ m, $g = 0.20$ m

$$F_I = 0.20 \times 5.20 = 1.04 \text{ m}^2$$

$$J_I^* = J_I = \frac{0.20 \times 5.20^3}{12} = 2.35 \text{ m}^4$$

(b) Stiffening wall II.

Data: $b = 5.20$ m, $b_0 = 1.80$ m, $d = 1.0$ m, $g = 0.12$ m.

$$F_{II} = 0.12(5.20 - 1.0) = 0.504 \text{ m}^2.$$

In order to read the graphs shown in Fig. 5.3.16, we first determine K_1, K_2 and K_3:

$$K_1 = \frac{6^2}{\left(\dfrac{19.50}{5.20}\right)^4} = 0.18; \qquad K_2 = \frac{1}{5.20} = 0.1925;$$

$$K_3 = \frac{1.80}{5.20} = 0.346.$$

For these parameters, the coefficient η is obtained from Fig. 5.3.16 as $\eta = 1.70$.

The moment of inertia of the equivalent cantilever is now determined from Eq. [5.3.80]:

$$J_{II}^* = \frac{1}{1.70} \times \frac{0.12 \times 5.20^3}{12} = 0.83 \text{ m}^4$$

(c) Stiffening wall III, with central door openings.

Data: $b = 5.20$ m, $d = 1.00$ m, $g = 0.20$ m.

For $K_1 = 0.18$, $K_2 = 0.1925$, $K_3 = 0$, the coefficient η is estimated from the graphs in Fig. 5.3.16 to be

$$\eta = 1.22$$

and therefore

$$J_{III}^* = \frac{1}{1.22} \times \frac{0.20 \times 5.20^3}{12} = 1.92 \text{ m}^4.$$

5.5.3.2. *Loads w_i^*.*

Knowing the values of J^* for each wall, the uniformly distributed loads can be determined from formula [5.3.75] as follows:

$$w_I^* = \frac{0.098 \times 24.8}{2} \times \frac{56.0 \times 10^4 \times 2.35}{56 \times 10^4 \times 2.35 + 2 \times 160 \times 10^4 \times 0.83 + 56 \times 10^4 \times 1.92}$$

$$= 0.313 \text{ T/m};$$

$$w_{II}^* = \frac{0.098 \times 24.8}{2} \times \frac{160 \times 10^4 \times 0.83}{56 \times 10^4 \times 2.35 + 2 \times 160 \times 10^4 \times 0.83 + 56 \times 10^4 \times 1.92}$$

$$= 0.316 \text{ T/m};$$

$$w_{III}^* = \frac{0.098 \times 24.8}{2} \times \frac{56 \times 10^4 \times 1.57}{56 \times 10^4 \times 2.35 + 2 \times 160 \times 10^4 \times 0.83 + 56 \times 10^4 \times 1.92}$$

$$= 0.254 \text{ T/m}.$$

5.5.3.3. Deflection f_{max}^*.

To determine the maximum deflection of the building, it is only necessary to calculate the deflection of a single wall.

Choosing wall I, we obtain from formula [5.3.76]

$$f_{max}^* = 0.313 \times \frac{18.0^2}{56 \times 10^4}\left(\frac{18.0^2}{4 \times 2.35} + \frac{2.8}{0.2 \times 5.20}\right) = 0.0067 \text{ m}.$$

To check the condition expressed by [5.3.77]

$$f_{max}^* = \frac{0.0067}{18.0} H = \frac{1}{2650} H < \frac{1}{2000} H.$$

Obtained value of f_{max}^* is satisfactory, however below will be done exact calculations in order to present the method described in chapter 5.3.3.

5.5.4. Exact Stiffness Calculations

5.5.4.1. Determination of redundant quantities and distribution coefficients a_i in a multi-storey frame system.

To clarify the calculations, the numerical values of the terms g (thickness of the wall) and E (elasticity modulus) will be introduced in the final stage of the calculations.
(a) For the unperforated wall I, Fig. 5.5.2a,

$$F = 5.20 \cdot g \text{ m}^2 \qquad J = 11.73 \cdot g \text{ m}^4$$

$$U_M = \frac{3.00^2}{12 \times 11.73} \times \frac{1}{E \cdot g} = 0.064 \frac{1}{E \cdot g}$$

$$U_Q = \frac{2 \times 1.4}{520} \times \frac{1}{E \cdot g} = 0.538 \frac{1}{E \cdot g}$$

and

$$a_I = \frac{3.00}{2} \times 36 \times 7 \times 19 \times 0.064\left[1 + \frac{0.538}{6 \times 19 \times 0.064}\right]\frac{1}{E \cdot g} = 492 \frac{1}{E \cdot g}$$

181

Putting

$$g = 0.20 \text{ m}, \quad E = 56 \times 10^4 \text{ T/m}^2$$

we obtain

$$a_{\mathrm{I}} = \frac{492}{0.20 \times 56 \times 10^4} = 43.9 \times 10^{-4}.$$

(b) For the stiffening wall II, with a single row of openings near one edge, Fig. 5.5.2b,

$$F_1 = 3.90 \cdot g \text{ m}^2 \qquad J_1 = 4.94 \cdot g \text{ m}^4$$
$$F_{\mathrm{p}} = 0.30 \cdot g \text{ m}^2$$
$$F_{\mathrm{r}} = 0.80 \cdot g \text{ m}^2 \qquad J_{\mathrm{r}} = 0.0427 \cdot g \text{ m}^4.$$

The redundant N_1 is obtained by using the auxiliary quantities from formulae [5.3.5], [5.3.6], [5.3.10], [5.3.19].

$$\overset{\circ}{A} = \frac{3.00 \times 3 \times 10^2}{4.94 \times g} + 3.0 \left(\frac{1}{3.90 \ g} + \frac{1}{0.30 \ g} \right) = 18.59 \times \frac{1}{g}$$

$$\overset{\circ}{B} = \frac{1.00}{3 \times 0.0427 \times g} (1.15^2 + 1.15 \times 0.15 + 0.15^2) + \frac{2.8}{0.80 \times g} = 15 \times 37 \frac{1}{g}$$

$$W^{\mathrm{N}} = \frac{3.10 \times 3.00^2}{2 \times 4.94 \times g} \ P = -2.82 \frac{P}{g}$$

$$\beta_6 = \frac{1}{10} \times \frac{7}{11} (3 \times 36 + 3 \times 6 - 1) = 7.954.$$

Then using equation [5.3.26], we obtain directly the relationship:

$$N_1 = \frac{2.82 \times 7.954}{18.59 \times 7.954 + 15.37} \ P = 0.152 \ P.$$

The distribution coefficient a_{II} is calculated from [5.3.27], whence,

$$U_{\mathrm{M}} = \frac{3.00^2}{12 \times 4.94} \times \frac{1}{E \cdot g} = 0.152 \frac{1}{E \cdot g}$$

$$U_{\mathrm{Q}} = \frac{2.8}{3.9} \times \frac{1}{E \cdot g} = 0.718 \frac{1}{E \cdot g}$$

$$a = \frac{3.00}{2} \times 36 \times 7 \times 19 \times 0.152 \left(1 + \frac{0.718}{6 \times 19 \times 0.152} \right) \frac{1}{E \cdot g} = 1134 \frac{1}{E \cdot g}$$

$$a_2 = 1134 - 0.152 \times 0.152 \times 3.00 \times 6 \times 7 (108 + 6 - 1) \frac{1}{E \cdot g} = 794 \frac{1}{E \cdot g}$$

Substituting $g = 0.12$ m, $E = 160 \times 10^4$ T/m^2, we obtain

$$a_{\mathrm{II}} = \frac{794}{0.12 \times 160 \times 10^4} = 41.3 \times 10^{-4}.$$

For the stiffening wall III, with a central row of openings, Fig. 5.5.2c,

$$F_1 = F_{\mathrm{p}} = 2.10 \ g \text{ m}^2 \qquad J_1 = J_{\mathrm{p}} = 0.772 \ g \text{ m}^4$$
$$F_{\mathrm{r}} = 0.90 \ g \text{ m}^2 \qquad J_{\mathrm{r}} = 0.0427 \ g \text{ m}^4.$$

The redundants N_1, T_1 and $\mathfrak{M}_1$ are obtained from the matrix in Table 5.3.2. The numerical coefficients needed are calculated from formulae [5.3.5] to [5.3.18]. The thickness of the wall g is omitted in all denominators.

$$\mathring{A} = \frac{3.00 \times 3.10^2}{0.772} + 2\,\frac{3.00}{2.10} = 40.24$$

$$\mathring{B} = \frac{1.00}{3 \times 0.0427}\,(2.05^2 + 2.05 \times 1.05 + 1.05^2) + 2.8\,\frac{1.00}{0.80} = 61.70$$

$$\mathring{C} = \frac{1.00}{0.047} \times \frac{1.00 + 2.10}{2} \times 3.00 = 54.35$$

$$\mathring{D} = \frac{3.00 \times 3.10}{0.772} = 12.07$$

$$\mathring{E} = \frac{1.00}{0.0427} \times \frac{1.00 + 2.10}{2} = 36.28$$

$$W^{\text{N}} = -\frac{3.10 \times 3.00^2}{2 \times 0.772}\,P = -18.07\ P$$

$$F = \frac{3.00^2}{6} \times \frac{1}{0.772} + 1.4 \times \frac{3.00}{2.10} \times 4.0 = 13.83$$

$$\mathring{G} = \frac{1.00}{0.0427} \times \frac{3.00^2}{4} = 52.70$$

$$\mathring{H} = \frac{1.00}{0.80} = 1.25$$

$$\mathring{L} = \frac{1.00}{0.0427} \times \frac{3.00}{2} = 35.10$$

$$W^{\text{T}} = \frac{3.00^2}{12 \times 0.772} + 2.8\,\frac{3.00}{2.10}\,P = 6.91\ P$$

$$\mathring{R} = \frac{2 \times 3.00}{0.772} = 7.77$$

$$\mathring{S} = \frac{1.00}{0.0427} = 23.40$$

$$W_{\mathfrak{M}} = \frac{3.00^2}{2 \times 0.772}\,P = -5.83\ P$$

and further, from Eqs. [5.3.19] and [5.3.20]:

$$\beta_6 = 7.954 \quad \text{and} \quad \gamma_6 = 0.318.$$

The matrix in Table 5.3.2 produces a system of simultaneous equations:

$$382.2\ N_1 + 54.3\ T_1 + 132.4\,\mathfrak{M}_1 = 143.8\ P$$

$$54.3\ N_1 + 57.2\ T_1 + 35.1\,\mathfrak{M}_1 = 2.2\ P$$

$$132.4\ N_1 + 35.1\ T_1 + 85.2\,\mathfrak{M}_1 = 46.3\ P$$

the solution being:

$$N_1 = 0.405\ P; \quad T_1 = -0.50\ P; \quad \mathfrak{M}_1 = 0.123\ P.$$

Proceeding to the calculation of the distribution coefficient a_1, we first determine the auxiliary quantities from [5.3.1]. These are:

$$U_M = \frac{3.00^2}{12 \times 0.772 \times E \times g} = 0.972\ \frac{1}{E \cdot g}$$

$$U_Q = \frac{2.8}{2.10 \times E \times g} = 1.333\ \frac{1}{E \cdot g}$$

$$a = \frac{3.00}{2} \times 36 \times 7 \times 19 \times 0.972 \left(1 + \frac{1.333}{6 \times 19 \times 0.972}\right) \frac{1}{E \cdot g} = 7057\ \frac{1}{E \cdot g}.$$

From equation [5.3.25], we have:

$$a_1 = \left\{ 7057 - \left[0.972\ (0.405 \times 3.00 + 0.123)\ 6 \times 7\ (108 + 6 - 1) - \right.\right.$$

$$\left.\left. - (0.972 + 1.333) \times \left(-\frac{0.50 \times 3.00}{2} \times 7 \times 6\right)\right]\right\} \times \frac{1}{E \cdot g} = 624\ \frac{1}{E \cdot g}.$$

Substituting: $g = 0.20$ m, $E = 56 \times 10^4$ T/m² we obtain

$$a_{III} = \frac{624}{0.20 \times 56 \times 10^4} = 55.7 \times 10^{-4}.$$

5.5.4.2. Distribution of wind loads between stiffening walls.

Using the values of the horizontal load per floor, W, and of the distribution coefficients a_I, a_{II} and a_{III} obtained previously, the share of the load carried by each wall is determined from formula [5.1.12]:

$$P_I = 7.30\ \frac{\dfrac{1}{43.9 \times 10^{-4}}}{\left(\dfrac{1}{43.9} + 2\,\dfrac{1}{41.3} + \dfrac{1}{55.7}\right)\dfrac{1}{10^{-4}}} = 1.86\ \text{T}$$

$$P_{II} = 7.30\ \frac{\dfrac{1}{41.3 \times 10^{-4}}}{\left(\dfrac{1}{43.9} + 2\,\dfrac{1}{14.3} + \dfrac{1}{55.7}\right)\dfrac{1}{10^{-4}}} = 1.98\ \text{T}$$

$$P_{III} = 7.30\ \frac{\dfrac{1}{55.7 \times 10^{-4}}}{\left(\dfrac{1}{43.9} + 2\,\dfrac{1}{41.3} + \dfrac{1}{55.7}\right)\dfrac{1}{10^{-4}}} = 1.47\ \text{T}$$

We are now ready to proceed to the determination of the deflection of the building and the magnitude of the internal forces in the most critical sections of the stiffening walls.

5.5.4.3. *Maximum deflection of the building.*

It has been previously established that the deflection of a closed system building is equal to the deflection of any randomly selected one of the three stiffening walls.

The maximum wall deflection is established from equations [5.3.1], [5.3.25], or [5.3.27].

From [5.3.1], for unperforated wall I,

$$f_{max} = 43.9 \times 10^{-4} \times 1.86 = 0.0082 \text{ m.}$$

Condition [5.1.1] must be checked. The height of the building being $H = 18.0$ m,

$$f_{max} = \frac{0.0082 \, H}{18.00} = \frac{H}{2190} < \frac{H}{2000}$$

and therefore the three-dimensional stiffness of this building in the transverse direction is satisfactory.

5.5.4.4. *Determination of internal forces.*

It was established in Section 5.3.1 that the critical sections in stiffening walls are the horizontal sections at the bases of the column segments, and the vertical section through the lintel band at the top of the second storey. The internal forces present in these sections will now be calculated.

(a) Unperforated wall I (Fig. 5.5.2a).

Concentrated force $P_I = 1.86$ T

For a section *A-A* at the base of the wall:

$$M = 1/2 \times 6 \, (6 + 1) \times 3.00 \times 1.86 = 117.20 \text{ Tm}$$

$$Q = 6 \times 1.86 = 11.16 \text{ T.}$$

(b) Stiffening wall II (Fig. 5.5.2b) with a single row of openings near one edge.

Concentrated force $P_{II} = 1.98$ T

Redundants at the base of the wall:

$$N_6 = 6^2 \times 0.152 \times P_{II} = 5.47 \times P_{II}$$

$$T_6 \approx 0; \quad \mathfrak{M}_6 \approx 0.$$

For a section *B-B* at the base of the narrow column segment, we obtain from formula [5.3.23]:

$$M \approx 0; \quad Q \approx 0;$$

$$S = 5.47 \times 1.98 = 10.84 \text{ T.}$$

Similarly, for the section *B-B* through the wide column segment, using formula [5.3.22], we have:

$$M = 1/2 \times 6 \times (6 + 1) \times 3.00 \times 1.98 - 5.47 \times 1.98 \times 3.10 = 91.2 \text{ Tm}$$

$$S = -5.47 \times 1.98 = -10.84 \text{ T};$$

$$Q = 6 \times 1.98 = 11.88 \text{ T.}$$

At the vertical section through the second lintel from the bottom (fifth from the top):

The redundant quantities are given by:

$$N_5 = 5^2 \times 0.152 \times P_{II} = 3.80 \, P_{II}$$

$$N_6 = 4^2 \times 0.152 \times P_{II} = 2.43 \, P_{II}.$$

For the section *C-C* at the face of the L.H. column, we obtain formulae [5.3.23]:

$$M = (3.80 - 2.43) \times (1.00 + 0.15) \times 1.98 = 3.12 \text{ Tm}$$

$$S \approx 0; \quad Q = (3.80 - 2.43) \, 1.98 = 2.71 \text{ T.}$$

(c) Stiffening wall III, with a central row of openings.

The concentrated force $P_{III} = 1.47$ T

The redundants are given by:

$$N_6 = 6^2 \times 0.405 \times P_{III} = 14.58\ P_{III}$$

$$T_6 = 6(-0.50)\ P_{III} = -3.00\ P_{III}$$

$$\mathfrak{M}_6 = 6^2 \times 0.123 \times P_{III} = 4.43\ P_{III}.$$

For the section *D-D* through the R.H. column, and from formulae [5.3.22]:

$$M = 3.00 \times 1.47\ \frac{3.00}{2} + 4.43 \times 1.47 = 13.1\ \text{Tm}$$

$$S = 14.58 \times 1.47 = 21.45\ \text{T}; \qquad Q = 3.00 \times 1.47 = 4.41\ \text{T}.$$

For a section *D-D* through the L.H. column, and from [5.3.21]:

$$M = 1/2 \times 6\ (6 + 1)\ 1.47 \times 3.00 - 14.58 \times 1.47 \times 3.10 -$$

$$- 3.00 \times 1.47 \times \frac{3.00}{2} - 4.43 \times 1.47 = 13.1\ \text{Tm}$$

$$S = -14.58 \times 1.47 = -21.45\ \text{T}$$

$$Q = 6 \times 1.47 - 3.00 \times 1.47 = 4.41\ \text{T}.$$

The redundants for the second lintel from the bottom (fifth from the top), are:

$$N_5 = 5^2 \times 0.405\ P_{III} = 10.13\ P_{III}; \qquad N_4 = 4^2 \times 0.405\ P_{III} = 6.48\ P_{III};$$

$$T_5 = 5(-0.50)\ P_{III} = -2.50\ P_{III}; \qquad T_4 = 4(-0.50)\ P_{III} = -2.00\ P_{III};$$

$$\mathfrak{M}_5 = 5^2 \times 0.123\ P_{III} = 3.08\ P_{III}; \qquad \mathfrak{M}_4 = 4^2 \times 0.123\ P_{III} = 1.97\ P_{III}.$$

Finally, for a section *E-E*, at the face of the L.H. column, and from formula [5.3.23]:

$$M = (10.13 - 6.48)\ 2.05 - (2.50 + 2.00)\ \frac{3.00}{2} + 3.08 - 1.97 = 3.80\ P_{III} = 5.58\ \text{Tm}$$

$$S = 2.50 - 2.00 = 0.50\ P_{III} = 0.73\ \text{T}$$

$$Q = 10.13 - 6.48 = 3.65\ P_{III} = 5.35\ \text{T}.$$

In designing the reinforcement of the lintel, the axial force *S* may be neglected and the lintel reinforced for pure bending only.

The shear stress τ and, if necessary, the stirrup section, are obtained with reference to the shearing force *Q*.

Knowing the magnitude of the internal forces at the critical sections of the wall, the load-carrying capacity at these sections can now be checked, or reinforcement introduced in accordance with normal r.c. procedure. The total forces acting on the horizontal cross-sections (in this example *A-A*, *B-B* and *C-C*) are the sum of the axial forces *S* due to the horizontal loading, and the axial forces due to the vertical loading (weight of the walls themselves and of the floor loads).

5.6. A NUMERICAL EXAMPLE OF THREE-DIMENSIONAL STIFFNESS CALCULATIONS FOR AN OPEN-SYSTEM BUILDING

5.6.1. Data

The subject of these calculations is a 12-storey skeleton-structure type building. Let us consider the lateral stiffness of an end segment, the plan of which is 42.0×11.1 m (Fig. 5.6.1), the height of each storey $h = 2.70$ m, and the total height of building $H = 32.40$ m.

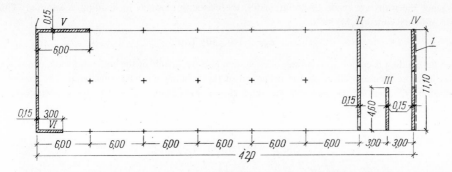

Fig. 5.6.1. Plan of the open system building used in the example for three-dimensional stiffness:
(I), (II), (III), (IV), (V), (VI) stiffening walls, (1) expansion joint

Three-dimensional stiffness is provided by three walls round the gable end of the building (L.H. side of Fig. 5.6.1), and a further three walls situated near the stairs and shown on the R.H. side of Fig. 5.6.1.

Wall I (Fig. 5.6.2a) has two symmetrical rows of windows near its centre. Wall II (Fig. 5.6.2b) also has two rows of openings, but they are not symmetrical. Wall III (Fig. 5.6.2c) is not perforated. Wall IV (Fig. 5.6.2d) has a central row of doors. Walls V and VI are solid.

All the walls are 15 cm thick and are made of ordinary concrete Mk. 170.

The longitudinal walls are connected to the cross walls only by means of ring beams at respective floor levels. They are therefore treated separately from the cross walls in these calculations.

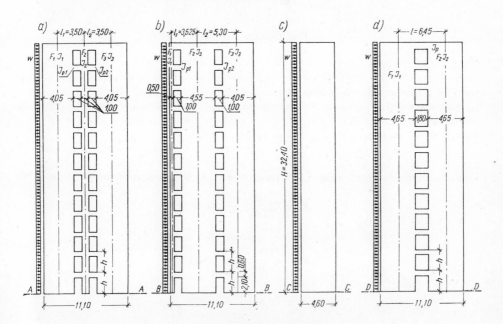

Fig. 5.6.2. Dimensions of the stiffening walls:
(a) wall I, (b) wall II, (c) wall III, (d) wall IV

187

Since the walls are made of prefabricates, the elasticity modulus in bending is adopted. Thus, for ordinary concrete Mk. 170

$$E_{br} = 160 \times 10^4 \ \text{T/m}^2.$$

As the building is constructed on the open system and the layout of the stiffening walls is not symmetrical, the torsional effect on the deflection of the building must be considered. The maximum deflection f_{max} will be the sum of f_z, as for a closed system building, and f_s, the deflection due to rotation of the building.

5.6.2. Horizontal Loading

The wind pressure w_f is read off from the graph in Fig. 5.1.4.
For a building 32.4 m high in exposure zone I,

$$w_f = 109.5 \ \text{kg/m}^2.$$

The equivalent horizontal unit pressure, due to the non-verticality of the wall units and columns, is taken from formula [5.1.4].
For $B = 11.10$ m, $h = 2.7$ m, $p = 200$ kg/m^2, and taking the unit weight of the structure as $G = 300$ kg/m^3, we obtain

$$w_p = \frac{11.10}{450} \left(300 + \frac{0.5 \times 200}{2.7} \right) = 8.3 \ \text{kg/m}^2.$$

The total horizontal load is then

$$w = w_f + w_p = 109.5 + 8.3 = 118 \ \text{kg/m}^2.$$

5.6.3. Preliminary Stiffness Check

5.6.3.1. *Deflection f_z as for the closed system building.*
The moments of inertia J^* are first determined from the geometric data shown on Fig. 5.6.2, and using the graphs in Figs. 5.3.16 and 5.3.20.
(a) Stiffening wall I — with two rows of openings arranged symmetrically about the centre line of the wall.
Data: $b = 11.1$ m, $d = 1.0$ m, $g = 0.15$ m, $b_1 = b_2 = 1.0$ m

$$F_I = 0.15(11.10 - 2.0) = 1.36 \ \text{m}^2.$$

In order to use the graph in Fig. 5.3.20, parameters K_1, K_2, K_4 and K_5 must first be obtained

$$K_1 = \frac{12^2}{\left(\dfrac{32.4}{11.1} \right)^4} = 1.98 \approx 2.0$$

$$K_2 = \frac{1.0}{11.10} = 0.09 \approx 0.1$$

$$K_4 = - \frac{1.00}{11.10} = -0.09$$

$$K_5 = \frac{1.00}{11.10} = 0.09.$$

188

For these parameters, the graph in Fig. 5.3.20c gives

$$\eta = 1.62$$

Further, from formula [5.3.80] the moment of inertia J^* is found to be

$$J_{\mathrm{I}}^* = \frac{1}{\eta} \times J = \frac{1}{1.62} \times \frac{0.15 \times 11.1^3}{12} = 10.55 \ \mathrm{m}^4$$

(b) Stiffening wall II—with two non-symmetrical rows of openings.

Data: $b = 11.1$ m, $d = 1.0$ m, $g = 0.15$ m, $b_1 = 4.55$ m, $b_2 = 1.00$ m

$$F_{\mathrm{II}} = 0.15 \ (11.1 - 2.0) = 1.36 \ \mathrm{m}^2$$

$$K_1 = \frac{12^2}{\left(\dfrac{32.4}{11.1}\right)^4} \approx 2.0$$

$$K_2 = \frac{1.00}{11.10} = 0.09 \approx 0.1$$

$$K_4 = -\frac{4.55}{11.10} = -0.41 \approx -0.40$$

$$K_5 = \frac{1.00}{11.10} = 0.09 \approx 0.1.$$

From the graph in Fig. 5.3.20c, we find

$$\eta = 1.75$$

and therefore

$$J_{\mathrm{II}}^* = \frac{1}{1.75} \times \frac{0.15 \times 11.1^3}{12} = 9.78 \ \mathrm{m}^4.$$

(c) Stiffening wall III — unperforated.

$$J_{\mathrm{III}}^* = J_{\mathrm{III}} = \frac{0.15 \times 4.60^3}{12} = 1.21 \ \mathrm{m}^4$$

(d) Stiffening wall IV — with a central row of openings.

Data: $b = 11.1$ m, $d = 1.80$ m, $g = 0.15$ m, $b_0 = 0$

$$F_{\mathrm{IV}} = 0.15 \ (11.10 - 1.80) = 1.39 \ \mathrm{m}^2.$$

Parameters K_1, K_2 and K_3 are

$$K_1 = \frac{12^2}{\left(\dfrac{32.4}{11.1}\right)^4} = 2.0$$

$$K_2 = \frac{1.80}{11.1} = 0.162$$

$$K_3 = 0.$$

From the graph in Fig. 5.3.16, we obtain

$$\eta = 1.5 + \frac{1.85 - 1.5}{0.05} \times 0.012 = 1.58$$

189

and therefore .

$$J_{IV}^* = \frac{1}{1.58} \times \frac{0.15 \times 11.10^3}{12} = 10.80 \text{ m}^4.$$

(e) Knowing the values of the moments of inertia J^* of all stiffening walls, we can now determine the share of the horizontal loading carried by each wall (formula [5.3.75]).

It is sufficient to find the deflection f_z^* for any given wall.

For wall I:

$$w_I^* = \frac{42.0 \times 0.118}{2} \times \frac{160 \times 10^4 \times 10.55}{160 \times 10^4 (10.55 + 9.78 + 1.21 + 10.8)} = 0.815 \text{ T/m};$$

$$a_I = \frac{H^2}{E}\left(\frac{H^2}{4 J^*} + \frac{2.8}{F}\right) = \frac{32.4^2}{160 \times 10^4}\left(\frac{32.4^2}{4 \times 10.55} + \frac{2.8}{1.36}\right) = 181 \times 10^{-4};$$

$$f_{zI}^* = a_I w_I^* = 181 \times 10^{-4} \times 0.815 = 147 \times 10^{-4} \text{ m}.$$

5.6.3.2. *Preliminary determination of the deflection f_s^* due to the torsional movement of the building.*

To find the centre of rotation, the moments of inertia J^* of the longitudinal stiffening walls must also be known.

(a) Stiffening wall V — unperforated.

Data: $b = 6.0$ m, $g = 0.15$ m

$$J_V^* = J_V = \frac{0.15 \times 6.0^3}{12} = 2.7 \text{ m}^4.$$

(b) Stiffening wall VI — unperforated.

Data: $b = 3.0$ m, $g = 0.15$ m

$$J_{VI}^* = J_{VI} = \frac{0.15 \times 3.0^3}{12} = 0.34 \text{ m}^4$$

(c) The centre of rotation of the building.

The coordinates of the centre of rotation are obtained from the formula [5.3.88]:

$$x_0 = \frac{\Sigma E_i \cdot J_i^* \cdot x_i}{\Sigma E_i \cdot J_i^*} = \frac{10.55 \times 0.075 + 9.78 \times 36.075 + 1.21 \times 39.075 + 10.80 \times 42.075}{10.55 + 9.78 + 1.21 + 10.80} = 26.70 \text{ m}$$

$$y_0 = \frac{\Sigma E_i \cdot J_i^* \cdot y_i}{\Sigma E_i \cdot J_i^*} = \frac{2.7 \times 11.075 + 0.34 \times 0.075}{2.7 + 0.34} = 9.90 \text{ m}.$$

The lever arms a_i^* of each wall relative to the centre of rotation are

$$a_I^* = 26.63 \text{ m} \qquad a_{IV}^* = 15.37 \text{ m}$$

$$a_{II}^* = 9.37 \text{ m} \qquad a_V^* = 1.15 \text{ m}$$

$$a_{III}^* = 12.37 \text{ m} \qquad a_{VI}^* = 9.80 \text{ m}.$$

(d) Position of the resultant of the horizontal forces.

After the centre of rotation of the building has been found, the lever arm of the resultant of the horizontal forces relative to the centre of rotation can be determined.

Thus, in the direction parallel to the x-axis

$$z_x = 26.7 - 0.5 \times 42 = 5.7 \text{ m.}$$

(e) Additional wall loading due to the torsion, w_s^*.

To find the additional forces acting on the individual walls and balancing the twisting moment,. coefficients β_i^* are first obtained from formula [5.3.90]:

$$\beta_1^* = \frac{160 \times 10^4 \times 10.55}{160 \times 10^4 \times 1.21} = 8.73$$

$$\beta_2^* = \frac{160 \times 10^4 \times 9.78}{160 \times 10^4 \times 1.21} = 8.08$$

$$\beta_3^* = \frac{160 \times 10^4 \times 1.21}{160 \times 10^4 \times 1.21} = 1.0$$

$$\beta_4^* = \frac{160 \times 10^4 \times 10.80}{160 \times 10^4 \times 1.21} = 8.93$$

$$\beta_5^* = \frac{160 \times 10^4 \times 2.7}{160 \times 10^4 \times 1.21} = 2.22$$

$$\beta_6^* = \frac{160 \times 10^4 \times 0.34}{160 \times 10^4 \times 1.21} = 0.278.$$

The additiona loading is found from formula [5.3.89]. For wall I:

$$w_{sI}^* = \frac{0.118 \times 42.0}{2} \times \frac{5.7 \times 26.63 \times 8.73}{(26.63^2 \times 8.73) + (9.37^2 \times 8.08) + (12.37^2 \times 1.0) +}$$

$$\overline{ + (15.37^2 \times 8.93) + (1.15^2 \times 2.22) + (9.8^2 \times 0.28)} = 0.357 \text{ T/m}$$

$$f_{sI}^* = 0.357 \times 181 \times 10^{-4} = 64.6 \times 10^{-4} \text{ m.}$$

5.6.3.3. Total maximum deflection, f_{max}^*.

The total deflection of wall I, the wall farthest from the centre of rotation, is

$$f_{max}^* = f_z + f_s = (147 + 64.6) \times 10^{-4} = 211.6 \times 10^{-4} \text{ m.}$$

To check condition [5.3.77]:

$$f_{max}^* = \frac{0.0211}{32.4} H \approx \frac{H}{1540} > \frac{H}{2000}.$$

It is therefore necessary to carry out exact calculations.

5.6.4. Exact Stiffness Calculations

5.6.4.1. Individual deflections f_z of the walls.

For greater clarity, the numerical values of the terms g and E are omitted from the calculation until the final stages ($g =$ thickness of the wall, $E =$ elasticity modulus).

(a) Wall I — with two symmetrical rows of openings, as in Fig. 5.6.2a.

$$l_1 = l_2 = 3.50, \quad g = 1.00 \text{ m}; \quad H = 2.70 \times 12 = 32.40 \text{ m}$$

191

$$J_1 = J_3 = \frac{1 \times 4.05^3}{12} = 5.52 \text{ m}^4; \quad F_1 = F_2 = 1 \times 4.05 = 4.05 \text{ m}^2$$

$$J_2 = \frac{1 \times 1^3}{12} = 0.084 \text{ m}^4; \quad F_2 = 1 \times 1 = 1.0 \text{ m}^2$$

$$J_r = J_{r2} = \frac{1 \times 0.6^3}{12} = 0.018 \text{ m}^4.$$

From formula [5.3.58] we obtain the quantities:

$$\lambda_{1,1} = \lambda_{2,1} = \left[\frac{l_1^2}{J_1 + J_2 + J_3} + \left(\frac{1}{F_1} + \frac{1}{F_2} \right) \right] \frac{12 J_{r1}}{h \, d_1^3}$$

$$= \left[\frac{3.5^2}{11.12} + \left(\frac{1}{4.05} + \frac{1}{1.0} \right) \right] \frac{12 \times 0.018}{2.7 \times 1.0^3} = 0.191$$

$$\lambda_{1,2} = \lambda_{2,2} = \left[\frac{l_1 \times l_2}{J_1 + J_2 + J_3} - \frac{1}{F_2} \right] \frac{12 J_{r1}}{h \, d_1^3}$$

$$= \left[\frac{3.5^2}{11.12} - \frac{1}{1.0} \right] \frac{12 \times 0.018}{2.7 \times 1.0^3} = 0.011$$

$$\mu_1 = \mu_2 = \frac{w \cdot l_1}{J_1 + J_2 + J_3} \frac{6 J_{r1}}{h \cdot d_1^3} = \frac{3.5^2 w}{11.12} \times \frac{6 \times 0.018}{2.7 \times 1.03} = 0.013 \ w$$

To calculate the deflections, auxiliary values D_i, $D_{1,i}$ and $D_{2,i}$ are first obtained from equation [5.3.61] for $i = 1$, 3 and 5 respectively:

$i = 1$,

$$D_1 = \left(\frac{1 \times 3.14}{2 \times 32.4} \right)^4 + 2 \times 0.191 \times \left(\frac{1 \times 3.14}{2 \times 32.4} \right)^2 + 0.191^2 - 0.011^2 = 0.0374$$

$$D_{1,1} = D_{2,1} = - \frac{2}{32.4} \left(\frac{2 \times 32.4}{1 \times 3.14} \right)^3 \times (2 - 1 \times 3.14) \times$$

$$\times \left[0.013 \ w \left(\frac{1 \times 3.14}{2 \times 32.4} \right)^2 + 0.191 - 0.013 \ w \times 0.011 \right] = 1.46 \ w$$

$$a_{1,1} = \frac{D_{1,1}}{D_1} = \frac{1.46 \ w}{0.0374} = 39.2 \ w$$

$$a_{1,1} \cdot l_1 \cdot 2 \cdot \left(\frac{2H}{i \cdot \pi} \right)^2 = 39.2 \ w \times 3.5 \times 2 \times \left(\frac{2 \times 32.4}{1 \times 3.14} \right)^2 = 116500 \ w$$

$i = 3$,

$$D_3 = \left(\frac{3 \times 3.14}{2 \times 32.4} \right)^4 + 2 \times 0.191 \times \left(\frac{3 \times 3.14}{2 \times 32.4} \right)^2 + 0.191^2 - 0.011^2 = 0.04589$$

$$D_{1,3} = D_{2,3} = - \frac{2}{32.4} \times \left(\frac{2 \times 32.4}{3 \times 3.14} \right)^3 \times (2 + 3 \times 3.14) \times$$

$$\times \left\{ 0.013 \ w \left[\left(\frac{3 \times 3.14}{2 \times 32.4} \right)^2 + 0.191 \right] - 0.013 \ w \times 0.011 \right\} = - 0.63 \ w$$

192

$$a_{1,3} = \frac{D_{1,3}}{D_3} = -\frac{0.63\, w}{0.0459} = -13.8\, w$$

$$a_{1,3} \cdot l_1 \cdot 2 \cdot \left(\frac{2\,H}{i\cdot\pi}\right)^2 = -13.8\, w \times 3.5 \times 2 \times \left(\frac{2\times32.4}{3\times3.14}\right)^2 = -4555\, w$$

$$i = 5,$$

$$D_5 = \left(\frac{5\times3.14}{2\times32.4}\right)^4 + 2\times0.191\left(\frac{5\times3.14}{2\times32.1}\right)^2 + 0.191^2 - 0.011^2 = 0.062$$

$$D_{1,5} = D_{2,5} = -\frac{2}{32.4}\left(\frac{2\times32.4}{5\times3.14}\right)^3 \times (2 - 5\times3.14) \times$$

$$\times \left\{0.013\,w\left[\left(\frac{5\times3.14}{2\times32.4}\right)^2 + 0.191\right] - 0.013\,w\times0.011\right\} = 0.18\,w$$

$$a_{1,5} = \frac{0.18\,w}{0.062} = 2.91\ w$$

$$a_{1,5}\cdot l_1 \cdot 2\cdot\left(\frac{2\,H}{i\cdot\pi}\right)^2 = 2.91\,w\times3.5\times2\left(\frac{2\times32.4}{5\times3.14}\right)^2 = 347\ w.$$

The deflection is calculated from [5.3.72]

$$f = \frac{1}{E\,(J_1 + J_2 + J_3)}\left[\frac{1}{8}\cdot w\cdot H^4 \mp \sum a_{1i}\,l_1\,2\left(\frac{2\,H}{i\cdot\pi}\right)^2\right] =$$

$$= \frac{1\cdot w}{E\cdot11.12}\left[137500 - (116500 + 4555 + 347)\right] = 1490\frac{w}{E}$$

or $g = 0.15$ m

$$f_z = \frac{1490\,w}{0.15\,E} = 9950\ \frac{w}{E}$$

whence $a_I = 9950$.

Ɔ) Stiffening wall II — with two asymmetrical rows of openings (Fig. 5.6.2b):

$$l_1 = 3.525 \text{ m}, \quad l_2 = 5.300 \text{ m}, \quad g = 1.00 \text{ m}, \quad H = 32.40 \text{ m}$$

$$J_1 = \frac{1\times0.5^3}{12} = 0.010 \text{ m}^4 \qquad F_1 = 1\times0.5 = 0.5 \text{ m}^2$$

$$J_2 = \frac{1\times4.55^3}{12} = 7.850 \text{ m}^4 \qquad F_2 = 1\times4.55 = 4.55 \text{ m}^2$$

$$J_3 = \frac{1\times4.05^3}{12} = 5.530 \text{ m}^4 \qquad F_3 = 1\times4.05 = 4.05 \text{ m}^2$$

$$J_{r1} = J_{r2} = \frac{1\times0.6^3}{12} = 0.018 \text{ m}^4.$$

From formulae [5.3.58] the following quantities may be determined:

$$\lambda_{1,1} = \left[\frac{l_1^2}{J_1 + J_2 + J_3} + \left(\frac{1}{F_1} + \frac{1}{F_2}\right)\right]\frac{12\,J_{r1}}{h\cdot d_1^3} = \left(\frac{3.5^2}{13.39} + \frac{1}{0.5} + \frac{1}{4.55}\right)\times\frac{12\times0.018}{2.7\times1.0^3} = 0.252$$

$$\lambda_{2,1} = \left[\frac{l_2^2}{J_1 + J_2 + J_3} + \left(\frac{1}{F_2} + \frac{1}{F_3}\right)\right]\frac{12\,J_{r2}}{h\cdot d_2^3} = \left(\frac{5.30^2}{13.39} + \frac{1}{4.55} + \frac{1}{4.05}\right) \times \frac{12 \times 0.018}{2.7 \times 1^3} = 0.205$$

$$\lambda_{1,2} = \lambda_{2,2} = \left[\frac{l_1 \cdot l_2}{J_1 + J_2 + J_3} - \frac{1}{F_2}\right]\frac{12\,J_r}{h\cdot d_1^3} = \left(\frac{3.5 \times 5.30}{13.39} - \frac{1}{4.55}\right) \times \frac{12 \times 0.018}{2.7 \times 1^3} = 0.094$$

$$\mu_1 = \frac{w \cdot l_1}{J_1 + J_2 + J_3} \times \frac{6\,J_{r1}}{h\cdot d_1^3} = \frac{w \times 3.5}{13.39} \times \frac{6 \times 0.018}{2.7 \times 1^3} = 0.0105\ w$$

$$\mu_2 = \frac{w \cdot l_2}{J_1 + J_2 + J_3} \times \frac{6\,J_{r2}}{h\cdot d_2^3} = \frac{w \times 5.85}{13.39} \times \frac{6 \times 0.018}{2.7 \times 1^3} = 0.016\ w$$

From the formula [5.3.61]:

$$i = 1$$

$$D_1 = \left(\frac{1 \times 3.14}{2 \times 32.4}\right)^4 + (0.252 + 0.205)\left(\frac{1 \times 3.14}{2 \times 32.4}\right)^2 + 0.252 \times 0.205 - 0.094^2 = 0.044$$

$$D_{1,1} = -\frac{2}{32.4}\left(\frac{2 \times 32.4}{1 \times 3.14}\right)^3 \times (2 - 1 \times 3.14) \times$$

$$\times \left\{0.0105\ w \left[\left(\frac{1 \times 3.14}{2 \times 32.4}\right)^2 + 0.205\right] - 0.016\ w \times 0.094\right\} = 0.43\ w$$

$$D_{2,1} = -\frac{2}{32.4}\left(\frac{2 \times 32.4}{1 \times 3.14}\right)^2 \times (2 - 1 \times 3.14) \times$$

$$\times \left\{0.016\ w \times \left[\left(\frac{1 \times 3.14}{2 \times 32.4}\right)^2 + 0.252\right] - 0.0105\ w \times 0.094\right\} = 1.89\ w$$

$$a_{1,1} = \frac{D_{1,1}}{D_1} = \frac{0.44\ w}{0.044} = 9.8\ w \qquad a_{2,1} = \frac{D_{2,1}}{D_1} = \frac{1.89\ w}{0.044} = 42.9\ w$$

$$(a_{1,1}\cdot l_1 + a_{2,1}\cdot l_2)\left(\frac{2\,H}{i\cdot\pi}\right)^2 = (9.8 \times 3.525 + 42.9 \times 5.30)\ w \times \left(\frac{2 \times 32.4}{1 \times 3.14}\right)^2 = 111500\ w$$

$$i = 3$$

$$D_3 = \left(\frac{3 \times 3.14}{2 \times 32.4}\right)^4 + (0.252 + 0.205) \times \left(\frac{3 \times 3.14}{2 \times 32.4}\right)^2 + 0.252 + 0.205 - 0.094^2 = 0.0529$$

$$D_{1,3} = -\frac{2}{32.4}\left(\frac{2 \times 32.4}{3 \times 3.14}\right)^3 \times (2 + 3 \times 3.14) \times \left\{0.0105\ w \times\right.$$

$$\times \left.\left[\left(\frac{3 \times 3.14}{2 \times 32.4}\right)^2 + 0.205\right] - 0.016\ w \times 0.094\right\} = -0.206\ w$$

$$D_{2,3} = -\frac{2}{32.4}\left(\frac{2 \times 32.4}{3 \times 3.14}\right)^3 \times (2 + 2 \times 3.14) \times \left\{0.016\ w \times\right.$$

$$\times \left.\left[\left(\frac{3 \times 3.14}{2 \times 32.4}\right)^2 + 0.252\right] - 0.0105\ w \times 0.099\right\} = -0.75\ w$$

$$a_{1,3} = \frac{D_{1,3}}{D_3} = -\frac{0.206\ w}{0.0529} = -3.89\ w$$

$$a_{2,3} = \frac{D_{2,3}}{D_3} = \frac{0.75\ w}{0.0529} = -14.15\ w$$

194

$$(a_{1,3} \cdot l_1 + a_{2,3} \cdot l_2)\left(\frac{2H}{i \cdot \pi}\right)^2 = -(3.89 \times 3.525 + 14.15 \times 5.30)\, w \times \left(\frac{2 \times 32.4}{3 \times 3.14}\right)^2 = -4200\ w$$

$$i = 5$$

$$D_5 = \left(\frac{5 \times 3.14}{2 \times 32.4}\right)^4 + (0.252 + 0.205)\left(\frac{5 \times 3.14}{1 \times 32.4}\right)^2 + 0.252 \times 0.205 - 0.094^2 = 0.0730$$

$$D_{1,5} = -\frac{2}{32.4}\left(\frac{2 \times 32.4}{5 \times 3.14}\right)^3 \times (2 - 5 \times 3.14) \times \Big\{0.0105\, w \times$$

$$\times \left[\left(\frac{5 \times 3.14}{2 \times 32.4}\right)^2 + 0.205\right] - 0.016 w \times 0.094\Big\} = 0.0762\ w$$

$$D_{2,5} = -\frac{2}{32.4}\left(\frac{2 \times 32.4}{5 \times 3.14}\right)^3 \times (2 - 5 \times 3.14) \times \Big\{0.016\, w \times$$

$$\times \left[\left(\frac{5 \times 3.14}{2 \times 32.4}\right)^2 + 0.252\right] - 0.0105\, w \times 0.094\Big\} = 0.232\ w$$

$$a_{1,5} = \frac{D_{1,5}}{D_5} = \frac{0.0762\, w}{0.0730} = 1.042\ w$$

$$a_{2,5} = \frac{D_{2,5}}{D_5} = \frac{0.232\, w}{0.0730} = 3.18\ w$$

$$(a_{1,5} \cdot l_1 + a_{2,5} \cdot l_2)\left(\frac{2H}{i \cdot \pi}\right)^2 = (1.042 \times 3.525 + 3.18 \times 5.30)\, w \times \left(\frac{2 \times 32.4}{5 \times 3.14}\right)^2 = 350\, w.$$

The deflection is obtained from [5.3.62]:

$$f_z = \frac{1}{(J_1 + J_2 + J_3) E}\left[\frac{1}{8} \cdot w \cdot H^4 - \sum (a_1 \cdot l_1 + a_2 \cdot l_2)\left(\frac{2H}{i \cdot \pi}\right)^2\right] =$$

$$= \frac{w}{13.39\, E}\,[137500 - (111500 + 4200 + 350)] = \frac{1530\, w}{E}$$

for $g = 0.15$ m

$$f_z = \frac{1530\, w}{0.15\, E} = \frac{10200\, w}{E}$$

whence

$$a_{II} = 10200.$$

(c) Stiffening wall III — unperforated.

The dimensions of this wall are shown in Fig. 5.6.2c, from which:

$$F_{III} = 0.15 \times 4.60 = 0.69\ \text{m}^2$$

$$J_{III} = \frac{0.15 \times 4.60^3}{12} = 1.21\ \text{m}^4.$$

The deflection is calculated according to formula [5.3.77]:

$$f_z = \frac{wH^2}{2E}\left(\frac{H^2}{4J} + \frac{2.8}{F}\right) = \frac{w \times 52.4^2}{2E}\left(\frac{32.4^2}{4 \times 1.21} + \frac{2.8}{0.69}\right) = 116000\,\frac{w}{E}$$

whence

$$a_{III} = 116000.$$

195

(d) Stiffening wall IV — with a single central row of openings.

The dimensions are given in Fig. 5.6.2d, from which:

$$J_1 = J_2 = \frac{1 \times 4.65^3}{12} = 8.4 \text{ m}^4; \quad F_1 = F_2 = 1 \times 4.65 = 4.65 \text{ m}^2$$

$$J_r = \frac{1 \times 0.6^3}{12} = 0.018 \text{ m}^4.$$

From formulae [5.3.44] and [5.3.45]:

$$\lambda = \left[\frac{l^2}{J_1 + J_2} + \left(\frac{1}{F_1} + \frac{1}{F_2}\right)\right]\frac{12\,J_r}{hd^3} = \left(\frac{6.45^2}{16.8} + \frac{1}{4.65} + \frac{1}{4.65}\right) \times \frac{12 \times 0.018}{2.7 \times 1.8^3} = 0.0398$$

$$\mu = \frac{w \cdot l}{2\,(J_1 + J_2)} \times \frac{12\,J_r}{hd^3} = \frac{w \times 6.45}{2 \times 16.8} \times \frac{12 \times 0.018}{2.7 \times 1.8^3} = 0.00263\ w.$$

From formulae [5.3.47] we obtain:

$i = 1$

$$a_1 = \frac{\mu\left[\dfrac{-2}{\left(\dfrac{i \cdot \pi}{2H}\right)^3} + \dfrac{2H}{\left(\dfrac{i \cdot \pi}{2H}\right)^2}\right]}{\dfrac{1}{2}H\left[\left(\dfrac{i \cdot \pi}{2H}\right)^2 + \lambda\right]} = \frac{0.00263\ w\left[\dfrac{-2}{\left(\dfrac{1 \times 3.14}{2 \times 32.4}\right)^3} + \dfrac{2 \times 32.4}{\left(\dfrac{1 \times 3.14}{2 \times 32.4}\right)^2}\right]}{\dfrac{1}{2}\,32.4\left[\left(\dfrac{1 \times 3.14}{2 \times 32.4}\right)^2 + 0.0398\right]} = 38.5\ w.$$

$i = 3$

$$a_3 = \frac{0.00263\ w\left[\dfrac{-2}{\left(\dfrac{3 \times 3.14}{2 \times 32.4}\right)^3} - \dfrac{2 \times 32.4}{\left(\dfrac{3 \times 3.14}{2 \times 32.4}\right)^2}\right]}{\dfrac{1}{2} \times 32.4\left[\left(\dfrac{3 \times 3.14}{2 \times 32.4}\right)^2 + 0.0398\right]} = -9.95\ w.$$

$i = 5$

$$a_5 = \frac{0.00263\ w\left[\dfrac{-2}{\left(\dfrac{5 \times 3.14}{2 \times 32.4}\right)^3} + \dfrac{2 \times 32.4}{\left(\dfrac{5 \times 3.14}{2 \times 32.4}\right)^2}\right]}{\dfrac{1}{2} \times 32.4\left[\left(\dfrac{5 \times 3.14}{2 \times 32.4}\right)^2 + 0.0398\right]} = 1.58\ w.$$

The deflection of the wall is given by [5.3.49]

$$f_z = \frac{1}{E\,(J_1 + J_2)}\left[\frac{1}{8}\,w\,H^4 \mp l\sum a_i\left(\frac{2H}{i \cdot \pi}\right)^2\right] = \frac{1}{16.8\,E}\left\{\frac{1}{8} \times 32.4^4 - 6.45\left[38.5 \times \left(\frac{2 \times 32.4}{1 \times 3.14}\right)^2 + \right.\right.$$

$$\left.\left. + 9.95\left(\frac{2 \times 32.4}{3 \times 3.14}\right)^2 + 1.58\left(\frac{2 \times 32.4}{5 \times 3.14}\right)^2\right]\right\} = 1695\,\frac{w}{E}.$$

196

For $g = 0.15$ m

$$f_z = \frac{1695\, w}{0.15\, E} = \frac{11300\, w}{E}$$

whence

$$a_{IV} = 11300$$

5.6.4.2. Distribution of horizontal loading between stiffening walls.

It can be deduced from formula [5.1.12] that the total uniformly distributed load is shared by the stiffening walls as follows:

$$w_I = \frac{0.118 \times 42.0}{9950\left(\dfrac{1}{9950} + \dfrac{1}{10200} + \dfrac{1}{116000} + \dfrac{1}{11300}\right)} = 1.69 \text{ T/m}$$

$$w_{II} = \frac{0.118 \times 42.0}{10200\left(\dfrac{1}{9950} + \dfrac{1}{10200} + \dfrac{1}{116000} + \dfrac{1}{11300}\right)} = 1.64 \text{ T/m}$$

$$w_{III} = \frac{0.118 \times 42.0}{116000\left(\dfrac{1}{9950} + \dfrac{1}{10200} + \dfrac{1}{116000} + \dfrac{1}{11300}\right)} = 0.145 \text{ T/m}$$

$$w_{IV} = \frac{0.118 \times 42.0}{11300\left(\dfrac{1}{9950} + \dfrac{1}{10200} + \dfrac{1}{116000} + \dfrac{1}{11300}\right)} = 1.49 \text{ T/m}$$

5.6.4.3. Deflection f_z of the building.

Knowing the manner in which the total horizontal load is divided between the stiffening walls, we can now determine that part of the deflection of the building which is due to the uniform deflection of all such walls; thus, only the deflection f_z of any one wall need be calculated.

For wall I, from formula [5.3.1]:

$$f_{z,1} = 9950 \times \frac{1.69}{160 \times 10^4} = 105.0 \times 10^{-4} \text{ m}.$$

5.6.4.4. Determination of the deflection f_s due to rotation of the floors.

To find the centre of rotation, values $\bar{a}$ for the longitudinal stiffening walls are also required.
(a) Wall V — unperforated

Data: $b = 6.0$ m, $g = 0.15$ m

$$F_V = 0.15 \times 6.0 = 0.9 \text{ m}^2$$

$$J_V = \frac{0.15 \times 6.0^3}{12} = 2.7 \text{ m}^4$$

The deflection of this wall is calculated from formula [5.3.77]

$$f_V = \frac{w \times 32.4^2}{2E}\left(\frac{32.4^2}{4 \times 2.7} + \frac{2.8}{0.9}\right) = 58000\frac{w}{E}$$

and therefore

$$a_V = 58000.$$

(b) Wall VI — unperforated

Data: $b = 3.0$ m, $g = 0.15$ m

$$F_{VI} = 0.15 \times 3.0 = 0.45 \text{ m}^2$$

$$J_{VI} = \frac{0.15 \times 3.0^3}{12} = 0.337 \text{ m}^4.$$

The deflection of this wall is taken from formula [5.3.76]

$$f_{VI} = \frac{w \times 32.4^2}{2E}\left(\frac{32.4^2}{4 \times 0.337} + \frac{2.8}{0.45}\right) = 411500\frac{w}{E}$$

$$a_{VI} = 411500.$$

(c) The coordinates of the centre of rotation are found from equations [5.1.14] and [5.1.15]

$$x_0 = \frac{\frac{1}{9950} \times 0.075 + \frac{1}{10200} \times 36.075 + \frac{1}{116000} \times 39.075 + \frac{1}{11300} \times 42.075}{\frac{1}{9950} + \frac{1}{10200} + \frac{1}{116000} + \frac{1}{11300}} = 25.70$$

$$y_0 = \frac{\frac{1}{411500} \times 0.075 + \frac{1}{58000} \times 11.075}{\frac{1}{411500} + \frac{1}{58000}} = 9.90 \text{ m.}$$

We can now find the eccentricity of the horizontal loading relative to the centre of rotation:

$$z = x_0 - \frac{1}{2}L = 25.7 - \frac{1}{2} \times 42.0 = 4.7 \text{ m.}$$

To find the force acting on any wall i and balancing the twisting moment, the coefficients $\bar{a}_i$ must first be found from formula [5.1.18]

$$\bar{a}_1 = \frac{116000}{9950} = 11.6 \qquad \bar{a}_4 = \frac{116000}{11300} = 10.2$$

$$\bar{a}_2 = \frac{116000}{10200} = 11.3 \qquad \bar{a}_5 = \frac{116000}{58000} = 2.0$$

$$\bar{a}_3 = \frac{116000}{116000} = 1.0 \qquad \bar{a}_6 = \frac{116000}{411500} = 0.3.$$

Using formula [5.1.19] the loads w acting on all the walls can now be calculated:

$$w_I = 42 \times 0.118 \times \frac{4.7 \times 11.6 \times 25.6}{11.6 \times 25.6^2 + 11.3 \times 10.4^2 + 1.0 \times 13.4^2 + 10.2 \times 16.4^2 + 2.0 \times 1.2^2 + 0.3 \times 9.8^2} =$$

$$= 0.001975 \times 11.6 \times 25.6 = 0.586 \text{ T/m}$$

$$w_{II} = 0.001975 \times 11.3 \times 10.4 = 0.232 \text{ T/m}$$

$$w_{III} = 0.001975 \times 1.0 \times 13.4 = 0.026 \text{ T/m}$$

$$w_{IV} = 0.001975 \times 10.22 \times 16.4 = 0.331 \text{ T/m.}$$

The maximum deflection will take place in the wall farthest away from the centre of rotation, i.e. wall I. This is given by:

$$f_{s,I} = 9950 \times \frac{0.586}{160 \times 10^4} = 36.4 \times 10^{-4} \ \text{m.}$$

5.6.4.5. *The total deflection of the building.*

The total deflection f_{max} is the sum of f_z and f_s:

$$f_{max} = f_z + f_s = 105 \times 10^{-4} + 36.4 \times 10^{-4} = 141 \times 10^{-4} \text{ m.}$$

Limiting condition [5.1.1], as the building is 32.4 m high:

$$f_{max} = \frac{141 \times 10^{-4}}{32.4} H = \frac{1}{2300} H < \frac{1}{2000} H.$$

Thus, the three-dimensional stiffness of the building is satisfactory.

5.6.4.6. *Determination of the internal forces.*

We have previously established that the sections which are critical, as far as the internal forces are concerned, are the horizontal sections at the bottom of the column strips and the vertical sections through a lintel nearest to a 1/3 of the height of the wall (from the bottom). We shall now proceed to establish the values of the internal forces at these sections.

(a) Stiffening wall I — Fig. 5.6.2a

Horizontal section at the base of the wall.

Uniformly distributed horizontal load on the wall

$$w_I = 1.69 + 0.586 = 2.28 \text{ T/m.}$$

Axial force is determined from formula [5.3.59]

$$T_1 = T_2 = 2.28 \left(39.2 \sin \frac{1 \times 3.14 \times 32.4}{2 \times 32.4} - 14.3 \sin \frac{3 \times \pi \times 32.4}{2 \times 32.4} + \right.$$

$$\left. + 2.91 \sin \frac{5 \times 3.14 \times 32.4}{2 \times 32.4} \right) = 128.7 \text{ T}$$

Bending moments are calculated from [5.3.54]–[5.3.56]

$$M_1 = M_3 = \left(\frac{2.28}{2} \times 32.4^2 - 128.7 \times 3.5 - 128.7 \times 3.5\right) \times \frac{5.32}{5.32 + 0.084 + 5.32} = 146 \text{ Tm}$$

$$M_2 = \left(\frac{2.28}{2} \times 32.4^2 - 128.7 \times 3.5 \times 2\right) \times \frac{0.084}{5.32 + 0.084 + 5.32} = 2.3 \text{ Tm.}$$

Section through the 4th storey lintel.

Bending moment at the face of the column strip, from [5.3.50]

$$M = \left(39.2 \sin \frac{1 \times 3.14 \times 24.3}{2 \times 32.4} - 14.3 \sin \frac{3 \times 3.14 \times 24.3}{2 \times 32.4} + \right.$$

$$+ 2.91 \sin \frac{5 \times 3.14 \times 24.3}{2 \times 32.4} - 39.2 \sin \frac{1 \times 3.14 \times 21.6}{2 \times 32.4} -$$

$$- 14.3 \sin \frac{3 \times 3.14 \times 21.6}{2 \times 32.4} - 2.91 \sin \frac{5 \times 3.14 \times 21.6}{2 \times 32.4} \Big) \times \frac{2.28 \times 1.0}{2} = 10.45 \ \text{Tm.}$$

(b) Stiffening wall II.

Section at the base of the wall.

The uniformly distributed horizontal load acting on this wall is $w_{II} = 1.64 + 0.232 = 1.87$ T/m. Axial forces are determined from formulae [5.3.59]:

$$T_1 = 1.87 \left(10.0 \sin \frac{1 \times \pi \times 32.4}{2 \times 32.4} - 4.10 \sin \frac{3 \times \pi \times 32.4}{2 \times 32.4} + 1.05 \sin \frac{5 \times \pi \times 32.4}{2 \times 32.4} \right) = 28.3 \ \text{T}$$

$$T_2 = 1.87 \left(42 \sin \frac{1 \times \pi \times 32.4}{2 \times 32.4} - 15 \sin \frac{3 \times \pi \times 32.4}{2 \times 32.4} + 3.10 \sin \frac{5 \times \pi \times 32.4}{2 \times 32.4} \right) = 105.2 \ \text{T}$$

Bending moments from equations [5.3.54], [5.3.56]:

$$M_1 = \left(\frac{1.87}{2} \times 32.4^2 - 28.3 \times 3.5 - 105.2 \times 5.25 \right) \times$$

$$\times \frac{0.0104}{0.0104 + 7.58 + 5.33} = 331 \times \frac{0.0104}{12.92} = 0.25 \ \text{Tm}$$

$$M_2 = 331 \times \frac{7.58}{12.92} = 194 \ \text{Tm}$$

$$M_3 = 331 \times \frac{5.33}{12.92} = 137 \ \text{Tm.}$$

Sections through the 4th storey lintels.

The bending moments at the face of the left hand column band from formula [5.3.50] are:

$$M_L = \left(10.0 \sin \frac{1 \times \pi \times 24.3}{2 \times 32.4} - 4.10 \sin \frac{3 \times \pi \times 24.3}{2 \times 32.4} + \right.$$

$$+ 1.05 \sin \frac{5 \times \pi \times 24.3}{2 \times 32.4} - 10.0 \sin \frac{1 \times \pi \times 21.6}{2 \times 32.4} +$$

$$\div 4.10 \sin \frac{3 \times \pi \times 21.6}{2 \times 32.4} - 1.05 \sin \frac{5 \times \pi \times 21.6}{2 \times 32.4} \Big) \times \frac{1.87 \times 1.0}{2} = 2.49 \ \text{Tm}$$

$$M_R = \left(42 \sin \frac{1 \times \pi \times 24.3}{2 \times 32.4} - 15 \sin \frac{3 \times \pi \times 24.3}{2 \times 32.4} + \right.$$

$$\cdot + 3.10 \sin \frac{5 \times \pi \times 24.3}{2 \times 32.4} - 42 \times \sin \frac{1 \times \pi \times 21.6}{2 \times 32.4} +$$

$$+ 15 \sin \frac{3 \times \pi \times 21.6}{2 \times 32.4} - 3.10 \sin \frac{5 \times \pi \times 21.6}{2 \times 32.4} \Big) \times \frac{1.87 \times 1.0}{2} = 9.03 \ \text{Tm.}$$

Having found the values of the internal forces at the critical sections, the load-carrying capacities can now be checked, or the necessary reinforcement designed (in accordance with current standards for r.c). In the case of horizontal sections, to the calculated values of the axial forces T resulting from the horizontal loading, must be added other axial forces, i.e. those due to the vertical loading (wall weight, floor loads, etc.).

Chapter 6

FLOORS, STAIRS AND ROOFS

6.1. TYPES OF CONSTRUCTION

6.1.1. General Introduction

Floors, stairs and roofs are the horizontal members of a building. Their structural requirements are basically identical and their constructional forms are therefore very similar, and lend themselves to a common discussion based on floor constructions.

In buildings made of large precast components the floors are usually made of reinforced concrete incorporating normal aggregates. Prestressed construction is seldom used, although lately some attempts have been made in this field.

The main application of lightweight concretes is in roofs, both flat and sloping.

With regard to the method of support and reinforcement, roofs fall into the following two main groups:
— slabs supported on two edges, reinforced in one direction (Fig. 6.1.1a);
— slabs supported on the whole perimeter or at the corners, and cross-reinforced (Fig. 6.1.1b, c).

The shape of the cross-section of floor slab components may be one of the following:
— solid (Fig. 6.1.2a);
— hollow or cored (multiduct) slabs (Fig. 6.1.2b);
— tray or pan (Fig. 6.1.2c);
— folded plate (Fig. 6.1.2d);
— ribbed with infilling (Fig. 6.1.2e).

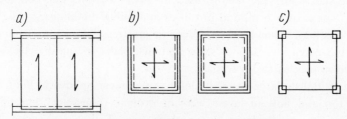

Fig. 6.1.1. Support and reinforcement of floor panels:
(a) panels simply supported on two edges, reinforced in one direction, (b), (c) cross-reinforced panels, supported on all four edges or on the corners

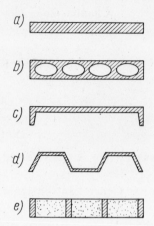

Fig, 6.1.2. Typical cross-sections of prefabricated floor panels:
(a) solid, (b) hollow (multiduct), (c) tray panel, (d) folded plate, (e) ribbed with infilling

Lightweight constructions are those in which the light concrete is designed to assist, wholly or in part, in the load-carrying function of the unit. Thus, ribbed slabs with light concrete block infilling between the ribs do not belong to this group.

Lightweight concrete slabs are as a rule of solid cross-section.

The types of concrete used are:
— cellular concrete (foamed or air-entrained);
— hollow or no-fines concretes, made without sand;
using clinker or crushed rock single-sized aggregates:
— dense concretes made with lightweight coarse aggregates;
— normal concrete with organic fillers, such as wood shavings or sawdust.

6.1.2. Solid Floor Slabs in Ordinary Concrete

Ordinary concrete slabs of solid cross-section are used:
— in beam-and-slab constructions, consisting of slabs supported on beams, or
— as floor slabs resting directly on the walls, or sometimes on columns.

Beam-and-slab floors are mainly used in blocks of flats built on the long-wall system with spans over 6 m, and in offices and public buildings.

Floor beams may be made of reinforced or prestressed concrete. Beams and slabs are generally treated in design as separate units. Slabs resting directly on the walls are designed mostly as two-way slabs.

In the first Polish large-panel building, three-layer sandwich floor slabs were tried. The top and bottom layers were of ordinary concrete 2 cm thick ($R_w = 170$ kg/cm^2). The middle layer 10 cm thick was of clinker concrete with $R_w = 25$ kg/cm^2. Thus the total thickness of the slab was 14 cm. The unit weight was assumed to be approx. 260 kg/m^2.

In practice, however, it was extremely difficult to keep the thickness of the ordinary concrete layers and the overall weight of the slab within the design figures. The finished units were up to 30 % heavier than allowed for in the calculations (especially after rain). In later buildings of the same project, the sandwich floor slabs were discarded in favour of homogeneous slabs made of ordinary concrete.

In the model PBU project, single layer slabs made of ordinary concrete were used ($R_w = 170$ kg/cm²). These are 9 cm thick and weigh 212 kg/cm² (Fig. 6.1.3). These slabs are cast horizontally. To avoid additional reinforcement against

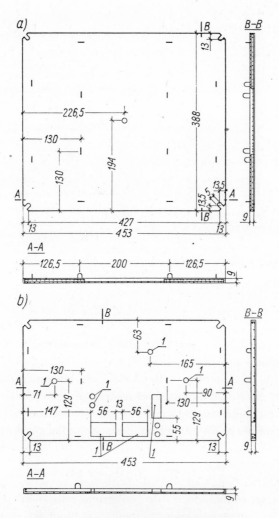

Fig. 6.1.3. Homogeneous r.c. floor panels:
(a) room-size panel, (b) bathroom panel
(1) services holes

203

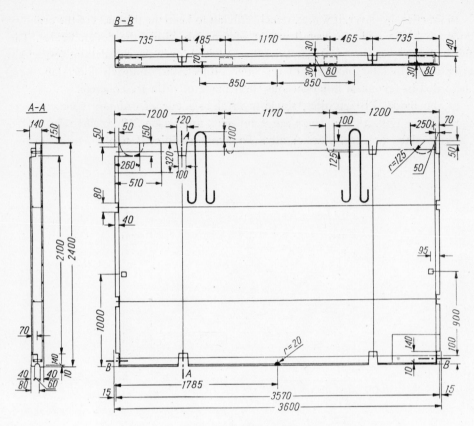

Fig. 6.1.4. A German solid floor panel, spanning one-way

Stage A conditions of loading, the units are lifted by means of eight lugs cast-in around the perimeter. The production of solid slab units of a single material is very simple. This kind of slab can also be cast in battery forms, which is a particularly economical solution.

Fig. 6.1.4 shows an example of a solid slab unit, spanning one-way, as used in a German project. Such slabs are made of concrete $R_{\square 20} = 160$ kg/cm². Their weight is 336 kg/cm², which includes the weight of reinforcement of 7.5 kg/m². Of special interest is the detail of the lifting points hidden in the thickness of the slab.

6.1.3. Multiduct Floor Slabs

The main advantage of multiduct slabs, compared with solid slabs, is that they utilise constructional materials more efficiently, without losing their flat surfaces, top and bottom.

The use of steel forms yields a smooth under-surface which does not need rendering.

Ducts in the slab may be of circular, oval or, sometimes, rectangular cross-section. As a rule, these run in the direction of the span. The ribs between the ducts are sufficiently stiffened by the top and bottom plates to make cross ribs superfluous.

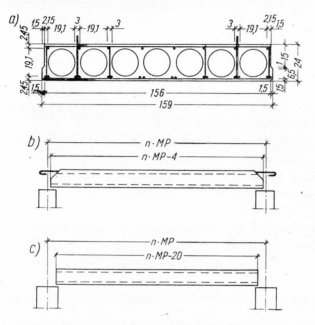

Fig. 6.1.5. Polish cored floor panels, so-called "Żerań brick":
(a) cross-section, (b) panel type A, designed to be supported directly on the walls, (c) panel type B, supported on the walls by means of r.c. dowels

The typical Polish slabs with circular ducts are produced nowadays in two varieties, classified according to the method used to support them on the walls. Type A slabs (Fig. 6.1.5b) are supported directly on the walls, while type B slabs (Fig. 6.1.5c) are supported by means of r.c. dowels.

Both types are made of ordinary concrete Mk. 170. The slabs are from 2.7 to 6.0 m long and from 0.89 to 1.48 m wide, depending on the module used. Their thickness is 24 cm, the duct diameter is 19 cm, and the total weight of the largest slab is 2.6 tonnes.

The prestressing of multiduct floor slabs results in a considerable saving in steel.

An example of a precast prestressed slab with oval ducts is shown in Fig. 6.1.6. This slab was designed in two versions:
— homogeneous, in Mk. 250 concrete, and
— two-layer casting, with the lower 3 cm consisting of Mk. 400 concrete and the remainder of Mk. 200 concrete.

The mean thickness of the slab is 11.6 cm. The reinforcement consists of twin-twisted wires of 2.5 mm dia. For a slab of 5.90 m $\times$ 1.49 m $\times$ 19 cm, the weight of

205

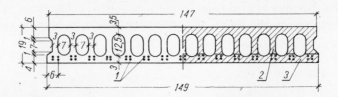

Fig. 6.1.6. A prestressed multiduct floor panel:
(1) 2×2.5 mm dia. strands, (2) concrete $R_{\phi16} = 200$ kg/cm²; (3) concrete $R_{\phi16} = 400$ kg/cm²

reinforcing steel is only 1.6 kg/m². The above slabs are manufactured on long stressing beds, using sliding placing plant.

Multiduct precast slabs, which represent one of the most economical solutions, are commonly used outside Poland.

In Czechoslovakia, 14 cm slabs are used for spans of up to 3.80 m, and 21.5 cm slabs for spans of up to 5.30 m.

Several types of multiduct precast slabs were developed in the Soviet Union. Fig. 6.1.7 illustrates one such slab which has oval ducts. This slab is lighter than a similar slab with ducts of circular cross-section (20 % saving in concrete), its production, however, is somewhat more difficult.

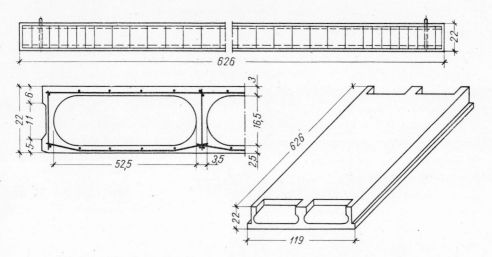

Fig. 6.1.7. A cored floor slab with oval ducts, widely used in the Soviet Union

An interesting solution is a Polish thin-walled floor slab made of air-free concrete, the weight of the 24 cm thick unit being only 200 kg/m² (Fig. 6.1.8). The slabs are cast in the vertical position, the deaeration being effected through the duct formers.

It should be pointed out that thin-walled castings are the best suited for deaeration, as thicker units are capable of forming only a thin skin of air-free concrete on the side facing the suction pump.

206

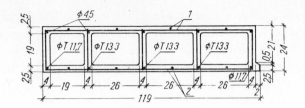

Fig. 6.1.8. A Polish floor panel, with thin deaerated concrete walls:
(1) top reinforcing mesh, 3 mm dia., (2) bottom mesh, 3 mm dia.

A British firm manufactures hollow multiduct floor slabs up to 2.30 m wide, in thicknesses ranging from 12.7–20.3 cm for reinforced concrete, and 13.3–61.0 cm for prestressed concrete. The cavities in the slab are formed by means of inflatable formers and are of roughly oval cross-section.

6.1.4. Tray or Pan Slabs

Tray-shaped precast floor panels fall into two general groups:
— narrow trays, several of which are required to floor one room (Fig. 6.1.9a), and
— wide trays, covering the whole room area (Fig. 6.1.9b).
Narrow tray slabs are also designed in an inverted form (pan panels), with a flat top face.

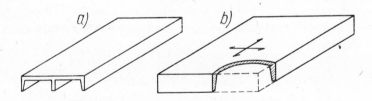

Fig. 6.1.9. Tray panels:
(a) narrow, (b) wide

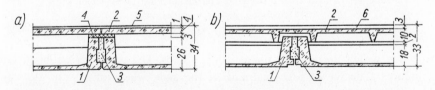

Fig. 6.1.10. Two forms of composite tray floors:
(a) the upper surface is obtained by laying additional flat r.c. panels on the longitudinal ribs,
(b) upper ribbed panels rest on the transverse ribs of the bottom panels
(1) tray panel, (2) floor panel, (3) stepped joint, (4) resilient pad, (5) linoleum, (6) block floor

207

The tray panels provide a ready-made ceiling surface. The upper surface is obtained by means of additional reinforced concrete panels supported on the main ribs (Fig. 6.1.10a), or on the cross-ribs (Fig. 6.1.10b). Tray construction is best combined with timber flooring, a common practice in the Soviet Union. Timber joists may be laid directly on the cross-ribs of the trays (Fig. 6.1.11), or on a loose fill of acoustic insulation.

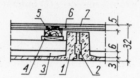

Fig. 6.1.11. Timber flooring supported by means of timber joists resting on the cross-ribs of the r.c. panels:
(1) tray panel, (2) stepped joint, (3) breeze fill, (4) resilient pad, (5) timber joist, (6) sub-floor (7) block floor

Timber flooring of this nature is seldom found in Poland due to the scarcity of timber.

With pan panels the ceiling is surfaced with plasterboard, fibreboard, or wet plaster applied to wire netting.

The most frequent application for narrow pan units occurs in sloping roofs and in the upper layers of ventilated flat roofs (section 6.1.10). In such cases ceilings are, of course, unnecessary.

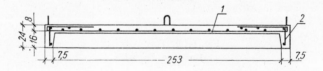

Fig. 6.1.12. Room-size inverted tray panels used in type SP buildings:
(1) horizontal mesh, (2) vertical mesh

Wide tray panels are akin to plain two-way slabs. The perimeter webbing, however, induces a degree of edge restraint in the slab, which offsets the decreased thickness. This stiffening effect on the upper surface of the slabs also tends to improve the acoustic insulation characteristics of the floor.

Unlike the narrow panels, the wide tray or pan units provide flat top and bottom surfaces.

208

An example of a wide pan unit of ordinary Mk. 170 concrete used in a Polish project is shown in Fig. 6.1.12. The weight of the panel itself is 215 kg/m²; the reinforcement for a panel 4.78×2.68 m weighed 5.0 kg/m².

A vibro-rolling method of production has recently been developed in the Soviet Union. Floor panels made in this way are either used singly, with plasterboard ceilings, or in pairs laid rib-to-rib (Figs. 6.1.13 and 6.1.14). To improve sound

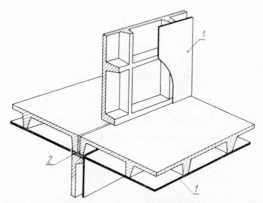

Fig. 6.1.13. Floor consisting of single "waffle" panels with plasterboard ceiling attached: (1) plasterboard, (2) resilient pad

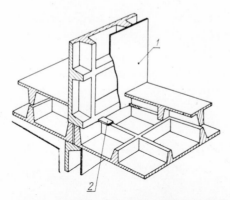

Fig. 6.1.14. Floor consisting of two-tray panels laid back-to-back: (1) plasterboard, (2) resilient pad

insulation, the panels are supported on the walls upon resilient pads. In the case of the twin floor, the upper panel rests on the lower one only at its perimeter.

The technical data of the twin floor are as follows: length 4.9 m, width 2.8 m, thickness 21.5 cm, mean thickness 8.6 cm, Mk. 300 concrete, steel ratio 5.8 kg/m², total weight 200 kg/m².

Fig 6.1.15 illustrates another Russian tray unit of room size dimensions with a remarkably low mean thickness of concrete (3.85 cm). The camber of the doubly

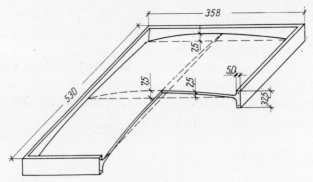

Fig. 6.1.15. Soviet room-size double curvature tray panel

curved plate is 7.5 cm and the underside is left exposed. This has not been widely used as yet, and is shown here as an academic example of the search for a solution resulting in the minimum consumption of materials.

6.1.5. Corrugated Plate or Trough Floor Slabs

In the search for the most economical floor unit, attempts have been made of late to develop thin-sectioned corrugated slabs. This form of construction is patterned on similar solutions often employed in the arched or shell roofs of industrial buildings.

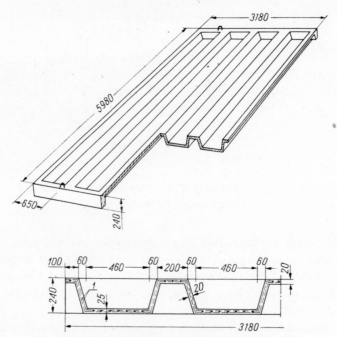

Fig. 6.1.16. A trough panel used in the Soviet building industry

210

The thickness of such units does not exceed 2–3 cm and they must therefore be made of cement-rich sand concrete or rich mortar.

An example of a trough panel, as used in the Soviet building industry, is shown in Fig. 6.1.16. For a span of 6.0 m the average thickness is 3.54 cm and the weight 85 kg/m². The reinforcement consists of closely spaced wires of 1.5 mm dia.

Another application, of Polish origin, possessing thicker horizontal walls, is reinforced with 10 or 12 mm dia. bars (Fig. 6.1.17).

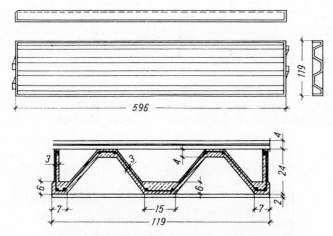

Fig. 6.1.17. A Polish design for a corrugated slab floor

The strength and stiffness of a panel are not the only criteria of its suitability. The fire-resistance, sound insulation, and, most important, the possibility of economical industrial production of the contemplated floor unit must also be considered in order to form a true picture of the suitability of a new idea in design. The last two examples, interesting though they are, must still remain of academic interest only.

6.1.6. Ribbed Floors with Infilling

The production of ribbed floors with infilling cannot be automated easily. In Polish practice, therefore, such floors are found to be best cast on the site, within reach of the erection crane, and with a minimum of special equipment.

The spaces between the ribs may be filled with ceramic tiles or with blocks of lightweight concrete or gypsum (Fig. 6.1.18).

Gas concrete blocks are particularly useful as fillers for two-way ribbed panels.

Specially light room-size panels, in which the infill blocks are laid after erection, have been developed in the Soviet Union for erection with a small capacity crane (Fig. 6.1.19).

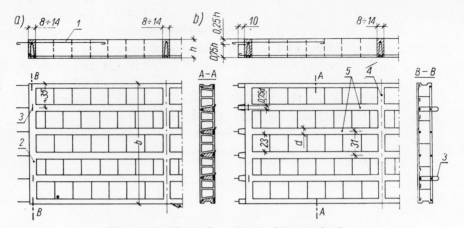

Fig. 6.1.18. Ribbed floor panels with ceramic tiles:
(a) to be rested on walls, (b) to be supported by in-situ concrete beams
(1) 3 mm dia. continuity bar, (2) ring rib, (3) lifting lug, (4) distribution rib, (5) main rib

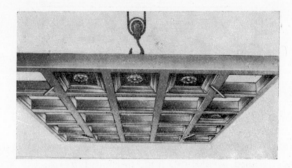

Fig. 6.1.19. A grid panel with gypsum inserts

Notwithstanding these attempts to use ribbed units in prefabricated buildings, they are not really suited to industrialised building.

6.1.7. Lightweight Concrete Floors

Floor panels in lightweight concrete may be homogeneous, or two- and three-layered.

Homogeneous slabs. The fabrication of such slabs is straightforward, but, keeping in mind the combined action of concrete and reinforcement, only gas concretes or dense concretes with lightweight aggregates are suitable for their production.

Autoclaved aerated concrete floor panels are commonly used in Sweden. The sheets (Fig. 6.1.20) may be self-faced or ready plastered, and have a width of 50 cm. The range of sheet thicknesses, with the corresponding maximum spans, is given in Table 6.1.1, taken from the makers catalogue (Siporex).

212

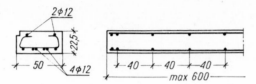

Fig. 6.1.20. A Swedish autoclaved gas concrete floor panel

A particular case of a single-layer panel is shown in Fig. 6.1.21; here, the gas concrete slab has been reinforced with prestressed inserts.

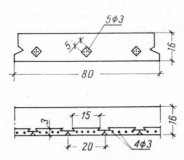

Fig. 6.1.21. Gas concrete panels reinforced with prestressed inserts

TABLE 6.1.1.

SIZES OF GAS CONCRETE FLOOR PANELS
(from the "Siporex" catalogue)

Type of concrete and superimposed loading (in addition to the weight of the panel itself) in kg/m²	Length of panel (m) for various thicknesses (cm)					
	12.5	15	17.5	20	22.5	25
05/300	2.75	3.5	4.25	5.0	5.5	6.0
05/400	2.75	3.5	4.25	4.75	5.0	5.5
07/300	3.0	3.75	4.5	5.25	6.0	6.0
07/400	3.0	3.75	4.5	5.25	5.5	5.75

Two-layer sandwich slabs. The reinforcement in such units is placed inside a thin layer (3–4 cm) of stiff cement mortar; the remainder of the slab (10–20 cm thick) consists of open-textured concrete, e.g. no-fines concrete with light aggregate. This construction is justified by the fact that a better bond is developed between the two types of concrete used than between porous concrete and reinforcement. Moreover, the coating of mortar protects the steel against corrosion (Fig. 6.1.22).

The reinforcing rods are sometimes pre-coated with cement mortar; in such cases the mortar layer is omitted.

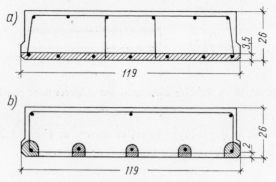

Fig. 6.1.22. Two-layer panels:
(a) panel with reinforcement laid in a thin layer of cement mortar, (b) panel with reinforcement laid within individual "sheaths" of cement mortar

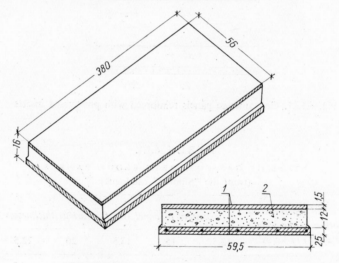

Fig. 6.1.23. A three-layer sandwich panel:
(1) layers of fine aggregate concrete, (2) expanded clay concrete (3) reinforcement

Three-layer slabs. Both outer skins of such units consist of cement mortar, the centre layer being of weak, light concrete. The lower layer of mortar embodies the reinforcement (Fig. 6.1.23), while the function of the top skin is to transfer the bending shears. The lightweight middle layer carries the principal stresses and ensures the joint action of the top skin and the reinforcement.

6.1.8. Balconies

Balconies in prefabricated buildings may be constructed by one of the following methods:

214

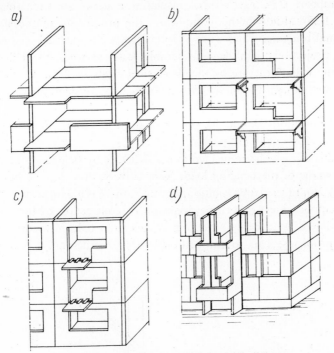

Fig. 6.1.24. Balconies in prefabricated buildings:
(a) balcony slab is an integral part of the floor panel, (b) balcony panel rests on cantilever brackets,
(c) balcony panel is connected to the structure by means of welded steel flats, (d) balconies supported
by a special structure

— continuation of the floor slab (Fig. 6.1.24a);
— separate balcony slab supported on brackets projecting from the wall or from the ring beam (Fig. 6.1.24b);
— separate slab attached to the structure by means of steel flats or plates (Fig. 6.1.24c);
— slab resting on a special structure jointed-off from the main building (Fig. 6.1.24d).

The first solution, which is the simplest, has a low thermal efficiency, and in an

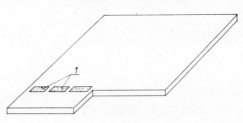

Fig. 6.1.25. Floor panel in which the balcony projection is partly separated by thermally insulating inserts

215

attempt to improve this, inserts of an insulating material are sometimes incorporated (Fig. 6.1.25), although this complicates the production of the slab.

Such thermal bridging, which always occurs where the external wall is punctured by concrete projections, can be considerably lessened when the balcony slab is attached to the main structure by means of steel cleats or flats. A solution of this nature, however, though thermally correct, leads to a considerable consumption of steel.

The steel connections should be protected from corrosion by a coating of 1:3 cement mortar, 2–3 cm thick.

Balcony slabs can also be connected to the structure by welded steel flats designed to carry the whole of the bending load. Alternatively, they may be hung from tie-rods (Fig. 6.1.26). In the latter solution, however, there is a danger of some cracking at the slab support due to thermal expansion or contraction of the tie-rods.

The provision of a separate structure to carry the balconies completely solves the thermal problems. This solution, though simple structurally, is comparatively expensive.

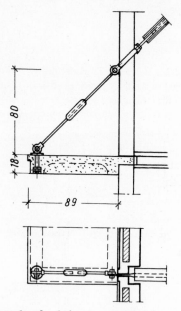

Fig. 6.1.26. Example of a balcony suspended by means of tie-rods

In balcony design, particular care must be taken to ensure proper drainage and to prevent the entry of water into the building. Although the ways of achieving the above are not very different from those used in traditional construction, instances of faults in prefabricated buildings are rather numerous.

216

6.1.9. Stairs

Stairs consist essentially of landings and flights.

Landing slabs are structurally identical to floor slabs except for a ledge formed along one side to support the flights. The latter are normally designed as solid slabs or tray panels.

Landing slabs may be supported by:

— half storey-height wall units (Fig. 6.1.27a);
— brackets on the wall slabs (Fig. 6.1.27b);
— perforated wall slabs (Fig. 6.1.27c).

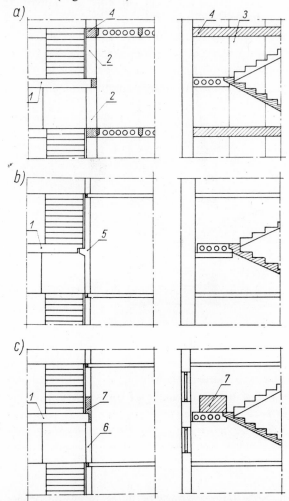

Fig. 6.1.27. Support for half-landing slabs provided by:
(a) using wall units of half storey-height, (b) wall units with brackets, (c) perforated wall units (1) half-landing slab, (2) half storey-height wall block, (3) full storey-height wall blocks, (4) r.c. ring beam, (5) bracketed wall panel, (6) perforated wall panel, (7) concrete filling

The first method is the one most commonly used in prefabricated buildings.

The bracket method is typical of the Scandinavian building industry, and allows the landing slab to be laid on acoustic insulation pads.

In Poland, landing slabs are usually keyed into perforated wall slabs (Fig. 6.1.28). For erection purposes, the opening is much taller than the thickness of the slab; when the latter is in position, the remainder of the pocket is concreted.

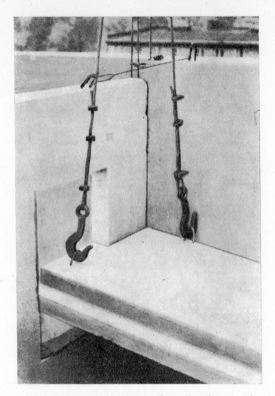

Fig. 6.1.28. Wall support for a landing panel

Figure 6.1.29 shows a staircase consisting of hollow slab landings and solid flights; the stairs in Fig. 6.1.30 are made of tray panels. The reinforcement in the landing panel was so designed that both solid and tray panel slabs could be supported. The weights of the units and of the reinforcement are shown in Table 6.1.2.

6.1.10. Roof Slabs

This section deals with roof structures and the ceilings to the top storeys. This is as distinct from the case where the ceiling is structurally independent; the structure supporting the weather skin is then known as an overroof.

Roofs may be ventilated (Fig. 6.1.31a,b), or unventilated (Fig. 6.1.31c).

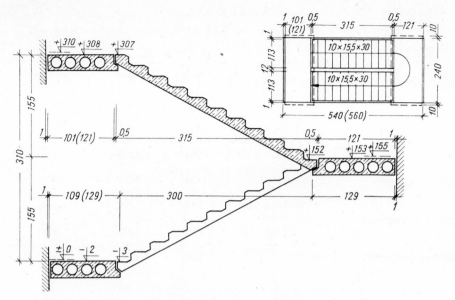

Fig. 6.1.29. Stairs consisting of hollow landing panels and solid flight panels

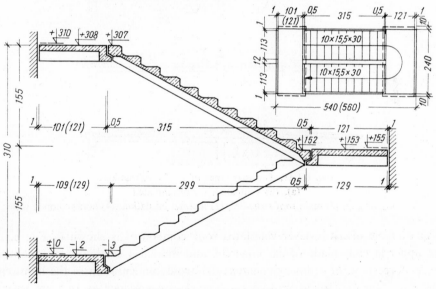

Fig. 6.1.30. Use of tray panels in stair construction

Unventilated roofs are less advantageous because of thermomoistural processes (cf. section 8.1.2), and should only be used over areas with a relative humidity not greater than 45 % (school rooms, offices). A damp-proof layer is as a rule provided underneath the thermal insulation of an unventilated roof, to protect it from condensation.

219

TABLE 6.1.2.

WEIGHTS OF STAIR COMPONENTS AND STEEL CONSUMPTION

Description of prefabricate		Weight of component		Consumption of steel per m² of plan area
		without terrazzo kg	with terrazzo kg	kg /m²
Cored landing panel	109 cm wide	835	960	6.77
	129 cm wide	960	1100	6.10
Solid flight panel		1450	1850	10.16
Ribbed landing slab	109 cm wide	730	835	10.68
	129 cm wide	850	995	9.10
Ribbed flight panel		970	1370	8.70

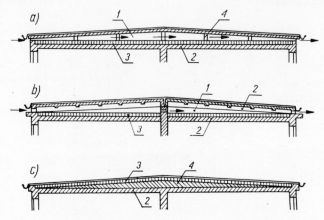

Fig. 6.1.31. The two types of roof construction:
(a), (b) ventilated, (c) unventilated
(1) air gap, (2) main roof structure, (3) thermal insulation, (4) honeycombed walls

An example of a two-layer ventilated roof component is shown in Fig. 6.1.32. The upper layer is made of gas concrete, and the 3.5–4 cm lower layer, housing the reinforcement, of ordinary concrete. To avoid condensation in the lightweight concrete, 5 cm dia. round ventilation channels are provided at 16.5 cm spacing.

Fig. 6.1.33 shows a ventilated roof in which the concrete overroof is supported on the ceiling slab by means of short piers. The thermal barrier consists of mineral wool.

Inward inclination of the roof is not practicable in Polish climatic conditions. Water drainage would be difficult in springtime, when the downpipe could easily be blocked by ice.

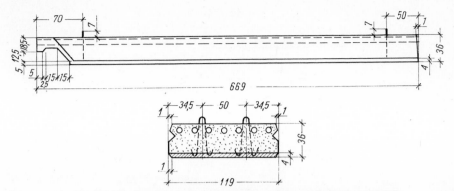

Fig. 6.1.32. Ventilated gas concrete panel used in roofs in the U.S.S.R.

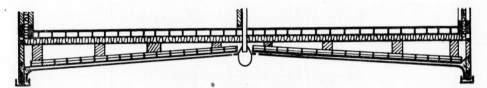

Fig. 6.1.33. Example of a roof in which the overroof structure is supported by the main ceiling slab by means of short piers

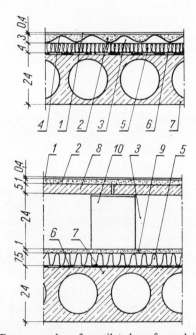

Fig. 6.1.34. Two examples of ventilated roofs used in Warsaw:
(1) two layers of roofing felt, (2) cement screed, (3) air gap, (4) corrugated asbestos-cement sheets, (5) woodwool slabs, (6) damp course, (7) hollow structural panel, (8) r.c. planks, (9) cement skim coat, (10) gas concrete spacer block

221

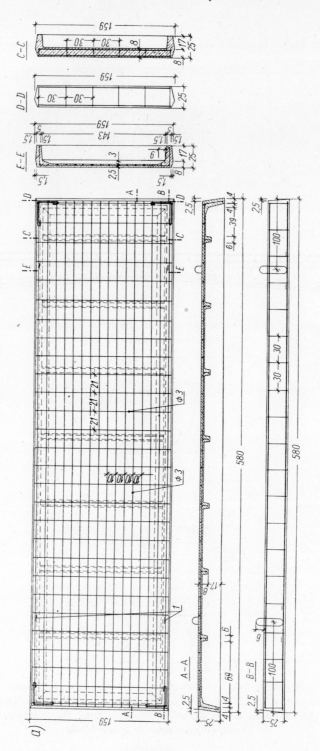

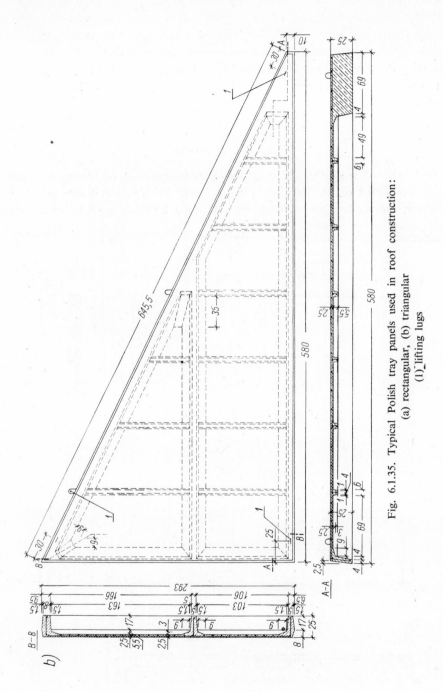

Fig. 6.1.35. Typical Polish tray panels used in roof construction:
(a) rectangular, (b) triangular
(1) lifting lugs

Two further examples of ventilated roofs in Warsaw are shown in Fig. 6.1.34.

In the first, the ventilated space is provided by the corrugations of asbestos-cement sheets laid on an insulating layer of woodwool. The total weight of the roof is 355 kg/m² and the thermal conductivity 650 cal/m²h°C.

In the second case, the void is created by resting an outer skin of precast concrete slabs on gas concrete spacers. The weight of this construction is 490 kg/m² and the conductivity 710 cal/m²h°C.

6.1.11. Overroofs

In prefabricated buildings the overroofs normally consist of reinforced concrete panels supported on loadbearing walls, columns or concrete beams and trusses. However, more advanced methods of traditional building, such as small precast components, are also used.

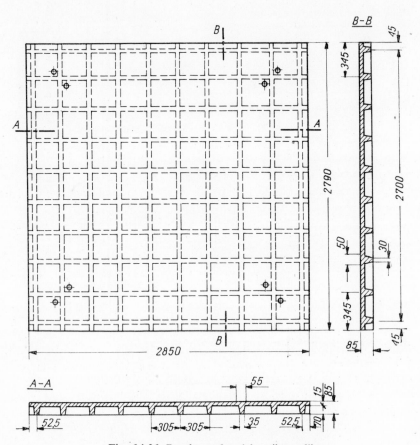

Fig. 6.1.36. Panels produced by vibro-rolling

224

Pan-shaped panels are often used for overroofs except where the span is small, when solid slabs may suffice. Attempts have also been made to produce suitable corrugated panels. Where the roof is to be tiled, some form of grid panel might be suitable.

Typical Polish pan-section units are illustrated in Fig. 6.1.35. Both rectangular and triangular panels are produced.

Another type of panel (Fig. 6.1.36) is made of Mk. 200 concrete by vibro-rolling. The mean thickness is 3.5 cm, and the weight of 4 mm dia. cold-rolled reinforcement is 2.6 kg/m².

An example of a corrugated overroof panel is shown in Fig. 6.1.37. This is used in double-slope roofs with 6 to 12 m spans. The thickness of the concrete varies between 1 and 1 1/2 cm, and the panel is made of sand concrete with normal or expanding cement. The mean thickness of the panel is 3.0 cm and the reinforcement weighs 3.9 kg/m². A coating of waterproof paint is applied to the concrete to make the rather thin walls impervious, and to prevent corrosion of the reinforcement.

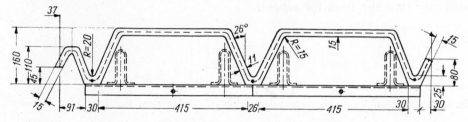

Fig. 6.1.37. Example of a sand concrete corrugated panel

In the design of prefabricated roofs special attention must be given to the configuration of joints with gable walls. Should the edge of the roof coincide with the face of the wall, rainwater will flow down the wall. If the water can penetrate into the roof ventilating spaces, the thermal insulation will become saturated, resulting in multiple damp spots inside the building and a sharp decrease in thermal protection.

6.2. DESIGN RECOMMENDATIONS

6.2.1. Edge Conditions

All beams and slabs should be designed with due regard to the actual edge conditions at the supports.

Components should only be designed as simply supported when free rotation at the support is assured. It must be added that the creation of this condition at the support may be injurious to the support component. Rotation at the support concentrates the load near its edge, which may cause premature wear of the support (Fig. 6.2.1a).

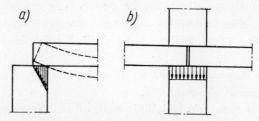

Fig. 6.2.1. Floor support conditions:
(a) loads concentrated near the edge of the support, (b) loading uniformly distributed

Where the conditions prevent rotation, a more efficient junction is obtained since the loading is uniformly transferred to the support (Fig. 6.2.1b).

Slabs fixed at the support must be reinforced to resist negative moments; the lack of such reinforcement may lead to the formation of wide cracks (Fig. 6.2.2), resulting in a greatly increased deflection of the panel. In the extreme case, the panel may even slip from the support.

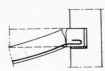

Fig. 6.2.2. Crack forming at the support due to lack of reinforcement against negative moments

By fixing the component at the support the bending moment in the span is correspondingly reduced. This reduction, however, may only be allowed for in calculations when:

— continuity of the slab over the support is assured and the panels are capable of developing the calculated support moment (section 6.3.3), or
— the slab is effectively fixed to the wall.

The conditions which must be fulfilled if the latter is to be assumed, are essentially the same as those applying to brick walls, namely:

— the width of the wall beam forming the actual supporting surface of the panel should not be less than 25 cm or 1/20 of the span;
— the supporting wall must be at least 25 cm thick and must be constructed of concrete not weaker than Mk. 50;
— the wall above the floor considered must be at least 2.50 m high and rigidly fixed at the top.

Walls made of hollow concrete blocks are not considered to satisfy the above requirements.

When floor panels are built into belt beams or supported by r.c. beams cast in-situ, the depth of the supporting beams should not be less than 5 cm (Fig. 6.2.3), to reduce the possibility of incomplete consolidation and of air gaps immediately

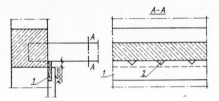

Fig. 6.2.3. The method of casting r.c. wall beams:
(1) profile, (2) notching

under the slab. With the same object in mind, the side formwork, on which the panel rests while the belt beam is being poured, should be notched as shown in Fig. 6.2.3.

6.2.2. Methods of Support and Length of Support

According to the Polish standards, the effective loadbearing area is measured as shown on Fig. 6.2.4, i.e. allowances must be made for the accuracy of the casting process (wall thickness) and for the end cover to the beam or slab reinforcement. The effective loadbearing area must not be smaller than the values given in Table 6.2.1.

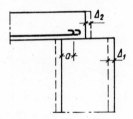

Fig. 6.2.4. Effective support of floor panels and beams

When the supporting wall is made of plain concrete not weaker than Mk. 140 with the upper edge reinforced, the minimum loadbearing area required to support floor panels is the same as if the walls were of reinforced concrete (see section 7.2.2).

Floor panels may bear on their supports over their whole width, or alternatively bearing lugs may be provided. If these lugs are staggered in the panels on either side of the wall, the loadbearing area may in effect be equal to the width of the wall (Fig. 6.2.5).

Lugs are often made of thickness smaller than that of the parent panel (Fig. 6.2.6). This makes possible the construction of a reinforced belt beam as wide as the supporting wall, which makes for the uniformity of wall stresses.

Top reinforcement, projecting from the present panel into the belt beam, allows the panel to be anchored more securely.

The total loadbearing area required when lugs are used is identical to that needed for floor beams.

227

TABLE 6.2.1.

THE MINIMUM EFFECTIVE SUPPORT OF FLOOR SLABS AND BEAMS, cm

Description of floor components		Type of wall		
		Reinforced concrete	*Wall from full bricks or ordinary concrete blocks*	*Wall from hollow bricks or lightweight concrete blocks*
Simply supported beams	$l \leqslant 3$ m	5	7	10
	$l > 3$ m	7	10	12
Fixed or continuous beams	$l \leqslant 3$ m	3	5	7
Panels supported at two edges, simply supported	$l > 3$ m	5	7	7
Slabs supported at two edges, fixed	$l \leqslant 3$ m	2	3	5
Panels supported at three or four edges		3	5	5

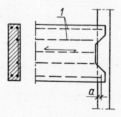

Fig. 6.2.5. Floor panel supported by means of bearing lugs
(1) reinforcement

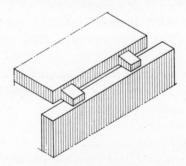

Fig. 6.2.6. Bearing lugs thinner than the floor panel

228

The hollow panels can be supported by means of reinforced concrete dowels cast in-situ (Fig. 6.2.7). Experiments show that this type of support provides partial anchorage which may be taken into account in the design.

The length of the dowel, measured from the edge of the panel, must not be less than 50 cm, or 40 diameters of the dowel reinforcing bars. It is essential to provide lateral reinforcement in the panel over the dowels to prevent their shearing through (Fig. 6.2.8).

The local bearing stresses must be checked if the floor beams are spaced more than 2.5 m apart, or when the floor panels are supported at the corners only. These

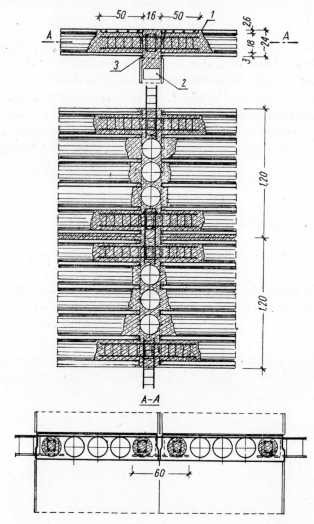

Fig. 6.2.7. Reinforced concrete dowels as a means of support for hollow floor panels: (1) vent hole, (2) paper plug, (3) thin timber strip

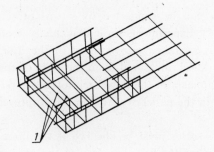

Fig. 6.2.8. Reinforcement in type B panels:
(1) transverse top reinforcement, to safeguard against r.c. dowels shearing through the walls of the panel

calculations must take into account the edge conditions and casting and erection tolerances. When a beam or a slab is supported immediately over a construction joint in the wall, only the area of the precast wall units should be taken into account in the calculations; the area of the grout or concrete infill should be neglected.

When prefabricated panels of spans greater than 6.0 m are used in the roof of the top storey, care must be taken to prevent the cracking of the joints with the external faces of the wall (Fig. 6.2.9), which is caused by the deflection of the panel.

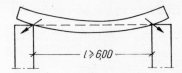

Fig. 6.2.9. Deflection of a large-span freely supported prefabricate

Floor panels should be laid on their supports in a cement mortar bedding of at least Mk. 50. The thickness of the mortar bed should not generally be more than 2.0 cm. A thicker bed is only allowed when the bearing stresses do not exceed the permissible stresses of the mortar used.

Bedding thicker than 2.0 cm may also be strengthened by the provision of reinforcement in the form of mesh or a flat helix of 4.5 mm dia. wire.

6.2.3. Structural Floor Thickness

The overall thickness of a structural floor panel must be sufficient to restrict its deflection under prolonged loading to a specified maximum value (section 6.3.5).

The following are general guide rules giving the minimum thicknesses of various panels.

Panels reinforced in one direction, simply supported:
— Roof panels — 3.5 cm or 1/35 of the span
— Other panels — 5.0 cm or 1/35 of the span.

Panels reinforced in one direction, fixed or continuous:
— Roof panels — 3.0 cm or 1/40 of the span
— Other panels — 4.5 cm or 1/40 of the span.
Cross-reinforced panels, simply supported:
— Roof panels — 3.0 cm or 1/45 of the span
— Other panels — 4.5 cm or 1/45 of the span.
Cross-reinforced panels, fixed or continuous:
— Roof panels — 2.5 cm or 1/50 of the span
— Other panels — 3.0 cm or 1/50 of the span.
Investigation of the deflection is essential when designing
— new types of construction;
— known constructions but using steel with a higher yield point than in the original solution.

In tray panels, the thickness of the very thin plate connecting the ribs should be sufficient to prevent its perforation by a concentrated load (e.g. heavy furniture or overroof supports).

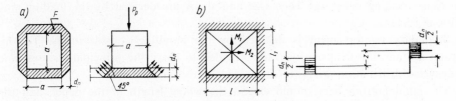

Fig. 6.2.10. Distribution of stresses in a thin plate due to concentrated loading:
(a) punching shear, (b) bending

The resistance of thin concrete plates to concentrated loads was investigated by R. N. Maceliński. The characteristics of the failure of test plates suggest that failure may occur through punching or as a result of local bending. Maceliński therefore proposes that the value of the critical load should be taken as the lower value obtained from the following formulae (Fig. 6.2.10):

$$P_p = 0.55 \, R_t(4 \, a \cdot d_n + 2 \, d_n^2) \qquad\qquad [6.2.1]$$

$$P_b = 0.42 \, d_n^2 \cdot R_b \qquad\qquad [6.2.2]$$

where P_p is the critical load, failure by punching shear, P_b the critical load, failure through local bending, R_t and R_b the tensile and bending strengths of the concrete, a the side of the cross-section of the metal cube through which the load is applied, and d_n is the thickness of the concrete plate.

The coefficients in formula [6.2.1] and [6.2.2] were obtained for rectangular plates the length of whose sides were in a ratio not greater than 1.5. The values of the critical loads are not dependent on the span of the plate.

231

6.2.4. Reinforcement in Floor Panels

The reinforcement in prefabricated components can be subdivided into main and secondary reinforcement (Fig. 6.2.11).

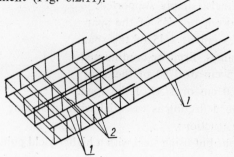

Fig. 6.2.11. Reinforcement in floor prefabricates:
(1) main reinforcement, (2) subsidiary reinforcement

Main reinforcement consists of bars in either the top or bottom face, designed to resist bending moments. Their size and shape are decided by the loading conditions in Stage C.

Secondary reinforcement is dictated by the handling considerations. To this group are added stirrups, which are provided to carry the principal stresses, and transverse distribution wires, often welded to the main bars.

The main bottom bars should extend the whole length of the panel, and the difference between this and the length of the bars should be no more than the cutting or bending tolerance. Greater end cover may lead to a shear failure of the panel at the support (Fig. 6.2.12). This danger is greatest in simply supported panels.

Some of the main reinforcements supporting the lower end of a unit may be terminated short of the support as implied by the bending moment diagram (Fig. 6.2.13); at least 4 bars per width of the panel, however, or 1/3 of their total number, must be taken as far as the support.

For units subject to a uniformly distributed loading, the distance of the cut-off point from the support may be obtained from the following formula:

$$x = \frac{l}{2}\left(\frac{1 - \sqrt{1 - a.}}{2}\right) - l_b. \tag{6.2.3}$$

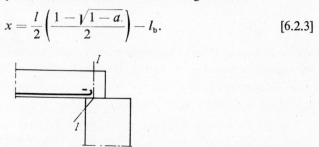

Fig. 6.2.12. Floor panel being sheared at the support due to the insufficient length of reinforcement

232

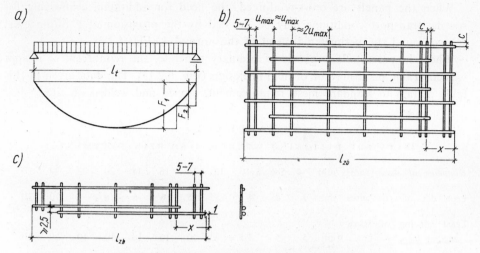

Fig. 6.2.13. The points of cut-off of some reinforcing bars:
(a) bending moment and reinforcing capacity diagram, (b) slab reinforcement, (c) rib reinforcement

For semi-fixed panels

$$x = \frac{l}{2}\left(\frac{1}{12} + \frac{1 - \sqrt{1 - a}}{2}\right) - l_b \qquad [6.2.4]$$

where $a = \dfrac{F_1}{F_2}$ = ratio of the total cross-sectional area of reinforcement at the support to that at mid-span, $l_b \geqslant 25d$ is the bond length of bars of diameter d.

Floor panels, designed as simply supported, but not completely free to rotate, should be given negative reinforcement at the support for a distance equal to approx. 1/7 of the span.

Precast components transported by lorries with insufficient platform lengths, should be provided with additional top reinforcement against the stresses induced during transportation. The amount of reinforcement necessary can be calculated from the bending moment according to:

$$M = \frac{1}{2} \cdot 1.5\, g \cdot l_w^2 \qquad [6.2.5]$$

where g is the weight of the unit per unit length, l_w is the length of the overhang (Fig. 6.2.14).

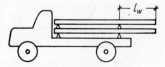

Fig. 6.2.14. Length of the overhang of a panel in transport

233

When the panels are cross-reinforced, the need for additional reinforcing for specific transport conditions may be avoided by the provision of 8 lifting eyes, spaced round the perimeter, instead of the normal 4 (Fig. 6.1.3).

When, in precast floor panels of ordinary concrete, the reinforcement is spot welded, Table 6.2.2 may be of help in design (Fig. 6.2.15). The data given in this table pertain to standard mesh reinforcement, lapped and welded on site.

TABLE 6.2.2.

DATA FOR DESIGNING WELDED MESH REINFORCEMENT

Diameter of main wires	mm	3–4	5–6	8–10	12	14	16	18	20	22	24	26
Least dia. of cross-wires	mm	3	4	4	5	5	6	6	8	8	10	10
Least spacing of wires $v_{min} = u_{min}$	cm	5	5	7.5	7.5	10	10	10	10	10	10	10
Maximum spacing of cross-wires u_{max}	cm	20	20	30	30	30	30	30	40	40	40	40
Maximum spacing of main wires v_{max}	cm	15	15	20	20	20	20	20	30	30	30	30
Projection of the wires beyond the last perpendicular wire												
c_{min}	cm	1.0	1.0	1.5	1.5	2.0	2.0	2.0	2.5	2.5	3.0	3.0
c_{max}	cm	2.5	2.5	3.0	3.0	4.0	4.0	4.0	4.0	5.0	5.0	5.0

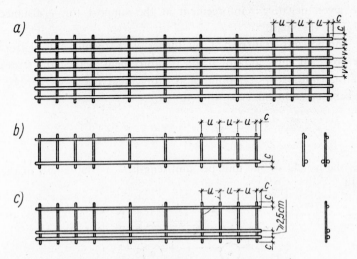

Fig. 6.2.15. Welded reinforcement in floor panels:
(a) slab reinforcement, (b), (c) rib reinforcement

In floor panels the value u_{max} governs the spacing of the three distribution wires nearest to the support (Fig. 6.2.15). Other cross wires are of little value as anchorage and may be spaced further apart, say 1 1/2–2 u_{max}.

6.2.5. Problems peculiar to Lightweight Concrete Panels

Compared with panels made of ordinary concrete, those of lightweight concrete are more easily deformed, more prone to corrosion of the reinforcement, and have much smaller total steel-to-concrete bond surface area.

The above disadvantages diminish with increasing strength and compactness of the concrete. Components designed in concrete stronger than 170 kg/cm², which is as a rule dense, may be treated as ordinary concrete components.

Concrete made with light aggregates, when used in homogeneous panels, should not be weaker than:

$$\text{for solid slabs} \qquad R_{\phi16} \geqslant 90 \text{ kg/cm}^2$$
$$\text{for hollow or ribbed slabs} \quad R_{\phi16} \geqslant 140 \text{ kg/cm}^2.$$

It is the author's opinion, that in the production of reinforced panels of light aggregate concrete, a dense structure is imperative. Concretes of semi-open and cellular structure are only applicable if the reinforcement is located in a special layer of dense mortar.

Light concretes of strengths lower than those shown above may be used in sandwich constructions, subject to their sufficient stability under given external conditions.

Cellular concretes used for reinforced panels must have a minimum air-dry strength $R_{\square10} = 35$ kg/cm² (10 cm test cubes).

As a rule, light concretes are reinforced with steel of low yield point, $Q_r = 2500$ kg/cm². The use of steels of higher yield point is not advisable, as the design would have to take into account the low bond stresses obtainable and the deflection criteria.

The German standard DIN 4223 allows the use of a steel with $Q_r = 4500$ kg/cm² in precast units made of steam-cured aerated concrete. At the same time, however, the value of the safety factor required is increased by 50% compared with its value for a steel with $Q_r = 2500$ kg/cm².

In panels of dense, light concrete, and in sandwich slabs with the reinforcement encased in ordinary concrete, the shape and layout of the reinforcement may be identical to that used in ordinary concrete. Thus, loose hooked bars may be used.

It is advisable, however, for the internal radius of curvature of hooks resting on bars thicker than $d = 8$ mm to be 2.5 d. With wire thickness $d < 8$ mm, the curvature of the hook may be only 1.25 d, as in ordinary concrete.

The anchorage of bars with diameter $d > 12$ mm should be strengthened by the provision of a transverse rod in the hook, the diameter of this bar being not smaller than that of the main bar. This is especially important in concretes with $R_{\phi 16} <$ < 120 kg/cm².

When the main reinforcement is thicker than 16 mm, all transverse wires should be spot welded to the main bars.

When working with cellular concrete, all transverse reinforcement should be welded to the main bars.

According to the instructions of the Swedish firm "Siporex", dealing with gas concretes Mk. 05 and 07, the diameter of the transverse anchor bars in floor panels should be equal to that of the main bars, and in any case should not be less than 7 mm. Vertical reinforcement, corresponding to the stirrups in beams, and also the top bars parallel to the main bars, should not be less than 5.5 mm in diameter. The spacing of anchor bars welded on near the support should be 20 cm, the first bar being as near to the end of the panel as possible. In panels up to 4.5 m long two anchor bars are provided, while in longer units, three are required. Other distribution bars, nearer to the centre of the panel, are less important structurally, but their diameter should not be less than 5.5 mm.

The German standard DIN 4223 specifies that the diameter of transverse reinforcement must not be less than 0.7 d and not more than 1.5 d, d being the diameter of the main bars.

The force Z, in main bars of diameter d is, in the limiting state, given as:

$$Z = 0.785 \, d^2 \cdot Q_r. \qquad [6.2.6]$$

This is to be transferred to the concrete through n bars of diameter d_1. The value of the anchorage is given in DIN 4223 as:

$$Z_a = s \times 50 \sqrt{n \cdot d_1 \cdot R_{\phi 10}} \qquad [6.2.7]$$

where s is the safety factor against failure of the steel at the yield point, $n \leqslant 6$, the number of anchor bars taken into account.

The lesser of the two forces obtained should be taken in calculations.

The size and spacing of anchoring bars should be so chosen that at least half of the ultimate tensile force is transferred to the concrete within a strip at one end, equal in width to four thicknesses of the panel.

The first transverse bar must not be further than 4 cm from the end of the panel, while the main reinforcement should stop 1.5 cm short of the end. Further crossbars should be spaced according to the shear force diagram, but in any case not more than 50 cm apart.

The Soviet code of practice dealing with the design of reinforced structures made in autoclaved cellular concretes gives the anchorage value of the welded crossbars as:

$$Z_a = 5n \cdot d_1 \cdot R_s \sqrt[3]{\frac{E_s}{E_c}} + R_\tau \cdot a_r \cdot u \qquad [6.2.8]$$

where n and d_1 are the number and diameter of cross-bars, R_s the $0.57\,R_{\square 10}$; E_s and E_c are the elasticity moduli of the steel and concrete used, R_τ is the bond stress: for plain bars, $R_\tau = 0.16\,R_{\square 10}$, for deformed bars, $R_\tau = 0.24\,R_{\square 10}$, u is the perimeter of the main bar.

All anchor bars must be located within a length a_r (Fig. 6.2.16), where the bending moment is smaller than the value M_r causing cracking in the tension zone (section 6.3.5.3).

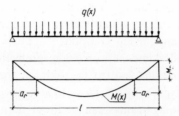

Fig. 6.2.16. The length a_r within which the lateral anchor bars must not be positioned: $M_{(x)}$ — bending moment, M_r — moment causing the formation of cracks

Main reinforcement should not be spaced closer than 5 cm apart. Not less than four anchor bars must be provided, at the same minimum spacing. At least the two outermost bars should overhang the support and the innermost bar must be 5 cm or more from the end of the strip a_r (Fig. 6.2.17).

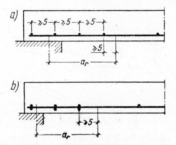

Fig. 6.2.17. Constructional conditions of the location of anchor bars: (a) lateral bars on one side of the main bars, (b) lateral bars on each side of the main reinforcement

The recommendation that stress should be transferred to the concrete within a non-cracking zone a_r, as described above is, in the author's view, extremely sound. However, the numerical value of the anchorage Z_a would seem to be more correctly obtained from formula [6.2.7] (Z_a should be proportional to $\sqrt{n}$ and not to n, as assumed in Eq. [6.2.8], and the contribution of the bond in cellular concrete is questionable, especially when the live loads on the panel are appreciable).

Reinforcement in lightweight concretes is protected from corrosion:
— in close-textured concretes, by ensuring a sufficient density of the material;
— in cellular concretes, by a protective coating.

It is pointless to increase the thickness of the protective covering layer beyond 2.5 cm.

Concrete of the required density is obtained, in addition to careful compacting, by a correct proportion of cement or by the addition of plasticising powders to the mix. In either case, proper grading of the aggregates is a basic essential.

The technical literature gives several examples of the good state of preservation of cement-weak close-textured light concretes. For example, M. I. Simonov mentions that in a number of buildings in Tiflis, floor slabs were cast in tough concrete using only 100 kg of cement per cubic metre. After twenty years, traces of rust were found only on the unrendered components. The application of a render to the prefabricates provided complete corrosion protection to the reinforcement.

This and similar observations lead to the opinion that due to the hygroscopic character of the smallest particles of most light aggregates, the cement content of concretes made of these aggregates can be lower than in the ordinary concrete.

It must be pointed out, however, that in graded aggregates the smallest particles are generally mixed with clay and other deleterious substances. Thus, unless special clean powdery additives are mixed with the matrix, the author considers that the cement content in light concrete reinforced components should not be lower than in ordinary concrete.

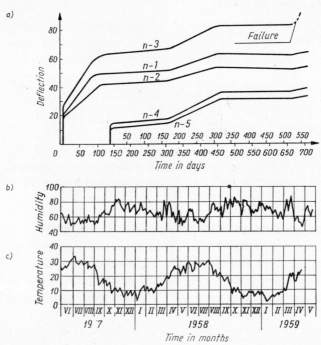

Fig. 6.2.18. Effect of atmospheric moisture on the deflection of floor slabs made of tough concrete: (a) increase in deflection with time, (b) relative humidity of air, (c) temperature

The method of compacting plays a vital role in the protection of reinforcing steel. It was found during the investigations by M. I. Simonov mentioned above, that corrosion was always more severe in hand-compacted than in mechanically vibrated samples.

The reinforcement in cellular concrete slabs may be encased in cement mortar, or it may be given a protective coating, usually bitumen or casein-based (Fig. 6.1.22).

Lightweight concretes are characterised by particularly large deformations. With time, these deformations increase under constant loading, but the humidity of the environment may accelerate them.

A typical example of the influence of atmospheric moisture on the deflection of a floor slab made of tough concrete is represented in Fig. 6.2.18.

The tests were made on panels 6.0 m × 0.50 m × 24 cm, with two ducts of 16 cm dia. The strength of the concrete was $R_{\square 20} = 60$ to 70 kg/cm². The loading, including the weight of the component itself, was 600 kg/m².

The chart shows that the relative humidity during the summer months was somewhat lower than in winter, but, allowing for the higher temperature, the absolute summer humidity was about 50 % higher than in winter.

The increased amount of water in the air always accelerates deflection.

The progressive increase in deflection may be lessened by providing a dense top layer of ordinary concrete (three-layer slabs, Fig. 6.1.27), or by secondary reinforcement in the compression zone.

Reinforcement of the compression zone is particularly necessary in autoclaved cellular concrete slabs. Not only does it decrease deflection under prolonged loading, but it also counteracts the shrinking deformations which occur during the curing of such slabs.

The Swedish firm Siporex provides, in its slabs, compression reinforcement equal to 20 % of the tension reinforcement, whilst in some German and Danish products this ratio reaches 50 % and more.

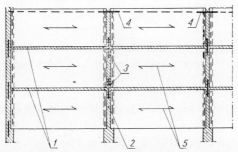

Fig. 6.2.19. Transformation of individual floor components into a rigid plate working together with the stiffening walls:
(1) side joints, (2) end joint over the support (panels joined in the direction of their main reinforcement), (3) connection of panels over the support in the direction perpendicular to their main reinforcement (r.c. ring beam), (4) perimeter joint (r.c. ring beam), (5) direction of the main reinforcement

6.2.6. Joints in Floor Panels

6.2.6.1. *General description.* Seperate floor components must be assembled to form a rigid platform, working efficiently together with the supporting walls. To this end one should (Fig. 6.2.19):

— join the panels along their side edges (parallel to the direction of the span);
— join the end faces of the panels over the support;
— effect proper anchorage of the whole floor to the supports in the direction perpendicular to the span;
— complete all peripheral jointing.

When self-supporting partitions are relied upon to assist in the stiffening of the building, it should be ensured that all horizontal forces are adequately transferred to these partitions.

The floor joints should be effected in such a manner as to prevent transmission of airborne noises and smells.

6.2.6.2. *Side joints between panels.* Two panels can be regarded as properly connected if the gap at the joint is completely filled with mortar and if the mortar is given a chance to dry out and harden. The shape of the joint (e.g. joggle) is of secondary importance and will not compensate for an incomplete penetration of mortar.

Cement mortar for longitudinal joints must not be weaker than Mk. 30.

The width of the filled part of the joint should be at least 3 cm, according to German and Soviet specifications (Fig. 6.2.20).

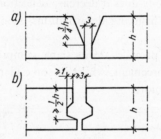

Fig. 6.2.20. Width of the structural part of the side joint, according to German and Soviet standards: (a) for smooth joint faces, (b) for joggled joints

The depth of the joint should be:
— in smooth-faced joints (Fig. 6.2.20a), not less than 3/4 of the thickness of the floor;
— in joggled or grooved joints (Fig. 6.2.20b), not less than 1/2 the thickness of the floor.

Polish regulations make grooved joints obligatory only when the live loads on the floor exceed 225 kg/m², including the weight of partitions.

The recommended joint width of 3 cm does not always ensure proper hardening of the mortar, and in the author's opinion, should be at least 5 cm. With a wider

240

joint and careful work, slabs could be effectively connected by a joint of structural depth equal to only one half the thickness of the slab.

A comparison of the distribution of loading, transversely through an in-situ hollow slab and a series of similar precast planks, is shown in Fig. 6.2.21.

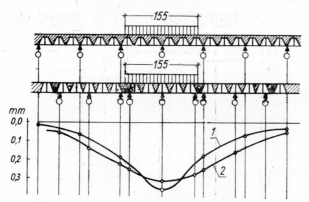

Fig. 6.2.21. Comparison of the deflection measurements carried out on an in-situ hollow floor and a similar floor made from prefabricated slabs:
(1) deflections of the in-situ floor, (2) deflections of the precast slab floor

The total thickness of the in-situ floor was 22 cm, including a 4 cm thick topping; there was no topping in the precast slabs and their thickness was 20 cm. The measured deflections of the precast slabs were reduced by a factor of 0.73 to make the comparison easier.

The results show that when one slab only was loaded, the neighbouring slabs deflected very similarily to the corresponding part of an in-situ floor of comparable construction; this offers good evidence of the load-spreading capability of the side joints.

Another example of load distribution is shown in Fig. 6.2.22. The mid-span deflections in a properly anchored slab of a hollow concrete floor were less than a third of the deflection of a single slab.

Many similar test results are given in Soviet technical literature.

A very strong side lap is obtained by welding projecting transverse reinforcements together (Fig. 6.2.23). This type of joint is not necessary under normal conditions but may be advisable in areas where there is a possibility of mining subsidence or earth tremors.

The joints are normally filled in after the floor slabs are laid, and access to the jointed floor should then be restricted for three days.

To speed up the hardening of the mortar, calcium chloride may be added, up to 4 % of the weight of cement.

6.2.6.3. *Support connections.* In order to achieve good three-dimensional stiffness of the building and to obtain uniform support of the loads, rigid joints are recom-

241

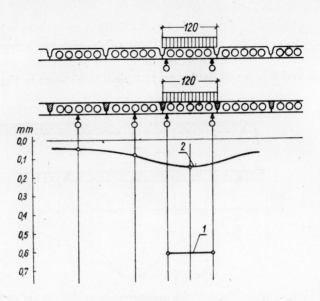

Fig. 6.2.22. Results of deflection observations on two cored slab floors:
(1) slab deflection with side joints not filled, (2) slab deflection after the side joints were filled with concrete

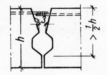

Fig. 6.2.23. An example of a very strong side joint between floor slabs

mended at the supports. This may be effected by anchoring the projecting panel reinforcement in a ring beam (Fig. 6.2.24a), or by the direct union of adjacent slabs (Fig. 6.2.24b, c).

The projecting length of reinforcing bars should be:

$$l_z = 0.25 \, d \, \frac{Q_r}{R_r + \sigma}$$
[6.2.9]

where d is the bar diameter, Q_r the yield point of the steel, R_r the tensile strength of the concrete, and σ the compression stress in the ring beam due to loads from the upper floors.

When adjacent panels are bolted or otherwise directly connected over the support, the width of the gap between them should be at least 3 cm. The strength of the mortar used to fill the joint and the thoroughness of the work contribute just as much to the final strength of the joint as does the welding of the lapping reinforcement.

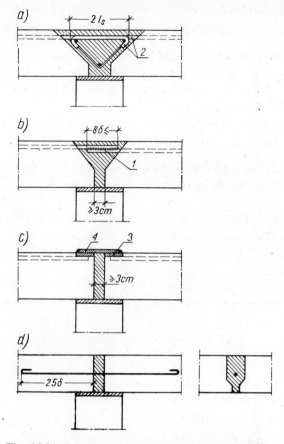

Fig. 6.2.24. Joints between floor slabs at the supports:
(a), (b), (c) rigid joints, (d) hinged joint
(1) reinforcing bars welded together, (2) slab reinforcement anchored in the ring beam, (3) flat
welded to the slab reinforcement, (4) linking flat

Should a hinged joint at the support be considered sufficient or advisable, it may be achieved by embedding anchor bars in the longitudinal joints (Fig. 6.2.24d). These bars should extend at least 25 diameters into the longitudinal joints, and their minimum c/s area should be 1 cm² per metre of the transverse joint.

The resistance to lateral movement between the panels meeting over the support is achieved by casting a reinforced concrete ring beam between them, or by means of welded cleats.

The cross-sectional area of the ring beam is dependent on the magnitude of the tangential forces at the junctions of wall components (section 7.6).

The longitudinal reinforcement in the ring beam (F_{zw}) should not be less than:

$$F_{zw} \geqslant 3 \text{ bars } (10 \text{ mm dia.}) \qquad [6.2.10]$$

$$F_{zw} \geqslant 0.006 \ P \ (\text{cm}^2) \qquad [6.2.11]$$

243

where P is the vertical load in tonnes per metre length of the wall

$$F_{zw} \geqslant 0.005\ F_w \qquad\qquad [6.2.12]$$

where F_w is the cross-sectional area of the belt beam.

The reinforcing bars must be given normal tension laps, but these should not coincide with the joints in the wall or floor units. 4.5 mm dia. stirrups must be provided at a maximum spacing of 50 cm.

When the floor panels are jointed by welding, the cross-sectional area of the splice plates or cleats must not be less than 1.5 cm².

6.2.6.4. *Peripheral joints.* The methods of connecting the whole floor area to the external walls and beams are in essence similar to those described in the preceding section.

The incidence of cracking in a ring beam bounding the floor seriously affects the floor stiffness. For that reason, when the spacing of the loadbearing cross-walls is greater than the width of the building, concrete Mk. 140 or better must be used for the ring beams.

6.3. Structural Calculations for Floor Slabs

6.3.1. Scope of the Calculations

Large prefabricated floor slabs may be treated on the same general lines as in-situ reinforced concrete floors. The aim is to determine the safety-factor s of the load-carrying capacity of the floor in Stage C. In some cases it may be necessary to check the safety factor of the slab under the loading conditions existing during Stages A and B.

In section 6.2.3 instances are given when it is also imperative to check the floor deflections under prolonged loading.

6.3.2. Effective Span of the Slab

The effective span of the panel, l_t, to be taken in the calculations is:
— for simply supported slabs, the distance between the midpoints of seating;
— for slabs fixed at the support, the theoretical point of support should be taken inside the wall at a distance equal to 2.5 % of the clear span. Should the value of l_t thus obtained be greater than the distance between the centres of supports, then the latter is taken as the effective span;
— for slabs continuous over the support, the theoretical point of support coincides with the centre of the wall.

6.3.3. Determination of Bending Moments

The bending moments to be considered as existing in Stage C are:

— *simply supported slabs*

in the span $\qquad M = M_{wg} + M_{wp}$ [6.3.1]

at the support $\qquad M = 1/3\ M_{wp}$ [6.3.2]

— *slabs partly fixed at one end*

in the span $\qquad M = M_{wg} + 4/5\ M_{wp}$ [6.3.3]

at the partly
fixed support $\qquad M = 3/4\ M_{zp}$ [6.3.4]

— *slabs partly fixed at both ends*

in the span $\qquad M = M_{wg} + 2/3\ M_{wp}$ [6.3.5]

at the supports $\qquad M = 3/4\ M_{zp}$ [6.3.6]

where M_{wg} and M_{wp} are the normal, simply supported bending moments caused by the weight of the slab itself and the applied loading respectively, M_{zp} is the theoretical fixed end moment for a span fully fixed at both ends and due to all loads other than the weight of the slab itself.

Provided the side joints between the slabs have been properly filled, the whole floor acts, practically speaking, as a monolithic structure (section 5.1.2). When only one slab is loaded, however, the adjacent slabs carry part of the load.

It is still debatable as to what extent this cooperation may be relied upon. In the author's opinion, with slabs 1.8 m wide and the side joints completely filled, it may be safely assumed that the loaded slab will carry 50 % and the adjacent panels 25 % each of the concentrated load, as shown in Fig. 6.3.1a (e.g. partition parallel to the span of the slabs). When the concentrated load occurs at the joint between two slabs, it may be assumed that they share the load equally (Fig. 6.3.1b).

The foregoing assumptions have been justified by research. Identical recommendations may be found in Soviet literature. Z.W. Kaplunov has found that when two slabs carry loads differing in their intensity by 400–450 kg/m², the shear stresses in the joint between them are of the order of 0.25–0.50 kg/cm².

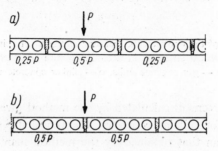

Fig. 6.3.1. Distribution of the concentrated load between neighbouring slabs:
(a) concentrated load at mid-width of slab, (b) load near the joint between the slabs

The whole problem of the cooperation of large jointed floor slabs under concentrated loads was investigated analytically by A. S. Kalmanok, who assumed the longitudinal joints to act as hinges. His conclusion was that the linear load due to a partition parallel to the span of the slabs may be considered to be uniformly distributed over a width of the floor equal to the span.

To guard against mistakes during erection, slabs should be reinforced symmetrically. Thus, when a slab is designed to be partly fixed at one end, it should be reinforced at *both* ends against the moment found from formula [6.3.4].

6.3.4. Reinforcement of Lightweight Concrete Slabs

The required cross-section of the reinforcement in lightweight concrete slabs is determined by the same methods as apply for ordinary concrete, the distribution of stresses in the compression zone being taken as rectangular. Experiments carried out in Poland and in the U.S.S.R. show that, provided the bond between the steel and concrete remains unbroken, this assumption gives a correct value of the load-carrying capacity of the component (Fig. 6.3.2).

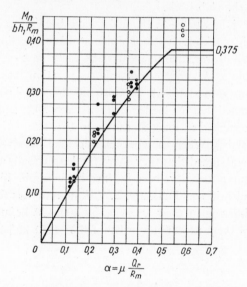

Fig. 6.3.2. Comparison of the experimental bending strengths of reinforced light concrete components with their theoretical strengths in accordance with the theory of plastic deformation: ● — gas concrete units, o — clinker concrete units

The area of reinforcement calculated by the method given in the German specification DIN 4223 for cellular concretes (parabolic stress distribution), is some 7 to 10 % higher than that obtained by the method mentioned above. However, when the safety factors called for by the Polish standard PN-56/B-03260 are compared with those of DIN 4223, the actual amounts of reinforcement are found to be equal.

246

The assumption of a triangular distribution of stresses, still used in some countries, results in somewhat heavier reinforcement, especially in components with a low percentage of steel. Where this value μ reaches 1.0%, the calculated value is the same for the rectangular and the triangular stress distribution methods.

The minimum area of reinforcement μ_{min} for lightweight concrete components is obtained (as for ordinary concrete) from the condition that a non-reinforced concrete section should possess strength equal to that of the same section reinforced, after cracks have appeared. As the safety factor required for the non-reinforced section is double that required for the reinforced section, we obtain, for concrete with $R_r/R_m = 0.10$, $\mu_{min} = 0.02\ R_m/Q_r$.

The question of the maximum permissible reinforcement μ_{max} in lightweight concretes is only of theoretical interest. Investigations have shown that formulae defining the value of μ_{max} for ordinary concrete, also apply to lightweight concretes.

The phenomenon of cracks appearing in the tension zone exerts some influence on the function of slabs made of open-textured light concretes, and is of the utmost importance in foam and gas concretes. Since the mechanism by which steel cooperates with these concretes is not yet fully understood, it is necessary to restrict the possibility of crack formation in the components of which they are the basis.

The effect of cracking on the functioning of the slab may be neglected in:

— roof panels   when $\mu < 0.10\ R_m/Q_r$,

— floor slabs   when $\mu < 0.08\ R_m/Q_r$

(live loads form the larger part of the total load).

Where compression reinforcement has been selected (not less than 25% of tensile steel), or in three-layer sandwich slabs (uppermost layer made of dense concrete of at least Mk. 140), the upper limit of the tensile reinforcement is of lesser importance. It is nevertheless advisable to observe the following limits:

— roof panels $\mu < 0.20\ R_m/Q_r$,

— floor slabs $\mu < 0.15\ R_m/Q_r$.

6.3.5. Deflection of Floor Slabs

6.3.5.1. *Maximum permissible values of deflections.* Polish standards do not specify maximum values of deflections, but only the minimum thickness of a floor (section 6.2.3); hence, Soviet standards, which limit the deflections in reinforced concrete components subject to prolonged loading to the following values, are often used:

Floors with flat soffit:

$$\text{when } l \leqslant 7\,\text{m} \quad f \leqslant \frac{l}{200}; \quad \text{when} \quad l > 7\,\text{m} \quad f \leqslant \frac{l}{300};$$

247

Floors with exposed ribs:

$$\text{when } l \leqslant 5 \text{ m} \quad f \leqslant \frac{l}{200}; \quad \text{when} \quad 5 \text{ m} < l \leqslant 7 \text{ m} \quad f \leqslant \frac{l}{300};$$

$$\text{when } l > 7 \text{ m} \quad f \leqslant \frac{l}{400}.$$

Maximum deflection calculated for the applied loads only should not be more than 1/350 of the span.

The introduction of a camber in the manufacture of a slab increases the permissible deflection by the value of the camber. It is advisable to make the camber equal to the calculated deflection under the dead load alone. It must be kept in mind, however, that the provision of a camber is equivalent to allowing the cracks in the tensile zone of the concrete to open wider.

The maximum permissible values of deflection in reinforced concrete floor slabs are thus comparable to those specified for steel or timber constructions.

6.3.5.2. *General principles of deflection calculations.* Values of maximum deflections are obtained by means of the general statics formulae, replacing the value of the flexural rigidity *EJ* by a suitable value *B* based on the size and shape of the cross-section.

Soviet standards state that, in a reinforced concrete component, the rigidity is constant between two points of contraflexure, and is equal to the rigidity at the point of the maximum bending moment in this part of the component.

In calculating the deflection of floor slabs, both simply supported and partly anchored, the problem may be simplified by assuming *B* to be constant over the entire span.

When the load is uniformly distributed:
— for simply supported slabs

$$f = \frac{5}{384} \times \frac{(g + p) l^4}{B} \tag{6.3.7}$$

— for slabs partly fixed at one end

$$f = \frac{1}{B} \times \left(\frac{5}{384} g + \frac{1}{110} p \right) \times l^4 \tag{6.3.8}$$

— for slabs partly fixed at both ends

$$f = \frac{1}{B} \times \left(\frac{5}{384} g + \frac{1}{155} p \right) \times l^4 \tag{6.3.9}$$

where *g* is the weight of the slab alone per unit area, *p* the load per unit area of the slab additional to its own weight.

248

Of the various methods of determining the stiffness of reinforced concrete components, those discussed here are the rules given in a Soviet standard, SNiP II-W 1-62, and the method of I. I. Ulicki.

The method of SNiP II-W 1-62, which has also been adopted in Poland, is based on the assumptions of W. I. Murashov, and assumes a rectangular distribution of the compression stresses.

I. I. Ulicki adopts the triangular stress diagram, as do Leonhardt and Yu and Winter. The triangular stress distribution seems to be more justified in stiffness considerations than the rectangular one (which is still fully adequate in strength calculations), and the author feels that future research into deflections will follow this line.

Table 6.3.1 gives an interesting comparison of the beam deflections calculated by various methods. The calculations were repeated over a wide range of beam strengths, varying both the concrete mix and the percentage of reinforcement.

6.3.5.3. *Deflection calculations in accordance with SNiP II-W 1-62.*

(a) *Deflection of an uncracked component* (*Phase I*)

The stiffness of an unweakened component (Phase I) is taken as:

$$B_k^I = 0.85 \ E_b \cdot J_i \qquad [6.3.10]$$

where E_b is the elasticity modulus under compression of the concrete, J_i the moment of the cross-section, taking into account the concrete used, and both the tension and the compression reinforcement.

Inclusion of the contribution of the reinforcement in the value of J_i is especially important when dealing with lightweight concretes.

The deflection f^I (under prolonged loading) of an uncracked r.c. unit is given by:

$$f^I = f_{k(k)}^I + f_{k(d)}^I \cdot C \qquad [6.3.11]$$

where $f_{k(k)}^I$ is the deflection due to transient loading, $f_{k(d)}^I$ the initial (short-lived) deflection due to prolonged loading, and C a coefficient allowing for the effect of creep.

The values $f_{k(k)}^I$ and $f_{k(d)}^I$ are calculated using the stiffness B_k^I from formula [6.3.10].

If the o/a depth of the panel is greater than $1/7$ of the span, the effect of lateral stresses should be allowed for by reducing the calculated value of B_k^I by 10 %.

Coefficient C is varied according to the humidity of the environment:

— in very dry surroundings $\qquad C = 3.0,$

— in normal conditions $\qquad C = 2.0,$

— in very humid conditions $\qquad C = 1.5.$

For prestressed components the formula for the deflection f^I is altered to:

$$f^I = f_{k(k)}^I + \left(f_{k(d)}^I - f_{k(s)}^I \right) \cdot C \qquad [6.3.12]$$

where $f_{k(s)}^I$ is the initial deflection due to prestress.

Loading diagram

Beam cross-section							
C/s area of reinforcement (cm²)			1.57 (2Ø10)			2.36 (3Ø10)		
Concrete strength (kg/cm²)			250	200	140	250	200	140
Variable point loads P (kg)			136	133	121	235	226	225
Deflection (cm)	According to SNiP II-W 1-62	f_k f_d	0.73 1.48	0.81 1.58	0.90 1.74	0.98 1.88	1.01 1.96	1.13 2.20
	By Ulicki's method	f_0 f_∞	0.68 1.52	0.75 1.55	0.83 1.67	0.92 1.82	0.95 1.85	1.07 2.09
	By Leonhardt's method	f_0 f_∞	0.84 1.39	0.85 1.43	0.86 1.48	0.90 1.61	0.92 1.62	0.97 1.81
	According to Yu and Winter	f_0 f_∞	0.55 1.70	0.84 1.79	0.78 1.97	0.77 2.46	0.84 2.51	1.03 2.74

The value $f_{k(s)}^{I}$ is obtained after due allowance is made for all prestress losses. As $f_{k(s)}^{I}$ greatly influences the final result, the author considers that it should be further decreased by some 20% to safeguard against unavoidable errors and inaccuracies in production.

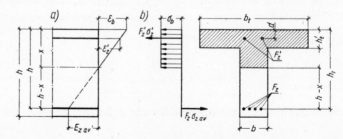

Fig. 6.3.3. Reinforced concrete cross-section after tensile cracks have appeared: (a) strain diagram, (b) stress diagram

DEFLECTION OBTAINED BY SEVERAL METHODS OF APPROACH

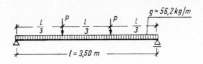

4.62 (3Ø14)			$F_z = F_z' = 1.57$ (4Ø10)			$F_z = F_z' = 2.36$ (6Ø10)			$F_z = F_z' = 4.62$ (6Ø14)		
250	200	140	250	200	140	250	200	140	250	200	140
485	465	455	144	142	140	250	248	246	525	523	521
1.30	1.31	1.44	0.71	0.79	0.91	0.97	0.98	1.01	1.12	1.15	1.20
2.64	2.76	3.24	1.24	1.43	1.59	1.66	1.70	1.75	1.99	2.07	2.24
1.15	1.20	1.28	0.73	0.80	0.94	1.00	1.05	1.14	1.33	1.36	1.50
2.46	2.57	2.80	1.40	1.45	1.57	1.66	1.69	1.78	2.05	2.12	2.34
1.07	1.08	1.16	0.87	0.88	0.91	0.93	0.94	0.95	1.02	1.07	1.12
2.24	2.26	2.62	1.17	1.19	1.21	1.26	1.27	1.29	1.51	1.54	1.69
1.10	1.18	1.42	0.56	0.64	0.80	0.78	0.84	0.94	1.04	1.10	1.46
4.27	4.30	4.56	1.08	1.14	1.23	1.34	1.36	1.38	1.60	1.64	1.70

(b) *Deflection in Phase II (Cracks developed)*

The stress and strain distribution in a cracked cross-section, in accordance with the assumptions in SNiP II-W 1-62, is shown in Fig. 6.3.3.

The elongation (strain) of the reinforcement $\varepsilon_{z\,av}$ is the average value between the elongation at the cracks, where the whole tensile force is taken by the reinforcement, and in the uncracked portions, where the concrete contributes to the tensile strength. W. I. Murashov gives the expression:

$$\varepsilon_{z\,av} = \psi_z \frac{\sigma_z}{E_z} \qquad [6.3.13]$$

where $\psi_z < 1$ is a coefficient allowing for the tensile stress in the concrete between cracks, σ_z the tensile stress in the reinforcement at the crack itself.

Similarly, SNiP II-W 1-62 introduces the notion of the average shortening of the concrete $\varepsilon_{b\,av}$, given by

$$\varepsilon_{b\,av} = \psi_b \frac{\sigma_b}{v \cdot E_b} \qquad [6.3.14]$$

251

where ψ_b is the ratio of the extreme fibre compression strain above the crack to that between the cracks, σ_b the extreme fibre compression stress in the concrete, and ν a coefficient expressing the ratio of the elastic compression strain in the extreme fibres, to the true strain, which allows for shrinking and creep in the concrete.

The compression stress σ_b immediately above the crack is

$$\sigma_b = \frac{M}{z \cdot F_b} \qquad [6.3.15]$$

where z is the lever arm, F_b the area of concrete under compression.

Substituting value σ_b from Eq. [6.3.15] into formula [6.3.14], we obtain:

$$\varepsilon_{b\,av} = \frac{\psi_b\,M}{\nu\,E_b \cdot z \cdot F_b} \qquad [6.3.16]$$

Similarly, the mean strain in the reinforcement can be expressed by

$$\varepsilon_{z\,av} = \frac{M}{z} \times \frac{\psi_z}{E_z \cdot F_z}. \qquad [6.3.17]$$

When, in addition to the bending moment M, the section considered is also acted upon by a compression force N perpendicular to the section, this force is assumed to act in the axis of the reinforcement under tension, and the moment M is increased by

$$\Delta M = N \cdot z_0 \qquad [6.3.18]$$

where z_0 is the eccentricity of the true axis of the load in relation to the reinforcement under tension.

From the above

$$\varepsilon_{b\,av} = \frac{(M + \Delta M) \cdot \psi_b}{z \cdot \nu \cdot E_b \cdot F_b} \qquad [6.3.19]$$

$$\varepsilon_{z\,av} = \left[\frac{(M + \Delta M)}{z} - N \right] \cdot \frac{\psi_z}{E_z \cdot F_z}. \qquad [6.3.20]$$

Knowing the values $\varepsilon_{z\,av}$ and $\varepsilon_{b\,av}$, the general relationship between the strains in the extreme fibres and the radius of curvature:

$$\frac{1}{\varrho} = \frac{\varepsilon_{z\,av} + \varepsilon_{b\,av}}{h_1} \qquad [6.3.21]$$

may by expressed:

$$\frac{1}{\varrho} = \frac{M + \Delta M}{z \cdot h_1} \left(\frac{\psi_z}{E_z \cdot F_z} + \frac{\psi_b}{\nu \cdot E_b \cdot F_b} \right) - N \frac{\psi_z}{E_z \cdot F_z \cdot h_1}. \qquad [6.3.22]$$

Formula [6.3.22] applies to both r.c. and prestressed members, whether the loading is transient or permanent.

In the absence of longitudinal forces, formula [6.3.22] is shortened to

$$\frac{1}{\varrho} = \frac{M}{B}$$

where

$$B = \frac{z \cdot h_1}{\dfrac{\psi_z}{E_z \cdot F_z} + \dfrac{\psi_b}{\nu \cdot E_b \cdot F_b}} \cdot \qquad [6.3.23]$$

The values z and F_b occurring in Eqs. [6.3.22] and [6.3.23] are, in SNiP II-W 1-62, expressed as a function of the ratio

$$\xi = \frac{x}{h_1},$$

where x is the depth of the compression area of the cross-section.

The value of ξ is found from the empirical formula

$$\xi = \frac{1}{1.8 + \dfrac{1 + 2.5\,G}{10\,\mu \cdot n}\,(1 + 5 \times L)} \pm \frac{1.5 + \gamma'}{11.5\,\dfrac{e_1}{h_1} \mp 5} \qquad [6.3.24]$$

in which the symbols represent:

$$\mu = \frac{F_z}{b \cdot h_1}, \qquad n = \frac{E_z}{E_b}$$

$$L = \frac{M}{b \cdot h_1^2 \cdot R_m},$$

$$G = \gamma'\left(1 - \frac{h_t'}{2\,h_1}\right),$$

$$\gamma' = \frac{(b_t' - b)\,h_t' + n' \cdot F_z'}{b \cdot h_1}$$

and where b_t' and h_t' are, respectively, the width and thickness of the compression flange of the T or I beam, F_z' is the area of the compression reinforcement, $n' = \dfrac{E_z}{\nu \cdot E_b}$, and e_1 is the longitudinal force (including the prestressing force), relative to the reinforcement under tension.

In formula [6.3.24] the first group of signs are applicable to eccentric compression and the second group to eccentric tension conditions.

The coefficient ξ calculated from Eq. [6.3.24] is valid for both transient and permanent loads.

The authors of SNiP II-W 1-62 stress that this assumption is not strictly true, but to date, research has not revealed a more correct solution.

The error resulting from accepting the same value of ξ for both types of load is to some extent reduced by the use of the coefficients ψ_z and ν.

For rectangular, T and I beams, the area of the compression zone F_b and the "lever arm" of the internal forces z is given by:

$$F_b = (\gamma' + \xi)\,b \cdot h_1 \qquad [6.3.25]$$

253

$$z = h_1 \left[1 - \frac{\dfrac{h_t'}{h_1} \gamma' + \xi^2}{2(\gamma' + \xi)} \right].$$ [6.3.26]

For rectangular members with compression reinforcement F_z', $2a'$ should be substituted for h_t' in [6.3.26], a' being the distance of the extreme compression fibres from the centre of the compression reinforcement.

The coefficient ψ_b, representing the ratio of the strain in the concrete just above a crack to that existing between the cracks, is taken in SNiP II-W 1-62 to be constant

$$\psi_b = 0.9.$$

Investigations have shown that in bent and eccentrically compressed r.c. units, in the strength range $R_{\square 20} = 330$ to 586 kg/cm², and with reinforcement percentages from 0.67 to 2.5 %, the value of the coefficient ψ_b varies with the load, remaining between the limits 0.8–1.0, irrespective of the duration of loading (Fig. 6.3.4). This justifies the assumption by SNiP II-W 1-62 of a constant value for ψ_b.

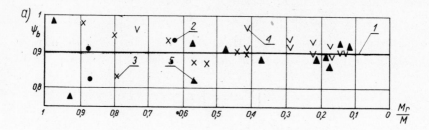

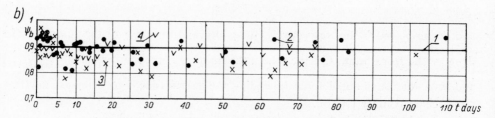

Fig. 6.3.4. Values of the coefficient ψ_b of reinforced concrete components in bending:
(a) under short-term loading, (b) under permanent loading
(1) value of ψ_b given in the Soviet standard SNiP II-W 1-62, (2), (3), (4) values of ψ_b obtained experimentally for $R_{\square 20} = 360$ kg/cm² and $\mu = 0.67$, 1.25 and 2.5% respectively, (5) values of ψ_b for $R_{\square 20} = 330$–586 kg/cm² and $\mu = 0.78\%$

The coefficient ψ_z, which takes into account the tensile resistance of the concrete between the cracks, is for non-prestressed components in bending:

$$\psi_z = 1.3 - s \cdot \frac{0.8 \ R_r \cdot W_r}{M}$$ [6.3.27]

for components under non-axial compression and for prestressed components:

$$\psi_z = 1.3 - s \cdot m - \frac{1-m}{6-4.5\,m} \qquad [6.3.28]$$

where s is a coefficient obtained experimentally, W_r a section modulus of the extreme tensile fibre, of the instant of cracking and allowing for the plastic properties of the concrete, $m = M_r/M$, M_r is the moment of internal forces, including the prestressing force, at the instant of cracking, calculated in relation to the resultant in the compression zone above the crack, and M is a similar moment, calculated for the conditions under which the deflection is being determined.

For both reinforced and prestressed concretes,

$$\psi_z \leqslant 1.$$

The section modules W_r is the first moment of the tensile area, neglecting the reinforcement, taken about the centre of gravity of the compression diagram, Fig. 6.3.5, and calculated from the expression:

$$W_r = \frac{2I_c}{h-x} + S_r \qquad [6.3.29]$$

where I_c is the moment of inertia of the compression area taken about the neutral axis, S_r the first moment of the tension area about the neutral axis, and $x = h/2$.

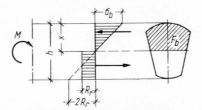

Fig. 6.3.5. Stress distribution in a cross-section of a bent concrete component at the instant of cracking

For a rectangular cross-section, the value of W_r calculated from [6.3.29] is

$$W_r = 0.292\ bh^2. \qquad [6.3.30]$$

For T and I sections the strength factors can be obtained from the formula:

$$W_r = \gamma_0 \cdot W_0 \qquad [6.3.31]$$

where γ_0 is a shape factor, dependent on the shape and dimensions of the section and tabulated in Table 6.3.2, and W_0 is the strength factor calculated from the geometry of the section.

The numerical value of the coefficient s occurring in formulae [6.3.27] and [6.3.28] depends on the type of reinforcement used and on the manner of loading. The following values are recommended:

SHAPE FACTORS γ_0 USED TO OBTAIN THE STRENGTH FACTOR

$$W_r = \gamma_0 \cdot W_0$$

Shape of cross-section	γ_0	Sketch
1. Rectangular	1.75	
2. T-section (flange under compression)	1.75	
3. T-section (flange in tension) when		
(a) $\dfrac{b_t}{b} \leqslant 2$ for all values of $\dfrac{h_t}{h}$	1.75	
(b) $\dfrac{b_t}{b} > 2$ and $\dfrac{h_t}{h} \geqslant 0.2$	1.75	
(c) $\dfrac{b_t}{b} > 2$ and $\dfrac{h_t}{h} < 0.2$	1.5	
4. Symmetrical I-section, when		
(a) $\dfrac{b'_t}{b} = \dfrac{b_t}{b} \leqslant 2$ for all values of $\dfrac{h'_t}{h} = \dfrac{h_t}{h}$	1.75	
(b) $2 < \dfrac{b'_t}{b} = \dfrac{b_t}{b} \leqslant 6$ for all values of $\dfrac{h'_t}{h} = \dfrac{h_t}{h}$	1.5	
(c) $\dfrac{b'_t}{b} = \dfrac{b_t}{b} > 6$ and $\dfrac{h'_t}{h} = \dfrac{h_t}{h} \geqslant 0.2$	1.5	
(d) $6 < \dfrac{b'_t}{b} = \dfrac{b_t}{b} \leqslant 15$ and $\dfrac{h'_t}{h} = \dfrac{h_t}{h} < 0.2$	1.25	
(e) $\dfrac{b'_t}{b} = \dfrac{b_t}{b} > 15$ and $\dfrac{h'_t}{h} = \dfrac{h_t}{h} < 0.1$	1.1	

for short-term loads:

$s = 1.1$ — for deformed bars

$s = 1.0$ — for plain bars;

for permanent loads:

$s = 0.8$ — irrespective of the type of bars.

Figs. 6.3.6 and 6.3.7 show experimentally obtained graphs of the relationship between the coefficient ψ_z and the parameter M_r/M, the ratio of the internal moment

Shape of cross-section	γ_0	Sketch

5. Non-symmetrical I-section, satisfying the condition $\dfrac{b'_t}{b} \leqslant 3$

when

(a) $\quad \dfrac{b_t}{b} \leqslant 2$ for all values of $\dfrac{h_t}{h}$ $\qquad$ 1.75

(b) $\quad 2 < \dfrac{b_t}{b} \leqslant 6$ for all values $\dfrac{h_t}{h}$ $\qquad$ 1.5

(c) $\quad \dfrac{b_t}{b} > 6$ and $\dfrac{h_t}{h} > 0.1$ $\qquad$ 1.5

6. Non-symmetrical I-section, satisfying the condition $3 < \dfrac{b'_t}{b} < 8$

when

(a) $\quad \dfrac{b_t}{b} \leqslant 4$ for all values $\dfrac{h_t}{h}$ $\qquad$ 1.5

(b) $\quad \dfrac{b_t}{b} > 4$ and $\dfrac{h_t}{h} \geqslant 0.2$ $\qquad$ 1.5

(c) $\quad \dfrac{b_t}{b} > 4$ and $\dfrac{h_t}{h} < 0.2$ $\qquad$ 1.25

7. Non-symmetrical I-section, satisfying the condition $\dfrac{b'_t}{b} \geqslant 8$

when

(a) $\quad \dfrac{h_t}{h} > 0.3$ $\qquad$ 1.5

(b) $\quad \dfrac{h_t}{h} < 0.3$ $\qquad$ 1.25

just before cracking ($M_r = 0.8\ R_r \cdot W_{zr}$) to the external bending moment M for which ψ_z is being determined. The graphs show that ψ_z increases with the bending moment, i.e. with decreasing ratio M_r/M.

The factor v, expressing the influence of the plastic deformation of the concrete should, according to SNiP II-W 1-62, be taken as:
for transient loads,
$v = 0.50$ — for reinforced sections in bending or under non-axial tension;
$v = 0.45$ — for sections under non-axial compression and for all prestressed sections;

257

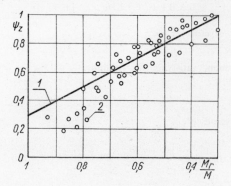

Fig. 6.3.6. Values of the coefficients ψ_z for reinforced concrete components in bending (plain round bar reinforcement):

(1) from standard SNiP II-W 1-62, (2) experimental results

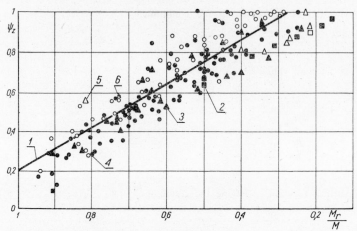

Fig. 6.3.7. Values of the coefficients ψ_z for reinforced concrete components in bending (deformed bar reinforcement):

(1) from standard SNiP II-W 1-62, (2), (3), and (4) experimental values obtained for rectangular beams by several researchers, (5) and (6) for T shaped beams with the flange in the tensile zone

for permanent loads, whatever the loading:

$v = 0.10$ — dry surroundings,

$v = 0.15$ — surroundings of normal humidity,

$v = 0.20$ — very humid surroundings.

Deflection f^{II} (*after cracking*). As in the case of f^{I}, so f^{II} may be calculated in the form of a sum. The components of the summation, however, are different.

Thus

$$f^{II} = f^{II}_{k(k+d)} - f^{II}_{k(d)} + f^{II}_{d(d)} \qquad [6.3.32]$$

where $f^{II}_{k(k+d)}$ is the inital deflection due to the total load, $f^{II}_{k(d)}$ the initial deflection under permanent loads, and $f^{II}_{d(d)}$ the permanent deflection under permanent loads.

When calculating values f_k and f_d, the coefficients ψ_z and ν should be taken for transient loads and permanent loads respectively.

When calculating the deflection of a hollow (multiduct) panel, the final value of f^{II} should be reduced by a factor of 0.8. In the case of slabs of thicknesses less than 16 cm, however, the final deflection f^{II} is multiplied by $4/\sqrt{h}$, where h is the thickness of the panel.

6.3.5.4. *I. I. Ulicki's method for deflection calculations.* The distribution diagrams of strains and stresses assumed by I. I. Ulicki are shown in Fig. 6.3.8.

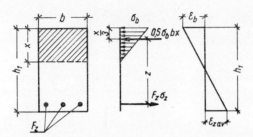

Fig. 6.3.8. Stresses and strains in a cross-section of a rectangular reinforced concrete beam

The relationship between the strains in the extreme fibres and their radii of curvature is given by

$$\frac{1}{\varrho} = \frac{\varepsilon_{z\,av} + \varepsilon_b}{h_1} = \frac{1}{h_1}\left(\frac{\sigma_z}{E_z}\psi_z = \frac{\sigma_b}{E_b}\right) \qquad [6.3.33]$$

where ψ_z is the same as in formula [6.3.27].

Unlike formula [6.3.21], no allowance is made here for the variation in compression strains immediately above the crack and in the uncracked portion.

The ultimate compression strains in the extreme fibres, after the completion of all long-term deformation are represented as:

$$\varepsilon_{b\,\infty} = \varepsilon_b (1 + \varphi_\infty) = \sigma_b \frac{1 + \varphi_\infty}{E_b} \qquad [6.3.34]$$

$$\varepsilon_z = \sigma_z \frac{\psi_{z\,\infty}}{E} = \sigma_z \frac{1}{E_z} \qquad [6.3.35]$$

where φ_∞ is the coefficient of creep, taken as a ratio between the ultimate strains and the immediate elastic strains.

Under prolonged loading, the original hairline cracks widen and new cracks form, and thus $\varepsilon_{z\,av}$ approaches ε_z. We can then accept in the calculations

$$\psi_{z\,\infty} = 1.$$

The preceding assumptions regarding long-term loading, when substituted into Eq. [6.3.33], convert it to:

$$\frac{1}{\varrho} = \frac{\varepsilon_z + \varepsilon_b (1 + \varphi_\infty)}{h_1}. \qquad [6.3.36]$$

259

Using the general equation for the relationship between the radius of curvature and the bending moment, and adopting the triangular distribution of stresses in the compression zone, the expression for the stiffness of a reinforced concrete section under a transient load is:

$$B_0 = \frac{z \cdot h_1}{\dfrac{\psi_z}{E_z \cdot F_z} + \dfrac{1}{0.5 E_b \cdot b \cdot x}} \qquad [6.3.37]$$

and under a permanent load of infinite duration:

$$B_\infty = \frac{z \cdot h_1}{\dfrac{1}{E_z \cdot F_z} + \dfrac{1 + \varphi_\infty}{0.5 E_b \cdot b \cdot x}} \cdot \qquad [6.3.38]$$

The depth of the compression zone and the "lever arm" are respectively given by:

$$x = \frac{n_{av} \cdot F_z}{b} \left(-1 + \sqrt{1 + \frac{2b \cdot h_1}{n_{av} F_z}} \right) \qquad [6.3.39]$$

$$z = h_1 - \frac{x}{3} \qquad [6.3.40]$$

where:

$$n_{av} = \frac{1}{\psi_z} \times \frac{E_z}{E_b} = \frac{1}{\psi_z} n. \qquad [6.3.41]$$

Assuming a triangular stress distribution, nearly all cross-sections encountered in practice can be regarded as rectangular for the purpose of deflection calculations.

TABLE 6.3.3.

VALUES OF THE MEAN COEFFICIENT OF CREEP φ_∞^{av}

Type of concrete	φ_∞^{av}
Ordinary coarse aggregate concrete:	
free cured	2.0
steam cured	1.8
Lightweight coarse aggregate concrete cured under normal conditions	2.5
Ordinary sand concrete:	
free cured	2.5
heated	2.0
Lightweight fine aggregate concrete cured under normal conditions	2.5
Re-activated concrete	2.5
Fine aggregate autoclaved concrete, cement-bonded	1.8
Autoclaved silicates:	
silicates, sand-limes	1.5
foamed and aerated silicates and sand-limes	2.5

The ultimate value of the coefficient of creep φ_∞ is given by Ulicki as:

$$\varphi_\infty = \varphi_\infty^{av} \cdot \eta_1 \cdot \eta_2 \cdot \eta_3 \qquad [6.3.42]$$

where φ_∞^{av} is the mean value of the coefficient of creep of the concrete, η_1 is a correction factor dependent on the humidity of the environment, η_2 a correction factor dependent on the least dimension of the cross-section of the component, and η_3 a correction factor governed by the age of the concrete at the time of loading.

Table 6.3.3 gives the mean values φ_∞^{av} of the coefficient of creep of the concrete, derived from a series of measurements taken at the Kiev Structural Institute. The "mean" conditions are:
— 50–60 % humidity,
— minimum sectional dimension of 20 cm,
— age of the concrete when loaded — 28 days.

For the above conditions, the values of the correction factors η_1, η_2 and η_3 are all equal to unity. Their values for other conditions are given in Tables 6.3.4, 6.3.5 and 6.3.6.

In the case of components in which the least lateral dimension is over 100 cm, and for all components completely encased in a dampproof skin, the factor η_1 is equal to unity, irrespective of the humidity of the surroundings.

In roof slabs carrying standard roof finishes, the value of factor η_2 is taken as if the slab had twice its thickness; when components are given a waterproof skin and are maturing freely, $\eta_2 = 0.40$ whatever their lateral dimensions.

TABLE 6.3.4
CORRECTION FACTOR η_1

Environmental conditions	Humidity of air,%	η_1
Very dry	<20	1.40
Dry	20—49	1.30
Normal	50—60	1.00
Damp	61—75	0.85
Humid	> 75	0.70

TABLE 6.3.5
CORRECTION FACTOR η_2

Minimum lateral dimension in cm	η_2	Minimum lateral dimension in cm	η_2
< 5	1.60	30	0.90
5	1.50	40	0.80
7	1.30	50	0.75
10	1.15	60	0.70
15	1.05	80	0.55
20	1.00	100	0.50
25	0.95	> 100	0.40

261

TABLE 6.3.6
CORRECTION FACTOR η_3

Age of concrete when loaded (days)	η_3	
	Concrete hardened under normal conditions	Concrete subjected to heat, steam, and autoclave
3	2.00	1.50
5	1.80	1.40
7	1.60	1.30
10	1.40	1.25
14	1.20	1.20
20	1.10	1.10
28	1.00	1.00
40	0.80	0.80
60	0.70	0.70
90	0.60	0.60
180	0.50	0.50
360	0.45	0.45

The compression reinforcement F_z' influences the magnitude of the stresses in the concrete and in the steel under tension, and tends to reduce both the creep coefficient and the ultimate deflection of a component under prolonged loading. To determine the effect of compression reinforcement on the coefficient of creep, the value φ_∞ should be replaced by $\overline{\varphi_\infty}$ taken from:

$$\overline{\varphi_\infty} = \frac{1}{n \cdot \mu_x'} (1 - e^{-\xi_x \varphi_\infty})$$ [6.3.43]

where

$$n = \frac{E_z}{E_b}; \quad \mu_x' = \frac{F_z'}{b \cdot x}; \quad \xi_x = \frac{n \cdot \mu_x'}{1 + n \cdot \mu_x'}.$$

To facilitate calculations, Table 6.3.7 and the graph in Fig. 6.3.9 show the value of $\overline{\varphi_\infty}$ as a function of the coefficient of creep φ_∞ and of the expression $n \cdot \mu_x'$. The

TABLE 6.3.7.
VALUES OF COEFFICIENTS $\overline{\varphi_\infty}$

φ_∞	$n \cdot \mu_x'$												
	0.00	0.05	0.10	0.15	0.20	0.25	0.30	0.40	0.50	0.60	0.70	0.80	1.00
0.0	0.00	0.00	0.00	0.00	0.00	0.00	0.00	0.00	0.00	0.00	0.00	0.00	0.00
1.0	1.00	0.93	0.86	0.81	0.77	0.73	0.69	0.62	0.56	0.52	0.48	0.45	0.39
2.0	2.00	1.82	1.66	1.53	1.42	1.32	1,23	1.09	0.97	0.88	0.80	0.74	0.63
3.0	3.00	2.67	2.40	2.16	1.97	1.80	1.67	1.44	1.26	1.12	1.01	0.92	0.78
4.0	4.00	3.46	3.05	2.71	2.44	2.20	2.01	1.70	1.47	1.29	1.15	1.04	0.86

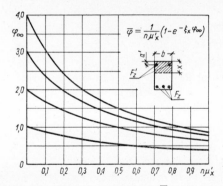

Fig. 6.3.9. Graphs of the dependence of coefficient $\overline{\varphi}_\infty$ on φ_∞ and the product of $n \cdot \mu'_x$

stiffness of a component with compression reinforcement is calculated from formulae [6.3.37] and [6.3.38], in which $\overline{\varphi}_\infty$ is substituted for φ_∞ and the depth of the compression zone x is obtained from:

$$x = r\left(-1 + \sqrt{1 + \frac{2s}{r^2}}\right)$$
[6.3.44]

where

$$r = \frac{n \cdot F'_z + n_{av} \cdot F_z}{b},$$

$$s = \frac{n \cdot F'_z \cdot a' + n_{av} F_z \cdot h_1}{b},$$

F'_z is the cross-sectional area of the compression steel, a' the distance of the C of G of the compression steel from the extreme concrete fibre in the compression zone.

The deflection under a permanent load (f^{II}) is calculated from formula [6.3.32].

6.4. EXAMPLES OF DEFLECTION CALCULATIONS

6.4.1. Deflection Calculations in Accordance with Soviet Standard SNiP II-W 1-62 for a Reinforced Concrete Slab working in Phase II

The slab (Fig. 6.4.1), was designed to be simply supported. The span, measured between the centres of supports, is $l = 5.96$ m. The properties of the concrete and steel used are:

Concrete $R_{\phi 16} = 200$ kg/cm²   Steel $Q_r = 2500$ kg/cm²
         $R_m = 180$ kg/cm² $E_z = 2100,000$ kg/cm²
         $R_r = 17.5$ kg/cm²
         $E_b = 290,000$ kg/cm²
         $n = \dfrac{E_z}{E_b} = 7.24$

Effective depth $h_1 = 24 - 2.5 = 21.5$ cm.

263

Loading

Dead load — 520 kg/m²
Live load — 200 kg/m²

Total — 720 kg/m²

Each 1 m length of the component 1.20 m wide carries
$1.20 \times 720 = 864$ kg/m or 8.64 kg/cm.

The bending moment for a simply supported slab is

$$M = \frac{1}{8} \times 8.64 \times 596^2 = 384 \times 10^3 \text{ kgcm.}$$

The required area of tensile reinforcement, with a safety factor $s = 1.5$, is $F_z = 11.03$ cm²; the reinforcement used was 6 bars of 16 mm dia., giving $F_z = 12.06$ cm².

Equivalent section (Fig. 6.4.1b):

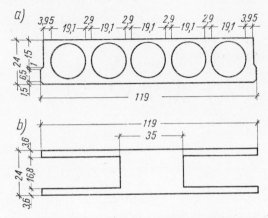

Fig. 6.4.1. Details of the cored panel used in the numerical example:
(a) cross-section, (b) equivalent section

Equivalent square holes

$$a = \frac{d}{2}\sqrt{\pi} = 0.88\,d = 0.88 \times 19.1 = 16.8 \text{ cm.}$$

Reduced width of the web

$$b = 119 - 5 \times 16.8 = 35 \text{ cm.}$$

Reduced thickness of flanges

$$h_t = h'_t = \frac{24 - 16.8}{2} = 3.6 \text{ cm.}$$

To calculate the magnitude of the central deflection under prolonged loading, the rigidity of the element B must be obtained from formula [6.3.23] for both transient and prolonged loading conditions.

The procedure is:
from Eq. [6.3.24] the value of ξ is obtained as:

$$\gamma' = \frac{(b'_t - b)\,h'_t + n' \cdot F'_z}{b \cdot h_1} = \frac{(119 - 25) \times 3.6}{30 \times 21.5} = 0.40$$

$$\mu = \frac{F_z}{b \cdot h_1} = \frac{12.06}{35 \times 21.5} = 0.016; \qquad n = \frac{E_z}{E_b} = 7.24$$

$$L = \frac{M}{b \cdot h_1^2 \times R_m} = \frac{384 \times 10^3}{35 \times 21.5^2 \times 180} = 0.13$$

$$G = \gamma' \left(1 - \frac{h_t'}{2h_1}\right) = 0.40 \left(1 - \frac{3.6}{2 \times 21.5}\right) = 0.37$$

$$\xi = \frac{1}{1.8 + \dfrac{1 + 2.5\,g}{10\,n}\,(1 + 5L)} = \frac{1}{1 + \dfrac{1 + 2.5 \times 0.37}{10 \times 0.016 \times 7.24}\,(1 + 5 \times 0.13)} = 0.22.$$

The area of the compression zone F_b is found from [6.3.25]:

$$F_b = (\gamma' + \xi) \cdot b \cdot h_1 = (0.40 + 0.22) \times 35 \times 21.5 = 450 \ \text{cm}^2$$

the "lever arm" z from [6.3.26] is given by:

$$z = h_1 \left[1 - \frac{\dfrac{h_t'}{h_1}\,\gamma' + \xi^2}{2\,(\gamma' + \xi)}\right] = 21.5 \left[1 - \frac{\dfrac{3.60}{21.50} \times 0.40 + 0.22^2}{2\,(0.40 + 0.22)}\right] = 19.56 \ \text{cm}$$

rom Eq. [6.3.27], coefficient ψ_z may be obtained, taking:
$s = 1.0$ for plain round bars, $\gamma_0 = 1.5$ for the equivalent symmetrical I-section (Table 6.3.2).

$$W_o = \frac{b_t \cdot h^3 - (b_t - b)\,(h - 2\,h_t)^3}{6\,h} = \frac{119 \times 24^3 - (119 - 35)(24 - 2 \times 3.6)^3}{6 \cdot 24} = 8660 \ \text{cm}^3$$

$$W_r = \gamma_0 \cdot W_o = 1.5 \times 8660 = 12990 \ \text{cm}^3$$

$$\psi_z = 1.3 - s'\frac{0.8\,R_r \cdot W_r}{M} = 1.3 - 1.0 \times \frac{0.8 \times 17.5 \times 12990}{384 \times 10^3} = 0.83.$$

Taking the coefficient $v = 0.50$ the above parameters are used to obtain the rigidity B_k^{II} under short-term loading

$$B_{k(k+d)}^{II} = \frac{z \cdot h_1}{\dfrac{\psi_z}{E_z \cdot F_z} + \dfrac{\psi_b}{v \cdot E_b \cdot F_b}} = \frac{19.56 \times 21.50}{\dfrac{0.83}{2.1 \times 10^6 \times 12.06} + \dfrac{0.90}{0.50 \times 2.9 \times 10^5 \times 450}} = 904 \times 10^7 \ \text{kg cm}^2.$$

The rigidities $B_{k(d)}^{II}$ and $B_{d(d)}^{II}$ are calculated similary to $B_{k(k+d)}^{II}$, but for the bending moment due to the dead load $-M = 0{,}125 \times 520 \times 1{,}20 \times 5{,}96^2 = 277 \times 10^3$ kgcm and taking:
for $B_{k(d)}^{II}$ the value ψ_z, found by $s = 1,0$, $\psi_z = 0{,}64$

$$B_{k(d)}^{II} = \frac{19.56 \times 21.50}{\dfrac{0.64}{2.1 \times 10^6 \times 12.06} + \dfrac{0.90}{0.50 \times 2.9 \times 10^5 \times 450}} = 1080 \times 10^7 \ \text{kgcm}^2$$

for $B_{d(d)}^{II}$ the value ψ_z, found by $s = 0,8$, is $\psi_z = 0{,}77$.

Taking coefficient $v = 0.15$:

$$B_{d(d)}^{II} = \frac{19.56 \times 21.50}{\dfrac{0.77}{2.1 \times 10^6 \times 12.06} + \dfrac{0.90}{0.15 \times 2.9 \times 10^5 \times 450}} = 550 \times 10^7 \text{ kg cm}^2$$

The magnitude of the deflection f^{II} due to prolonged loading is calculated from formula [6.3.32] as follows:

— deflection due to short action of the total load

$$f_{k(k+d)}^{II} = \frac{5}{384} \times 8.64 \times \frac{596^4}{904 \times 10^7} = 1.57 \text{ cm.}$$

The initial deflection due to permanent load is given by:

$$f_{k(d)}^{II} = \frac{5}{384} \times 6.24 \times \frac{596^4}{1080 \times 10^7} = 0.95 \text{ cm.}$$

The total deflection due to permanent load is:

$$f_{d(d)}^{II} = \frac{5}{384} \times 6.24 \times \frac{596^4}{550 \times 10^7} = 1.86 \text{ cm.}$$

The total maximum deflection f^{II} will be:

$$f^{II} = (1.57 - 0.95 + 1.86) \times 0.8 = 1.98 \text{ cm.}$$

The deflection-span ratio is:

$$\frac{f^{II}}{l} = \frac{1.98}{596} = \frac{1}{302} < \frac{1}{200}.$$

6.4.2. Phase I Deflection in a Prestressed Component (by the SNiP II-W 1–62 method)

The span, loading and the cross-section of the slab are the same as in the last example.

The physical properties are:

Concrete	Steel
$R_{\phi 16} =$ 300 kg/cm²	$R_r =$ 21000 kg/cm²
E_b = 340000 kg/cm²	$E_z =$ 2100000 kg/cm²

$$n = \frac{E_z}{E_b} = 6.18.$$

Prestressing was applied via 6 strands of seven 2.5 mm dia. wires, as follows:

$$F_z = 6 \times 7 \times 0.049 = 2.06 \text{ cm}^2.$$

The prestress $\sigma_{zs} = 12000$ kg/cm² and thus the total prestressing force is given by:

$$S_s = 2.06 \times 12000 = 24700 \text{ kg.}$$

The bending moments:

due to loading — as in the previous example —

$$M = 384 \times 10^3 \text{ kg cm}$$

266

due to prestressing (eccentricity $e_s = 12 - 2.5 = 9.5$ cm)

$$M_s = S_s \times e_s = 24700 \times 9.5 = 235 \times 10^3 \text{ kg/cm.}$$

To find the deflection f^{I} from formula [6.3.12], we obtain:
— the equivalent moment of inertia of the cross-section J_i

$$J_i = \frac{b_t \cdot h^3}{12} - 2\,\frac{\dfrac{(b_t - b)}{2}(h - 2h_t)^3}{12} + n \cdot F_z\left(\frac{h}{2} - a\right)^2 =$$

$$= \frac{119 \times 24^3}{12} - 2\,\frac{\dfrac{(119 - 35)}{2} \times (24 - 2 \times 3.6)^3}{12} + 6.18 \times 2.06\left(\frac{24}{2} - 2.5\right)^2 = 105 \times 10^3 \text{ cm}^4$$

— rigidity B_k^{I} for an uncracked section from [6.3.40]

$$B_k^{\mathrm{I}} = 0.85 \times E_b \times J_i = 0.85 \times 340 \times 10^3 \times 105 \times 10^3 = 30.36 \times 10^7 \text{ kg cm}^2$$

— deflection $f_{k(k)}^{\mathrm{I}}$, due to a short load $g = 1.20 \times 2.00 = 2.4$ kg/cm

$$f_{k(k)}^{\mathrm{I}} = \frac{5}{384} \times 2.4 \times \frac{596^4}{30.36 \times 10^7} = 0.130 \text{ cm}$$

— initial deflection $f_{k(d)}^{\mathrm{I}}$, due to the permanent load $p = 1.20 \times 5.20 = 6.24$ kg/cm

$$f_{k(d)}^{\mathrm{I}} = \frac{5}{384} \times 6.24 \times \frac{596^4}{30.36 \times 10^7} = 0.337 \text{ cm}$$

— initial deflection $f_{k(s)}^{\mathrm{I}}$, due to the prestress

$$f_{k(s)}^{\mathrm{I}} = \frac{1}{8} \times \frac{M_s \cdot l^2}{B_k^{\mathrm{I}}} = \frac{1}{8} \times \frac{235 \times 10^3 \times 596^2}{30.36 \times 10^7} = 0.344 \text{ cm.}$$

Taking $C = 2.0$ (normal atmospheric conditions) and reducing the above value of $f_{k(s)}^{\mathrm{I}}$ by 20%, the total maximum deflection is:

$$f^{\mathrm{I}} = f_{k(k)}^{\mathrm{I}} + f_{k(d)}^{\mathrm{I}} = 0.8 f_{k(s)}^{\mathrm{I}} \cdot C = 0.130 + (0.337 - 0.8 \times 0.344) \times 2.0 = 0.254 \text{ cm.}$$

The deflection-span ratio is

$$\frac{f^{\mathrm{I}}}{l} = \frac{0.254}{596} = \frac{1}{2350}.$$

A comparison of the results just obtained with those found in the preceding example will show that the deflection of the prestressed slab is approx. 10 times smaller than that of the reinforced concrete slab.

6.4.3. Example of Deflection Calculations using I. I. Ulicki's Method

In order to determine the magnitude of deflection f^{II} the short-term load rigidity B_0 is obtained from formula [6.3.37] and the permanent load rigidity B_∞ from formula [6.3.38].

The procedure is as follows:
From Eq. [6.3.41], the value of n_{av} is obtained, taking coefficient $\psi_z = 0.83$ (as in the previous example):

$$n_{av} = \frac{1}{\psi_z} \cdot n = \frac{1}{0.83} \times 7.24 = 8.72,$$

the depth of the neutral axis x is calculated from Eq. [6.3.39] and the "lever arm" from Eq. [6.3.40]

$$x = \frac{n_{av}\, F_z}{b}\left(-1 + \sqrt{1 + \frac{2\, bh_1}{n_{av}\, F_z}}\right) =$$

$$= \frac{8.72 \times 12.06}{119}\left(-1 + \sqrt{1 + \frac{2 \times 119 \times 21.50}{8.72 \times 12.06}}\right) = 5.32 \text{ cm}$$

$$z = h_1 - \frac{x}{3} = 21.50 - \frac{5.32}{3} = 19.73 \text{ cm}.$$

From the parameters obtained above, the value of B_0 is derived as follows:

$$B_0 = \frac{z \cdot h_1}{\dfrac{\psi_z}{E_z \cdot F_z} + \dfrac{1}{0.5\, E_b \cdot b \cdot x}} = \frac{19.73 \times 21.50}{\dfrac{0.83}{2.1 \times 10^6 \times 12.06} + \dfrac{1}{0.5 \times 2.9 \times 10^5 \times 119 \times 5.32}}$$

$$= 970 \times 10^7 \text{ kg cm}^2.$$

To find B_∞, the slab rigidity under permanent loading, the ultimate value of the coefficient of creep is evaluated from formula [6.3.42], taking $\varphi^{av}_\infty = 2.0$, $\eta_1 = 1.0$, $\eta_2 = 0.95$ and $\eta_3 = 1.0$.

$$\varphi_\infty = \varphi^{av}_\infty\, \eta_1\, \eta_2\, \eta_3 = 2.0 \times 1.0 \times 0.95 \times 1.0 = 1.90.$$

Assuming $\psi_{z\infty} = 1$,

$$B_\infty = \frac{z \cdot h_1}{\dfrac{1}{E_z \cdot F_z} + \dfrac{1 + \varphi_\infty}{0.5\, E_b \cdot b \cdot x}} = 596 \text{ kg cm}^2.$$

The deflection f^{II} due to the prolonged loading is obtained from formula [6.3.32]:
— deflection due to the short action of the total loading

$$f^{II}_{k(k+d)} = \frac{5}{384} \times 8.64 \times \frac{596^4}{970 \times 10^7} = 1.46 \text{ cm}$$

— initial deflection due to the permanent load
(in the formula for B_0 is taking the value $\psi_z = 0.64$ like on the page 265; then $B_0 = 1610 \times 10^7$ kgcm^2)

$$f^{II}_{k(d)} = \frac{5}{384} \times 6.24 \times \frac{596^4}{1610 \times 10^7} = 0.64 \text{ cm}$$

— total deflection due to the permanent load

$$f^{II}_{d(d)} = \frac{5}{384} \times 6.24 \times \frac{596^4}{596 \times 10^7} = 1.71 \text{ cm}.$$

Finally, the total magnitude of the deflection will be

$$f^{II} = (1.46 - 0.64 + 1.71) \times 0.8 = 2.02 \text{ cm}.$$

The deflection-span ratio is

$$\frac{f^{II}}{l} = \frac{2.02}{596} = \frac{1}{296} < \frac{1}{200}.$$

The value of f^{II} just obtained is very close to that found using the method recommended in SNiP II-W 1-62.

Chapter 7

WALLS

7.1. TYPES OF WALLS

7.1.1. General Notes

There are many ways in which walls built of prefabricated components could be classified. From the point of view of design, however, walls are distinguished according to their function in the building, and also according to the structure of the prefabricates.

With regard to their function, therefore, walls may be external or internal, structural or non-structural.

Depending on the materials used in their production, walls, as all prefabricates, may be homogeneous or composite (see also section 1.2).

Thin skins of internal or external rendering, bonded to the body of the prefabricate in an identical manner to the renderings of traditional brick walls, do not affect the classification of the prefabricates. Thus, for example, clinker concrete blocks rendered on both faces are still regarded as homogeneous.

Internal structural walls are generally built of homogeneous blocks or panels of ordinary or clinker concrete, or, more rarely, of other lightweight concretes. Composite prefabricates are only occasionally used in these walls.

Partition walls differ fundamentally from internal structural walls. They are, more often than not, constructed from other materials, suitably lighter than ordinary concrete.

In view of their thermal-insulating functions, there is little difference between structural and non-structural components used in external walls. They are normally homogeneous blocks or panels, composite panels, or, less often, skeletal panels.

External walls made of materials other than concrete, such as light curtain walls with metal, timber or asbestos-cement framing, belong to a separate class.

7.1.2. Large-Block Internal Walls

Large-block internal walls are as a rule made of homogeneous components. The layout of the blocks in a wall is shown in Fig. 7.1.1.

In Polish practice, block walls extend the full storey-height, the reinforced concrete ring beam at the floor levels being cast in-situ.

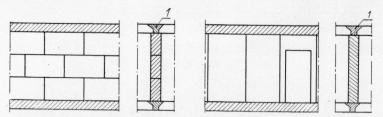

Fig. 7.1.1. Arrangement of blocks in internal loadbearing walls:
(1) in-situ ring beam

In the Soviet Union ring beams are often prefabricated, the separate units being welded together after positioning. The wall thus consists of two types of components—the beams themselves, and vertical blocks somewhat lower than storey-height.

In Polish long-wall large-block buildings (Fig. 2.2.1), internal loadbearing walls are normally built of clinker concrete blocks, as are the external walls. Because of the extra wall strength required, Mk. 90–100 clinker concrete with an admixture of sand aggregate is often used. The density of this concrete in the air-dry state is about 1.6–1.8 T/m³.

In cross-wall buildings (Fig. 2.2.14), internal loadbearing wall blocks are normally made from Mk. 140–170 ordinary concrete, or from Mk. 90–100 clinker concrete.

Cored blocks are widely used in Poland in such walls (Fig. 7.1.2). These blocks, which are made of Mk. 170 ordinary concrete, are mechanically produced using the same plant used to make hollow floor panels (section 6.1.3). In cases when

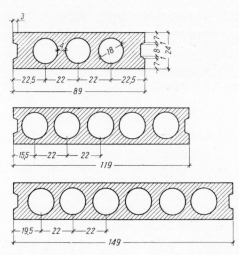

Fig. 7.1.2. Internal loadbearing wall of cored blocks, so-called "Żerań bricks"

270

walls of particularly high strength are called for, some ducts are omitted in production, or a stronger concrete is used, but not stronger than is Mk. 250.

Prefabricated masonry blocks are widely employed in the Soviet Union and in Czechoslovakia. The advantages of this method are the coalescence of a large number of bricks into single units and the possibility of increasing the strength of the wall by the use of vibration during the production of the blocks (section 7.5.4).

The door openings in large-block walls are situated in special, suitably reinforced prefabricates, normally made of ordinary concrete (Fig. 7.1.3).

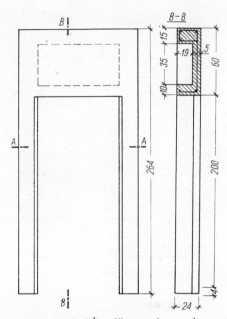

Fig. 7.1.3. "Żerań" type door unit

Similarly, special hollow prefabricates, with recesses designed to house meter-cupboards, etc., are also made of ordinary concrete (Fig. 7.1.4).

7.1.3. Large-Panel Internal Walls

Panels for internal walls are usually homogeneous and made of ordinary concrete.

Originally, such panels were fully reinforced, with steel mesh extending over the entire area of the panel. Experience and laboratory research have proved, however, that the reinforcement can be drastically reduced, and that, in fact, there is no reason why panel walls should not be designed—for Stage C conditions—as plain concrete walls, similar to block walls.

It is essential, however, to design reinforcement for wall panels which will be sufficient to withstand the stresses of transportation and erection.

271

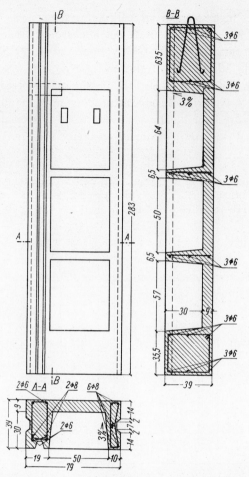

Fig. 7.1.4. Special unit with recess to house service meters

Technologically speaking, the method which allows the highest degree of mechanisation of production, is to cast the wall panels in upright battery forms. Because of the smoothness of the form walls, such panels do not need to be rendered. In addition, the extra reinforcement normally provided to resist the stresses set up when lifting panels cast in horizontal forms becomes superfluous.

The "classic" wall panel is a room-sized panel. If a door opening occurs in the wall, there are three possible variations (Fig. 7.1.5).

In the first of these (Fig. 7.1.5a), the opening is in the centre of the panel. With the opening situated to one side of the panel, the distance between the door and the edge of the panel is sometimes so narrow, that a column member is provided.

In the extreme case, as in Fig. 7.1.5b, the lintel part of the panel is designed as a cantilever. The shape of the panel is then reasonably simple, but carpentry work around the door is made somewhat difficult.

272

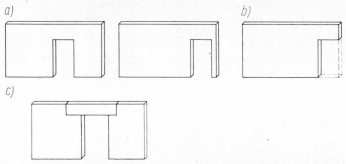

Fig. 7.1.5. Position of the door opening relative to the loadbearing wall panel:
(a) opening in the centre of the panel, (b) panel forming a cantilever lintel over the door, (c) door between two panels with a special prefabricate forming the lintel

The door opening may also be placed between two wall panels, as shown in Fig. 7.1.5c. This solution, however, has the disadvantage of using a larger number of types of prefabricates, one of them much lighter than the rest.

Ordinary concrete internal wall panels of sections other than rectangular are only very occasionally used. One such example, used in the building pictured in Fig. 2.2.29, is shown in Fig. 7.1.6. These panels, the top edges of which are recessed, work on the girder-wall principle. They are bent in the vertical plane, under their own weight and the floor loading of one storey only. The loading from higher storeys is distributed only through the thickened end sections. The thickness of the central part of the panel is 4 cm. Party walls between flats, where good sound insulation is required (50 db), are constructed of two panels side-by-side.

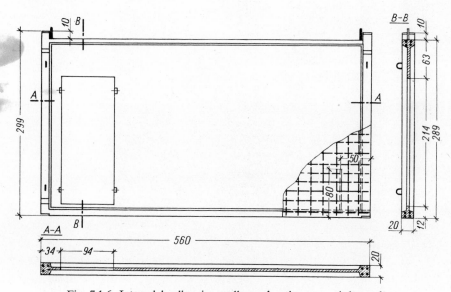

Fig. 7.1.6. Internal loadbearing wall panel acting as a girder wall

273

An example of a skeletal panel is shown in Fig. 7.1.7. The production of such panels has now been discontinued in the U.S.S.R., but they are still employed in Czechoslovakian buildings (Fig. 2.2.2). The structural part of this panel is the prestressed frame, which is stressed on a special turntable. The inner part of the panel (expanded clay concrete), has no structural significance. The technology of production of this type of panel was found to be too complex and uneconomic.

Double panels form a separate class of wall panels.

A Soviet example of this construction is shown in Fig. 7.1.8. Two ribbed panels, made by the vibro-rolling process, are brought together, ribs inwards, and sepa-

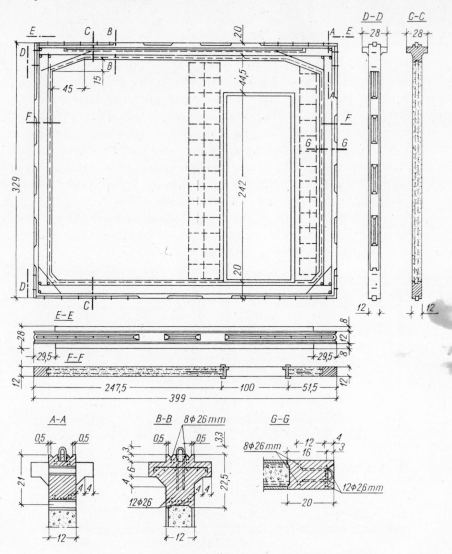

Fig. 7.1.7. A skeletal panel used in internal loadbearing walls

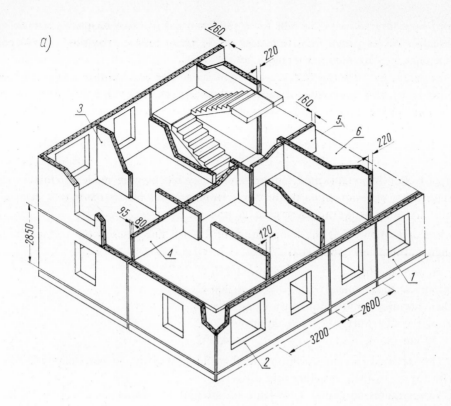

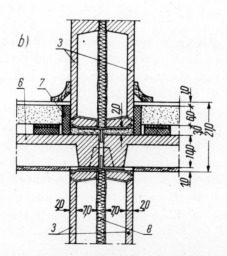

Fig. 7.1.8. Building constructed of compound walls:
(a) diagrammatic view, (b) joint between loadbearing walls and floor panels
(1) and (2) external wall panel, (3) internal loadbearing wall panels, (4) longitudinal loadbearing
wall panels, (5) party wall, (6) floor panel, (7) acoustic insulation, (8) fibrebroad panel

275

rated by a layer of felt. The ribs are at 30 cm centres in two directions parallel to the edges of the panels. The thickness of the panel between the ribs is 1.5–4 cm, depending on the required strength of the wall.

The areas between the ribs are not reinforced. The only reinforcement are bars in the ribs, which are welded together to form a mesh. The two halves of the panel are joined by welding.

7.1.4. Chimney Blocks

In early Polish prefabricated buildings, chimney blocks were made of clinker concrete with a clay pot lining to the flues. Homogeneous blocks made of special fire resistant concrete are however used at present.

Research shows that the temperature of kitchen flue gases is on average when burning low grade coal

— at the flue inlet   — approx. 250°C
— 50 cm above inlet   —   ,,   200°C
when burning wood in quantity (long flames)
— at the flue inlet   — approx. 620°C
— 50 cm above inlet   —   ,,   450°C.

The repeated thermal cycling of kitchen flues gives rise to particular difficulties with regard to their structure and properties.

Temperatures up to 300 °C increase the strength of concretes made with Portland cement. In higher ranges of temperature, 350–800 °C, cement mortar loses up to 85 % of the chemically combined water, and, as a result, its strength is greatly reduced.

The strength of a concrete is again increased at temperatures above 1100 °C, when the hydraulic structure of set cement becomes ceramic.

Concretes in which high alumina cements are used, withstand high temperatures without undergoing great physical changes.

Polish regulations require that chimney blocks must be made from concrete resistant to temperatures up to 500 °C. A concrete is considered to be fire-resistant if, after 25 cycles of heating and cooling, no cracking or crumbling takes place, and if the strength of the samples after treatment is not less than 50 % of the strength of the unheated samples, and, in any case, not less than 40 kg/cm².

A concrete which satisfies the above conditions has the following composition, the total quantity being 1 m³:

Portland cement	275 kg	
brick dust up to 0.25 mm	235 kg	crushed common bricks
brick sand 0.25–4 mm	500 kg	
brick chips 4–20 mm	640 kg	
water	320 kg	

The addition of a micro-filler in the form of brick dust is essential, since it not only helps to produce a very dense concrete, but also improves its resistance to fire, since the brick dust chemically binds the dehydration products of the set cement.

The brick dust should be premixed with the cement. Brick aggregates are first moistened in the mixer with part of the required water, and cement, premixed with brick dust is then added with the remainder of the water.

The brick aggregates should be as pure as possible. Particles of lime are very harmful, and so are admixtures of mineral sand, due to the lack of thermal stability of quartz.

Laboratory tests on concrete made according to the above specifications have given 28 day strength of 180–200 kg/cm². Under service conditions, however, much lower results were obtained, approx. 110 kg/cm².

Allowing for repeated heating and cooling, the design strength of this concrete should be taken as

$$R = 50 \ \text{kg/cm}^2.$$

It must also be stressed that not all types of Portland cement are equally suitable for use in fire-resistant concretes. Of the several chemical components of Portland cement, tricalcium-silicate (C_3S) is the least stable at high temperatures.

To prevent excessive heating of the external faces of the chimney block, the thickness of the external walls of the flue should not be less than 7 cm. If the blocks, in addition to their own weight, also carry floor loads, the sides of the flues should be thicker (10–12 cm).

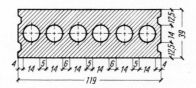

Fig. 7.1.9. A flue block used in Warsaw projects

A typical chimney block, used in Warsaw, is shown in Fig. 7.1.9.

7.1.5. External Block Walls

A classification of the components of large-block external walls as found in long-wall buildings is shown in Fig. 7.1.10.

Three basic types of prefabricates are used: vertical blocks, sill blocks and lintels. Floor slabs rest directly on lintel units which have an L-shaped section.

From the constructional point of view, the classification of the components of external loadbearing walls into the above three types is quite logical, since it faithfully

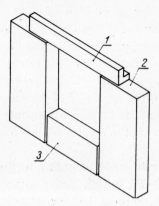

Fig. 7.1.10. Division of the external loadbearing wall in large-block buildings:
(1) lintel, (2) vertical block, (3) sill block

follows the particular structural function of each type of component, while leaving a measure of freedom in window design. The disadvantage of this arrangement is the considerable difference in weights of the prefabricates.

Loadbearing wall blocks are usually made of clinker concrete weighing $1.5–1.7$ T/m³. The aggregates used are furnace clinker of foamed slag.

To reduce the weight of the vertical blocks, they are sometimes produced hollow, with vertical ducts. It must be added, however, that the presence of ducts greatly reduces the strength of the blocks (section 7.5.4), and has little practical effect on the thermal properties of the wall.

The provision of ducts increases the cost of producing the blocks. It may be roughly stated that the provision of ducts in blocks is only economical if the cross-sectional area of the ducts is not less than 1/3 of the cross-sectional area of the block.

Besides the three basic types of blocks, other components are used in many Polish buildings. These take the form of reinforced concrete window or balcony frames, made of ordinary concrete (Fig. 7.1.11). Such prefabricated frames allow all carpentry to be carried out in the factory, but are inefficient thermally, since they form heat escape bridges and greatly increase the total length of construction jointing which must be made weather-proof.

Wall blocks made of two different materials are not often used, but may be suitable for the gable walls of cross-wall buildings. In order to keep the structure of the building uniform, gable walls are usually constructed from blocks similar to those used in the internal walls, but with an external insulating skin.

The arrangement of the blocks in non-loadbearing external walls was discussed in section 2.2.2. Because of the lower loads, blocks in such walls can be made from suitably lighter concretes.

Particularly useful in this context are blocks made of autoclaved aerated concretes. An example of a foamed silicate block is given in Fig. 7.1.12. This block can be

278

Fig. 7.1.11. A view of a large-block external wall with an additional prefabricated window frame

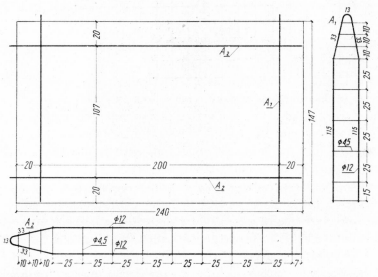

Fig. 7.1.12. A foamed silicate block used in a building near Katowice

adapted for either vertical or horizontal use. The consumption of steel is rather high — 4.4 kg/m² for a block 600 kg in weight.

A gas concrete block, shown in Fig. 7.1.13, is produced in the USSR. This is provided with anti-crack reinforcement, which also protects the block from damage during demoulding and transportation. The vertical edges are provided with notches which are filled in with mortar after erection.

Autoclaved cellular concrete blocks do not require rendering, as both surfaces are perfectly smooth after demoulding. The external finish is normally applied in the form of emulsion paints, which are permanent and allow the concrete to "breathe". Internal surfaces are painted with distemper.

279

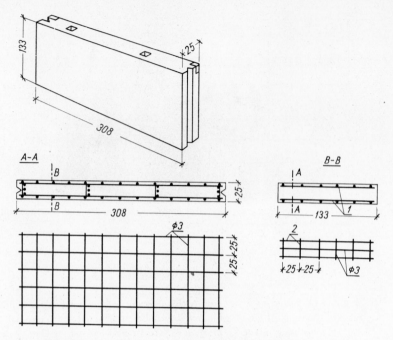

Fig. 7.1.13. A Soviet gas concrete block for external walls

7.1.6. External Large-Panel Walls

7.1.6.1. *Division of the wall into panels.* Loadbearing external walls may only be divided into panels in the manner illustrated in Fig. 7.1.14.

The shape of the panel follows from its loadbearing function. The floor loading applied to the panel at the upper edge is transferred to the lower storeys through the pillars on either side of the window (reinforcement normally required).

In cross-wall buildings or in skeleton structures, the external walls can be freely divided. The usual arrangement is the "classic" panel arrangement (Fig. 7.1.14a), but of late, other patterns have been used more frequently, e.g. "two-room" panel (Fig. 7.1.14c).

The examples shown in Fig. 7.1.15 show the results of the tendency to reduce to the minimum the length of the exposed joints between panels.

7.1.6.2. *Homogeneous panels.* Homogeneous panels are used in non-loadbearing and non-structural walls, but only very seldom in loadbearing walls. They are made of concretes normally not heavier than 1300 kg/m³. With heavier concretes, the thickness and, in consequence, the weight of the panel, become excessively large.

Panels made from concrete with lightweight aggregates are given an external skin of cement rendering or of decorative concrete. In order not to hinder the natural permeation of moisture during the winter months, this external skin must have low diffusion resistance.

280

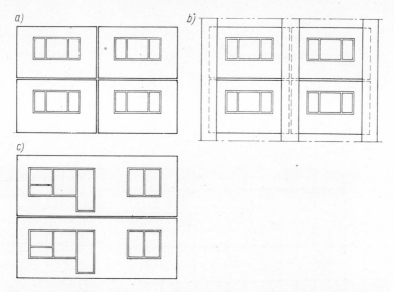

Fig. 7.1.14. Division of the external loadbearing wall in large-panel buildings:
(a) the "classic" division, (b) wall with the vertical joints covered by additional prefabricates forming pilasters, (c) division into "two-room-size" panels

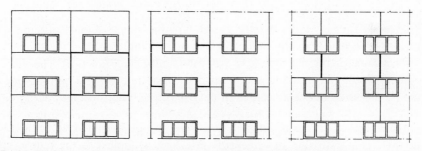

Fig. 7.1.15. Divisions of a large-panel external wall (non-load-bearing), aiming at the shortest possible length of exposed joints (Explanation in text)

Brick prefabricates, which represent a different class of homogeneous panel, are widely used in the Soviet Union and in France.

A homogeneous panel suitable for non-loadbearing walls (German type VW) is shown in Fig. 7.1.16. This panel is made of foamed slag concrete and weighs 1200 kg/m³. Vertical strands of the erection reinforcement project from the upper surface of the panel and serve as handling lugs.

A Soviet homogeneous panel, made of expanded clay aggregate concrete, is shown in Fig. 7.1.17 (Weight: 900–1000 kg/m³). The sill part of the panel houses central heating coils.

281

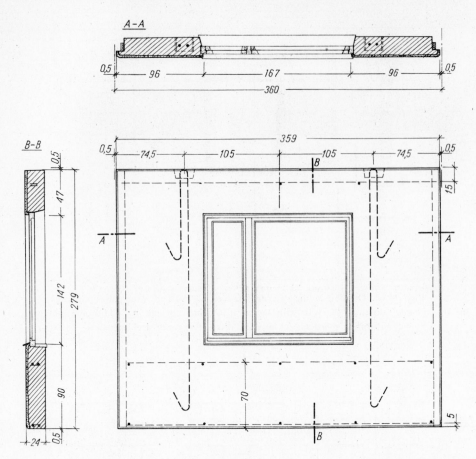

Fig. 7.1.16. Homogeneous external wall panel (self-supporting), made from foamed slag concrete

On the external face, the panel is given a 2 cm skin of decorative concrete. On the inside there is a 1 cm skin of cement paste, which is applied to the bottom of the mould before casting.

In the U.S.S.R., recent advances have featured the production of homogeneous panels from autoclaved gas concrete. These are composed of two separately produced "semi-panels", each of half storey-height (Fig. 7.1.18). The length of the panels, 5.56 m, is a feature of particular interest.

The height of the "semi-panels" was dictated by the size of the autoclave. Before erection, the "semi-panels" are joined together by welding the projecting steel flats.

A French panel made of hollow clay tiles, shown in Fig. 7.1.19, is finished externally with 2 cm of concrete and internally with a 1.5 cm skin of gypsum plaster. Panels of this type are also used in loadbearing walls (Fig. 7.1.20).

As the firm which produces these panels builds houses in the south of France and in Spain, the thermal bridges in the panels are of little importance.

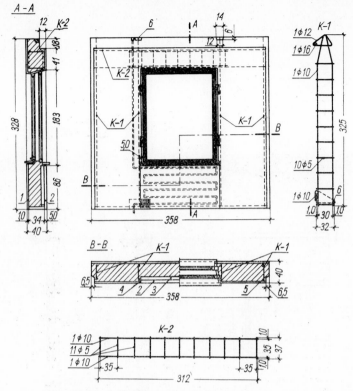

Fig. 7.1.17. A Soviet expanded clay concrete panel:
(1) external concrete rendering, (2) layer of insulation, (3) heated panel, (4) 4 mm wide expansion gap, (5) internal rendering, (6) lifting lugs

7.1.6.3. *Sandwich panels*. Sandwich panels may comprise the following layers: structural, insulating and decorative. In curtain walls, in which the decorative skin is also structural, additional internal cladding is normally to be found.

In loadbearing walls, the structural layer is usually of solid slab construction; in other walls a ribbed cross-section is sometimes used.

The structural layer is most often made of ordinary concrete, or occasionally of clinker concrete. In structural walls, this layer is normally 12–14 cm thick; in curtain walls, where there are no stiffening ribs, 8–10 cm thick.

The insulating layer may consist of very light concretes, expanded polystyrene, mineral wool, glass wool, etc.

Panels for structural walls are normally made complete in one production cycle, with their separate layers adhering closely to each other.

In the case of curtain walls, because of their structural peculiarities and the variety of the materials used, the technology of production is often more complex.

A typical Polish sandwich wall is shown in Fig. 7.1.21. The thermal insulation is in this case provided by a layer of expanded polystyrene.

283

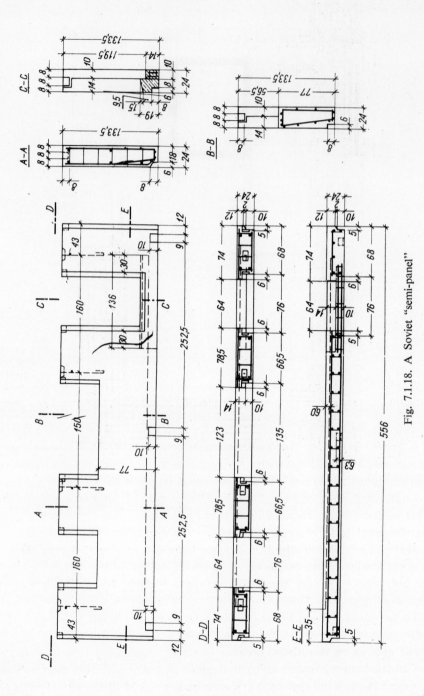

Fig. 7.1.18. A Soviet "semi-panel"

284

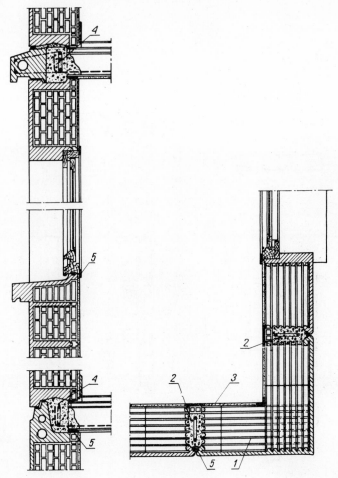

Fig. 7.1.19. Sections through loadbearing panels made from hollow clay tiles by the French firm "Fiorio":

(1) hollow clay tiles, (2) in-situ concrete, (3) gypsum plaster, (4) in-situ ring beam, (5) elastic seal

A panel constructed by the French firm of R. Camus, is illustrated in Fig. 7.1.22. The thickness of the structural layer was reduced to 8 cm in the sill portion of the panel, which reduced the weight of the whole. The external skin has a thickness of 7 cm. The required texture was obtained by sand-blasting the external face.

The French firm of E. Coignet uses loadbearing panels with the thermal insulation on the inside (Fig. 7.1.23), though in the Polish climate this solution is not recommended. The internal layer, reinforced by welded mesh, is connected to the thick external layer by means of steel spikes.

An example from Swedish industry is given in Fig. 7.1.24. The structural layer is 10 cm thick, and the mineral wool insulation 8–12 cm thick. The external layer of coloured or exposed aggregate concrete is 5 cm thick. The outer layers are con-

Fig. 7.1.20. Assembly of a school building with loadbearing external walls consisting of "Fiorio" ceramic prefabricates

nected by means of stainless steel dowels. An air-gap of 1.5 cm is left between the structural layer and the thermal insulation.

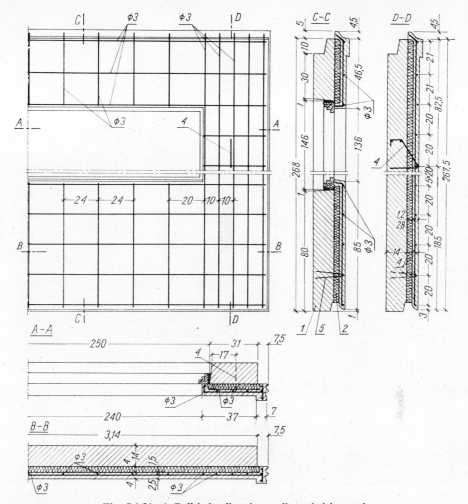

Fig. 7.1.21. A Polish loadbearing wall sandwich panel:
(1) structural layer of ordinary concrete, (2) expanded polystyrene insulation, (3) external skin
(ordinary concrete reinforced with 3 mm dia. mesh)

On the edges of the decorative layer there are ribs, which give additional protection to the joints.

A Russian panel, used for self-supporting walls, is shown in Fig. 7.1.25. Both outer layers are of ordinary, mesh-reinforced concrete; the insulation is of mineral wool. The outer skins are joined through ribs formed on the edges of the panel and around window openings. To avoid forming thermal bridges, these ribs are made of lightweight concrete.

A French curtain wall panel is shown in Fig. 7.1.26. The structural skin is of ordinary concrete and the panels are 4.5 m long. It is interesting to note the ventilated air space and the details of the attached woodwork shown in Fig. 7.1.27.

287

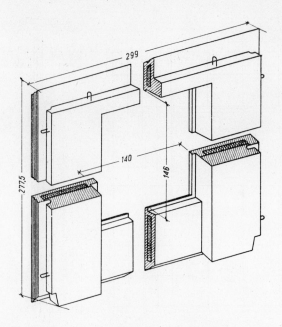

Fig. 7.1.22. Loadbearing wall sandwich panel produced by Messrs. R. Camus

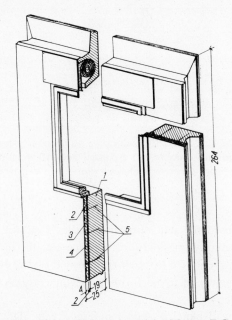

Fig. 7.1.23. A sandwich panel used by Messrs. E.Coignet:
(1) external layer, (2) expanded polystyrene insulation, (3) internal skin, (4) welded mesh, (5) steel dowels connecting individual layers

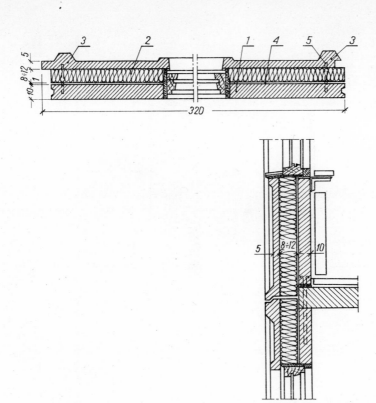

Fig. 7.1.24. A loadbearing wall sandwich panel used in the Scandinavian building industry:
(1) structural layer, (2) mineral wool, (3) decorative external skin, (4) air gap, (5) stainless steel
dowels

One of the Soviet curtain wall panels is illustrated in Fig. 7.1.28. This panel consists of a thin concrete external skin, clad in ceramic mosaic, an insulating layer, and internal finishing plaster coat 1 cm thick. The weight of 1 m² of the panel is 150 kg.

Other Soviet curtain wall panels are generally three-layered. The outer skins are normally made of concrete, and the thermal insulation consists of mineral wool.

7.1.6.4. *Skeletal panels.* In panels of skeletal construction the load-carrying part consists of vertical reinforced concrete ribs. No structural value is attached to the material filling the spaces between the ribs (lightweight concrete, ceramic or gypsum hollow tiles).

In France, panels composed of hollow tiles are often cast on a floor slab, in the immediate neighbourhood of their final positions, and are then slid into place by tilting the forms, Fig. 7.1.29.

A particular example of a skeletal panel is one in which the structure is limited to a peripheral frame.

An example of such a panel is given in Fig. 7.1.30. The area bounded by the frame

289

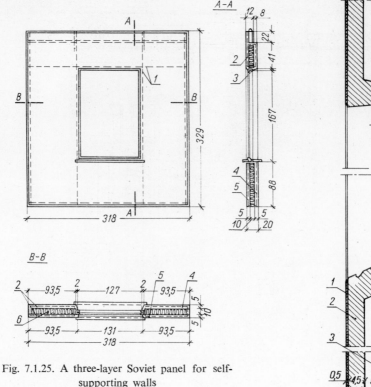

Fig. 7.1.25. A three-layer Soviet panel for self-supporting walls

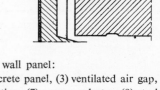

Fig. 7.1.26. Example of a French curtain wall panel:
(1) ceramic mosaic, 2×2 of 5×5 cm, (2) ribbed reinforced concrete panel, (3) ventilated air gap, (4) galvanised mesh, (5) mineral wool, (6) gypsum thermal insulation, (7) gypsum plaster, (8) steel flat, (9) floor slab, (10) timber spacers

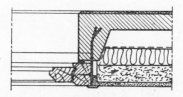

Fig. 7.1.27. Detail of a window woodwork fixing device in the panels shown in Fig. 7.1.26 (horizontal section)

290

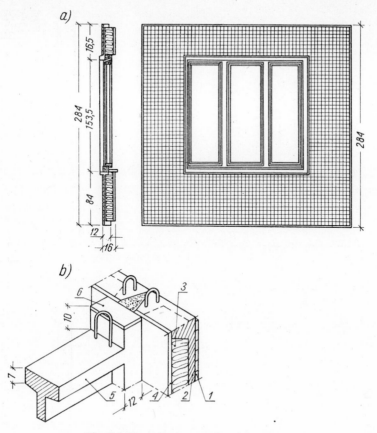

Fig. 7.1.28. A Soviet curtain wall panel:
(a) elevation and section, (b) detail at the joint of the external wall with the cross-wall
(1) ceramic mosaic, (2) reinforced concrete panel, (3) thermal insulation, (4) plasterboard, (5) cross-wall prefabricate, (6) steel plate

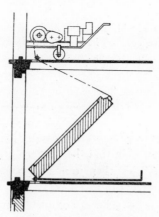

Fig. 7.1.29. Example of a wall-panel being produced next to its final position

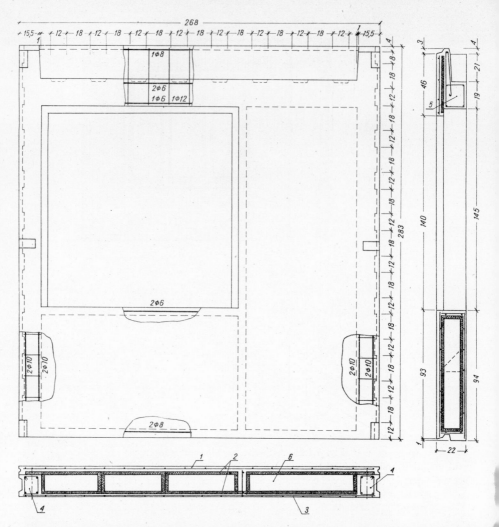

Fig. 7.1.30. A skeletal wall panel with insulation in the form of expanded polystyrene boxes: (1) external skin, (2) polystyrene box, (3) internal skin, (4) load-carrying mullions, (5) spandrel beam, (6) air space

is filled with foam concrete boxes. The external skin of the panel is designed similarly to other sandwich panels.

7.1.6.5. *Compound wall panels.* Panels referred to in this book as "compound" panels differ from "composite" panels in that their several layers are produced separately, and the "semi-prefabricates" are then joined together, still in the factory, or, in some cases, during actual erection.

In both cases, the aim is to achieve completely mechanised production of the components.

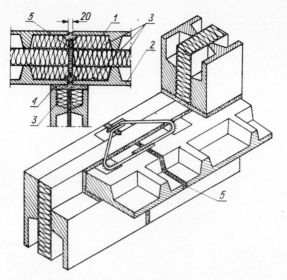

Fig. 7.1.31. Compound wall panels used in Russia:
(1) and (2) external and internal vibro-rolled ribbed panels, (3) mineral wool insulation layer,
(4) mortar, (5) tarred rope

Fig. 7.1.32. A Swedish compound wall panel made by Messrs. Siporex-Ytong:
(a) view of the panel, (b) wall during erection

It is often easier to mechanise the production of separate "semi-prefabricates" than of entire sandwich panels. It is thought that in this field real industrialisation will be achieved.

As an example of a compound panel assembled in the factory, we have the Soviet panel shown in Fig. 7.1.31. The external wall panels consist of two identical "waffle" sections produced by vibro-rolling. These panels are joined together, ribs facing inwards, with mineral wool insulation between them.

293

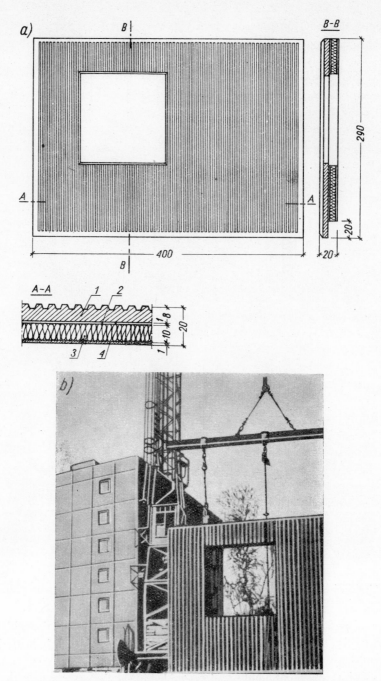

Fig. 7.1.33. A Swedish external wall compound panel, erected in two stages:
(a) elevation and sections of the panel, (b) view during erection
(1) external panel erected first, (2) air gap, (3) mineral wool thermal insulation, (4) internal skin of fibrolite sheets

A Swedish compound panel, in which two gas concrete "semi-prefabricates" are glued to the polystyrene insulating slab, is shown in Fig. 7.1.32. In addition to the glue, the outer panels are joined by means of steel cramps driven into their end faces.

In the second type of compound panel, the prefabricates are erected in two stages: the concrete facade panels are first fixed to the structure, and the internal part (insulation and lining) is then erected from the inside.

An example taken from Sweden is shown in Fig. 7.1.33. The wall here consists of concrete facade panels, mineral wool cladding and an internal lining of fibrolite sheets. The facade panels are separated from the insulation by an air gap.

The concrete panels are corrugated on the outside, which prevents the diagonal flow of rain water into vertical joints. The corrugations are obtained by lining the moulds with thin wood sheets to which hardwood lathing is nailed.

7.2. STRUCTURAL PRINCIPLES

7.2.1. Factors governing the Construction of Loadbearing Walls

Loadbearing walls in three-dimensionally rigid buildings (see Chapter 5), are considered to be effectively supported laterally along their horizontal edges by floor slabs, the joints being regarded as non-sliding hinges.

Structural walls may be regarded as similarly supported along their vertical edges if they satisfy certain definite conditions. These conditions are:
— that the wall is connected to another wall at right angles to it in such a way that it is impossible for the edges of the wall to shift horizontally,
— that the thickness and the width of the second wall are sufficient for it to be regarded as a stiffening wall,
— that the wall is monolithic over the whole width under consideration.

A wall, or part of a wall, is monolithic:
— when it consists of only one prefabricate (room-size panels);
— when it consists of several prefabricates so connected that the flexural rigidity of the wall at the joints is practically the same as between the joints.

Walls in which vertical joints run the full height of the storey should not be regarded as being monolithic (as far as the stiffening of the vertical edges is concerned).

Any opening higher than 1/3 of the height of a wall must be considered to be a break in the wall.

Joints between stiffening walls may allow of a certain degree of rotation. It is not essential to have joints which are absolutely rigid and which allow no rotation or horizontal shift.

The thickness of the stiffening wall must not be less than
— 12 cm, if made of lightweight concrete,
— 8 cm, if made of ordinary Mk. 140 concrete, or stronger.

The width of the stiffening wall should not be less than 1/3 of the storey height.

295

TABLE 7.2.1.

Type of concrete	Stiffening at vertical edges	Minimum thickness of the wall (cm)
Lightweight	unstiffened	20
	stiffened	15
Ordinary Mk. 140 concrete or stronger	unstiffened	12
	stiffened	10

The minimum thicknesses of homogeneous walls and of the loadbearing layers of composite panels are given in Table 7.2.1.

If the ratio of the width of the wall, b, to the storey height, l, is:

$b/l > 2$ — for walls laterally supported along both their vertical edges, or

$b/l > 1$ — for walls laterally supported along one vertical edge only,

then the thickness of the wall should not be less than the minimum thickness given in Table 7.2.1 for unstiffened walls.

In the case of ribbed walls, in which the spaces between ribs are filled with hard and stable materials, the recommendations of Table 7.2.1 also apply, but the characteristics of the infilling should also be taken into consideration when choosing the thickness of the wall. Ribbed walls with a reinforced plate not thinner than 1/30 of the spacing of the ribs, may be considered as if filled with a hard and stable material.

In case of unfilled ribbed walls (open waffle), or walls filled with insufficiently rigid materials (aerated concrete lighter than 500 kg/m², woodwool slabs, etc.), the width of the loadbearing ribs should not be less than 1/20 of the spacing of the horizontal distribution ribs, and in any case not less than 6 cm. The thickness of the wall should not be less than the minimum value given for lightweight concrete walls.

7.2.2. Reinforcement of Wall Prefabricates

As a rule, the walls in buildings made of large prefabricates are designed as unreinforced concrete members. Consequently, the reinforcement in wall components is restricted to the provision of lifting attachments and to erection reinforcement, which will prevent part of the component breaking away in case of accidental cracking.

Additional reinforcement is normally needed in the facade layers of sandwich panels (section 7.3.2).

In wall blocks, and in narrow panels ($b \leqslant 2/3\, l$), the rods used to form lifting eyes may also serve as vertical erection reinforcement (Fig. 7.2.1). In such cases,

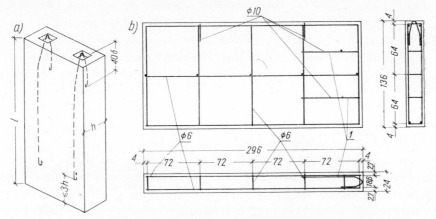

Fig. 7.2.1. Reinforcement of wall blocks:
(a) ordinary or clinker concrete, (b) autoclaved cellular concrete
(1) lifting eyes

these rods should extend to within a distance, from the bottom of the component, equal to 3 d, where d is the minimum horizontal dimension of the component.

Components made from autoclaved cellular concretes are reinforced with welded mesh (Fig. 7.2.1b). To prevent spalling of the concrete covering the reinforcing rods under compression, the latter should be located at the centre of the panel.

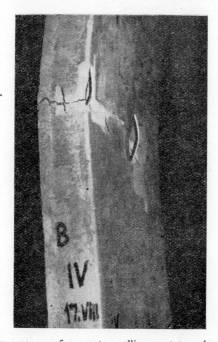

Fig. 7.2.2. The phenomenon of concrete spalling next to a bar under compression

297

In thicker walls, where two layers of reinforcement are provided, the buckling length of the vertical rods should be reduced by means of horizontal links.

The phenomenon of spalling of concrete in the vicinity of a compressed reinforcing bar is particularly frequently observed in components made of lightweight concretes (Fig. 7.2.2), but is not unknown even in components made of ordinary concrete.

Buckling of the vertical bars may reduce the strength of the prefabricates by as much as 20 % and more.

Moreover, in case of fire, if the reinforcement is covered with a concrete layer of insufficient thickness, the latter may spall (section 8.3.2).

The presence of vertical reinforcement, therefore does not always increase the load-carrying capacity of the wall components, and this must be borne in mind when designing them.

In wall panels wider than $b > 2/3\ l$, horizontal erection reinforcement is also necessary (Fig. 7.2.1). This reinforcement should consist of not less than two 8 mm dia. bars.

Wall panels with door or window openings should have reinforcement around the openings (Fig. 7.2.3). The cross-sectional area of this reinforcement should be at least 1 cm², and the wires should project at least 25 diameters beyond the opening.

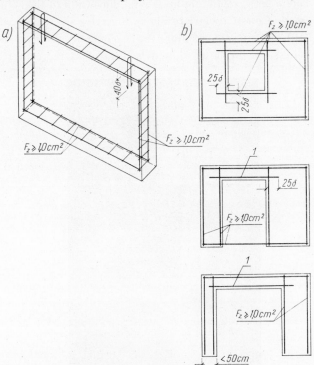

Fig. 7.2.3. Reinforcement of wall panels:
(a) unperforated wall, (b) wall with a window opening
(1) lintel reinforcement, area F_z to be calculated

298

In the case of door panels, it is not necessary to reinforce along the bottom edge of the panel. Lifting lugs should be carefully positioned in perforated panels, due attention being paid to the centres of gravity of the latter.

The general principles governing the design and incorporation of lifting devices have already been discussed in section 4.1.2.

In wall panels, any vertical bands narrower than 50 cm should be reinforced with at least four 12 mm dia. bars and with stirrups at 20 cm intervals, unless heavier reinforcement is indicated by the results of calculations.

Examples of the reinforcement in wall panels of autoclaved cellular concrete are shown in Figs. 7.1.12, 7.1.13, and 7.1.18.

The cross-section area of any additional reinforcement necessary (other than lifting devices or the nominal erection reinforcement just discussed), should be determined according to normal reinforced concrete design procedure.

In the case of wall panels cast in the horizontal position, the possibility of cracks forming during lifting or tilting to the vertical position must be checked by calculation. Production methods, which might result in the formation of cracks on the external face of a facade panel, should be avoided (section 7.3.2).

Ribbed wall panels are designed as reinforced concrete components. The cross-section area of the reinforcement in the horizontal distribution ribs should not be less than half of that used in the vertical ribs and, in any case, not less than 2 bars of 6 mm dia.

Thin-walled panels in compound walls are reinforced with welded mesh.

7.2.3. Jointing of Prefabricates in Structural Walls

7.2.3.1. *General considerations.* The constructional requirements governing the jointing of prefabricates depend on the participation of the wall in the functions of the building as a whole. The joints must be able to withstand the same forces as would exist in the corresponding sections of a monolithic wall.

In view of the participation of the walls in the function of the structure, horizontal joints are mainly acted upon by normal forces, and vertical joints by tangential forces.

Joints at which floor slabs are supported on walls, are subject to additional local stresses due to the deformation of the floor slabs (rotation at the supports).

Joints may be of plain concrete, reinforced concrete or of steel. Plain concrete joints are, in principle, capable of dealing with normal compression forces or with tangential forces. Reinforced concrete and steel joints will, moreover, transfer normal tensile stresses.

Joints in internal walls, in addition to their structural functions, should form effective barriers against air-borne noise and the penetration of smells. Joints in external walls must also be weatherproof and must not form thermal bridges which result in heat losses from the building.

As a result of these considerations, the joints in external walls (other than those made from homogeneous components) normally consist of a structural component similar to those used in internal walls, insulation, and weatherproofing.

The problem of protection from wind and rain-water penetration is more fully discussed in section 7.3, and the aspects of thermal insulation in section 8.1.

7.2.3.2. *Horizontal joints.* The function of a horizontal joint in a structural wall is to transfer loads from the upper storeys and from floor slabs which may be supported at the joint.

The designer should aim at spreading the load from an upper component over the whole area of the joint with the lower prefabricate (Fig. 7.2.4a, b). It is not advisable to provide joints in which the load is transferred at two or more levels, since there is no guarantee that, in fact, the whole of the load will not concentrate at only one level (Fig. 7.2.4c). For the same reason, joints in which the load is applied in one plane, but through two types of concrete, of different compressibility, are also to be avoided (Fig. 7.2.4d).

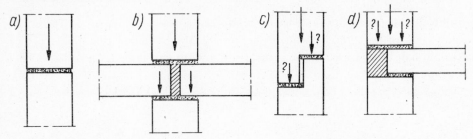

Fig. 7.2.4. Transfer of load from upper storey wall prefabricates to lower storey prefabricates: (a), (b) load transferred on to the whole support area, (c) load transferred at two levels — incorrect solution, (d) loading transferred through concretes of different elasticity — not recommended

In loadbearing walls, loads from the upper components are normally transferred to the lower components through the built-in portions of floor slabs, and this results in concentrations of stresses in the lower walls near the joint.

If the floor slabs are monolithic and continuous over the wall support, the conditions of load transfer through the joint are not, in effect, different from those occurring in the horizontal joint between two wall components meeting directly. The load-carrying capacity of the wall is little affected by this method of floor support.

When the floor slab is free to rotate at the support (simply supported), the load transfer conditions are much less favourable. In extreme cases, the load-carrying capacity of the wall may be reduced to 1/3 or even 1/4 of its capacity when loaded uniformly.

The effect of the distance along which simply supported slabs are directly supported, and of the strength of the material used for filling the joint, is given by G. A. Shapiro in the form of an equation:

300

$$m_0 = \frac{N'}{F \cdot R} = 0.8 \left[0.6 \left(\frac{a}{0.5\,h} \right)^{3/2} + 0.4 \frac{R_z}{R_s} \right] \qquad [7.2.1]$$

where a is the breadth of the supporting structure, h the thickness of the wall, R_z the strength of the mortar used in the joint, measured on 7 cm cubes, and $R_s = 0.8\,R$ — strength of the concrete under direct compression.

The values obtained from Eq. [7.2.1] are on average 12 % higher than the experimental results, and since the joints were free to deform laterally during these experiments, the values of m_0 obtained from Eq. [7.2.1] may be considered to be minimum values (Fig. 7.2.5).

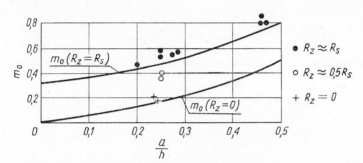

Fig. 7.2.5. Influence of the length along which the panel is supported, a, and of the strength of the mortar R_z, on the load-carrying capacity of the wall in the immediate neighbourhood of the joint

Shapiro also investigated the effect of the lateral reinforcement in the wall on the load-carrying capacity of the joint. When the wall was reinforced with three layers of mesh, failure in the components occurred outside the joint area. Lateral reinforcement of the wall with only one layer of mesh was not sufficient to improve the load-carrying capacity of the joint.

A. Shishkin investigated the load-carrying capacity of joints in which floor slabs were laid dry on the wall components. The gap between the slabs meeting at the joint was filled with mortar. The upper wall was also laid in a layer of mortar.

When the slab is supported over a greater length (narrow gap between the slabs) the strength of the mortar when set has relatively little influence on the load-carrying capacity of the wall:

$$\text{for } R_z \leqslant 10 \text{ kg/cm}^2 \qquad m_0 = 0.35$$

$$\text{for } R_z > 10 \text{ kg/cm}^2 \qquad m_0 = 0.45.$$

When the mortar is still fresh, the value of m_0 is only 0.25.

When the slabs are "laid dry" and supported over a short distance ($a/h = 0.25$),

301

the effect of the strength of the mortar is dominant. Shishkin puts the value of m_0 in this case in the form of an equation:

$$m_0 = 0.8 \left(1 - \frac{0.285}{0.425 + \dfrac{R_z}{R}} \right) \qquad [7.2.2]$$

provided that $R \leqslant R_z$.

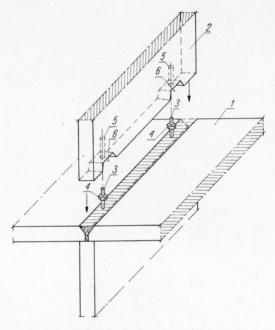

Fig. 7.2.6. Erection of structural wall panels by resting them on bolts projecting from the panel below:

(1) floor panel, (2) wall panel, (3) steel bolt, (4) nut, (5) ferrule, (6) recess permitting nut adjustment

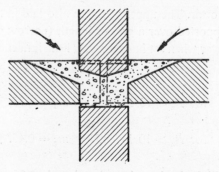

Fig. 7.2.7. Detail of the seating, ensuring axial transfer of loading from the loadbearing wall panel and facilitating proper mortar filling

When slabs are laid "dry" on the supporting wall, cracks appear in the wall after a relatively short period of time. With strong mortar between the slabs, cracking occurred under loads equal to 0.3–0.4 N. This places severe limitations on the possibility of applying this method in practice.

The influence of the method used to support the slabs on the load-carrying capacity of the wall is taken into consideration in structural calculations (section 7.5.8).

Load-carrying joints in prefabricated walls must be completely filled with cement mortar over their entire area. This is an essential condition, for the capacity of the wall does not depend so much on the strength of the mortar, as on its workability, proper compacting, and on the shape of the joint itself.

In Polish practice, prefabricates are laid on a layer of wet mortar, the verticality

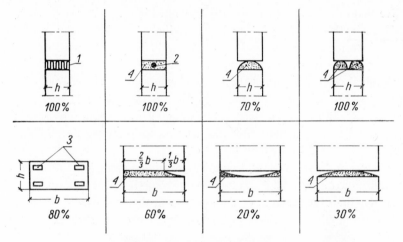

Fig. 7.2.8. The effect of incomplete grouting or packing of the joint with mortar on the load-carrying capacity of the wall:
(1) woodwool panel, (2) round bar, (3) wedges left in the joint, (4) mortar, h — wall thickness; b — width of wall

Fig. 7.2.9. Premature failure of the wall due to the wedge action of the mortar

303

of erection being adjusted by wedges. When the wall is plumb, the mortar in the joint must be carefully rammed tight. After the mortar has hardened, the wedges are removed and the voids filled with more mortar.

In Scandinavia structural wall panels are often laid on nuts threaded onto bolts projecting from the lower panels (Fig. 7.2.6). After the verticality of the panel is adjusted by turning the nuts, the joint is filled with mortar. When this has hardened, the nuts are lowered and the spaces around them also filled with mortar.

The bottom edge of the panel is sometimes shaped as shown in Fig. 7.2.7. The purpose of this is to ensure axial loading of the wall below, and to facilitate efficient grouting of the joint.

The effect of bad grouting on the load-carrying capacity is illustrated in Fig. 7.2.8. The percentages given express the ratio of the strength of the wall with the joint shown, to that of a similar wall with a solidly filled joint.

As shown in this illustration, careless grouting of the joint may result in a loss of 80 % of the load-carrying capacity of the wall. Non-withdrawal of the erection wedges also results in a loss of strength.

Longitudinal reinforcement in the joints does not affect the strength of the wall, provided that the joint itself is properly filled with mortar. However, with bars larger than, say, 12 mm in diameter there is a danger of erecting the panel unevenly and of incomplete compacting of the mortar. In addition to the decrease in strength, such a joint would not be air-tight (section 7.3.3).

Any grooves in the faces of the prefabricates meeting at the joint affect the strength of the wall unfavourably. If the compression strength of the mortar in the joint is much greater than the strength of the concrete in the wall panel, the wedge action of the mortar may lead to failure of the wall in the groove (Fig. 7.2.9).

Fig. 7.2.10. Example of the failure of a lightweight concrete component due to the action of an ordinary concrete reinforced ring beam

A similar effect in lightweight concrete walls may be caused by a reinforced ring beam made of ordinary concrete, as illustrated in Fig. 7.2.10. The formation of vertical cracks as shown in Fig. 7.2.10, can be prevented by horizontal reinforcement along the edge of the panel, as shown in Fig. 7.2.11.

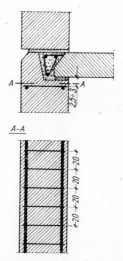

Fig. 7.2.11. Reinforcement inhibiting formation of vertical cracks under ring beams

According to Polish regulations, the mortar used should not be weaker than Mk. 30. To increase the workability of the mortar, the addition of lime is advocated.

German and Soviet standards permit the use of weaker mortars in large-block walls ($R_{\text{中}10} = 10$ or 15 kg/cm²).

For practical reasons, wall components are often laid in mortar similar to that used in floor slab construction, i.e. $R_z \geqslant 30$ kg/cm².

The thickness of the joint should be approx. 1.5 cm, with a tolerance of ±0.5 cm. When, in order to compensate for inaccuracies, a thicker joint is required, it should be reinforced with wires of 4.5 mm diameter laid in the form of a ladder with rungs at 10 cm crs., or in the form of a flat spiral.

It is normally unnecessary to provide reinforced concrete or welded joints at the horizontal junctions of the wall components. They should only be given consideration when calculations reveal the presence of large horizontal tangential forces, or of vertical tension.

In any case, the presence of large vertical tensile forces in structural walls is undesirable, as they may cause gaps to appear at the joints. Instead of introducing elaborate reinforced concrete or welded joints, it is advisable to increase the three-dimensional stiffness of the building.

When designing reinforced concrete or welded horizontal joints, it must be borne in mind that practically all of the vertical loading may be concentrated at the welds or near the reinforcement, because of the rheological deformations (creep, shrinkage) occurring in fresh mortar under the dead weight of the upper wall. This condition is particularly dangerous in the case of welded connections which may crack due to overstress.

The effect of rheological deformations may be greatly reduced by providing additional welded connections some 10–14 days after erecting the walls.

7.2.3.3. Vertical joints. In buildings made up of large prefabricates, vertical joints in the walls normally extend from floor to floor. Depending on the construction of the building, the vertical joints may be called upon to transfer:
— vertical tangential forces, occurring as a result of the wall bending in its own plane under the action of horizontal loads (Fig. 7.2.12), or because of the unequal loading of adjoining components (Fig. 7.2.12 a–c),
— horizontal tensile and tangential forces due to the buckling tendencies of adjoining walls (Fig. 7.2.12d, e).

The joints should be so constructed as to inhibit the formation of cracks in the walls themselves. Besides satisfying the structural requirements, vertical joints must also ensure the thermal and acoustic continuity of the wall.

At floor levels, the components forming the structural walls should be connected by means of welded lugs, or, in the author's opinion preferably by means of reinforced concrete ring beams. These beams, in addition to contributing to the three-dimensional stiffness of the structure (section 5.1.2), should resist part of the vertical tangential forces at the joints.

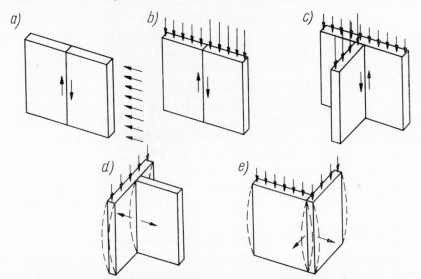

Fig. 7.2.12. Forces occurring in the vertical joints of structural wall panels:
(a) vertical tangential forces due to the action of horizontal forces, (b), (c) vertical tangential forces due to uneven loading of the walls, (d), (e) horizontal tensile and tangential forces due to the bending of the adjoining walls

In early large-block buildings, no correct solution was to be found for the problem of the differential movement of unequally loaded walls meeting at a joint.

Unloaded cross walls embodying ventilation ducts were connected to the loadbearing longitudinal walls by means of flexible ties. This type of connection, whilst preventing the walls from coming apart in the direction of the ties, does not control the vertical or lateral movements of the walls in relation to each other. As a result, cracks appeared at the corners (Fig. 7.2.13).

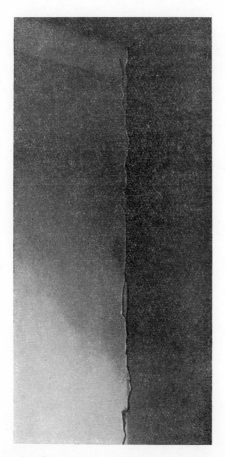

Fig. 7.2.13. Example of a crack at the junction of unequally loaded walls

If the difference in the mean stresses occurring in two walls meeting at a joint is greater than 15 % of the strength of the materials used, or if the two walls are made of different types of concrete, the load-carrying capacity of the joint with respect to the vertical tangential forces must be checked by calculation.

Vertical forces due to the differential deformation of unequally loaded components must be added to the vertical tangential forces caused by horizontal loading.

(a) *Concrete joints*. The load-carrying capacity of a concrete joint depends on the strength of the concrete in the joint and on the adhesion of this concrete to the prefabricate.

The part of the joint intended to be filled with concrete should be at least 5 cm wide and its cross-section at least 100 cm², or, when the thickness of the wall, h, is smaller than 20 cm, given by the formula $F = 5\,h$ cm². With these proportions, the volume of concrete in the joint is sufficient for its strength not to be affected unduly by the loss of moisture to the prefabricates as it dries.

The provision of narrow, concrete-filled joints is strongly discouraged. On the one hand, it is not easy to fill and compact such a joint completely, and on the other, the loss of water will be very large in relation to the volume of the joint, and will cause shrinkage-cracking over the whole width of the joint.

In considering the mutual effects of the concrete in the joint and that of the prefabricate, only the mechanical union of the two concretes should be relied upon. Shrinkage of the fresh concrete in the joint always decreases its adhesion to at least one of the prefabricates.

Ordinary concrete prefabricates normally have smooth joint surfaces. In order to form a joint capable of resisting vertical forces, these faces should be suitably shaped (Fig. 7.2.14).

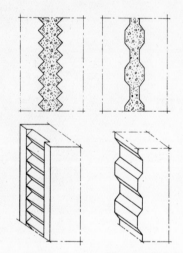

Fig. 7.2.14. Concrete filled joggle joints

The strength of the joggle joint N_T, with respect to the vertical force acting in the plane of the joint, may be obtained from the expression:

$$N_T = F_{sp} \cdot R_{ts} \qquad [7.2.3]$$

where F_{sp} is the shear area of the concrete in the joint, and R_{ts} the ultimate direct shear stress of the mortar or concrete filling the joint.

308

The following values may be taken in calculations:

for cement mortar $\qquad R_{ts} = 0.12\ R_{\phi 8}$

for concrete $\qquad R_{ts} = 0.15\ R_{\phi 16}.$

The area F_{sp} should be taken at the most unfavourable section through the joint, taking into account only that part of the fill which will be loaded via a direct mechanical bond, despite the formation of shrinkage gaps.

In Scandinavia, the joint surface of one of the prefabricates is sometimes coated with asphalt to induce the formation of the shrinkage gap at that surface. This creates conditions favourable to good bonding of the fresh joint concrete with the other prefabricate. The Danish firm Larsen and Nilsen uses this type of joint to join non-structural external walls to the cross-walls (Fig. 7.2.15).

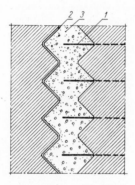

Fig. 7.2.15. A concrete joint with one joint face treated with asphalt:
(1) dowel bars protruding from one of the prefabricates, (2) asphalt coated surface, (3) concrete infilling

In the case of prefabricates made of lightweight concretes with an open or semi-open texture, there is normally no need to shape the joint surfaces. They are sufficiently rough to create a good mechanical bond with the fresh concrete. On the other hand, the porous surface of the prefabricates impedes the complete filling of the joint with mortar. For this reason, it is advisable to use a suitably reduced value of F_{sp}, equal to 0.5–0.7 of the theoretical area, when calculating the load N_T.

Any part of the joint narrower than 5 cm should be neglected in determining F_{sp}.
(b) *Reinforced concrete joints.* In reinforced vertical joints, horizontal wires project from the prefabricates into the joint. In order to resist the horizontal tensile forces, these wires are normally bent to form loops and are often anchored around a vertical bar (Fig. 7.2.16a). Occasionally, horizontal dowel bars are welded together inside the joint (Fig. 7.2.16b).

In order to utilise directly the shear resistance of the joint concrete, the joint faces of the prefabricates are shaped as in the case of plain concrete joints (Fig. 7.2.17).

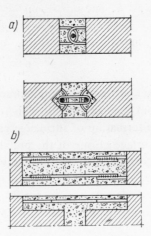

Fig. 7.2.16. Reinforced concrete joints between wall prefabricates:
(a) joints with reinforcement anchored around a vertical bar and projecting from the prefabricates,
(b) a joint with projecting reinforcing bars welded together

Fig. 7.2.17. A wall panel with characteristically shaped joint edge

The joints should be filled with cement mortar not weaker than $R_{\phi 8} \geqslant 100$ kg/cm² or with concrete $R_{\phi 16} \geqslant 160$ kg/cm².

For calculation purposes, joints in which the area of reinforcement F_z is greater than 0.2 % of the total cross-sectional area of the joint are regarded as reinforced concrete joints.

The load-carrying capacity of a reinforced concrete joint may also be obtained from Eq. [7.2.3] using, instead of the value R_{ts}, the appropriate shear strength as taken from normal r.c. specifications.

The material used to fill a reinforced concrete joint must be sufficiently compact to protect the reinforcement from corrosion. Lightweight concrete with a porous texture is not suitable for this purpose. According to A. Shishkin, reinforcing rods

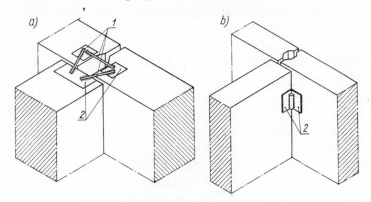

Fig. 7.2.18. Two types of welded joint:
(a) joint with tie-bars, (b) rigidly welded joint
(1) slender tie-bars, (2) steel flats

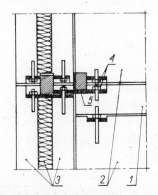

Fig. 7.2.19. Example of prefabricates joined by bolting:
(1) floor panel, (2) internal loadbearing wall, (3) external wall, (4) factory bolted steel connectors joining individual ribbed panels (the vertical flat of the connector fitted to the lower wall panel fits into a slot in the upper wall panel assembly), (5) connector joining the lower wall panel with the floor (the vertical steel flat fits into a gap between the panels)

311

in a joint filled with expanded clay concrete were covered with a 0.1 mm thick layer of rust only two years after the completion of the building.

(c) *Steel joints*. Steel joints may take the form of thin tie-bars (Fig. 7.2.18a), rigid welded brackets (Fig. 7.2.18b) or, less often, bolted connections (Fig. 7.2.19).

Thin tie-bars ensure resistance to tensile forces parallel to them, but shearing forces can only be guarded against by connections of the rigid type.

In considering the strength of the joint, only the cross-sectional area of metal is taken into account. Thus the strength of a welded joint is equal to the strength of the welds.

The purpose of the mortar filling in welded joints is to close the gap and to protect the metal parts from corrosion.

Mortar of Mk. 50 is not sufficient; neither are any mortars with a porous structure. Adequate safety will be given by mortars of Mk. 80 or stronger, i.e. at least 400 kg of cement per cubic metre of mortar.

This sort of filling is not always possible and protective coats must then be applied to the metal. Welded connections in external walls are particularly susceptible to corrosion.

A coat of bitumen paint is not a sufficient protection against corrosion. Adhesion of the paint to the metal is too weak and, besides, the paint is not resistant enough to wear and impact. Bitumen-covered brackets in several buildings in Moscow were found to be rusted to a depth of 0.3 mm, after the paint had flaked.

When bars smaller in diameter than $d \leqslant 12$ mm are used, good results are obtained by galvanizing. For welds, however, acidcoated electrodes must be used.

In the case of welded connections, there is one additional factor contributing to the corrosion of the steel. High temperatures generated during welding destroy the concrete immediately behind the welded metal, forming small cavities in which moisture will collect. This then attacks the metal from behind.

(d) *Glued joints*. Prefabricates with smooth, closely-fitting surfaces may be joined with the aid of adhesives. This method is widely used in Scandinavia and in Western Germany to join cellular concrete blocks.

The gaps between glued blocks should not be wider than 2–3 mm, and to ensure this, the joint faces are often polished.

This method of joining, however, is only applicable to relatively small sized units.

7.2.3.4. *Stiffening of walls along their vertical edges*. Walls can be stiffened along their vertical edges by the suitable configuration of the surface of the wall, resulting in direct support, or by providing concrete, r.c. or welded joints.

The geometrical conditions governing the degree of support are relatively easily satisfied when four walls meet at one point. Fig. 7.2.20a shows a joint which as a result of the edges of all four walls are stiffened; in the case illustrated in Fig. 7.2.20b, however, only walls marked I and II are satisfactorily stiffened.

Adequate stiffness of all walls can be obtained by casting a concrete core in the joint, as shown in Fig. 7.2.21.

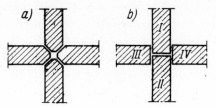

Fig. 7.2.20. Joints in which the geometrical arrangement of the walls results in the stiffening of their vertical edges:
(a) bevelled edges ensure perfect stiffness of all wall edges, (b) only walls I and II are fully stiffened

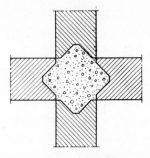

Fig. 7.2.21. A concrete joint in which the edges of all four walls meeting at the joint are stiffened

When less than four walls meet at one point, reinforced concrete or welded joints are normally used.

Fig. 7.2.22 illustrates a reinforced concrete joint typical of those used to join external walls to cross-walls. The stiffness of both walls is ensured if the spacing

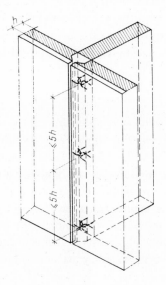

Fig. 7.2.22. A characteristic reinforced concrete joint between external wall and cross-wall

313

of the steel reinforcement projecting into the joint does not exceed 6–8 thicknesses of the external wall. In the case of composite external walls, this condition applies to the thickness of the structural skin.

The reduction in the spacing of the reinforcement protruding from internal walls into the joints reduces the buckling length of the walls at their edges.

7.3. Weather Protection of External Walls

7.3.1. General Observations

In discussing the weather protection of external walls, we must consider:
— the impermeability of the outside skin of the wall;
— the imperviousness of the joints;
— the accuracy of fit of the window carpentry and of the metal flashings round window and door openings.

The demands made on the outside skin of the wall also depend on the material from which the wall is made, and on the type of prefabricates used.

Cracks are never welcome in external walls, but only in the case of sandwich prefabricates are they absolutely inadmissible.

The construction of the prefabricates and the materials used are also of essential importance in the design of joints.

The immunity of the joints to water and wind penetration must be reasonably permanent and, in addition, the joints must retain an acceptable appearance both from the outside and from the inside. The joints must also satisfy certain structural requirements (section 7.2.3) and those of thermal insulation.

The principles of window carpentry and water protection are the same as in traditional building, but the thinness of the walls, normally consisting, as they do, of nonabsorbent materials, makes precision of execution particularly important.

7.3.2. Outside Skin

7.3.2.1. *Walls made of homogeneous prefabricates*. The outside skin of a homogeneous prefabricate is very strongly bonded to its backing and, as in the case of rendered brickwork, is not free to move in relation to the backing. Shrinkage or thermal deformation, which are not the same in the lightweight concrete backing and in the outside skin, may lead to the formation of cracks.

The degree of protection against water penetration, which the external skin of a homogeneous unit must provide, is in principle the same as that required of the outside rendering on a brick wall. Cracks in this skin are undesirable, as they allow water to penetrate into the wall, but they are not so harmful as to necessitate their complete elimination.

The less water the outside skin allows through, and the more easily it enables the wall to dry out later, the better it is. Good drying conditions are particularly important for lightweight concrete prefabricates, which dry out more slowly than brick walls.

The formation of hair cracks is encouraged by the use of too much cement of other fine-particled materials (e.g. limestone dust) and by drying too quickly during the initial hardening. These factors should be avoided during the production or prefabricates.

The thickness of the rendering should be small. In thin skins, numerous fine hair cracks will form. With increased thickness, fewer but wider cracks will occur, and this favours water penetration. In addition, a thin skin makes subsequent drying-out easier.

The surface of the external skin should be as smooth as possible, to facilitate the quick flow of water. Any unevenness, particularly horizontal grooving, tends to slow down the vertical flow of rainwater and contributes to its penetration into the wall.

Prefabricates are sometimes given a water-repelling coating, which is applied with a brush or sprayed on. If the surface of the basic wall material is sufficiently smooth, such a coating can replace the external skin.

Water-repellent coatings are especially recommended for cellular concrete prefabricates. These dry out relatively slowly and, when wet, are very prone to frost damage. For this reason a skin of cement rendering, which makes drying difficult, is less advantageous.

7.3.2.2. *Walls made of composite components.* The degree of water protection expected from the external skin in composite prefabricates is much greater than in the case of homogeneous components.

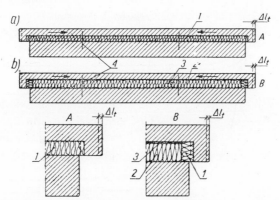

Fig. 7.3.1. Diagrams showing the shape of flanges designed to allow the free movement of the external skin of a panel:
(a) horizontal section of a panel with easily deformed insulating material, (b) horizontal section of a panel with more rigid insulating material;
(1) easily deformed insulating material, (2) rigid insulating material, (3) paper separation, (4) steel wire bracket connecting the facade skin to the structural layer

When this protective skin is in direct contact with the thermal insulation, no cracking is admissible.

Unlike the external render on homogeneous components, the outside skin of sandwich panels forms a suitably thick concrete slab which is free to deform independently of the other layers. The degree of this freedom depends on the material used for thermal insulation.

When easily deformed insulating material, such as polystyrene or woodwool, is used, the design of the components should include edge flanges, flexible in the plane of the panel (Fig. 7.3.1a). Any cracks in the flanges, resulting from the movements of the external skin, should be localised on the inside, beyond the waterproofing seal. The details of flange design are discussed in section 7.3.3.

When the insulating material is stiffer than polystyrene, e.g. foamed glass or cellular concrete, and easily bonded to the concrete, separation of the two layers by a layer of paper during production is recommended (Fig. 7.3.1b). A narrow strip of polystyrene, on the inside of the flange, gives additional protection to the flange.

It is essential that the paper used to separate the two layers should not be impervious to water vapour. Thick paper or paper impregnated with bitumen or grease should not be used, as it would form an unwanted obstacle to the movement of vapour, and could lead to the dampening of the insulation layer through condensation.

The external skin is normally made of ordinary Mk. 170–200 concrete. Its thickness depends on the conditions and accuracy of production.

For general economy, and to facilitate vapour movement, the thickness of the external skin should be reasonably small. On the other hand, it should be sufficient to ensure good concrete hardening conditions, by avoiding excessive drying and shrinkage cracking. In addition, it should be thick enough to afford good corrosion

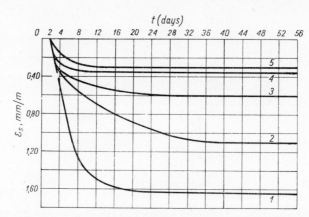

Fig. 7.3.2. Shrinkage in thin concrete and mortar plates, tested in controlled average atmospheric conditions:

(1) cement paste sample, (2) 1:2.3 cement-sand mortar, (3) unreinforced concrete plate, (4) plate reinforced with welded mesh, 3 mm dia. wires at 20 cm centres ($\mu = 0.14\%$), (5) plate reinforced with welded mesh, 3 mm dia. wires at 6.7 mm ($\mu = 0.42\%$)

protection to the reinforcing steel. After allowing for production errors, the reinforcement should be covered by a layer of not less than 1.5 cm on the outer face, and 0.5 cm on the inside.

Allowing for a discrepancy of minus 1.0 cm, the nominal thickness of the external skin should not be less than 4.0 cm (for exposed aggregate slabs, 5.0 cm).

The reinforcement normally consists of a mesh of 3 mm diameter wires at 25–30 cm centres. Where a concentration of stresses is expected, mainly near the corners of window and door openings, the spacing of the wires should be reduced to 10 cm.

One of the functions of the reinforcement is to prevent parts of the slab falling away in case of accidental damage. Care must be taken to ensure that the wires are properly lapped, so that when a large crack occurs, the panel does not separate into two parts.

The second function of the wires is to resist the formation of shrinkage cracks. The relationship between the volume of reinforcement used and the incidence of shrinkage cracks in thin concrete panels has still not been fully determined.

Investigations by L. F. Illarionova (Fig. 7.3.2) show that even relatively wide mesh ($\mu = 0.14\%$) will in normal conditions considerably reduce the shrinkage of concrete.

Moisture and temperature changes of the environment cause further increases in the deformation of the concrete. After ten cycles of temperature changes (from $-70\,°C$ to $+90\,°C$) it was found (Fig. 7.3.3) that reinforcement really only affects the final value of the movements involved when the wires are spaced at 10 cm centres.

The outer layer is connected to the structural layer by means of mild steel wire brackets.

In Scandinavian countries these brackets are made of stainless steel. If ordinary steel is used, the diameter of the wires should be 2 mm larger than that indicated by calculation.

The brackets must be made from wire of not less than 12 mm in diameter. Any part of the wire bracket projecting from the structural layer must be coated with a bitumen or cement slurry to protect it from corrosion.

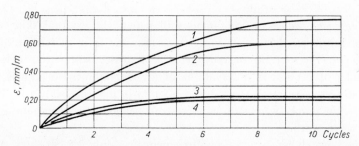

Fig. 7.3.3. Shrinkage of concrete after 10 cycles of cooling to $-70\,°C$ and heating to $+90\,°C$: (1) unreinforced concrete plate, (2) plate reinforced, with mesh, wires spaced at 20 cm centres ($\mu = 0.14\%$), (3) reinforcing wires at 10 cm centres ($\mu = 0.28\%$), (4) reinforcing wires at 6.7 cm centres ($\mu = 0.42\%$)

317

The size of the steel bracket is calculated from the forces acting on it, taking as the permissible stress in steel the value $\sigma = 1000$ kg/cm².

When the upper arm of the bracket (tension) is inclined at 30° to the plane of the panel, and the lower arm (compression) at 90°, as in Fig. 7.3.4, the cross-section area of the bracket steel may be obtained from the expressions:

$$F \geqslant \frac{1.12\,G}{n} \quad \text{and} \quad F > \frac{G}{\beta \cdot n} \quad \text{cm}^2 \qquad [7.3.1]$$

where G is the weight of the external skin (tonnes), n the number of brackets per panel (min. 2), and β the buckling factor.

When the length of the compression member is less than 10 bar diameters, we may take $\beta = 1$.

The brackets should be so distributed in the panel that they offer the least possible resistance to the movements of the outside skin, but, at the same time, prevent sections of it from falling off in case of serious damage.

A horizontal bar 8–10 mm in diameter is located in the bends of the brackets and the reinforcing mesh of the outside skin is attached to this. The method of anchoring the bracket in the structural layer is shown in Fig. 7.3.4. The part under tension should be embedded to a depth of at least 25 bar diameters, and the compression part, 10 diameters.

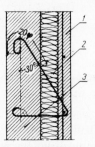

Fig. 7.3.4. Wire bracket connecting the individual layers of a composite panel:
(1) external skin, (2) thermal insulation, (3) structural layer

7.3.2.3. *Compound walls*. In compound wall panels the external skin consists of separate prefabricates. Most frequently these take the form of reinforced concrete ribbed panels (Fig. 7.1.32) or corrugated asbestos-cement sheets (Fig. 7.1.33).

The results of prolonged observations of the development of cracks in ribbed panels reinforced with mesh (bars 3 and 6.5 mm in dia.) are shown in Fig. 7.3.5.

As a rule, the cracks were more numerous in panels with a southern aspect than in those facing north.

When the cover lying over the reinforcement was only 0.5 cm thick, rust stains 5–20 cm long appeared along the reinforcing wires (mainly vertical), when the widths of the cracks were only 0.05 mm. With increased cover thickness, 1.0 cm, large rust spots were only observed when the cracks were 0.2 mm wide.

318

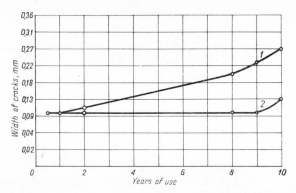

Fig. 7.3.5. Widening of the cracks in reinforced concrete facade panels, measured over a period of ten years:

(1) south wall, (2) north wall

Increasing the size of the wires to 6 mm had no influence on crack development. On the other hand, cracking is successfully controlled by reducing the spacing of the reinforcing wires, or by prestressing.

7.3.3. Joints between Prefabricates

7.3.3.1. *Working conditions and functions.* For the proper solution of the problem of preventing water penetration through the joints between prefabricates it is essential to have information concerning the variations in the widths of those joints due to temperature changes and to shrinkage.

In Polish climatic conditions, the temperature range may be taken to be approx. 50 °C. Since the coefficient of thermal expansion of concrete is 1×10^{-5}, the resulting strains are $\varepsilon_t = 50 \times 10^{-5}$. This value is considerably in excess of the limiting tensile strains of concrete, which are approximately equal to 20×10^{-5}.

If the outside skin of the prefabricate is free to deform independently of the structural layer, the total increase in the width of the panel will result in a corresponding decrease in the width of the joint. Over a length l, the change in the width of the joint Δl_t will be

$$\Delta l_t = 5 \times 10^{-4} l.$$

Thus, with a panel 4.0 m wide, the variation in the width of the joint will be approximately $\Delta l_t = 5 \times 10^{-4} \times 4000 = 2.0$ mm.

Experimentally measured variations of the widths of joints between prefabricates made of different materials are shown in Fig. 7.3.6. The temperatures shown are air temperatures, and the temperature variations at the wall faces were in fact a little lower. In homogeneous units, when small cracks appear on the surface of the outside skin, the variations in the widths of the joints are somewhat smaller.

319

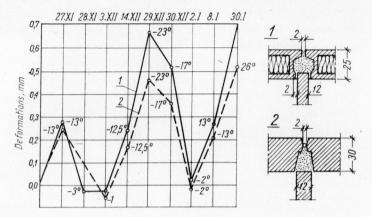

Fig. 7.3.6. Changes in the widths of the joints between wall panels in a Moscow building, caused by temperature and humidity changes:
(1) sandwich panels with an insulation layer, (2) homogeneous panels made from expanded clay concrete

Temperature variations on the inside face of the wall normally do not exceed 10 °C, and this face is therefore not directly subjected to the formation of thermal cracks.

A correctly designed joint between two prefabricates should remain watertight even under the worst possible conditions, so that water not only will not appear on the inside of the wall in the form of stains or wet patches, but will cause neither corrosion of the reinforcement nor dampening of the thermal insulation.

It has been observed that the worst conditions correspond to rain accompanied by squally winds. A thin sheet of water flowing down the normally non-absorbent external face of the wall is forced by the wind into all crevices and gaps.

In hair-cracks up to 0.5 mm wide the water is drawn into the wall by capillary action (Fig. 7.3.7a).

In cracks from 0.01 to 4 or 5 mm wide, backed by an impermeable inner layer (e.g. structural concrete layer), water penetration is caused by a phenomenon which could be called "pumping" (Fig. 7.3.7b). Due to wind pressure, there is a pressure difference between the inner and outer surfaces of the wall. This difference causes the water sheet on the face of the wall to be momentarily broken, and water is

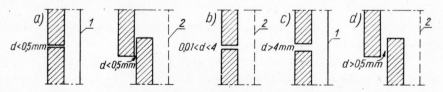

Fig. 7.3.7. Penetration of water into the wall by:
(a) capillary action, (b) "pumping", (c) oblique driving rain, (d) wind pressure
(1) impervious layers, (2) permeable layers

320

forced into the crack. The pressures are now in equilibrium, but immediately the crack is closed again by the water flowing down and the cycle is then repeated. The result is a sort of mechanism similar to a rhythmic pump.

In wider gaps the "pumping" no longer takes place. With widths of the gap greater than 4–5 mm, direct "driving" of the rain is the decisive factor (Fig. 7.3.7c).

When overhangs are provided at the horizontal joints, water may be forced up by the wind pressure (Fig. 7.3.7d). The height to which the water may rise is equal to the wind pressure p expressed in mm w.g.; to a close approximation

$$p = 0.0625 \ v^2 \tag{7.3.2}$$

where v is the wind velocity in m/sec.

To protect the joint against this action, the height of the overlap, after allowing for the tolerance, must be at least

$$h_p = 2 \ p. \tag{7.3.3}$$

Of fundamental importance to the impermeability of a horizontal joint, however, is not so much the shape or the height of the overhang, but the width of the joint.

It has been shown by Isaksen that this width must not be less than 4 mm. In narrower joints conditions exist which may easily give rise to "pumping" or even to a capillary action.

With the wind blowing at an angle to the face of the wall, the amount of water penetrating into a vertical joint is several times larger than the product of the area of the joint and the quantity of water per unit area of the wall. D. Bishop has discovered that a factor of 5–10 is normally involved, though this may be as high as 40 in extreme cases. Screening of the joint by suitably designed flanges (Fig. 7.3.8) decisively reduces the penetration of water.

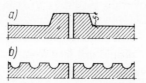

Fig. 7.3.8. Amount of water entering the vertical joint reduced by shaping the external surface of the wall:
(a) projecting flange, (b) vertical groving of the surface

With no capillary action in the joint, very little water penetrates deeper than about 5 cm. The results of Bishop's research on this matter are shown in Fig. 7.3.9.

Statistical data collected over several decades show that, in Warsaw, squalls and rainstorms are accompanied by winds slower than 10 m/sec. Allowing for local gusts, the height of the overhang, h_p, in Warsaw should not be less than

$$h_p = 2 \times 2 \times 0.0625 \times 10^2 = 25 \ \text{mm}.$$

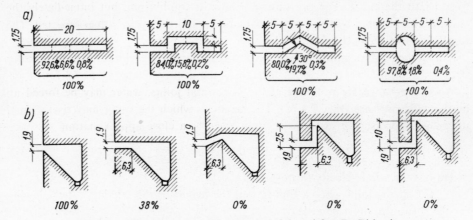

Fig. 7.3.9. The penetration of water into joints (after D. Bishop):
(a) vertical joints (the figures given show the amounts of water collected in successive control containers), (b) horizontal joints (the figures given show the amount of water collected in the control containers, related to the penetration through the vertical joints)

When designing the joint, h_p should be made more than 2.5 cm to allow for unavoidable errors of production, say $h_p = 3$ or 4 cm.

As previously mentioned in section 7.3.1, in addition to being waterproof, the joints should also be airtight, otherwise:

(a) infiltration of cold air would reduce the temperature of the interior, and

(b) air movement would facilitate water penetration.

In principle, the amount of air penetrating through the external walls of a building constructed from prefabricates should not be greater than the amount of air entering a traditional building under identical conditions.

The specific requirements of walls in blocks of flats depend on the climatic conditions.

The most stringent requirements are encountered in Norway, where correctly built walls in timber buildings should not let through more air than 2 m³/hour·m², for a difference of air pressure of 70 mm w.g. This corresponds to a coefficient of air penetration:

$$i_p = 0.036 \text{ kg/hour} \cdot \text{m}^2 \cdot \text{mm of water.}$$

For Polish conditions, these requirements are too severe.

In the U.S.S.R. the regulations are complied with when, taking the mean wind velocity v_{mean} of the coldest month, the air passing through the wall should not exceed a rate of approximately 0.4 m³/hour · m². Thus, in the Russian plains, where $v_{mean} = 5$ m/sec (corresponding to a pressure of 1.5 mm w.g.), we obtain

$$i_p = 0.25 \text{ kg/hour} \cdot \text{m}^2 \cdot \text{mm w.g.}$$

In more exposed regions, where $v_{mean} = 7$ m/sec,

$$i_p = 0.13 \text{ kg/hour} \cdot \text{m}^2 \cdot \text{mm w.g.}$$

322

Similar requirements are set by Polish regulations. In coastal and mountain regions, $v_{\text{mean}} = 7$ m/sec, elsewhere $v_{\text{mean}} = 5$ m/sec.

Concrete wall panels in prefabricated buildings may be considered to be completely airtight. Air can only penetrate through the joints.

In considering the amount of air which is allowed to pass through per unit length of a joint, the coefficient i_p given above should be divided by the ratio of the total length of jointing to the total area of the wall, or, on average, multiplied by 1.5.

Joints which are satisfactory with regard to the movement of cold air may be considered airtight, provided the movement of air does not facilitate the penetration of water.

7.3.3.2. *Waterproof joints*. Joints may be protected from rainwater penetration by:
— filling the gap between the prefabricates with a suitable sealing compound, or
— suitably shaping the edges of the prefabricates, so that after they are assembled the shape of the joint will prevent the penetration of water.

In the first case a filled joint is obtained (Fig. 7.3.10a). In the second case we have an open joint (Fig. 7.3.10b), or a sealed open joint (Fig. 7.3.10c).

The design of filled joints assumes that the space between the prefabricates is filled so efficiently that water will not penetrate beyond the external surface of the wall and will flow down the surface of the joint.

This function of the joint will be fulfilled, provided that the material used to fill the gap is truly waterproof and either permanently elastic, so as to fill the gap completely, or permanently plastic and well bonded with the concrete. Due to

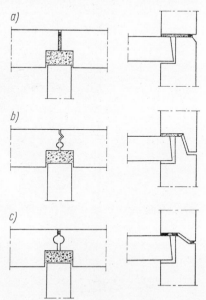

Fig. 7.3.10. Types of joints with respect to protection against water penetration: (a) filled joint, (b) open joint, (c) sealed open joint

323

temperature variations, changes of up to 2 mm in the width of the joint must be allowed for (section 7.3.3.1). The sealing compound must be capable of such deformations despite its relatively small volume.

It must be stressed that the sealing compound is subjected to particularly high tensile stresses in winter; during the summer, the stresses which occur in the joints are compression stresses.

Various types of putty are generally used as the sealing compound, while elastic inserts made from synthetic materials are occasionally used.

The suitability of the putties used in joints is very variable. In some cases faults are discovered after a few months, and in others not until a few years later. On the whole, judging from the reports of many research institutes, most of the putties or mastics do not fulfil their functions properly and new varieties are continually in demand.

The polysulphide group of putties (Thiokol) are quite different from the usual oil-based mastics. They are characterised by their capacity for elongation (200 % when fresh) and the very good bond they form with concrete. They are also very stable, but costly, and because of their toxicity, their use is limited and requires special precautions.

Cement mortar is not suitable for this type of joint. Its use would inevitably

Fig. 7.3.11. Cracks in cement mortar used for filling joints

Fig. 7.3.12. Hardened putty falling out of a joint

lead to cracking (Fig. 7.3.11). In prefabricated buildings, the use of cement mortar as a joint sealer is only allowed in the case of very thick walls (over 30 cm), composed of relatively small blocks.

Occasionally, joints sealed with putty are pointed on the outside with cement mortar. This is not recommended, however, as the uneven surface of the pointing will slow down the flow of water, which is always undesirable.

When placed too near the surface of the wall, putties other than those of prime quality will, when brittle and cracked with age, fall out from the joint similarly to mortar (Fig. 7.3.12).

In *open joints* some water is allowed to penetrate past the face of the wall. The shape of the inside of the joint, however, ensures that this water will quickly flow out again.

The open joint in Fig. 7.3.10b is not sealed at all. The penetration of water is prevented, in the horizontal part by a suitably high overhang, and in the vertical joint by a proper depth of the gap and by the decompression channel.

The function of the decompression channel is to counteract the "pumping" action and to form a vertical pipe, down which any water forced in by the wind will flow. For this reason, this type of joint is also called a "self-draining" joint.

To reduce the effects of driving rain, open joints can be further protected by suitably shaping the edges of the panels. The joint may also be covered by overlapping neighbouring panels (as in the case of horizontal joints) or by providing special cover plates.

Water in the decompression channel should be drained off at each floor level.

325

To achieve this, special stainless steel or plastic gutters are located in horizontal joints to take the water to the outside face of the wall.

In place of a decompression channel, diagonal grooves may be made in the joint surfaces (Fig. 7.3.13). Additional protection is given by joint flanges, projecting from the wall face.

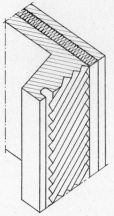

Fig. 7.3.13. Diagonal grooves in joint surfaces

Open joints are, unfortunately, not really airtight. Other disadvantages of open joints, which are, however, less important than the latter include the collection of dust and nesting of insects.

Wind penetration through open joints can largely by restricted by an additional seal near the outside face of the joint.

This additional sealing strip may be made of stainless steel (England, Norway), plastic, usually neoprene (France, Sweden), or even putty, if carefully applied.

Instead of placing the sealing strips inside the joint, various external seals (Fig. 7.3.14) may be provided. These are mostly made from plastics, or from stainless steel or zinc sheeting. Aluminium sheeting should not be used because of corrosion caused by its contact with the concrete.

Sealed open joints are nowadays most frequently used in Western Europe. In the author's opinion this type of joint is also to be recommended for use under Polish conditions.

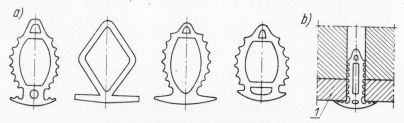

Fig. 7.3.14. Plastic seals protecting open joints:
(a) several cross-sections, (b) seal placed in the joint;
(1) outer surface of the wall

326

An idea of the effectiveness of various types of sealed open joints is given by the results of tests carried out by the Norwegian Institute of Building Research in Trondheim. Of four types of joints shown in Fig. 7.3.15, joint II was the least watertight (no decompression channel). Water appeared on the inside face of the wall after only 15 minutes of simulated rain. The remaining three types were found to be watertight and, practically speaking, of equal efficiency.

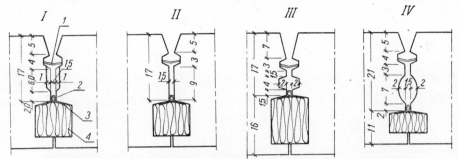

Fig. 7.3.15. Joints tested at the Institute of Building Research at Trondheim:
(1), (2) plastic seals, (3) bitumen impregnated tape, (4) mineral wool

No advantage was gained by increasing the size of the decompression channel (joint IV). Diagonal grooving (joint I) was as effective as the decompression channels (joints III and IV).

It is very important to see that all surfaces inside a joint are perfectly smooth. Experiments have confirmed that decompression channels with rough surfaces can be insufficiently effective in very strong rain.

7.4. EXAMPLES OF WALL JOINTS

7.4.1. Walls made of Homogeneous Prefabricates

The joints in a wall made of large clinker concrete blocks are shown in Fig. 7.4.1. This solution is recommended by the Polish Building Institute.

The horizontal joints in the external walls (Fig. 7.4.1a) are protected by drip-channels in the facade concrete skin. Misalignment of the blocks by 1 or even 2 cm (a fault often encountered in practice) is still not serious enough to cause water penetration.

The blocks are suitably bevelled to avoid damage to sharp corners in transit.

Vertical joints in the external walls are filled with clinker concrete similar to that from which the blocks were made (Fig. 7.4.1b). The large cross-sectional area of the joint (approx. 190 cm²) ensures proper hardening conditions for the concrete infilling. From the outside, the joint is sealed with tarred hempen rope. The shallow recess visible on the inside face of the joint is to allow for a thickening of the internal finishing plaster.

327

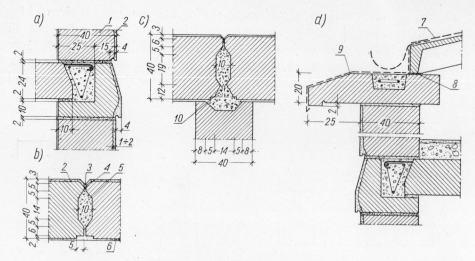

Fig. 7.4.1. Joints in large-block walls:
(a) horizontal junction of external wall and floor, (b) vertical joint between external wall blocks,
(c) vertical joint between internal and external walls, (d) vertical section through joints at the level
of the loft
(1) clinker concrete, (2) decorative concrete skin, (3) mortar, (4) tarred rope, (5) clinker concrete
weighing approx. 1500 kg/m³, (6) internal rendering, (7) roof covering, (8) two layers of roofing
felt, (9) metal flashing, (10) joint widened by hammering off the edges of the blocks

At the junction of the internal and the external walls, the gap between the external blocks should be enlarged (Fig. 7.4.1c). Such a joint, when filled with concrete, will successfully resist the formation of cracks at the junction of walls subjected to different loadings (section 7.6).

In ventilated roofs (Fig. 7.4.1d), overroof panels should be connected to the structural walls by sliding joints (section 4.4.2). A reinforced ring beam can be

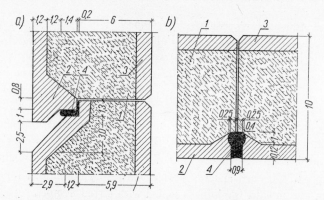

Fig. 7.4.2. Joints in external walls made of wood-shavings concrete panels:
(a) horizontal joint, (b) vertical joint
(1) wood-shavings concrete, (2) cement mortar external skin, (3) internal rendering, (4) putty

328

cast in the groove in cornice slabs, as shown in Fig. 7.4.1d, or in a groove in the wall blocks immediately beneath the cornice. In the latter case, the cornice slabs will have vertical holes through which the ring beam will be concreted.

Joints in external walls built with wood-shavings concrete, made by the Yugoslavian firm of "Komgrap", are shown in Fig. 7.4.2. The horizontal joints are in this case also protected by drip-channels formed in the upper panels.

The panels are fitted together dry. A seal is made with putty forced into the joint from the outside.

Some examples of welded joints, as used in East Germany, are given in Fig. 7.4.3.

The external walls are made from very light foamed slag concrete. The design weight of the concrete is 1.20 T/m³.

With this material, a wall 24 cm thick is sufficient in Germany. The required strength of concrete was $R_{\square 20} = 40$ kg/cm². The building was designed on a cross-wall plan, with self-supporting longitudinal walls.

The floor slabs are fixed to the gable walls by welding the top bars projecting from the slabs to the anchor bars concreted into the wall components (Fig. 7.4.3a).

It is very interesting to note the method of joining wall panels. At the top corners of the prefabricates, there are perforated metal flats welded to the horizontal reinforcement, with cavities under the flats.

During erection, the prefabricates are temporarily joined together by driving 10 mm dia. cramps into the perforations in the metal flats. These cramps are later welded to the flats.

The wide joints in the external walls (Fig. 7.4.3c, d, e) are filled with foamed slag concrete similar to that used in the manufacture of wall panels.

7.4.2. Walls made of Sandwich Prefabricates

Joints between sandwich panels as used on a Polish project are illustrated in Fig. 7.4.4.

The panels are joined by filling the wide gap between them with ordinary concrete, at least Mk. 140 (Fig. 7.4.4a). From the internal wall, 8 mm dia. loops project into the joint every 70 cm. Additional reinforcement is provided in the form of a ladder made of wires 6 mm in dia., with "rungs" every 50 cm.

The trapezoidal shape of the joint and the reinforced concrete in it improves the bond between the components.

The seal consists of expanded PVC beading, forming a barrier against the direct action of driving rain, and a decompression channel through which any water penetrating behind the PVC is led away.

The width of the joint is 2 cm on the outside, and only 1 cm on the inside of the wall. Thus, even if the panels were erected too close together, there would still be a gap on the outside into which the PVC could be forced.

The outside skin of the panel is quite free to deform independently of the structural

329

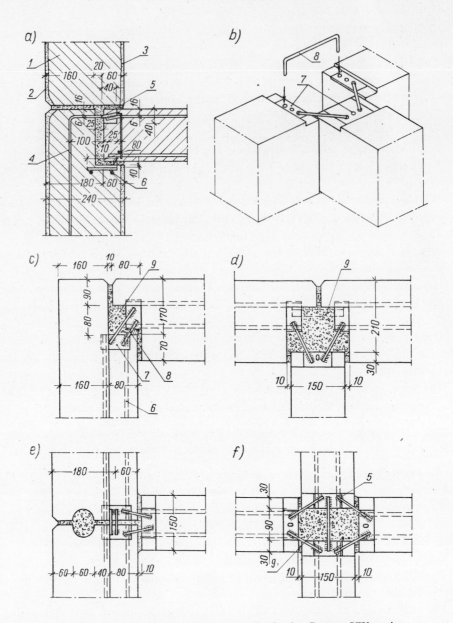

Fig. 7.4.3. Welded joints in large-panel walls, in the German VW project:
(a) junction of gable wall with floor, (b) method of steadying prefabricates during erection by
means of cramps, (c) vertical joint between gable wall and external longitudinal wall, (d) vertical
joint between external and internal walls, (e) vertical joint between gable wall and internal wall,
(f) junction between internal walls
(1) clinker concrete, (2) external skin, (3) internal rendering, (4) anchor bar, (5) weld, (6) perimeter
reinforcement, (7) steel flat, (8) connecting cramps, (9) clinker concrete

330

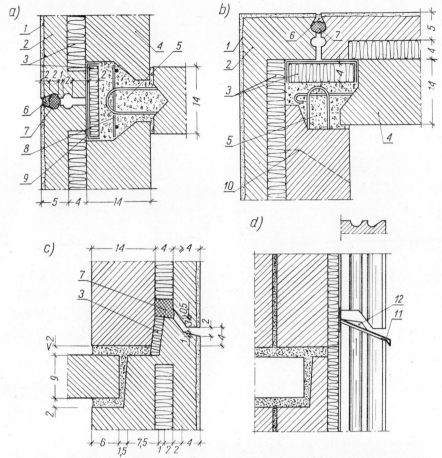

Fig. 7.4.4. Examples of joints used in sandwich panel walls in a Polish project:
(a) vertical joint, (b) vertical corner joint, (c) horizontal joint (section outside the vertical joint),
(d) section through the vertical joint
(1) rendering on the outside layer, (2) outside layer, (3) expanded polystyrene insulation, (4) structural layer, (5) in-situ joint concrete, (6) cement mortar, (7) PVC beading, (8) welded reinforcing "ladder", (9) sealing tape, (10) notching, (11) metal flashing, (12) profile of the step in the panel outside the vertical joint

layer. The two layers are connected by wire brackets, as in Fig. 7.3.4 (not shown in Fig. 7.4.4).

The corner joint is in essence similar to the one just described. Here, however, because of the forces acting at the corner, reinforcement must project from both panels (Fig. 7.4.4b).

The gable wall panel has two notches on its vertical edge, through which it is possible to manipulate the expanded polystyrene joint insulation (inserted from the top).

331

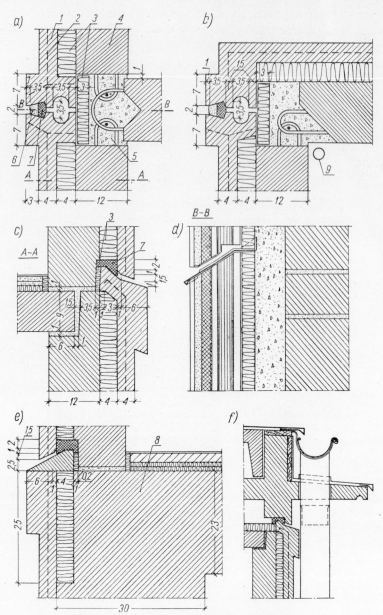

Fig. 7.4.5. Joints in a sandwich panel wall:

(a) vertical joint, (b) vertical corner joint, (c) horizontal joint and section of the extension of the vertical joint, (d) vertical section through the vertical joint, (e) vertical section through the joint between the first panel and the structure below ground level, (f) vertical section through the joints at the edge of the loft

(1) facade skin, (2) 3 mm dia. wire mesh, (3) expanded polystyrene insulation, (4) structural layer, (5) in-situ concrete filling the joint, (6) cement mortar, (7) soft PVC seal, (8) in-situ concrete wall (below ground), (9) central-heating pipe

The horizontal joints (Fig. 7.4.4c) are waterproofed by screening a step in the lower panel by a beak formed in the upper panel. To prevent damage during transportation, the lower edge of the beak is still some 4 cm above the bottom edge of the structural layer.

The joint is made airtight by a roll of foamed PVC glued to the bottom edge of the upper panel. After erection, this roll is compressed by the step in the lower panel.

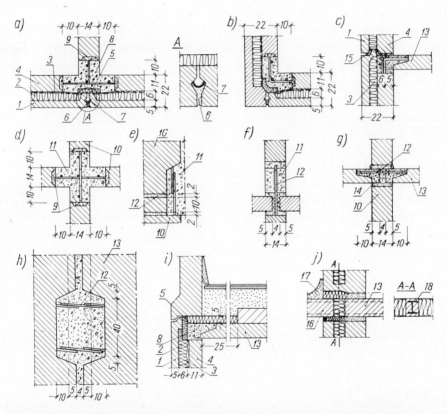

Fig. 7.4.6. Joints in large-panel buildings in the Rumanian earthquake zone:
(a) vertical joint, (b) vertical corner joint, (c) horizontal joint, (d) vertical joints at the junction of four internal walls, (e) horizontal joint in the internal walls (section parallel to the plane of the wall), (f) horizontal joint in the internal walls (section at right angles to the plane of the wall), (g) floor support, (h) joints between floor panels, (i) junction of the external wall and roof, (j) connection of the balcony slab to the floor panel
(1) external skin, (2) mineral wool thermal insulation, (3) damp-proofing in the form of bitumen-impregnated cardboard, (4) structural layer, (5) expanded polystyrene, (6) cement mortar, (7) PVC seal (tube cut in two), (8) concrete in the joint, (9) recesses in the wall joint faces, (10) internal walls, (11) concrete in the joint between the walls, (12) bars joined by welding, (13) floor, (14) floor bearing lug, (15) horizontal joint seal (mortar and tarred rope), (16) balcony slab, (17) cement cove, (18) I-section cantilever

At the meeting point of horizontal and vertical joints (Fig. 7.4.4d) the step in the lower panel is bevelled for 5 cm on each side of the vertical joint. The vertical joint is at this point bridged by a zinc plate, which deflects the water from the decompression channel. The bevelled edges of the step stem the lateral flow of this water.

The panels meeting at the joint shown in Fig. 7.4.5a are connected by loops of 6 mm dia. wire let into the joint at approx. 70 cm intervals. The vertical edges of the panels were made 3 cm thicker, thus forming a barrier, which prevents water flowing into the joint from the sides (section 7.3.9).

For architectural reasons the top edges of the panels were also thickened. The drip channel thus formed is very convenient, as it throws clear of the wall any water flowing down from above.

Examples of joints used in the Rumanian earthquake zone are given in Fig. 7.4.6.

Continuity of the horizontal and vertical wall reinforcement, and of the wall and floor reinforcement, is structurally essential here. Structural joints were designed sufficiently wide in this case, to make welding of the reinforcement in them easy.

The joints are filled with ordinary concrete $R_{\Box 20} = 200$ kg/cm². The bond between the fresh concrete and the old can be further improved by making notches on the vertical edges of the panels.

The principles on which the design of the waterproofing was based were the same as in the preceding examples. Of particular interest is the simple way in which mortar was used to seal the joint without clogging the decomposition channel.

A PVC pipe, cut in half, was forced from the outside into the channel. This piece in springing back, prevented the mortar from filling the channel. The shape of the joint stops the hardened mortar from falling out.

Joints used by the Danish firm "Larsen and Nielsen" in cross-wall buildings are shown in Fig. 7.4.7.

A joggle joint connects the external walls to the cross-wall (Fig. 7.4.7a) and loops of 6 mm wire are let into the joint from the latter.

The vertical joint is sealed with a strip of neoprene. In addition, the outside face of the wall is grooved vertically.

The decompression channel is rectangular. It is closed from the inside by a polystyrene plate, which renders the joint airtight and breaks the thermal bridge.

The horizontal joint is screened by a 13 cm overhang, this being an extension of the external skin of the panel (Fig. 7.4.7b, c).

The wall panels are stood on adjustable nuts, as described in section 7.2.3. and shown in Fig. 7.4.7b, d.

Cored floor panels are laid "dry" on a layer of roofing felt, without mortar (Fig. 7.4.7c, d). This construction requires a very high degree of accuracy.

The floors are connected to the gable walls by means of 8 mm dia. wires projecting from the floor slabs into the joint. A reinforced concrete ring beam is then cast at floor level.

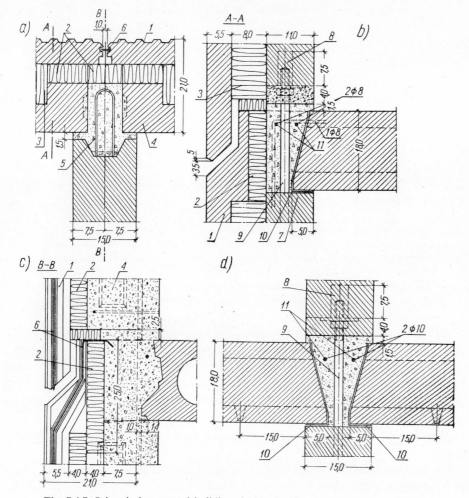

Fig. 7.4.7. Joints in large-panel buildings by the Danish firm of Larsen and Nielsen:
(a) vertical joint, (b) horizontal joint between floor and loadbearing gable wall, (c) horizontal
joint in the non-structural external wall, (d) horizontal joints between floor panels and loadbearing
internal wall
(1) external skin with grooved outer face, (2) layer of expanded polystyrene protecting the joint,
(3) main thermal insulation layer, (4) structural layer in the curtain wall, (5) concrete filler in the
joint, (6) neoprene strip, (7) structural layer of the gable wall, (8) ferrule capping on steel bolt,
(9) steel bolt with adjustable nut, (10) roofing felt, (11) ring beam reinforcement

Two further examples of joints used in the Danish building industry are given
in Fig. 7.4.8.

Curtain wall panels rest on brackets cast into the internal loadbearing walls
(Fig. 7.4.8a, b, c) or are hung from these walls by grouting special construction
joints (Fig. 7.4.8d). In both cases, the curtain wall panels are interconnected by

335

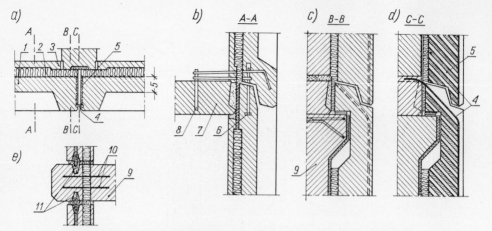

Fig. 7.4.8. External wall joints used in the Danish building industry:
(a) diagonally grooved vertical joint, (b) horizontal joint—section *A-A*, (c) horizontal joint—section
B-B, (d) horizontal joint—section *C-C*, (e) junction of a curtain wall with a cross-wall
(1) external skin, (2) thermal insulation, (3) inner skin, (4) neoprene strip, (5) inclined grooving
on the side edge of the panel, (6) steel dowel in the wall panel, (7) floor panel, (8) steel dowel in the
floor, (9) cross-wall, (10) connecting steel bars, (11) asphalt covered surfaces

dowelling, and are joined to the floor by anchoring the protruding horizontal wires round dowel bars cast into the floor panels.

In the case of panels resting on brackets, the vertical joints are diagonally grooved to throw off any water (section 7.3.3). To obtain the necessary depth of grooving, the panels were thickened at the edges to 12 cm, the flanges giving additional protection against the inflow of water from the sides.

A further safeguard is a strip of neoprene inserted under the upper panel at floor level.

The horizontal joints are protected by drip channels formed in the upper panels and overlapping the steps in the lower panels.

When the panels are hung as in Fig. 7.4.8e, an ingenious construction precludes the formation of thermal or shrinkage cracks in the concrete infilling.

The contingent surfaces are shaped to form notches. Closely spaced (15 cm) 4.5 mm dia. loops project from the curtain wall panels. The surfaces of the cross-wall is given a coat of bitumen at the joint. Although the mortar fill is well bonded with the curtain wall panel, it will not stick to the bitumen treated surface and any gaps will be hidden and will not diminish the resistance of the joint to vertical tangential forces.

Thus, although the joint is executed "wet", it allows some independent movement of the external panels relative to the structure of the building.

Another curtain wall joint, used in France, is shown in Fig. 7.4.9.

External wall panels are connected to the loadbearing cross-wall by a wide, concrete-filled joint (Fig. 7.4.9a). Reinforcing bars project from the external panels

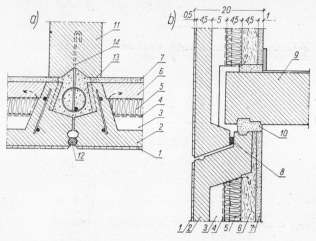

Fig. 7.4.9. Joints in curtain walls, in the French project SSTP:
(a) vertical joint, (b) horizontal joint

(1) 2×2 cm ceramic mosaic, (2) concrete panel, (3) ventilated gap, (4) galvanised wire mesh, (5) mineral wool thermal insulation, (6) gypsum thermal insulation, (7) gypsum finishing coat, (8) seal broken to release condensation water, (9) floor, (10) joint filled with gypsum mortar, (11) internal wall, (12) elastic seal, (13) spiral of 6 mm dia. wire, (14) anchor bar

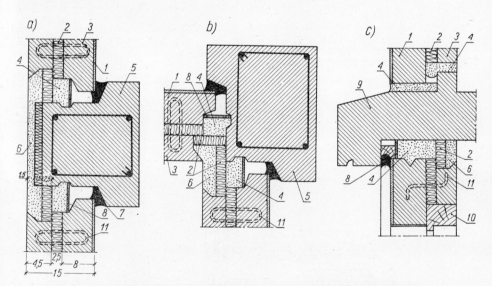

Fig. 7.4.10. Joints in curtain walls by the French firm "Agglogiro":
(a) vertical joint, (b) vertical corner joint, (c) horizontal joint

(1) external concrete panel, (2) expanded polystyrene, (3) internal concrete plate, (4) cement mortar, (5) prefabricated column forming a pilaster, (6) gypsum mortar, (7) mastic, (8) strip of asbestos-cement, (9) floor overhang, (10) window frame, (11) dowels connecting the two concrete skins

337

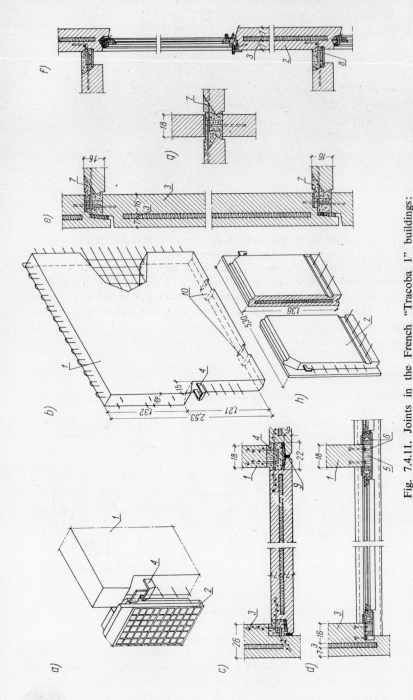

Fig. 7.4.11. Joints in the French "Tracoba 1" buildings:

(a) detail of suspension of the curtain wall on the cross-wall, (b) loadbearing panel of the cross-wall, (c) horizontal section through the junctions of the curtain wall with the gable wall and the cross-wall, (d) horizontal section through the external wall at window level, (e) vertical section through the gable wall, (f) vertical section through the curtain wall, (g) junction of the floor with the cross-wall, (h) curtain wall panel

(1) cross-wall, (2) curtain wall, (3) gable wall, (4) fixing hoop, (5) insulation, (6) asbestos-cement plates, (7) floor support lugs, (8) plywood, (9) mastic, (10) recesses in the wall panels above floor-support lugs

338

into the joint. The trapezoidal shape of the joint and the notches on the edges of the external panels ensure that the concrete in the joint forms a mechanical bond with the panels. Additional reinforcement is provided in the shape of a spiral made of 4.5 mm dia. wire.

A slight disadvantage of this joint, the fact that it forms a relatively efficient thermal bridge, is of secondary importance in the French climate. In Poland some form of thermal insulation would be necessary in the joint.

The horizontal joint (Fig. 7.4.9b), as in other examples, is protected by an over-hang from the upper panel. The thermal bridge in this joint is easily broken by attaching a strip of expanded polystyrene to the front edge of the floor panel.

Another French joint is illustrated in Fig. 7.4.10.

The vertical joints are protected by a precast pilaster (Fig. 7.4.10a, b), and the horizontal joints by the projecting parts of the floor panels. Strips of cardboard prevent the mortar from being forced too far into the joint.

As in the previous example, extra thermal insulation would be necessary in Polish climatic conditions.

Details of joints between prefabricates used by the French firm "Tracoba" are shown in Figs. 7.4.11 and 7.4.12.

The curtain wall panels are first hung on hooks projecting from the internal wall panels. After final positioning, the wires projecting from each panel are welded together and both the vertical and the horizontal construction joints are filled with mortar.

The vertical joint is sealed with mastic.

There are no horizontal joints between the prefabricates forming the longitudinal walls. In the gable walls these joints are protected by long drip-channels formed in the upper panels.

Characteristic of the "Tracoba" projects is the joint between the floor panels and the loadbearing walls (Fig. 7.4.12).

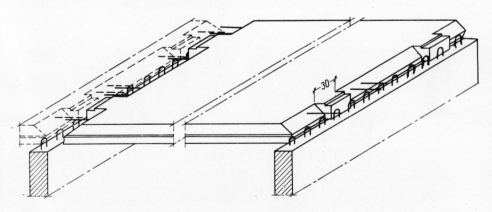

Fig. 7.4.12. Method of floor support used in the "Tracoba 1" system

The floor panels rest on the walls on four lugs, 2 cm thinner than the floor itself. The bottom edge of the wall panel above is recessed above the lugs, so that the whole load from above is transferred directly on to an "in-situ" ring beam. As the width of this ring beam is wider at the top than the wall thickness, and the bottom edge of the wall is slightly below the top of the beam, it can be well filled with concrete and thoroughly compacted.

Joints in external walls constructed from gas concrete planks, taken from the catalogue of Messrs. Siporex-Ytong, are shown in Fig. 7.4.13.

The wall consists of storey-height vertical planks and special sill panels. The vertical planks are erected on a 1 cm layer of mortar spread on the floor panels, and are connected to the floor above by dowel bars dropped through holes in the floor panel into the vertical joints between the planks.

The external gas concrete skin (0.5 T/m³) projects upwards to insulate the front edge of the floor panel.

Two types of vertical joints are found in the wall.

On the inside, there are wide, concrete-filled joints opposite the internal cross-walls. Looped reinforcement projects from the cross-walls into the joints. On the

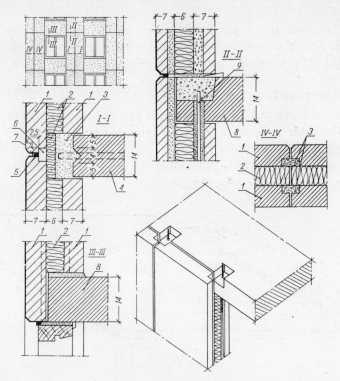

Fig. 7.4.13. Joints in the external wall composed of gas concrete planks:
(1) gas concrete type 07, (2) expanded polystyrene, (3) in-situ concrete, (4) cross-wall, (5) mastic, (6) decompression channel, (7) external rendering, (8) floor panel, (9) anchor bar

outside, the gap is left unfilled, forming a decompression channel, and is sealed with mastic.

The intermediate vertical joints are relatively narrow and are filled with mortar, forming, in fact, a monolithic panel. However, as the two skins of gas concrete are only connected by wall-ties, and there are open joints opposite the cross-walls, the outside skin of the wall has sufficient freedom.

The horizontal joint between the planks is not stepped (as is normal in walls consisting of sandwich panels), the seal consisting only of a thin strip of expanded polystyrene and a run of mastic filling the outside of the joint. According to Swedish reports this is sufficient, thanks perhaps to the rough texture and relatively good absorption of the gas concrete forming the outside skin of the wall.

To facilitate the downward flow of rainwater, the external surfaces of gas concrete prefabricates are treated with water-repellent chemicals.

Joints used in the external walls of buildings constructed by the Swedish firm of "Sundth" are shown in Fig. 7.4.14.

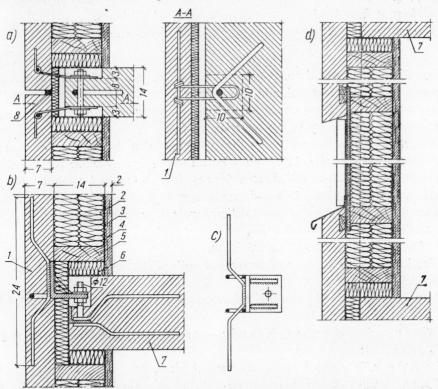

Fig. 7.4.14. Joints in compound external walls as used in buildings by the Swedish firm of "Sundth": (a) vertical joint, (b) horizontal joint, (c) angle cleat with anchors, (d) vertical section through the wall
(1) external concrete panel, (2) layer of mineral wool, (3) plastic foil, (4) plasterboard, (5) timber frame, (6) polystyrene, (7) floor panel, (8) mastic

341

The walls consist of external concrete panels fixed to the cross-walls and to the floors with the aid of bolts, and of an internal skin of mineral wool in timber framing and plasterboard.

Of particular interest is the very careful thermal protection at the points where the external panels meet the structural components of the building.

7.5. LOAD-CARRYING CAPACITY OF LARGE-COMPONENT WALLS

7.5.1. General Considerations

In structural calculations, the load-carrying capacity of a wall is estimated at two horizontal sections:

N_n — the l.c. capacity at mid-height, and

N'_n — in the immediate vicinity of the floor supports.

The determination of N_n forms the basic part of the calculations. The other value, N'_n, represents a certain limitation of the l.c. capacity due to the support conditions at floor level or to the concentration of the loads.

The l.c. capacity N_n of a wall is taken in calculations to be a product

$$N_n = F \cdot R \cdot \varphi \qquad [7.5.1]$$

where F is the horizontal cross-sectional area of the wall or pier, R is the design strength of the wall material, and φ a coefficient, expressing the effect on the l.c. capacity of the initial eccentricity of the load e_0, allowing for the geometric conditions and the elasticity of the material, $d\sigma/d\varepsilon$.

The value of φ is determined on the assumption that the wall is hinged along its stiffened edges (section 7.2.1) and is loaded with a force N acting parallel to the plane of the wall with an initial eccentricity e_0. It is also taken for granted that the building is sufficiently rigid three-dimensionally as described in section 5.1.

Depending on the type of construction involved, walls may be:
— unstiffened at the vertical edges, or
— stiffened at one or both vertical edges.

The load-carrying capacity of unstiffened walls is calculated as for a long strut (Fig. 7.5.1a).

In the case of stiffened walls, they behave as plates supported at three (Fig. 7.5.1b) or four edges (Fig. 7.5.1c).

When the width of the wall, b, in relation to the clear height between the floors, l, is more than:

$b/l > 2$ for walls stiffened along two vertical edges, or

$b/l > 1$ for walls stiffened along one vertical edge only, the l.c. capacity of the wall is calculated as for an unstiffened wall.

The initial eccentricity e_0 is a sum of the technical eccentricity e_t, not allowed for in the design, and the construction eccentricity e_k, resulting from the planned distribution of the loads.

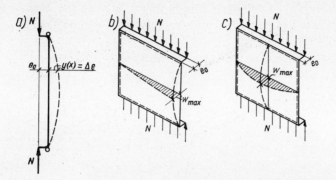

Fig. 7.5.1. Work diagrams of loadbearing walls:
(a) wall unstiffened along its vertical edges, (b) wall stiffened along one vertical edge, (c) wall stiffened along both vertical edges

Thus, when the wall is intended to be axially loaded, and $e_k = 0$, then the l.c. capacity is nevertheless calculated as for an eccentrically loaded wall, and $e_0 = e_t$. This makes allowance for unavoidable errors of production and erection.

The influence of the geometric conditions, mainly of the slenderness ratio

$$\lambda = \frac{l}{h}$$

and in the case of walls restrained along the vertical edges, also of the ratio

$$\gamma = \frac{l}{b}$$

is manifested by an increase in the initial eccentricity e_0 by a quantity Δe, as a result of the buckling of the wall under the force N (Fig. 7.5.1).

The work diagram assumed in Fig. 7.5.1 represents the least favourable conditions for a given value of e_0. In other variants, the increment Δe due to the same force N may be much smaller (Fig. 7.5.2).

The initial eccentricity e_0 may also vary along the horizontal edges of the wall (Fig. 7.5.3), which also decreases the value of the increment Δe.

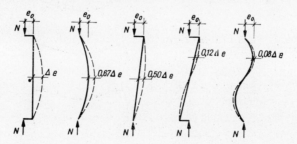

Fig. 7.5.2. Work diagrams for loadbearing walls

343

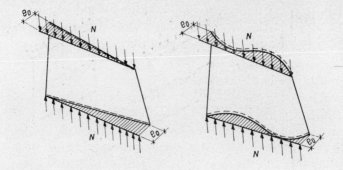

Fig. 7.5.3. Variation in the initial eccentricity e_0 in the horizontal direction

In exploratory structural calculations, the true manner in which the wall will buckle is unknown, and therefore, the least favourable conditions are assumed to hold. The picture is quite different when the l.c. capacity of a wall is tested in the laboratory. Knowing, by measurement at several sections, the strains in the extreme fibres, or the deflections corresponding to various loadings we are able to define the true working diagram of the tested component and to interpret the results accordingly.

Some authors suggest that the l.c. capacity of walls should be based on the assumption that they deform as vertical members of a frame (Fig. 7.5.4), and not as long struts. In this case the eccentricity of loading would be the result of the floor being fixed to the wall.

This assumption is doubtless well founded for buildings with few floors and with large floor spans, particularly when constructed in-situ. For prefabricated buildings, the assumptions shown in Fig. 7.5.1 seem to be nearer to the true conditions existing in the limiting state.

When the slenderness ratio is small—$\Delta e \approx 0$. In determining the capacity of such squat units, the effect of slenderness may be neglected.

The elasticity of the wall material governs the distribution of stresses and the flexural rigidity of the wall.

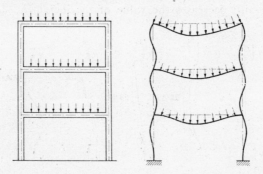

Fig. 7.5.4. Multistorey frame assumption for the work of floors and loadbearing walls

In addition to the deformations occurring immediately, or within a short time, after the application of the load, other deformations take place under prolonged loading. These are known collectively as rheological deformations.

Rheological deformations cause further deflections of a component, in excess of the value Δe due to immediate deformations, and, as a result, the load-carrying capacity of the unit is quite appreciably decreased.

The problem of the effect of the rheological deformations on the l.c. capacity of eccentrically loaded units is very complex and has not, to date, been sufficiently investigated. An additional difficulty is found in the fact that some of the loads in a building are short-term, and others long-term (section 4.1.4).

In design calculations the problem of the rheological deformation of the material used is treated by a very simplified method.

Polish and Soviet regulations state that the l.c. capacity of a component should be calculated as if all the loading was short-term. The rheological effect is allowed for by a numerical increase of the permanent loading, taking into account the slenderness of the component and the material used (section 7.5.2).

The load-carrying capacity next to the floor supports N_n', is given by the equation

$$N_n' = m_0 \cdot F \cdot R \qquad\qquad [7.5.2]$$

where $m_0 < 1$ is a coefficient expressing the effect on the l.c. capacity of the wall of the non-uniform distribution of loading at the joint (section 7.5.8), or of concentrated loads (section 7.5.9).

The safety factor s for the section next to the floor support is calculated without increasing the long-term part of the total load.

When the calculated safety factor s is smaller than is normally acceptable, the wall must be reinforced transversely in the joint (section 7.2.3.2).

The conditions of load transfer at the floor wall joint are of special importance in rather squat walls. With a larger slenderness ratio, a decisive role is normally played by the increase of eccentricity due to the bending of the wall at mid-height (buckling).

7.5.2. Design Loading

Under Polish regulations, the design load N_0 used to determine the safety factor s, should be obtained from the formula

$$N_0 = m_{d1} \cdot N_{d1} + N_{kr} \qquad\qquad [7.5.3]$$

where N_{d1} and N_{kr} are respectively the long-term and the short-term loadings (section 4.1.4), and m_{d1} is a coefficient defining the effect of the long-term loading on the value of N_0:

— When calculating the safety factor next to the floor support, $m_{d1} = 1.0$, but

TABLE 7.5.1
LONG-TERM LOAD FACTOR m_{d1}

| $\dfrac{l_0}{h}$ | Type of concrete | | | |
| | ordinary concrete | | lightweight concrete | |
	Unreinforced components	Reinforced components	Unreinforced components	Reinforced components
8	1.00	1.00	1.00	1.00
10	1.04	1.00	1.05	1.04
12	1.09	1.04	1.11	1.09
14	1.14	1.08	1.18	1.14
16	1.19	1.12	1.25	1.19
18	1.25	1.18	1.33	1.25
20	1.33	1.24	1.43	1.30
22	1.41	1.28	1.54	1.37
24	1.47	1.35	1.67	1.45

for the mid-height section $m_{d1} > 1$, depending on the ratio of the effective length of the unit l_0 to its thickness h (Table 7.5.1).

The effective length l_0 of the component, for the purpose of the calculations, is taken as:

— for walls unstiffened along their vertical edges:

$$l_0 = l \qquad\qquad [7.5.4]$$

— for walls stiffened along one vertical edge $(b/l < 1)$:

$$l_0 = \frac{l}{1 + \dfrac{l}{4\,b}} \qquad\qquad [7.5.5]$$

— for walls stiffened along two vertical edges $(b/l < 2)$:

$$l_0 = \frac{l}{1 + \dfrac{l}{b}} \qquad\qquad [7.5.6]$$

where l is the storey height, and b the width of the wall.

The height of the section is taken as being equal to the thickness of the wall, irrespective of the shape of the cross-section. For example, in T-shaped walls, the height of the section is taken to be the sum of the height of the rib and the thickness of the table.

For lightweight concrete prefabricates, in which lightweight sand was used, the values of m_{d1} given in Table 7.5.1 for lightweight concretes should be increased by 20%.

346

For prefabricates made of sand concrete, the values of m_{d1} are taken as for light-weight concretes.

In squatter walls, say $l_0/h < 14$, there is no need to differentiate between the long and short-term loadings, and m_{d1} can be applied to the total load (section 4.3.2). For more slender walls, this method would result in an unnecessarily high safety factor.

The load acting on the wall is normally computed for a width equal to the width of one wall component.

The load N_0 for the mid-height section is computed from the following:

N_g — the load transferred by the next wall above (including both N_{d1} and N_{kr} loads),

N_{s1} and N_{s2} — the loads from the floors resting directly on the given width of wall (N_{d1} and N_{kr});

N_p — the concentrated load (e.g. beam reaction) (N_{d1} and N_{kr});

G — the dead weight of one storey height of the wall (N_{d1} only);

N_w — the force due to the participation of the wall in the three-dimensional rigidity of the structure (N_{kr} only).

In wall calculations, the superimposed floor loading for private dwellings may be reckoned as follows:
— the roof, attics, and top living floor 100 % of the useful load
— 2nd floor from the top   80 % „ „   „   „
— 3rd floor from the top   60 % „ „   „   „
— 4th and all other floors   50 % „ „   „   „

In the case of floor panels supported on their whole perimeter (cross-reinforced), instead of a triangular or trapezoidal distribution of the loading on the walls, an equivalent uniformly distributed load q may be used:

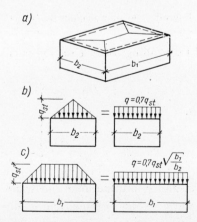

Fig. 7.5.5. Equivalent uniformly distributed load on walls supporting slabs spanning in two directions:
(a) diagram of slab support, (b) triangular loading, (c) trapezoidal loading

347

— for trapezoidal loads

$$q = 0.7 \, q_{st} \sqrt{\frac{b_1}{b_2}} \qquad\qquad [7.5.7]$$

where — as shown on Fig. 7.5.5:
q_{st} is the maximum intensity of the load applied by the floor, b_1 and b_2 are the floor dimensions, provided that

$$2 \geqslant \frac{b_1}{b_2} \geqslant 1$$

— for triangular loads:

$$\text{if } \frac{b_1}{b_2} \leqslant 2 \qquad q = 0.7 \, q_{st}$$

$$\text{if } \frac{b_1}{b_2} > 2 \qquad q = q_{st}.$$

When an opening occurs in a wall panel, only the net area of the cross-section is considered (Fig. 7.5.6).

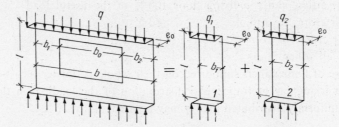

Fig. 7.5.6. Equivalent loading diagram for a perforated wall

The share of the total load falling to each section is calculated according to the expressions:

$$\left.\begin{array}{l} q_1 = q \, \dfrac{b_1 + 0.5 \, b_0}{b_1} \\[3mm] q_2 = q \, \dfrac{b_2 + 0.5 \, b_0}{b_2} \end{array}\right\} \qquad [7.5.8]$$

where, as in Fig. 7.5.6: q_1 and q_2 are the load unit width of the panel section, of width b_1 or b_2; b_0—the width of the opening, and q—the load per unit width of the whole panel.

Concentrated loads are considered to be spread through a wall at a gradient of 4 in 1.

348

When the concentrated load is due to the reaction of a cantilever beam or bracket working in the plane of the wall, the width of the wall over which this load is considered to be spread may be increased by twice the height of the cantilever beam (or of the ring beam, if the cantilever is an extension thereof) (see Fig. 7.5.7).

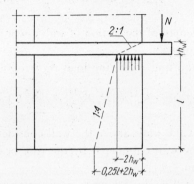

Fig. 7.5.7. Distribution of the concentrated load through the wall

The force N_w should only be taken into account if the wall has been designed as a stiffening wall (section 5.2). The safety factor is then checked only for the extreme sections of the wall.

The force N_w can be calculated from the equation

$$N_w = F \frac{M \cdot z}{J}$$

[7.5.9]

where, as shown in Fig. 7.5.8, F is the area of an extreme section of the wall, M the moment of the extreme horizontal forces about the section considered, J the moment of inertia of the cross-section considered, and z the distance of the centre of gravity

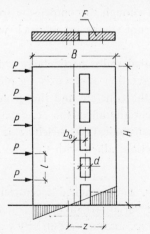

Fig. 7.5.8. Diagram used for determining the force N_w

349

of the external section considered, from the centre of gravity of the whole cross-section of the wall.

If the wall is not weakened by openings, this force is expressed as

$$N_w = 6\ m\ (1-m)\frac{M}{B} \tag{7.5.10}$$

where $m = b/B$, b is the length of the section of wall under consideration, and B the total width of the stiffening wall.

In the case of self-supporting walls, the load N_0 is obtained as the sum:

$$N_0 = m_{d1} \cdot N_{d1} = \left(N_g + \frac{G}{2} + \sum T\right) m_{d1} \tag{7.5.11}$$

where N_g is the weight of the walls above the wall considered, and $\sum T$ the sum of the forces imparted to the wall considered by the ring beams connecting it to the loadbearing walls (section 7.6.1).

If the self-supporting wall is also acting as a stiffening wall, then in load N_0, in addition to the N_{d1} load components, there is also a load $N_{kr} = N_w$ due to the work of the wall in resisting horizontal forces.

7.5.3. Initial Eccentricity

7.5.3.1. *General observations.* The initial eccentricity e_0, as used in structural calculations, is the sum of a technical eccentricity e_t and the constructional eccentricity e_k (section 7.5.1).

When calculating the loadbearing capacity of brick walls, the effect of e_t is neglected. The design strength of the wall in this case is not the strength of the material $R = R(\varepsilon_R)$, but a strut strength R_s. As stated in section 4.2.2, $R_s < R$.

The difference between R_s and the strength R which really determines the l.c. capacity of the wall, is large enough to compensate for the effects of inaccuracies of erection. These effects are not significant in brick walls, which are normally at least 25 cm thick.

In the design of prefabricated walls, particularly ordinary walls of 12 to 16 cm thick, a more accurate interpretation of the existing phenomena is necessary. Non-uniformity and elasticity of the concrete and the geometrical inaccuracies of production and erection, all essentially affect the l.c. capacity of the wall.

The necessity to allow for a technical eccentricity e_t is thus a specific characteristic of large-prefabricate construction, allied with the small thickness of the structural walls.

7.5.3.2. *Technical eccentricity.* The technical eccentricity e_t is treated as the sum of an eccentricity e_{t1} due to variations in the elasticity of the material over the cross-section of the component, and an eccentricity e_{t2} caused by deviations from the shape or positioning of the wall assumed in design.

350

Variations in the elasticity of various points in the wall bring out a disagreement between the diagram of the mean stresses

$$\sigma_0 = \frac{P}{F}$$

and the diagram of the mean strains

$$\varepsilon_0 = \frac{\varepsilon_1 + \varepsilon_2}{2}.$$

This is illustrated by Fig. 7.5.9.

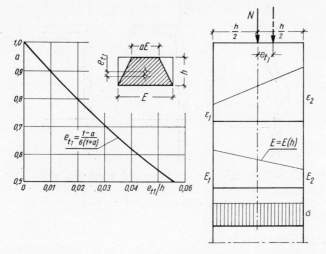

Fig. 7.5.9. Eccentricity e_{t1} caused by elasticity variations within the material: (a) graph of the relationship between e_{t1}/h and a, (b) stress and strain diagrams for an axially loaded section, taking into account elasticity variations along its height h

If, in a rectangular section of height h, the modulus of elasticity varies uniformly from a value E at one edge to a value $a \cdot E$ at the other edge ($a > 1$), then the axis of the mean stresses in the section will be separated from the axis of the mean strains (i.e. from the geometrical axis of the section) by a distance e_{t1} equal to

$$e_{t1} = \frac{1 - a}{6(1 + a)} h. \qquad [7.5.12]$$

The elasticity variations within the thickness of a wall are especially noticeable in horizontally cast prefabricates, i.e. cast at right angles to the direction of loading, although they also occur in prefabricates cast in vertical moulds.

The magnitude of e_{t1} may be obtained by laboratory tests. One method used is to find by trial and error the position of the component in the testing machine which gives equal strains on all sides. The distance between the geometrical axis of the component and the load axis is then measured directly.

351

The value e_{t1} may also be calculated, without the need for laborious shifting of the component in the machine, by measuring the strains on all faces of the component. For small stresses, sufficient accuracy will be obtained by assuming the linearity of the function $\sigma(\varepsilon)$.

Since samples prepared for laboratory tests are normally produced more carefully than general production units, the test results are increased by some 30–50%.

The eccentricity e_{t2} may be caused by dimensional errors of production (particularly warped surfaces), by divergence from the truly vertical, or by a horizontal shift of the wall relative to the upper or lower storeys (Fig. 7.5.10).

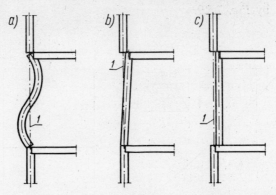

Fig. 7.5.10. Irregularities in the shape and positioning of the wall:
(a) warped panel, (b) panel out of plumb, (c) panel displaced horizontally
(1) theoretical position of the wall

The design assumption is that

$$e_t = |e_{t1}| + |e_{t2}| \qquad [7.5.13]$$

although, with equal probability, the actual condition may be

$$e_t = |e_{t1}| - |e_{t2}| \qquad [7.5.14]$$

The magnitudes of e_{t1} vary within the range 0.01–0.05 h.

Tests carried out by the Polish Building Institute have given the following mean values of e_{t1} for 24 cm thick "flat" cast panels:

ordinary concrete	0.02 h
clinker concrete	0.04 h
autoclaved gas concrete	0.03 h.

Other authorities have suggested that e_{t1} should be taken as a set fraction of the radius of gyration of the section; for concrete $e_{t1} = 1/6\ i$, i.e. for a rectangular section, $e_{t1} = 0.048\ h$.

The magnitude of the eccentricity e_{t2} due to inaccuracies of production and erection is set in relation to the tolerances allowed. If the building is erected by a highly experienced team, e_{t2} can be correspondingly reduced.

Polish regulations demand that the following eccentricities should be allowed for in design:

e_{t1}

— for prefabricates made from ordinary concrete (not weaker than Mk. 140)
$$e_{t1} = 0.03 \; h$$
— for close-textured lightweight concretes (e.g. clinker concrete)
$$e_{t1} = 0.05 \; h$$

e_{t2}

— for walls stiffened along one vertical edge, or panels of width b larger than storey height l $\qquad e_{t2} = 0.7$ cm
— for walls made of narrow components ($b < l$) $\qquad e_{t2} = 1.0$ cm.

For prefabricates cast in timber moulds or in field factories, the value of e_{t1} should be increased by at least 30 %.

According to Soviet standards, e_t should be taken as 2.0 cm, irrespective of the material used or the dimensions of the prefabricates.

7.5.3.3. *Constructional eccentricity.* The magnitude of the constructional eccentricity e_k of prefabricated walls is determined as for other types of loadbearing walls in blocks of flats. It is given by:

$$e_k = \frac{\sum M}{\sum N} \qquad\qquad [7.5.15]$$

where $\sum M$ is the sum of the moments of vertical loads, taken about the axis of the wall, and $\sum N$ the sum of the vertical loads on the wall (Fig. 7.5.11).

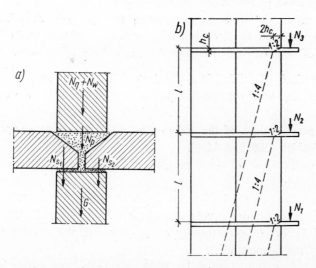

Fig. 7.5.11. Points of application of various loads, assumed for the purpose of determining e_k: (a) in the direction of the thickness of the wall, (b) in the direction perpendicular to the thickness of the wall

For this purpose, the true values of N are used, without increasing the long-term loads.

The forces N_g, G and N_w (section 7.5.2) are considered to be acting axially.

The points of application of the floor loads N_s are assumed, depending on the type of support, to be at a distance from the edge of the wall equal to:
— when freely supported — 1/3 of the length of the slab support
— with the floor partly fixed in the wall — 1/6 of the support length
— with continuous floors (internal supports) — 1/6 of the thickness of the support for each span.

When the spans l_t of neighbouring slabs differ by less than $0.25\ l_t$ of the larger span, it may be taken that the total load

$$N_s = N_{s1} + N_{s2}$$

acts along the axis of the wall.

The points of application of concentrated loads are determined in the same way as those of N_{s1} and N_{s2}.

Loads from the upper storeys can be considered to act axially.

7.5.4. Strength of Walls

7.5.4.1. *Types of walls.* In considering the strength R of the wall, two kinds of walls can be distinguished:
— walls made from prefabricates of full storey height, and
— walls made from prefabricates of less than storey height, i.e. large-block walls.

Walls made from prefabricates extending from the top of the lower floor to the underside of the lintel may be included in the first category. A suitably reinforced lintel, rigidly attached to the floor, is in this case considered to be part of the floor slab.

In a class of their own are prefabricates made from brick-work.

7.5.4.2. *Walls made of full-height prefabricates.* Such walls are, in effect, uniform concrete walls, and their strength is equal to that of the concrete from which they are made.

The appropriate values of the design strength of a concrete were discussed in section 4.2 (Tables 4.2.5 and 4.2.6).

When the wall consists of cored panels, a value $R_\mu < R$ is taken as the strength of the wall.

The effect of ducts on the load-carrying capacity of prefabricates is very complex. Not only are there factors devolving from effectively bi-axial stressing, but also technological factors (non-uniformity of the material, fine crazing caused by the withdrawal of the formers, etc.).

The results of an investigation by W. A. Kamiejko are shown in Fig. 7.5.12, where the relationship between R_μ and the gross cross-section area of the component are represented as follows:

$$R_\mu = \mu \cdot R \cdot \frac{F_n}{F_{br}} \qquad\qquad [7.5.16]$$

where $\mu < 1$ is an experimental coefficient, R the strength of the concrete from which the component is made, and F_n and F_{br} are respectively the net and gross areas of the cross-section of the component.

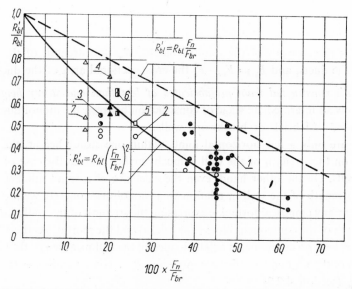

Fig. 7.5.12. Effect of vertical ducts on the strength of wall blocks (after W. A. Kamiejko): (1) thin-wall ordinary concrete blocks, (2) ordinary concrete blocks with circular ducts, (3) ordinary concrete blocks with narrow air gaps, (4) silica blocks with narrow air gaps, (5) clinker concrete blocks with circular ducts (6) clinker concrete blocks with air gaps, (7) silica blocks with internal circular canals

If no tests have been made of a particular type of cored panel, the value of μ for the panel may be taken as

$$\mu = \frac{F_n}{F_{br}} \qquad\qquad [7.5.17]$$

whence

$$R_\mu = R\left(\frac{F_n}{F_{br}}\right)^2. \qquad\qquad [7.5.18]$$

As can be seen in Fig. 7.5.12, for $F_n/F_{br} < 0.70$, most of the test results lie above the curve of equation [7.5.18].

The test result obtained for Żerań blocks (Fig. 7.1.2) of Mk. 170 ordinary concrete, $F_n/F_{br} = 0.535$, was $\mu = 0.75$, which is approximately

$$\mu = \sqrt{\frac{F_n}{F_{br}}}. \qquad\qquad [7.5.19]$$

355

Polish research work has confirmed the view taken by the Soviet standards that, if the joints are properly designed and formed, the quality of the mortar does not significantly affect the loadbearing capacity of large-block walls, although some relationship doubtless exists. This effect of the strength of the mortar on the strength of the wall is more apparent in walls made of clinker blocks (Fig. 7.5.13a), than in walls made of ordinary concrete blocks, which are normally stronger than the former type (Fig. 7.5.13b).

Important, however, is the effect of the height of the individual blocks (and therefore of the number of joints) on the ratio of the strength of the wall R_{sm} to the strength of the blocks themselves R_{bl}. It can be seen from Fig. 7.5.14 that R_{sm}/R_{bl} for a wall consisting of two blocks, say 75 cm high, will differ considerably from the ratios R_{sm}/R_{bl} of walls consisting of larger numbers of smaller blocks. The author considers that the limiting height of the block, above which the wall can be considered a large-block wall, is at least 70 cm.

During tests, cracks were noticed in the mortar, in some cases as early as $0.6\,N_n$. These cracks did not however affect the general pattern of wall failure. Our research did not disclose any reduction in the ratio R_{sm}/R_{bl} with increasing R_{bl}, as would have been expected from formula [7.5.24].

From a series of 26 tests, in which clinker concrete blocks of $R_{\phi16} = 50-150$ kg/cm² were used, the following functions were deduced:

$$R_{sm} = 0.89\ R_{\phi16} - 6\ \text{(kg/cm}^2\text{)} \qquad [7.5.25]$$

or

$$R_{sm} = 0.605\ R_{\phi16}^{1.065}\ \text{(kg/cm}^2\text{)} \qquad [7.5.26]$$

The agreement of the test results with equations [7.5.25] and [7.5.26] is illustrated by Fig. 7.5.15. Equation [7.5.26] seems to conform more closely to the test results,

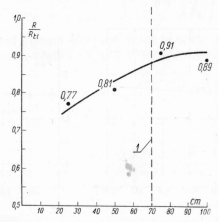

Fig. 7.5.14. Effect of the height of the blocks on the strength of a wall:
(1) limiting height of blocks in large-block walls

358

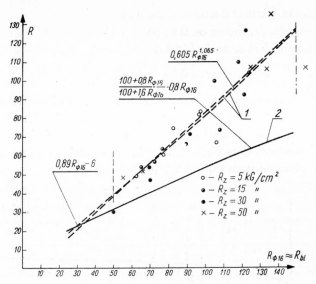

Fig. 7.5.15. Relationship between the strength of individual blocks and the load-carrying capacity of a wall:

(1) after research by the Building Establishment of the Polish Academy of Sciences, (2) from Onishchik's formula

but the differences in R_{sm} are very small, and in the range $R_{\phi16} = 50-150$ kg/cm² they do not exceed ±0.5 kg/cm².

In Fig. 7.5.16, the graph of equation [7.5.24] is also shown, substituting, in agreement with Eq. [4.2.2]

$$R_{\text{s}} = 0.8\ R_{\phi16}.$$

It is evident that the values of R_{sm} obtained from equation [7.5.24] are much lower than the mean test results represented by equations [7.5.25] and [7.5.26]. This difference is approx. 30 % for $R_{\phi16} = 120$, and even more for stronger blocks.

At $R_{\phi16} < 50$, the values of R_{sm} obtained from Eqs. [7.5.25] and [7.5.26] are close to the results of earlier research by S. A. Sementzov, who gave the following expression for clinker concrete block walls, with $R_{\square20} < 40$ kg/cm²:

$$R_{\text{sm}} = 0.75\ R_{\square20} \approx 0.7\ R_{\phi16}.\qquad\qquad [7.5.27]$$

The problem of the basic strength of large-block walls is now being re-investigated in the Soviet Union. The aim of the research is to establish as accurately as possible the experimental coefficients in formula [7.5.21].

A wide range of experiments in this field has been carried out by W. W. Kamejko. He suggests the use of the following coefficients:

Coefficient A (in formula [7.5.22])

for solid blocks in ordinary concrete $\qquad\qquad A = 0.9$

for solid blocks in clinker and cellular concretes $\qquad\qquad A = 0.8$

359

The formulae for functions $\varphi(e, \lambda, \gamma)$, derived from the relationship $\sigma(\varepsilon)$ are somewhat complex, particularly when the geometrical relations are strictly accounted for. In practical work they are not convenient, and suitable tabulated values are used.

The use of tables, instead of formulae, cannot be considered a fault of this method. It is rather a normal consequence of the use of stricter assumptions, and is unavoidably tied to progress in the technique of calculation.

The simplified methods. These are in the main empirical. Normally, they are generalisations of a certain number of experimental results, and sometimes also of results obtained by calculations (by the basic methods).

The great advantage of the simplified methods is the very simple equations they give for calculating the load-carrying capacity of a structure.

The load-carrying capacity $N(e, \lambda, \gamma)$ is normally expressed in the form

$$N(e, \lambda, \gamma) = \varphi(e) \cdot \varphi(\lambda) \cdot \varphi(\gamma) \cdot F \cdot R \qquad [7.5.30]$$

or alternatively

$$N(e, \lambda, \gamma) = \varphi(e) \cdot \varphi(\lambda') \cdot F \cdot R_m \qquad [7.5.31]$$

where $\lambda' = \lambda(\gamma)$.

Arrangement of function $N(e, \lambda, \gamma)$ in the form [7.5.30] or [7.5.31] helps to determine the required coefficients. In building specifications, the values of φ, and particularly of $\varphi(\lambda)$, are given mostly in tabular form, rather than in the form of equations.

The main disadvantage of the simplified methods is that they really should be used only within the tabulated range. Any extrapolation is likely to lead to additional errors. As the simplified methods are mostly based on the results of experiments, the picture is further clouded by the lack of knowledge of the actual test conditions. On the other hand, if the test results are correctly interpreted and used within the tested range, the results obtained by simplified methods may, in fact, be nearer the truth than those calculated by the basic methods.

From the scientific point of view, and that of the economy of construction, the basic methods, based directly on function $\sigma(\varepsilon)$, are normally valued more highly than the simplified methods. It must be pointed out, however, that to make possible the practical utilisation of the coefficients $\varphi(e_0, \lambda, \gamma)$, derived by the basic methods, it is necessary to introduce some mean numerical values of the experimental parameters of the function $\varepsilon(\sigma)$. In consequence, the coefficients $\varphi(e_0, \lambda, \gamma)$ also become approximations. As a rule, however, they are more accurate than those obtained by the simplified methods.

Polish specifications stipulate that, if the loadbearing capacity is based on calculations carried out by the basic methods, then the required safety factor may be decreased by 10 %.

7.5.6. The Basic Method

7.5.6.1. General observations. Several fundamental theories, based on the function $\varepsilon(\sigma)$, may be found in the technical literature. This problem is very wide, as it concerns not only concrete walls, but also masonry walls and axially loaded reinforced concrete components.

Provided that the correct strength R of the concrete is used, the numerical values of the parameter φ obtained by various methods, are generally very close. Larger differences only occur when the assumptions differ widely.

There follows a method of determining the effects of slenderness and non-axiality of loading on the load-carrying capacity of a wall. This method, developed by the author, differs from other methods in that its approach to the problems of the characteristic strength of the concrete R, and of changes in the flexural rigidity of the wall, is stricter. Unlike other solutions, the change in flexural rigidity is only considered in the zone in which cracking is likely to occur. Due to this assumption, a more accurate analysis of the function of the component after cracking is possible.

7.6.6.2. Relationship $\varepsilon(\sigma)$. The relationship between the strains ε and stresses σ is expressed by the following functions:

when the stresses are compression stresses, i.e. $\sigma \geqslant 0$

$$\varepsilon\,(\sigma) = -\frac{k}{a}\,\log_e\left(1 - \frac{\sigma}{k \cdot R}\right) \qquad [7.5.32]$$

and when the stresses are tensile stresses, i.e. $\sigma \leqslant 0$

$$\varepsilon\,(\sigma) = -\frac{k}{a_r}\,\log_e\left(1 - \frac{\sigma}{k_r \cdot R_r}\right) \qquad [7.5.33]$$

with

$$a_r = \frac{k \cdot R}{k_r \cdot R_r}\,a \qquad [7.5.34]$$

and where a, k, k_r are the experimental parameters, and R, R_r are respectively the compression and tensile strengths of the concrete.

Substituting

$$n = \frac{k_r \cdot R_r}{k \cdot R} \qquad [7.5.35]$$

formulae [7.5.32] and [7.5.33] may be rewritten in a general form

$$\varepsilon\,(\sigma) = -\frac{n \cdot k}{a}\,\log_e\left(1 - \frac{\sigma}{n \cdot k \cdot R}\right) \qquad [7.5.36]$$

where for $\sigma \geqslant 0$, $n = 1$; and for $\sigma < 0$, $n < 0$.

363

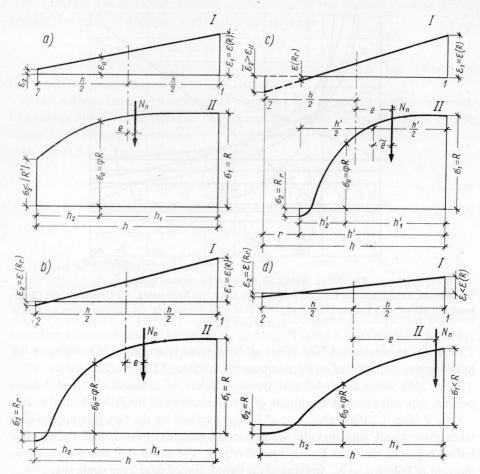

Fig. 7.5.19. The three modes of failure of an eccentrically loaded section:
(a) Case I, (b) limiting case, when $\sigma_1 = R$ and $\sigma_2 = R_r$, (c) Case II, (d) Case III;
(I) strain diagram, (II) stress diagram

In *Case III* (Fig. 7.5.19d), when $e > e^{**}$, the instantaneous extension of the crack is so large that the state $P = N_r$ is also the state of ultimate capacity, i.e. $N_r = N_n$.

The limiting values of e, governing the mode of failure, and also the magnitude of the ultimate load N_n, are related to the function $\sigma(\varepsilon)$.

The variability of the function $\varphi(e)$ for a rectangular section, with $k = 1.01$ and $n = -0.15$, is shown in Fig. 7.5.20.

The parameter a does not affect the function $\varphi(e)$.

The three ranges of e, representing the manner of failure, are divided on the graph by broken lines, $e^* = 0.11\ h$ and $e^{**} = 0.44\ h$.

Within the range $e^* < e < e^{**}$ there are two values:

force N, and is therefore variable along the length of the strut,

$$D = D(e_0 + y).$$

The geometry of the strut, after a crack has formed and the cross-section of the strut has been weakened over a part of its length, is shown in Fig. 7.5.25.

The variability $\varphi(e, \lambda)$ is a function of all three parameters α, k, and n, occurring in formulae [7.5.32] and [7.5.36].

In further calculations this variability will be expressed in the form

$$\frac{N[e, \bar{\lambda}(\alpha)]}{F \cdot R} = \varphi[e, \bar{\lambda}(\alpha)] \tag{7.5.40}$$

where $\bar{\lambda}(\alpha)$ is the so-called reduced slenderness of the component given by

$$\bar{\lambda} = \frac{l}{h\sqrt{\alpha}} \tag{7.5.41}$$

where α is the elastic characteristic of the concrete used, given in Tables 4.2.6 and 4.2.7.

The parameters k and n are still taken as $k = 1.01$, $n = 0.15$.

The graph of the function $\varphi(e, \bar{\lambda})$ for struts with rectangular cross-section is given in Fig. 7.5.26. This graph is used to determine the load-carrying capacity of walls unstiffened along their vertical edges.

As was the case with the graph $\varphi(e)$, we can also distinguish here the boundaries of the three modes of failure (section 7.5.6.3).

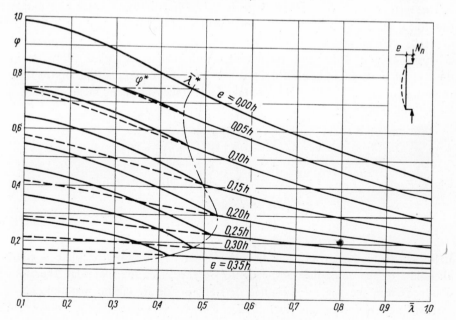

Fig. 7.5.26. Function $\varphi(e, \bar{\lambda})$ for rectangular columns and walls unstiffened along their vertical edges

371

Characteristically, the second case, when $N_r < N_n$, occurs only in components having a relatively small slenderness ratio, when $\bar{\lambda} < \bar{\lambda}^*$. With greater slenderness, irrespective of the initial eccentricity of the load, failure occurs once the strain ε_{Rr} is reached.

These inferences are fully confirmed by laboratory findings.

For medium strength concretes, with $a = 1000$, the value of $\bar{\lambda}^*$ can be said to be approx. $l/h = 15$.

Similar graphs for T-shaped cross-sections, and for a rectangular cross-section weakened by a circular duct, are shown in Figs. 7.5.27 to 7.5.29.

7.5.6.5. *Walls stiffened along their vertical edges.* To determine their load-carrying capacity, walls stiffened along one or both their vertical edges are considered to behave as eccentrically loaded plates.

This assumption is valid until the first crack appears in the loaded wall. As a rule it is a vertical crack caused by the horizontal deformations of the wall reaching the critical value of ε_{Rr}. These cracks may occasionally be horizontal.

The existence of vertical cracks destroys the horizontal continuity of the wall, and therefore reduces the effect of stiffening along the vertical edges on the load-carrying capacity of the wall. In other words, after the vertical cracks appear, the wall stops behaving as a plate, and becomes a slender strut, behaving as if unstiffened.

The attainment of the critical strains $\varepsilon(R_r)$ in the vertical direction (horizontal cracking) is also considered to be the limiting state, as far as the plate-like behaviour of the wall is concerned.

The further work of the wall is only taken into account when the parameter $\varphi(e, \lambda, \gamma)$, calculated for a plate, is smaller than $\varphi(e, \lambda)$ for a strut (wall unstiffened along its vertical edges).

This limitation of the range in which the wall behaves as a plate allows the introduction of a very essential simplification into the determination of the flexural rigidity B of the plate. This value is taken as a function of the mean stresses, $\sigma_0 = N/F$, of the form:

$$B(\sigma_0) = \frac{E(\sigma_0) \cdot b \cdot h^3}{12 [1 - \nu(\sigma_0)^2]} \qquad [7.5.42]$$

where $E(\sigma_0) = \dfrac{d\sigma}{d\varepsilon} = a \cdot R\left(1 - \dfrac{\sigma}{k \cdot R}\right)$, $\nu(\sigma_0)$ is Poisson's ratio, taken as

$$\nu(\sigma_0) = 0.1 + 0.23 \frac{\sigma_0}{R}. \qquad [7.5.43]$$

It follows from this assumption that the flexural rigidity of the plate is equal at all points of the component. The deflection $f(x, y)$ of the plate can therefore be obtained from the general formulae derived for ideally elastic materials.

A wall stiffened along one vertical edge. This behaves as a plate as shown in Fig. 7.5.1b.

372

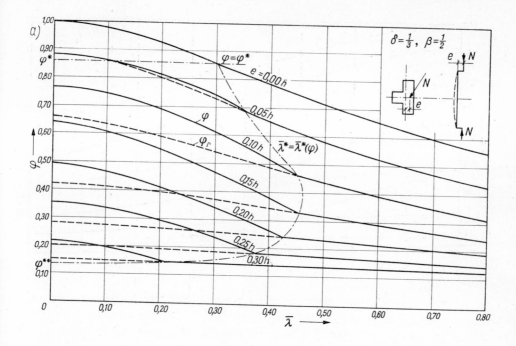

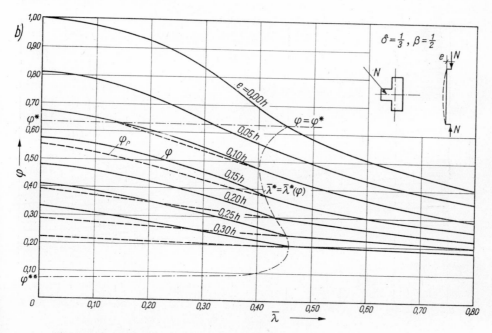

Fig. 7.5.27. Function $\varphi(e, \lambda)$ for T-shaped columns with $\delta = 1/3$ and $\beta = 1/2$:
(a) eccentric force N on the flange side, (b) force N on the rib side

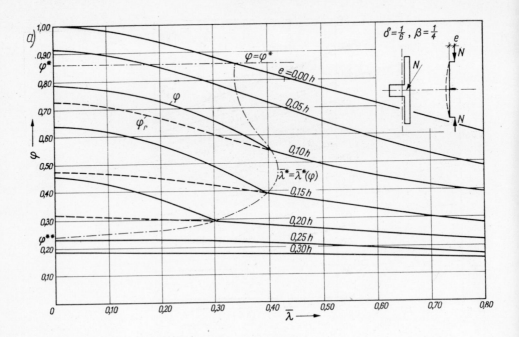

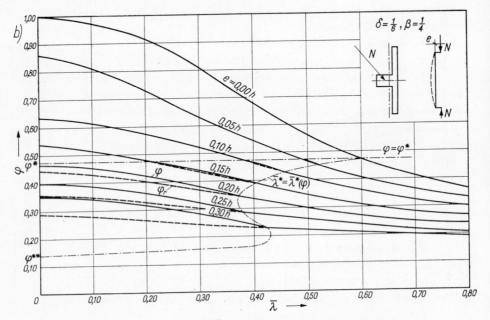

Fig. 7.5.28. Function $\varphi(e, \bar{\lambda})$ for T-shaped columns with $\delta = 1/6$ and $\beta = 1/4$:
(a) eccentric force N on the flange side, (b) force N on the rib side

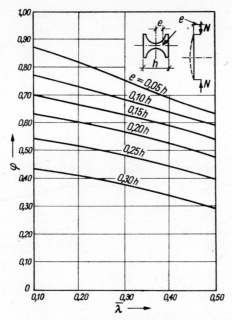

Fig. 7.5.29. Function $\varphi(e, \bar{\lambda})$ for hollow walls

The maximum deflection f_{max} occurs at the mid-height of the free edge. The calculation of f_{max} for $N = N_n$ is very complex, and normally warrants the use of an electronic digital computer.

Graphs of the parameter $\varphi(e, \bar{\lambda}, \gamma)$ in the form of $\varphi_\gamma(e, \bar{\lambda})$ for $\gamma = 1$ and $\gamma = 2$ are given in Fig. 7.5.30.

For $\gamma = 1.0$ the stiffening along one edge has a very small effect upon the load-bearing capacity of the wall. But for $\gamma = 5.0$ this effect is so great that, practically speaking, the effect of the slenderness on the l.c. capacity of the wall may be neglected.

Thus, when calculating the l.c. capacity of a wall stiffened along one edge, the parameter φ_γ is obtained as follows:

for $\gamma < 1.0$ — as for a rectangular strut, from the graph in Fig. 7.5.26;

for $\gamma > 5.0$ — from the graph in Fig. 7.5.20, as for a rectangular strut (neglecting the effect of slenderness);

for $1.0 < \gamma < 5.0$ — by linear interpolation between the values in the graphs in Figs. 7.5.20 and 7.5.30.

A wall stiffened along both vertical edges. This behaves like the plate shown in Fig. 7.5.1c. The maximum deflection f_{max}, caused by the non-axial action of the load, occurs at the centre of the plate.

The magnitude of f_{max} is defined by a relatively simple formula

$$f_{max} = \frac{4e}{\pi} \frac{\chi^2}{(1 + \gamma^2)^2 - \chi^2} \qquad [7.5.44]$$

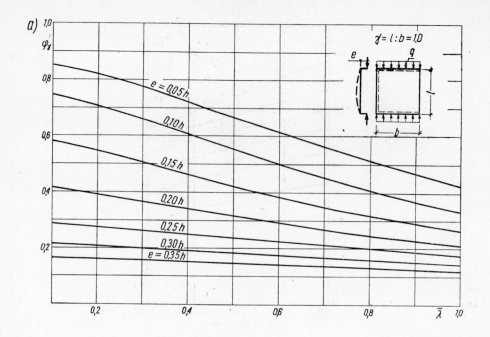

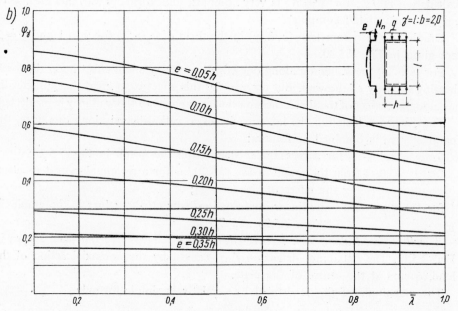

Fig. 7.5.30. Function $\varphi_\gamma(e, \lambda)$ for walls stiffened along one vertical edge:
(a) $\gamma = 1$, (b) $\gamma = 2$

376

where

$$\chi^2 = \frac{N}{B(\sigma_0) \dfrac{\pi^2}{l^2}}$$

and $B(\sigma_0)$ is taken from formula [7.5.42].

Making use of formula [7.5.44], the relationship $\varphi(e, \bar{\lambda}, \gamma)$ may now be expressed in the form $\varphi(e, \bar{\lambda}_\gamma)$, where

$$\bar{\lambda}_\gamma = \bar{\lambda} \cdot \frac{1}{1 + \gamma^2}. \qquad [7.5.45]$$

The graph of the function $\varphi(e, \bar{\lambda}_\gamma)$ is given in Fig. 7.5.31.

In design calculations, when $\gamma < 0.5$ the effect of stiffening along the vertical edges of the wall is neglected, and when $\gamma > 2.5$ the effect of slenderness is also neglected. Therefore, just as in the case of the wall stiffened along one edge, the parameters φ are obtained as follows:

For $\gamma < 0.5$ — from the graph in Fig. 7.5.26;
for $\gamma > 2.5$ — from the graph in Fig. 7.5.20;
for $0.5 < \gamma < 2.5$ — from the graph in Fig. 7.5.31, for a suitable value of $\bar{\lambda}_\gamma$,
calculated from formula [7.5.45].

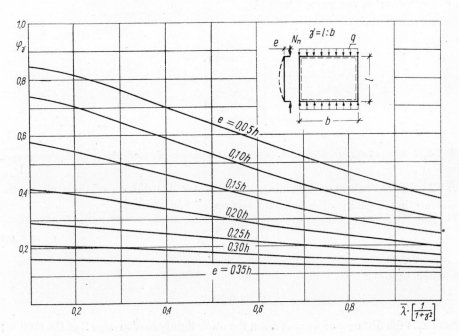

Fig. 7.5.31. Function $\varphi_\gamma(e, \bar{\lambda}_\gamma)$ for walls stiffened along both vertical edges

377

7.5.7. The Simplified Method

7.5.7.1. *General observations.* There is quite a wide scope for simplifying calculations of the load-carrying capacity of concrete walls.

For example, on the basis of the results of laboratory research, Z. Ćwiok suggests that the l.c. capacity N_n under (technically) axial loading, for walls of width b more than half the height l, with a slenderness ratio $l/h \leqslant 30$, to be calculated, irrespective of the slenderness ratio, from the formula:

$$N_n = 0.78 \cdot b \cdot h \cdot R_{\phi 16}. \qquad [7.5.46]$$

This proposition could be accepted, if $a \pm 25\%$ accuracy of the calculated value of N_n was sufficient, and if the required safety factor was accordingly increased. The fluctuations in the assumed strength R represent a separate problem. However, when designing a structure, we must obtain a more accurate value of N_n.

The Polish Guiding Regulations give a simplified method of calculation based on a rectangular distribution of stresses over the section of a non-axially loaded unit. The effect of slenderness is allowed for by multiplying the value $N(e) = \varphi(e) \cdot F \cdot R$ by a reduction coefficient $\varphi(\lambda)$, determined empirically.

The rectangular distribution of stresses (Fig. 7.5.32) is a close approximation to the true distribution of the stresses in the limiting state of failure, and is commonly adopted by other authors in their simplified methods. Large differences between individual methods, and therefore between the calculated values of N_n, occur in the conception of the parameter $\varphi(\lambda)$.

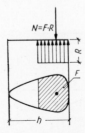

Fig. 7.5.32. Rectangular stress diagram in the cross-section of an eccentrically loaded component

7.5.7.2. *Squat component.* Assuming a rectangular distribution of the stresses, the load-carrying capacity of a concrete section of any shape is

$$N(e) = \frac{S_b}{e_2} R \qquad [7.5.47]$$

provided that

$$S_b \geqslant 0.20 \, S_0$$

where e_2 is the distance of force N from the more lightly loaded edge 2 of the section; for a rectangular section:

$$e_2 = \frac{h}{2} + e.$$

S_b is the first moment of the area of the compression zone in the concrete, calculated for edge 2, and S_0 the first moment of the area of the whole section, calculated for edge 2.

For a rectangular section, formula [7.5.47] simplifies to

$$N\left(e\right) = \left(1 - 2\frac{e}{h}\right) b \cdot h \cdot R \qquad [7.5.48]$$

The use of formula [7.5.48] is limited by the condition

$$e \leqslant 0.45\ h.$$

The coefficient $\varphi(e)$, which describes the influence of the eccentricity e on the l.c. capacity of the section, is given by the following formulae:

for any shape of the cross-section

$$\varphi\left(e\right) = \frac{N\left(e\right)}{F \cdot R} = \frac{S_b}{e_2 \cdot F} \qquad [7.5.49]$$

for a rectangular cross-section

$$\varphi\left(e\right) = 1 - 2\frac{e}{h}. \qquad [7.5.50]$$

When $S_b < 0.20\ S_0$ or, for rectangular sections, $e > 0.45\ h$, Polish specifications suggest the use of reinforced concrete components.

The Soviet standard SNiP II-W 1–62 limits the range of use of formula [7.5.48] to $e < 0.30\ h$. With larger eccentricities, the l.c. capacity should be calculated with respect to the tensile strength of the concrete R_r, namely:

$$N_n = \frac{1.75}{6\dfrac{e}{h} - 1} \cdot b \cdot h \cdot R_r. \qquad [7.5.51]$$

Graphs of the function $\varphi(e) = N(e)/b \cdot h \cdot R$ for rectangular sections, calculated according to Polish specifications SNiP II-W 1-62, and also by the previously discussed basic method, are given in Fig. 7.5.33. It can be seen, that the differences between the curves are very small.

7.5.7.3. *The effect of slenderness.* The parameter $\varphi(\lambda)$, which is used in the simplified method, is expressed by the ratio

$$\varphi\left(\lambda\right) = \frac{\sigma_{kr}}{R}. \qquad [7.5.52]$$

379

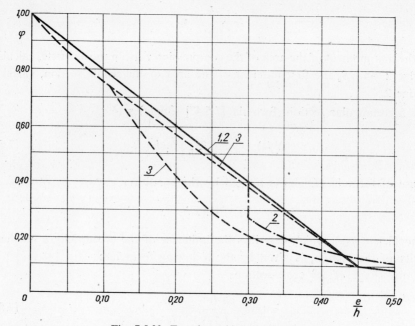

Fig. 7.5.33. Function $\varphi(e)$ according to:
(1) Polish "Guiding Regulations", (2) SNiP II-W 1-62, (3) the basic method

Into the equation

$$\sigma_{kr} = \pi^2 \left(\frac{i}{l}\right)^2 E\left(\sigma_{kr}\right) \qquad [7.5.53]$$

we substitute from expression [7.5.37]

$$E\left(\sigma_{kr}\right) = a \cdot R \left(1 - \frac{\sigma_{kr}}{R}\right).$$

Putting into equation [7.5.53]

$$\pi^2 \cdot a \cdot \left(\frac{i}{l}\right)^2 = \varphi_0 \qquad [7.5.54]$$

we obtain

$$\varphi\left(\frac{l}{i}\right) = \frac{\varphi_0}{1 + \varphi_0} \qquad [7.5.55]$$

or

$$\varphi\left(\frac{l}{i\sqrt{a}}\right) = \frac{\bar{\varphi}_0}{1 + \bar{\varphi}_0}. \qquad [7.5.56]$$

380

where

$$\overline{\varphi}_0 = \pi^2 \left(\frac{i \sqrt{a}}{l} \right)^2 \qquad [7.5.57]$$

and i is the radius of gyration of the section.

For rectangular sections

$$\overline{\varphi}_0 = \frac{0.823}{\overline{\lambda}^2}. \qquad [7.5.58]$$

L. I. Onishchik suggested that formula [7.5.52] be used only for components loaded axially (in the technical sense).

It has been discovered, however, by calculating a number of examples, that, to a reasonable approximation,

$$N(e, \lambda) = \varphi(e) \cdot \varphi(\lambda) \cdot F \cdot R \qquad [7.5.59]$$

where $N(e, \lambda)$ is the load-carrying capacity of a wall with a slenderness ratio λ and loaded with an initial eccentricity e, where $\varphi(e)$ is taken from Eq. [7.5.47], and $\varphi(\lambda)$ from Eq. [7.5.52].

This method has been included in the Soviet standards.

For very slender walls, and also for larger initial eccentricities, formula [7.5.59] rather overestimates the load-carrying capacity of the wall.

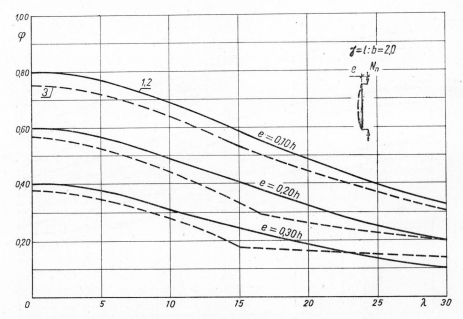

Fig. 7.5.34. Function $\varphi(e, \lambda)$ for walls unstiffened along their vertical edges:
(1) according to the Polish "Guiding Regulations", (2) according to SNiP II-W 1-62, (3) by the basic method

381

For this reason, in the new Soviet standard SNiP II-W 1-62, an empirical correction factor has been introduced into the formula [7.5.57], in the form

$$k = 1 - \frac{e}{h}(0.06\lambda - 0.2).$$ [7.5.60]

The Polish specifications give the same simplified method as SNiP II-W 1-62.

The graphs of $\varphi(e) \cdot \varphi(\lambda) \cdot k$ are given in Fig. 7.5.34. For comparison, graphs of function $\varphi(e, \lambda)$, calculated by the basic method discussed in section 7.5.6, are also shown.

7.5.7.4. *The effect of stiffening at the vertical edges.* When walls are stiffened along their vertical edges, the Polish regulations suggest the use of formulae [7.5.59] and [7.5.60], using a suitably reduced value of the effective height l_0, according to the ratio l/b.

For a wall stiffened along one vertical edge, with $b \leqslant l$

$$l_0 = \frac{l}{1 + \dfrac{l}{4b}}$$ [7.5.61]

and for walls stiffened along both vertical edges, with $b \leqslant 2l$

$$l_0 = \frac{l}{1 + \dfrac{l}{b}}.$$ [7.5.62]

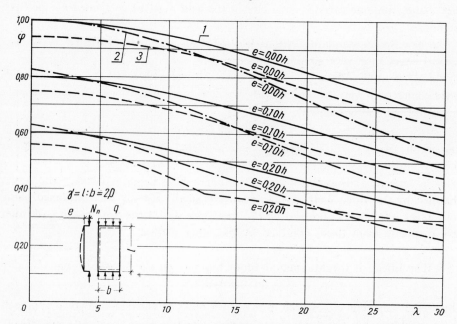

Fig. 7.5.35. Function $\varphi(e, \lambda)$ for walls stiffened along one vertical edge, according to:
(1) the "Guiding Regulations", (2) SNiP II-W 1-62, (3) the basic method

382

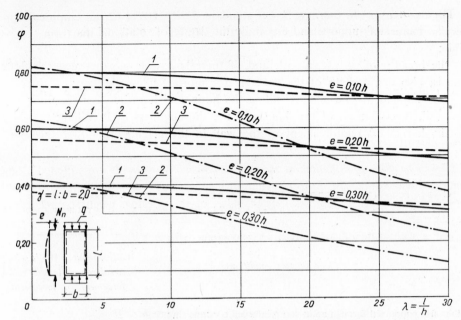

Fig. 7.5.36. Function $\varphi(e, \lambda)$ for walls stiffened along two vertical edges, according to: (1) the "Guiding Regulations", (2) SNiP II-W 1-62, (3) the basic method

The simplified formulae may be used only when $e \leqslant 0.20\ h$. When greater eccentricities occur, the load-carrying capacity of the wall must be calculated by the basic method.

The new Soviet standard SNiP II-W 1-62 deals with walls stiffened along their vertical edges in a very simplified manner.

The N_n of walls stiffened along one vertical edge, with $b \leqslant 1.5\ l$, and walls stiffened along both vertical edges, with $b \leqslant 2.0\ l$, are treated in the same manner as unstiffened walls, but with

$$l_0 = 0.9\ l.$$

The graphs of $\varphi(e) \cdot \varphi(\lambda_\gamma) = \varphi_\gamma(e, \lambda_\gamma)$, as calculated by the two simplified methods and by the basic method, are given in Figs. 7.5.35 and 7.5.36.

In the case of walls stiffened along one edge, the differences between the curves obtained by the three methods are relatively small, but for walls stiffened along both edges, the curves obtained by the method given in the Soviet standard differ very distinctly from those obtained by the other methods.

7.5.8. The Effect of the Manner of Floor Support on the Load-carrying Capacity of the Wall

The present day state of research does not yet make possible an analytical approach to this problem, but the fundamental factors affecting the l.c. capacity are already known.

They are:

— the manner of support, and especially the degree of rotational movement possible;

— the breadth of direct support, and, if there is a wide gap between the floor panels, also the strength of the concrete (or mortar) filling the gap;

— the character of the material filling the horizontal joint between the floor and the wall, the thickness of this joint and the thoroughness of its filling;

— the horizontal reinforcement of the wall in the neighbourhood of the joint.

TABLE 7.5.3.

COEFFICIENT m_0 EXPRESSING THE EFFECT OF THE FLOOR SUPPORT CONDITIONS ON THE LOAD-CARRYING CAPACITY OF THE WALL

	Floor support conditions	*Coefficient m_0*	
		Walls without lateral reinforcement	*Walls with lateral reinforcement*
Floor slab supported through an in-situ reinforced concrete ring beam, extending over the whole width of the wall (Fig. 7.5.37a)		0.80	0.80
Floor slab laid on a bed of cement mortar 1 to 1.5 cm thick ($R_z \geqslant 30$ kg/cm²)	internal supports of continuous slabs and fixed supports (Fig. 7.5.37b)	0.70	0.80
	end supports of continuous slabs and simply supported slabs (Fig. 7.5.37c)	0.50	0.70

Tests indicate that the structural details of the joint, and its consequent freedom of rotation, have a particularly great effect on the load-carrying capacity of the wall. The Polish regulations allow for this by prescribing that the values m_0 given in Table 7.5.3 should be used in formula [7.5.2] (Fig. 7.5.37).

When the floor panels are laid in mortar weaker than $R_z = 30$ kg/cm², or when the construction of the joint is non-standard, experimental data must be obtained before the value of m_0 is decided.

Some guidance in this matter may be obtained from formulae [7.2.1] and [7.2.2].

The Soviet standard SNiP II-W 1-62 expresses the condition [7.5.2] in the form

$$N'_n = m_0 \cdot R_s \cdot F = 0.8 \; m_0 \cdot R \cdot F \qquad [7.5.63]$$

For buildings erected in normal atmospheric conditions, m_0 is taken to be equal to 0.9; but in the winter months, when there is a chance of the fresh mortar freezing, $m_0 = 0.5$.

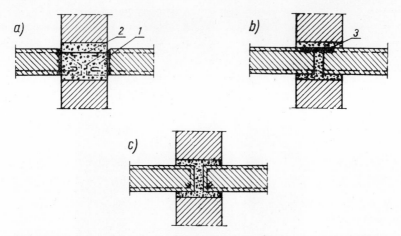

Fig. 7.5.37. Three basic methods of supporting floor panels (cf. Table 7.5.3):
(1) loadbearing portion of the floor panel, (2) lapped reinforcement, (3) steel splice plate

7.5.9. The Effect of Concentrated Loads

When the load is applied to a prefabricated component over a relatively small part of its top surface, it may fail due to the overstress in the concrete next to the point of application of the load.

Examples of the failure of concrete components under concentrated loads are shown in Fig. 7.5.38. Characteristic wedges of strain form immediately under the loads, leading to the ultimate destruction of the components.

When the concentrated load is applied somewhere near the mid-width of the wall, the manner of failure is in essence the same as when it occurs near the edge of the wall. However, near the edge, the wedge of deformation is not restrained horizontally by the bulk of the wall, and the failure load is smaller.

With a larger area of direct support (and with a component of sufficient height), the load-carrying capacity of an eccentrically loaded component is decided by the function of the whole cross-section (Fig. 7.5.39).

The load-carrying capacity of a concrete component loaded over a part of its top surface is determined by empirical formulae. Solutions based on Hooke's law do not embrace the whole of the problem and are of little use.

The Polish Guiding Regulations give, for the load-carrying capacity of a wall loaded over a part of its directly supported area, the formula

$$N_n = m_e \cdot F_d \cdot \gamma \cdot R \qquad [7.5.64]$$

where $m_c \leqslant 1$ is a coefficient expressing the degree of uniformity of the loading, i.e. for a uniformly distributed load $m_c = 1$, with non-uniform distribution of the load over the supporting area, e.g. reaction of a simply supported beam; $m_c =$

385

Fig. 7.5.38. Two examples of the failure of concrete components due to the application of concentrated forces near their edges

$= 0.75$; F_d is the area of direct support, and γ a parameter expressing the increase in the strength of the concrete due to the restraint to horizontal deformation offered by those portions of the component lying outside the region of direct loading.

The parameter γ is obtained from the formula:

$$\gamma = 0.8 \sqrt[3]{\frac{F}{F_d}} \geqslant 1.0 \qquad [7.5.65]$$

where F is the effective area of support, as shown in Fig. 7.5.40.

The Soviet standard SNiP II-W 1-62 limits the value of γ to:

$\gamma_{max} = 1.6$, for the cases shown in Fig. 7.5.40a, b, c

$\gamma_{max} = 1.2$, for the cases shown in Fig. 7.5.40d, e.

For lightweight concretes ($R_{\varphi 20} < 75$ kg/cm²), the value of γ_{max} should be decreased by 20%.

The breadth of the support of a beam (measured from the face of the wall) should not be taken, in calculations, as more than 20 cm.

Values of the function $\gamma(F/F_d)$ obtained from formula [7.5.65] are approx. 10% too low (Fig. 7.5.41).

Fig. 7.5.39. Failure of a tall concrete component (eccentrically loaded)

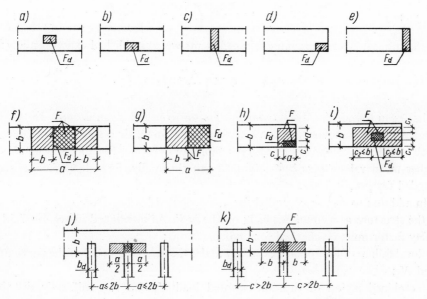

Fig. 7.5.40. The effective area of support F to be used in formula [7.5.65] (explanation in text)

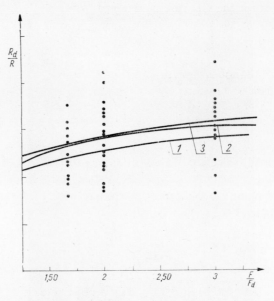

Fig. 7.5.41. Graph illustrating the agreement of experimental results with theoretical calculations for concrete components loaded with concentrated forces; curves obtained: (1) from formula [7.5.65], (2) from formula [7.5.66], (3) from formula [7.5.67]

The same figure shows the curves of two similar functions. The first one was obtained in accordance with the theory of least squares:

$$\gamma = 0.88 \sqrt[3]{\frac{F}{F_d}}.$$ [7.5.66]

In the other function, the numeral coefficients were established experimentally:

$$\gamma = 1.40 + 0.14 \sqrt{\frac{F_d}{F}} - 0.74 \frac{F_d}{F}.$$ [7.5.67]

It has been found that the standard deviation from the mean is some 15 % higher, when testing components under a concentrated force, than the standard deviation of the results of compression tests on samples of concrete. For this reason, although higher mean values have been obtained experimentally, formula [7.5.65] is recommended for practical use.

In addition to the concentrated force, distributed loading from other components in the structure acts simultaneously on the wall. As mentioned in section 7.5.1, the safety factor must be checked for two conditions:

— local failure of the concrete, directly under the area of support of the concentrated load N_d;

— combined action of the concentrated load N_d and the uniformly distributed load q.

The safety factor for the first case is obtained from

$$s = \frac{N_n}{N_d}$$ [7.5.68]

where the value N_d is not affected by long-term loading.
In the second case

$$s = \frac{N_n}{N_0}$$ [7.5.69]

where N_0 is the load, calculated in accordance with section 7.5.2.
The load-carrying capacity of the wall is calculated for a component under a load N_n, acting at the point of application of the resultant of the concentrated force N_d and the distributed load q (Fig. 7.5.42).

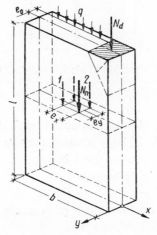

Fig. 7.5.42. Force distribution diagram for calculating the load-carrying capacity of a wall acted upon by a concentrated load and a distributed load

N_n is obtained from the empirical formula

$$N_n = \frac{1}{\dfrac{1}{N_n(e_x, \lambda_x)} + \dfrac{1}{N_n(e_y, \lambda_y)} - \dfrac{1}{N_n(0)}}$$ [7.5.70]

where $N_n(e_x, \lambda_x)$ and $N_n(e_y, \lambda_y)$ are, respectively, the load-carrying capacity of the component, calculated for a force acting with eccentricity e_x (slenderness λ_x), and for a force acting with eccentricity e_y (slenderness λ_y), $N_n(0)$ the load-carrying capacity under an axial load, neglecting the effect of slenderness.
The points of application of the forces $N_n(e_x, \lambda_x)$ and $N_n(e_y, \lambda_y)$ are marked in Fig. 7.5.42 with broken lines.

389

7.6. CALCULATIONS CONCERNING THE JOINTS BETWEEN UNEVENLY LOADED WALLS

7.6.1. The Function of the Joint

The function of a joint between unevenly loaded walls can be represented in a simplified way with the aid of the two blocks shown in Fig. 7.6.1.

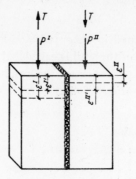

Fig. 7.6.1. The work of two joined blocks loaded with unequal vertical forces

The two blocks are side by side, their cross-sectional areas are F^I and F^{II}, they are made of materials having elasticity moduli E^I and E^{II}, and they are loaded with forces P^I and P^{II}. If there is no joint between the two blocks, the strains in them are ε^I and ε^{II}. In fact, however, the joint between them is filled with mortar, or else they are connected by a ring beam.

No crack will form in the joint if it is capable of transferring a force T, the magnitude of which will make the deformations of both blocks equal.

Instead of the forces P^I and P^{II}, the blocks should be acted upon by forces $P^{I\prime}$ and $P^{II\prime}$, such that

$$\frac{P^{I\prime}}{F^I \cdot E^I} = \varepsilon^{I\prime} = \varepsilon^{II\prime} = \frac{P^{II\prime}}{F^{II} \cdot E^{II}}. \qquad [7.6.1]$$

From Fig. 7.6.1:

$$\left. \begin{array}{c} P^{I\prime} = P^I - T \\[4pt] P^{II\prime} = P^{II} + T \end{array} \right\} \qquad [7.6.2]$$

whence

$$\frac{P^I - T}{F^I \cdot E^I} = \frac{P^{II} + T}{F^{II} \cdot E^{II}} \qquad [7.6.3]$$

The force T, which must be transferred by the joint, can now be obtained from equation [7.6.3].

The quantities E^I and E^{II} should really be considered as functions of the stresses

$$\sigma_1 = \frac{P^I - T}{F^I} \quad \text{and} \quad \sigma_2 = \frac{P^{II} + T}{F^{II}}$$

respectively, in the general function $\sigma(\varepsilon)$ of the concrete. As the principle of the function of the joint we have assumed is very simple, it would be pointless to complicate the calculations by adopting complex basic functions. Besides, under practical working conditions, the lengths of the walls being joined are much larger than in the basic diagram (Fig. 7.6.1), and the ring beam loads only those parts of the walls close to the joint and affects the mean stresses existing in the main bodies of the walls very little. Therefore, when calculating the force T, we may replace the moduli $E^I(\sigma_1)$, $E^{II}(\sigma_2)$, by the initial values

$$E^I = a^I R^I \quad \text{and} \quad E^{II} = a^{II} R^{II} \qquad [7.6.4]$$

where a and R represent, respectively, the elasticity characteristic and the design strength of the concrete (section 4.2.8).

The magnitude of T, therefore, is taken as

$$T = \frac{P^I - P^{II} \dfrac{E^I \cdot F^I}{E^{II} \cdot F^{II}}}{1 + \dfrac{E^I \cdot F^{II}}{E^{II} \cdot F^{II}}}. \qquad [7.6.5]$$

Equation [7.6.5] is used when the prefabricates are loaded directly, and not by means of a ring beam.

In our basic model (Fig. 7.6.1), we have accepted that F^I and F^{II}, i.e. the areas on which force T acts, are known.

When considering the joint in large-block walls as in Fig. 7.6.2, L. I. Onishchik and A. W. Jolkin assumed that a joint formed by means of a ring beam affects the whole area of the external pier block (between windows), and that its action

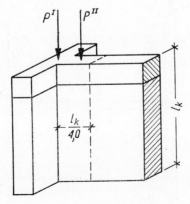

Fig. 7.6.2. The point of contact of the loadbearing external wall and a self-supporting cross-wall (stiffening wall)

391

extends into the internal cross-wall to a depth of $l_k/4.3$, where l_k is the storey height and h the thickness of the wall. The Polish regulations assume that the force T penetrates to a depth of $l_k/4$.

Substituting into formula (7.6.5)

$$F^{II} = \frac{h \cdot l_k}{4} \text{ and also } P^I = \sigma^I \cdot F^I \text{ and } P^{II} = \sigma^{II} \cdot F^{II} \text{ we obtain}$$

$$T = \frac{\left(\sigma^I - \sigma^{II}\dfrac{E^I}{E^{II}}\right)F^I}{1 + 4\dfrac{F^I}{h \cdot l_k} \cdot \dfrac{E^I}{E^{II}}} \cdot \qquad [7.6.6]$$

In multistorey buildings, there are several corresponding forces acting at each floor level (Fig. 7.6.3); each ring beam intercepts a force T, thus relieving wall I and additionally loading part of wall II (originally the more lightly loaded wall).

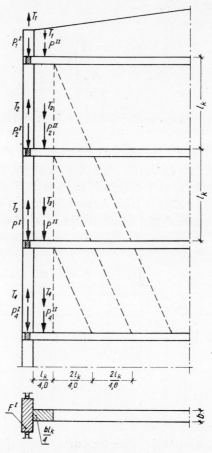

Fig. 7.6.3. Distribution through the wall of stresses caused by forces T acting at floor levels

392

At the level of the floor slab above the $(n+1)$th storey from the top wall I is then acted upon from above by a force

$$P_{n+1}^{I} = P_{n+1}^{I(0)} - \sum_{1}^{n} T \qquad [7.6.7]$$

where $P_{n+1}^{I(0)}$ is the force acting on wall I at the $(n+1)$th storey, calculated without allowing for the interaction at the joint.

Similarly, wall II is acted upon by a force P_{n+1}^{II} correspondingly larger than the force $P_{n+1}^{II(0)}$. Assuming that the ring beams distribute the loading as shown in Fig. 7.6.3, we obtain

$$P_{n+1}^{II} = P_{n+1}^{II(0)} + \frac{4F^{I}}{h \cdot l_{k}} \left(\frac{1}{3} T_{n} + \frac{1}{5} T_{n-1} + \dots + \frac{1}{2n-1} T_{1} \right). \qquad [7.6.8]$$

After substituting the values of P_{n+1}^{I} and P_{n+1}^{II} into equation [7.6.6], this formula, which gives the force T_{n+1} acting on the joint between the walls of the $(n+1)$th storey from the top, becomes

$$T_{n+1} = \frac{\left(\sigma_{n+1}^{I} - \sigma_{n+1}^{II} \dfrac{E^{I}}{E^{II}} \right) F^{I} + \Delta T_{n+1}}{1 + 4 \dfrac{F^{I}}{h \cdot l_{k}} \cdot \dfrac{E^{I}}{E^{II}}} \qquad [7.6.9]$$

where σ_{n+1}^{I} and σ_{n+1}^{II} are the stresses in the pier section of the self-supporting external wall and in the adjoining section of the loadbearing internal wall, at the $(n+1)$th storey from the top, calculated for the case when the two walls act independently; F^{I} is the cross-sectional area of the pier section of the external wall; h the thickness of the internal wall; l_{k} the clear storey height; E^{I}, E^{II} are, respectively, the elasticity moduli of the materials from which the external and the internal walls are made, and ΔT_{n+1} is a factor expressing the effect on the joint considered, of the forces T transferred to wall II by the joints of n upper storeys.

$$\Delta T_{n+1} = - \sum_{1}^{n} T_{n} - 4 \frac{F^{I}}{h \cdot l_{k}} \cdot \frac{E^{I}}{E^{II}} \left(\frac{1}{3} T_{n} + \frac{1}{5} T_{n-1} + \dots + \frac{1}{2n-1} T_{1} \right). \qquad [7.6.10]$$

In the case of hollow walls, instead of the thickness h, a reduced thickness h_{red} is used. This is given by:

$$h_{red} = h \frac{F_{net}}{F_{gross}}.$$

Formula [7.6.9] is normally sufficient to yield the forces T occurring at the join. between the walls due to unequal loading and/or materials of different elasticity. In some cases it is necessary to include also the effect of shrinkage of the material.

393

This effect may be allowed for in formula [7.6.9] by calculating the equivalent stresses $\overline{\sigma}_{sk}$ due to shrinkage

$$\overline{\sigma}_{sk} = \varepsilon_{sk} \cdot E \tag{7.6.11}$$

and adding these stresses (at each floor) to the stresses due to loading. Thus, into formula [7.6.9] we substitute,

$$\sigma'_{n+1} = \sigma_{n+1} + \overline{\sigma}_{sk}. \tag{7.6.12}$$

The shrinkage effect must be taken into consideration, when non-loadbearing prefabricated walls are joined to in-situ loadbearing walls.

For ordinary concrete, the shrinkage strain ε_{sk} may be taken to be approx. 2×10^{-4}. Assuming that the prefabricates will be erected not earlier than a fortnight after casting the in-situ walls, only half the total shrinkage need be allowed for in calculating σ_{sk}, i.e. $\varepsilon_{sk} = 1 \times 10^{-4}$.

The calculation of the forces T is begun at the force T_1. In this case $\Delta T = 0$, and formula [7.6.9] takes the form

$$T_1 = \frac{\left(\sigma^{\mathrm{I}} - \sigma^{\mathrm{II}} \cdot \dfrac{E^{\mathrm{I}}}{E^{\mathrm{II}}}\right) F^{\mathrm{I}}}{1 + 4 \dfrac{F^{\mathrm{I}}}{h \cdot l_k} \cdot \dfrac{E^{\mathrm{I}}}{E^{\mathrm{II}}}}. \tag{7.6.13}$$

After force T_1, the force T_2 is obtained from [7.6.9], taking $n = 1$; force T_3 follows and so on.

7.6.2. The Load-carrying Capacity of a Vertical Joint

To prevent cracking at the point of contact of two walls unequally loaded, or made from different concretes, the load-carrying capacity of the joint between them, with respect to the vertical tangential force, should be at least $s_r \geqslant 1.8$ times bigger than the value of the force T occurring at this point.

The force T may be transferred by the joint itself, or, as is often the case, by the joint and a ring beam together.

The constructional requirements for joints, and their load-carrying capacity with respect to the forces acting in their planes, were discussed in section 7.2.3.

When the joint between adjoining prefabricates is tied with a ring beam, then the whole or a part of the force T may be transferred to the latter.

It has been discovered, in the course of research at the Polish Building Institute, that whilst cracking occurred in concrete joints without ring beams when

$$T = T_{rs} = F_{sr} \cdot R_{ts} \tag{7.6.14}$$

where F_{sr} is the area of the shear surface of the joint, R_{ts} the direct shear strength of the mortar or concrete filling the joint, when the vertical joints were tied with ring beams, cracking occurred when a force

$$T < F_{sr} \cdot R_{ts} + F_w \cdot R_{tw} \qquad [7.6.15]$$

is reached, where R_{tw} is the direct shear strength of the reinforced ring beam, and F_w the cross-sectional area of the ring beam.

When blocks joined without ring beams were tested, cracks appeared in the joint (Fig. 7.6.4) under a load $T = T_{rs}$ (formula [7.6.4]), calculated for $R_{ts} = 0.15\ R_{\phi 8}$ (mean). But when ring beams were used, the cracks appeared between the panels when T was

$$T_{rs} = F_{sp} \cdot 0.15\ R_{\phi 8} + F_w \cdot k \cdot R_{tw} \qquad [7.6.16]$$

where k varies between 0.38 and 0.84.

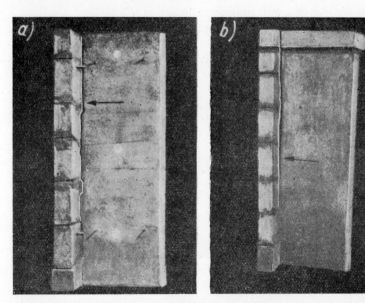

Fig. 7.6.4. Cracks in the joints of T-shaped junctions between blocks:
(a) joint without ring beam, (b) joint with a reinforced concrete ring beam

Cracks in the ring beams themselves only appeared when T was much larger

$$T_{rw} = 1.10 - 1.25\ T_{rs}.$$

Neglecting the contribution of the joint between the panels, which was already badly cracked, the shear stresses R_{tw} in the ring beam, corresponding to the force T_{rw}, were

$$R_{tw} = 0.17 - 0.19\ R_{\phi 16}$$

i.e. 10 to 25 % more than the design shear strength of reinforced concrete beams.

395

Thus, even a ring beam strong enough to resist cracking does not fully protect the joint between the panels below it. When checking the safety factor s_r of the shear capacity of the joint, only part of the shear capacity of the ring beam should be taken into consideration.

The Polish regulations demand that the joint should be so designed, that

$$s_r \cdot T \leqslant F_{sp} \cdot R_{ts} + 0.3 \ F_w \cdot R_{tw} \qquad [7.6.17]$$

where $s_r = 1.8$.

In actual calculations, a reduced value of F'_{sp} is normally inserted into formula [7.6.17] (section 7.2.3.3)

$$F'_{sp} < F_{sp}.$$

When the joint being designed occurs within a stiffening wall (e.g. connection between the flange and the web of a wall considered to act as a T section), the force T should be increased by the addition of an appropriate shear force due to the function of the wall in resisting horizontal loading.

The safety factor with respect to this combined vertical shear force may be reduced to 1.6.

7.7. NUMERICAL EXAMPLES OF WALL CALCULATIONS FOR A CROSS-WALL BUILDING

7.7.1. Description of the Building

The check presented below relates to a 5-storey building (Fig. 7.7.1), with loadbearing cross-walls and light curtain walls on the long elevations.

(a) *General data*:
— width of the building (central lines of external walls)—10.80 m;
— length of the building — 57.00 m (5 staircases) — no expansion joints;
— spacing of the loadbearing cross-walls-centres — 5.70 m, clear — 5.46 m;
— storey height — 2.80 m o/a, 2.56 m clear.

(b) *Roof*:
cored panels, insulated by lightweight rubble (0.8 T/m³), forming a single slope 1 in 50, and covered by two layers of roofing felt. Dead weight $g = 750$ kg/m², superimposed load $p = 60$ kg/m².

(c) *Floor slabs and balconies*:
Floors — made of standard cored panels with smooth lower surfaces, no plaster, supported on walls by means of reinforced concrete dowels cast in-situ, $g = 465$ kg/m², $p = 150$ kg/m².
Balconies — cored panels supported on in-situ reinforced concrete cantilevers which are prolongations of ring beams on the cross-walls, $g = 410$ kg/m², $p = 500$ kg/m².

(d) *Stairs*:
Landings — cored panels spanning between the cross-walls.
Flights — solid slabs.

(e) *Internal loadbearing walls*:
made of storey height prefabricates of three types:
— cored blocks, with diameter of the core 18 cm;

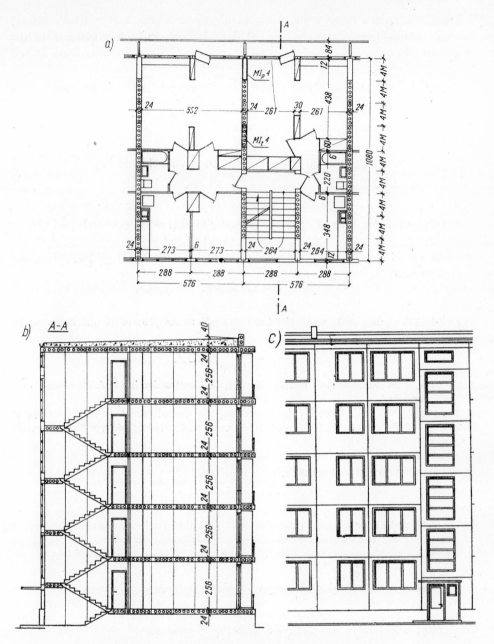

Fig. 7.7.1. A block of flats built on the cross-wall system:
(a) central portion of a typical floor plan, (b) vertical section, (c) part elevation

— solid blocks, carrying the balcony loads;
— door blocks, reinforced.

The thickness of all blocks was 24 cm; they were made of Mk. 170 ordinary concrete.

(f) *External walls*:

— Gable walls and longitudinal walls in the end bays — cored blocks, insulated with a 12 cm layer of gas concrete;

— other longitudinal walls — curtain walling on a timber frame.

(g) *Underground part of the building — monolithic.*

(h) *The three-dimensional stiffness of the building is provided by*:

— in the long direction — external structural walls in the end bays;

— in the short direction — loadbearing cross-walls.

7.7.2. Internal Cross-Walls, Extreme Blocks—Solid

Block dimensions: $b = 119$ cm, $h = 24$ cm, $l = 256$ cm.

Ratio $l/h = \dfrac{256}{24} = 10.7 > 8$. Hence, the effect of long-term loading must be considered.

The net cross-sectional area of the block, subtracting the area of side grooves, is given by:

$$F_b = 24 \times 119 - 210 = 2650 \text{ cm}^2$$

The basic strength of the block is the design strength of the concrete used, i.e. for Mk. 170 concrete, from Table 4.2.5

$$R = 170 \text{ kg/cm}^2,$$

$$a = 1750.$$

The reduced slenderness of the wall is given, at right angles to the plane of the wall, by the expression:

$$\bar{\lambda} = \frac{10.7}{\sqrt{a}} = \frac{10.7}{\sqrt{1750}} = 0.256.$$

In the plane of the wall, however, because of the type of construction involved, the effect of slenderness is neglected, and $\bar{\lambda}_y = 0$.

The quantity N'_n, which limits the load-carrying capacity depending on the type of floor support used, is taken as for a joint (ring beam) made in-situ and extending the full width of the wall (section 7.5.8):

$m_0 = 0.80$

$N'_n = 0.80 \times 2650 \times 170 = 360{,}400$ kg.

The first storey block involves the following calculations:

(a) *Loading*

The block carries all its loading on a strip of wall 1.20 m wide. The loading consists of the weight of the external wall and the reaction from the balcony cantilever (Fig. 7.7.1b).

The load on a 1.20 m strip of wall, given by the forces $N_g + 1/2$ G can be found as follows:

Roof

$$2 \times \frac{5.46}{2} \times 1.20 \times 705 = \qquad 4620 \text{ kg}$$

$$2 \times \frac{5.46}{2} \times 1.20 \times 60 = \qquad\qquad 390 \text{ kg}$$

Floors

$$4 \times 2 \times \frac{5.46}{2} \times 1.20 \times 465 = \qquad 12250 \text{ kg}$$

$$4 \times 2 \times \frac{5.46}{2} \times 1.20 \times 150 = \qquad\qquad 3940 \text{ kg}$$

Wall blocks from 4 1/2 storeys

$$4.5 \times 1725 \qquad\qquad\qquad\qquad 7750 \text{ kg}$$

R.c. ring beams

$$5 \times 300 \qquad\qquad\qquad\qquad 1500 \text{ kg}$$

$$N_{\text{d}1} = 26120 \text{ kg} \qquad 4330 \text{ kg}$$

Reduction of superimposed load

$$(0.2 + 0.4 + 0.5) \times 2 \times \frac{5.46}{2} \times 1.20 \times 150 \qquad\qquad - 1080 \text{ kg}$$

$$N_{\text{kr}} = 3250 \text{ kg}$$

Thus $N_{\text{g}} + 1/2\ G = 26120 + 3250 = 29370$ kg.

Loading from the balcony cantilevers and external walls: The force N_5 is given by

Parapet wall

$$2 \times \frac{5.70}{2} \times 2.09 \qquad 1190 \text{ kg}$$

Slab overhang over the top storey balcony

$$2 \times \frac{5.70}{2} \times 440 \qquad 2510 \text{ kg}$$

$$2 \times \frac{5.70}{2} \times\ 60 \qquad\qquad\qquad 340 \text{ kg}$$

$$3700 \text{ kg} \qquad 340 \text{ kg}$$

$$N_5 = 3700 + 340 = 4040 \text{ kg.}$$

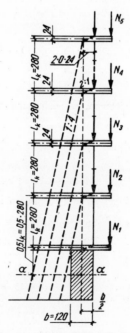

Fig. 7.7.2. Distribution through the cross-wall of the effect of the concentrated loading (the weight of the external wall and of the balconies)

Forces $N_4 = N_3 = N_2 = N_1$
Balcony

$$0.90 \times 2 \times \frac{5.70}{2} \times 410 \qquad\qquad 2100 \text{ kg}$$

$$0.90 \times 2 \times \frac{5.70}{2} \times 500 \qquad\qquad\qquad 2560 \text{ kg}$$

Dividing wall panel $\qquad\qquad\qquad\qquad\qquad\qquad \underline{420 \text{ kg}}$

$$\qquad\qquad\qquad\qquad\qquad\qquad\qquad 2520 \text{ kg} \quad 2560 \text{ kg}$$

$$N_4 = N_3 = N_2 = N_1 = 2520 + 2560 = 5080 \text{ kg.}$$

As is evident from Fig. 7.7.2, the block under consideration supports a load

$$N_{p,\text{d}l} = \left(\frac{3700}{4 \times \dfrac{2.80}{4} + 2 \times 0.24} + \frac{2520}{3 \times \dfrac{2.80}{4} + 2 \times 0.24} + \frac{2520}{2 \times \dfrac{2.80}{4} + 2 \times 0.24} + \right.$$

$$\left. + \frac{2520}{\dfrac{2.80}{4} + 2 \times 0.24} \right) \times 1.20 + 2520 = 6700 + 2520 = 9220 \text{ kg.}$$

$$N_{p,\text{kr}} = \left(\frac{340}{3.28} + \frac{2560}{2.58} + \frac{2560 \times 0.8}{1.88} + \frac{2560 \times 0.6}{1.18} \right) \times 1.20 + 2560 = 4140 + 2560 = 6700 \text{ kg.}$$

Design load N_0, for which the safety factor is checked:

For a slenderness ratio $l/h = 10.7$, the coefficient $m_{\text{d}l}$ is obtained from Table 7.5.1 as:

$$m_{\text{d}l} = 1.06.$$

The force N_0 is obtained as the sum

$$N_0 = (26120 + 9220) \times 1.06 + (3250 + 6700) = 47450 \text{ kg.}$$

(b) *Initial eccentricity*

Constructional eccentricity:

There is no eccentricity in the x direction, perpendicular to the plane of the wall, and therefore

$$e_{x,k} = 0.$$

In the other direction, parallel to the plane of the wall, the eccentricity is $e_{y,k} = 0$, and the following forces are present:

$$N_g + 1/2 \ G = 29370 \text{ kg}$$

together with components of the forces $N_5, N_4, N_3,$ and N_2, calculated previously

$$N_5 + N_4 + N_3 + N_2 = N_{p,\text{d}l} + N_{p,\text{kr}} = 6700 + 4140 = 10840 \text{ kg.}$$

There is, however, a force N_1 equal to $2520 + 2560 = 5080$ kg, representing the loading from the second storey balcony cantilever, and acting with an eccentricity

$$e_{y,k} = \frac{b}{2} + a = \frac{1.20}{2} + 0.45 = 1.05 \text{ m.}$$

The resultant eccentricity $e_{y,k}$ is

$$e_{y,k} = \frac{5080 \times 105}{29370 + 10840 + 5080} = 11.8 \text{ cm.}$$

400

The technical eccentricity is only considered in the x direction:
— eccentricity e_{t1} for ordinary concrete prefabricates

$$e_{t1} \doteq 0.03 \; h = 0.03 \times 24 = 0.72 \text{ cm}$$

— eccentricity e_{t2} for walls constructed of narrow prefabricates

$$e_{t2} = 1.0 \text{ cm.}$$

Total eccentricities (Fig. 7.7.3):

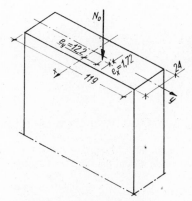

Fig. 7.7.3. Loading on the extreme block of the cross-wall

— in the x direction — only the technical eccentricity:

$$e_x = e_{x,t} = 0.72 + 1.0 = 1.72 \text{ cm}$$

$$\frac{e_x}{h} = \frac{1.72}{24} = 0.07$$

— in the y direction — only the constructional eccentricity:

$$e_y = e_{y,k} = 11.8 \text{ cm}$$

$$\frac{e_y}{b} = \frac{11.8}{119} = 0.10.$$

(c) *Determination of the load-carrying capacity of the block*
    The l.c. capacity is obtained from formula [7.5.70] as

$$N_n = \frac{1}{\dfrac{1}{N_n\,(e_x,\,\lambda_x)} + \dfrac{1}{N_n\,(e_y,\,\lambda_y)} - \dfrac{1}{N_n\,(0)}}.$$

The values $N_n(e_x, \lambda_x)$ and $N_n(e_y, \lambda_y)$ are, according to the basic method:

for $\dfrac{e_x}{h} = 0.07$ and $\lambda_x = 0.256$ $\qquad$ $\varphi_x = 0.76$

for $\dfrac{e_y}{b} = 0.10$ and $\lambda_y = 0.0$ $\qquad$ $\varphi_y = 0.75$

and therefore,

$N_n\,(e_x, \lambda_x) = 0.76 \times 2650 \times 170 = 342{,}380 \text{ kg}$

$N_n (e_y, \lambda_y) = 0.75 \times 2650 \times 170 = 337{,}870$ kg

$N_n (0) = 2650 \times 170 = 450{,}500$ kg

and finally

$$N_n = \cfrac{1}{\dfrac{1}{342380} + \dfrac{1}{337870} - \dfrac{1}{450500}} = 271{,}500 \text{ kg.}$$

Safety factors:
  actual

$$s = \frac{271{,}500}{47450} = 5.73$$

  required $- 2.5 \times 0.9 = 2.25$.

7.7.3. Internal Cross-Walls—Cored Blocks W4

Dimensions of the blocks: $b = 119$ cm, $h = 24$ cm, $l = 255$ cm.
  There are 5 vertical ducts per block, 18 cm dia. at 22 cm centres.
  The ratio $l/h = \dfrac{256}{24} = 10.7$

and the long-term and short-term loads are therefore considered separately.
  The cross-sectional area of the block, allowing for the side grooves, is given by:

$$F_{br} = 24 \times 119 - 210 = 2650 \text{ cm}^2$$

$$F_n = 2650 - 5 \times \frac{3.14 \times 18^2}{4} = 1464 \text{ cm}^2.$$

For Mk. 170 ordinary concrete, from Table 4.2.5,

$$R = 170 \text{ kg/cm}^2 \qquad a = 1750.$$

The basic strength of the cored blocks is given by the formula

$$R_\mu = \mu \cdot R.$$

For the type of block used, where $F_n/F_{br} = \dfrac{1464}{2650} = 0.55, \mu = 0.75$ (see section 7.5.4),

and, therefore,

$$R_\mu = 0.75 \times 170 = 127.5 \text{ kg/cm}^2.$$

The value N'_n limiting the load-carrying capacity of the block (section 7.5.8) is

$$N'_n = 0.80 \times 1464 \times 127.5 = 149200 \text{ kg.}$$

The stiffening along the vertical edges is neglected in calculations of the load-carrying capacity
  The first storey block involves the following computations:

(a) *Loading*
  The block carries the loads from: roof, floors and the dead weight of the wall over a strip 1.20 m
wide, and also some of the balcony load.

402

Loading on 1.20 m width of the wall:

Roof (as with the previous full block)		4620 kg	390 kg
Floors	ditto	12250 kg	3940 kg
Ring beams 5×300		1500 kg	
Wall blocks 4.5×915		4110 kg	

$$N_{d1} = 22{,}480 \text{ kg} \qquad 4330 \text{ kg}$$

The reduction of the superimposed load is:

$$(0.2 + 0.4 + 0.5) \times 2 \times \frac{5.46}{2} \times 1.20 \times 150 \qquad\qquad - 1080 \text{ kg}$$

$$N_{kr} = 3250 \text{ kg}$$

Balcony loading (Fig. 7.7.2):

The forces N_5, N_4 and N_3 are determined as for the full extreme block, distinguishing between N_{d1} and N_{kr}. The force N_3 though, acts only on a part of the width of the block, this part width being

$$b' = 2 \times \frac{2.80}{4} + 2 \times 0.24 - 1.20 = 0.68 \text{ cm.}$$

The effect of the eccentricity of this force is neglected however.

The force N_2 does not act on the block under consideration.

$$N_{p,d1} = \left(\frac{3700}{4 \times \dfrac{2.80}{4} + 2 \times 0.24} + \frac{2520}{3 \times \dfrac{2.80}{4} + 2 \times 0.24} \right) \times 1.20 +$$

$$+ \frac{2520}{2 \times \dfrac{2.80}{4} + 2 \times 0.24} \times 0.68 = 3450 \text{ kg.}$$

$$N_{p,kr} = \left(\frac{340}{3.28} + \frac{2560}{2.58} \right) \times 1.20 + \frac{0.8 \times 2560}{1.88} \times 0.68 = 2056 \text{ kg.}$$

For $l/h = 10.7$, from Table 7.5.1, by interpolation

$$m_{d1} = 1.06.$$

Force N_0 is then given by

$$N_0 = (22480 + 3450) \times 1.06 + (3250 + 2056) = 37810 \text{ kg.}$$

The value to be adopted when checking the safety factor with respect to N'_n (section 7.5.8) is given by:

$$N'_0 = 22480 + 3450 + 3250 - 2056 = 31240 \text{ kg.}$$

(b) *Initial eccentricity*

Constructional eccentricity:

As the wall is symmetrically loaded,

$$e_k = 0.$$

The technical eccentricity (section 7.5.3.2), is as for the full blocks previously calculated,

$$e_t = e_{t1} + e_{t2} = 0.7 + 1.0 = 1.7 \text{ cm.}$$

Total eccentricity

$$e = e_k + e_t = 0 + 1.7 = 1.7 \text{ cm}$$

$$\frac{e}{h} = \frac{1.7}{24} = 0.07.$$

403

(c) *Determination of the load-carrying capacity of the wall, using graphs prepared by the basic method*

From the graph in Fig. 7.5.29, for $\dfrac{e}{h} = 0.07$ and for

$$\bar{\lambda} = \frac{256}{24\sqrt{1750}} = 0.256$$

we find

$$\varphi = 0.76$$

and therefore

$$N_n = \varphi \cdot F_n \cdot R_\mu = 0.76 \times 1464 \times 127.5 = 142000 \text{ kg}.$$

Safety factor

$$s = \frac{142000}{37810} = 4.32 > 2.5.$$

(d) *Determination of the l.c. capacity of the wall by the simplified method (section 7.5.7)*
To determine $\varphi(e)$, we shall consider a part of the cross-section of the block as shown in Fig. 7.7.4

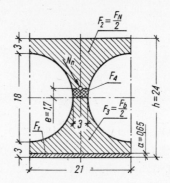

Fig. 7.7.4. Part-horizontal section through a cross-wall block to assist in calculating the value S_b

The coefficient $\varphi(e)$ is obtained from formula [7.5.47]

$$\varphi(e) = \frac{S_b}{e_2 \cdot F}$$

To determine S_b, the area of the compression zone of the concrete, F_b, must first be found.
A force N_n, acting with eccentricity $e = 1.7$ cm, is applied at the C. of G. of the area F_b, and therefore:

$$F_2 = F_3 = \frac{F_b}{2}.$$

This condition will be satisfied if

$$F_1 = 2 \times F_4$$
$$22 \times a = 2 \times 3.2 \times 1.7$$

whence

$$a = 0.65 \text{ cm}.$$

404

The value of the first moment of the area S_b is now calculated as a difference between the first moment of the area of the gross rectangular compression zone (neglecting the duct) and the first moment of the area of the duct section.

$$S_b = 22(24 - 0.65) \times \left(\frac{(24 - 0.65)}{2} + 0.65 \right) - 3.14 \times 9^2 \times \frac{24}{2} = 3270 \text{ cm}^3.$$

The value of e_2 in formula [7.5.47] is given by:

$$e_2 = \frac{h}{2} + e = 12 + 1.7 = 13.7 \text{ cm}^2.$$

The area F of the block is:

$$F = 22 \times 24 - 3.14 \times 9^2 = 274 \text{ cm}.$$

$\varphi(e)$ then becomes

$$\varphi(e) = \frac{3270}{13.7 \times 274} = 0.872$$

The coefficient $\varphi\left(\frac{l}{i}\right)$ is obtained from formula [7.5.55]

$$\varphi\left(\frac{l}{i}\right) = \frac{\varphi_0}{1 + \varphi_0}$$

whence, from formula [7.5.54]

$$\varphi_0 = \pi^2 a \left(\frac{i}{l}\right)^2.$$

The radius of gyration is given by:

$$i = \sqrt{\frac{J_n}{F_n}} = \sqrt{\frac{0.0833 \times 119 \times 24^2 - 5 \times 0.25 \times 3.14 \times 9^2}{1464}} = 8.7 \text{ cm}$$

and

$$\varphi_0 = 3.14^2 \times 1750 \times \left(\frac{8.7}{256}\right)^2 = 20.0$$

whence

$$\varphi\left(\frac{l}{i}\right) = \frac{20}{1 + 20} = 0.954.$$

The coefficient k from formula [7.5.60] is given by

$$k = 1 - \frac{e}{h}(0.06 \, \lambda - 0.2).$$

For a rectangular cross-section, $i = 0.289 \, h$. The slenderness of the cored block is then taken as

$$\lambda = \frac{256}{8.7} \times 0.289 = 8.8.$$

Coefficient k is now determinate:

$$k = 1 - 0.07 \times (0.06 \times 8.8 - 0.2) = 0.98.$$

405

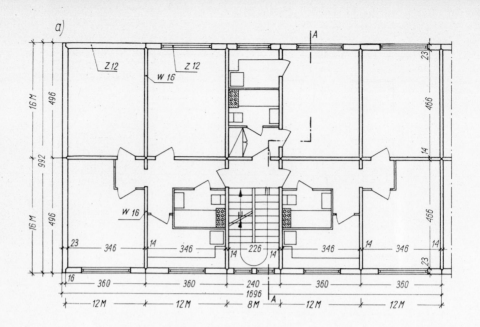

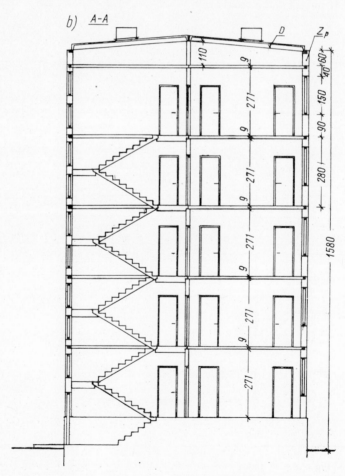

Fig. 7.8.1. (see also next page)

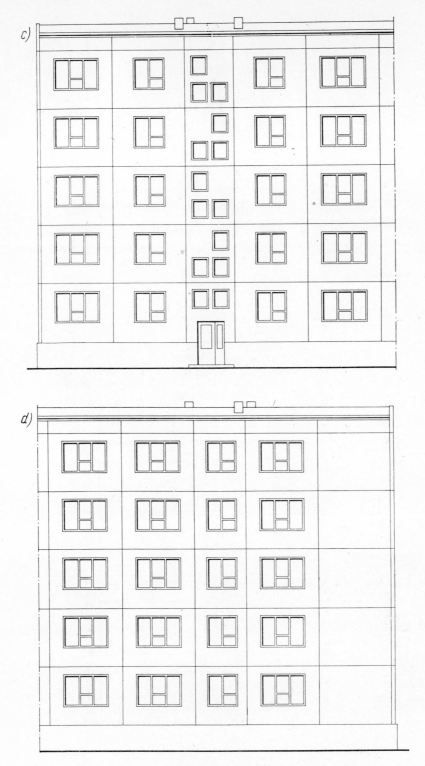

Fig. 7.8.1. A block of flats built on the two-way span system:
(a) end portion of a typical floor plan, (b) vertical section, (c), (d) part elevations

The product of the coefficients is:

$$\varphi\,(e) \cdot \varphi\left(\frac{l}{i}\right) \cdot k = 0.872 \times 0.954 \times 0.98 = 0.815$$

and the load-carrying capacity N_n of the block is

$$N_n = 0.815 \times 1464 \times 127.5 = 153000 \text{ kg}$$

$$N_n > N_n' = 149200 \text{ kg}.$$

The safety factor with respect to N_n is:

$$s = \frac{153\,000}{32\,810} = 4.66 > 2.5$$

and with respect to N_n' (no increase in the long-term loading)

$$s = \frac{149\,200}{31\,240} = 4.77.$$

7.8. NUMERICAL EXAMPLE OF WALL DESIGN IN A BUILDING CONSTRUCTED ON THE TWO-WAY SPAN SYSTEM

7.8.1. Description of the Building

The building in question is a five storey, two bay block of flats with non-utilised loft (Fig. 7.8.1).
(a) General data:
— width of the building — 9.60 m between the centre lines of the external walls, 9.92 m o/a;
— length of the building — 67.56 m (four staircases);
— centre of walls — longitudinal, 4.80 m; cross-walls 3.60 and 2.70 m;
— storey height — 2.80 m finish-to-finish; 2.71 m clear;
— height of loft — from 0.60 m to 1.0 m.
(b) Roof:
symmetrical, double-sloped (8 %) roof, constructed from uninsulated "waffle" panels, with two layers of roofing felt, dead load $g = 213$ kg/m², superimposed load $p = 60$ kg/m².
(c) Floors:
simply supported solid panels, ordinary concrete, cross reinforced, 9 cm thick.
"Floating" finish: 2 cm layer of hardboard, 3 cm concrete screed, rubber tiles.
Loft floor — $g = 291$ kg/m², $p = 50$ kg/m².
Other floors — $g = 375$ kg/m², $p = 150$ kg/m².
(d) Stairs:
landing panels resting on cross-walls, both landings and flights being of solid panels.
(e) External walls:
"room-size" sandwich panels, 22 cm thick; individual layers:

$$\text{Mk. 170 ordinary concrete} - 14 \text{ cm,}$$

$$\text{expanded polystyrene} \qquad - 4 \text{ cm,}$$

$$\text{facing concrete} \qquad - 4 \text{ cm.}$$

The weight of the external loft panels is 1080 kg, and that of the main external wall panels 2910 kg.
(f) Internal walls:
"room-size" panels, 14 cm thick, of Mk. 170 ordinary concrete.

408

Panels W 16 — 4650 kg,

Panels W 16d — 4045 kg.

(g) The underground structure, cellar walls and foundation beds are of traditional, monolithic construction.

(h) The three-dimensional stiffness of the building is ensured by the pattern of the loadbearing walls.

7.8.2. Window Panels in External Walls

Clear storey height $l = 271$ cm, thickness of the structural layer 14 cm.

Width of the panel $b = 3.46$ m, width of the window 2.26 m, width of the pier $b_s = 60$ cm (Fig. 7.8.2).

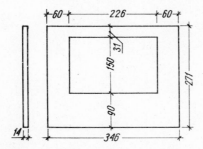

Fig. 7.8.2. Window panel in an external wall—dimensions of the structural leaf

To decide the value of coefficient m_{d1} from Table 7.5.1, the slenderness ratio l_0/h is used, where l_0 is obtained from formula [7.5.5]:

$$l_0 = \frac{1}{1 + \dfrac{l}{4b}} = \frac{271}{1 + \dfrac{271}{4 \times 60}} = 127 \text{ cm}$$

$$l_0 = \frac{127}{14} = 9.1 > 8.0.$$

As the pier is reinforced for production reasons with four 10 mm dia. bars, for this value of l_0/h the effect of long-term loading may still be neglected in practice. For the purpose of this example, however, a distinction between long-term and short-term loading will be made.

For Mk. 170 ordinary concrete, from Table 4.2.5,

$$R = 170 \text{ kg/cm}^2$$

$$a = 1750.$$

The reduced slenderness of the wall is given by:

$$\bar{\lambda} = \frac{271}{14\sqrt{1750}} = 0.464.$$

The loads acting on the panel are carried by the side piers. Each pier may be considered to be a wall, 60 cm wide, stiffened along one vertical edge.

The cross-sectional area of the pier is given by:

$$F_b = 60 \times 14 = 840 \text{ cm}^2.$$

409

The load from the pier is then transferred to a section of an area much larger than that of the pier itself. In this situation, the requirement that $N_n > N'_n$ (section 7.5.8) does not apply.

The 1st storey panel may be treated as follows:

(a) *Loading*

Forces acting axially

	long-term	short-term
roof		
$3.60 \times \dfrac{4.66}{2} \times 213 =$	1760 kg	
$3.60 \times \dfrac{4.66}{2} \times 60 =$		500 kg
loft floor slab		
$0.7 \times \dfrac{3.46^2}{2} \times 291 =$	1220 kg	
$0.7 \times \dfrac{3.46^2}{2} \times 50 =$		210 kg
other floor slabs		
$3 \times 0.7 \times \dfrac{3.46^2}{2} \times 375 =$	4700 kg	
$3 \times 0.7 \times \dfrac{3.46^2}{2} \times 150 =$		1950 kg
loft wall panel	1080 kg	
repeating wall panels $4\,5 \times 2910 =$	13100 kg	
	21860 kg	2660 kg

Reduction of the superimposed loading

$$(0.2 + 0.4) \times 0.7 \times \frac{3.46^2}{2} \times 150 = \qquad\qquad -380 \text{ kg}$$

$$2280 \text{ kg}$$

The 2nd storey floor load, acting with an eccentricity of 5 cm, is given by:

$$0.7 \times \frac{3.46^2}{2} \times 375 = 1600 \text{ kg}$$

$$0.7 \times \frac{3.46^2}{2} \times 150 = 650 \text{ kg}$$

$$2250 \text{ kg.}$$

The total loads on the panel are:

$$N_{d1} = 21860 + 1600 = 23460 \text{ kg}$$
$$N_{kr} = 2280 + 650 = 2930 \text{ kg}$$
$$26390 \text{ kg.}$$

From Table 7.5.1 for $l_0/h = 9.1$ and for ordinary concrete,

$$m_{d1} = 1.02$$

410

whence
$$N_0 = 23460 \times 1.02 + 2930 = 26860 \text{ kg.}$$

(b) *Initial eccentricity*

Constructional eccentricity:

$$e_k = \frac{5.0 \times 2250}{26390} = 0.4 \text{ cm.}$$

Technical eccentricity:

— e_{t1} as for ordinary concrete prefabricates. N.B.—the governing ratio of width to height is $b_s < l$, and

$$e_{t1} = 0.03 \text{ h} = 0.03 \times 14 = 0.42 \text{ cm}$$

— e_{t2}, for a "room-size" element

$$e_{t2} = 0.7 \text{ cm}$$

total technical eccentricity

$$e_t = e_{t1} + e_{t2} = 0.42 + 0.70 = 1.1 \text{ cm}$$

Total eccentricity:

$$e = e_k + e_t = 0.4 + 1.1 = 1.5 \text{ cm}$$

$$\frac{e}{h} = \frac{1.5}{14} = 0.11.$$

(c) *Determination of the load-carrying capacity of the wall from graphs prepared by the basic method* (*section 7.5.6*)

For the ratio

$$\gamma = \frac{l}{b} = \frac{271}{60} = 4.5$$

the value of the parameter φ may be obtained by interpolation from the graphs in Figs. 7.5.30 and 7.5.20, using the ratio $e/h = 0.11$.

For $\gamma = 2.0$ $\quad \overline{\lambda} = 0.464$ $\quad$ we find $\varphi = 0.61$
for $\gamma = 5.0$ $\quad \overline{\lambda} = 0.0$ $\qquad\qquad \varphi = 0.78$
whence
for $\gamma = 4.5$ $\quad \lambda = 0.464$ $\qquad\qquad \varphi = 0.75.$

The load-carrying capacity (two piers) is given by:

$$N_n = 0.75 \times 2 \times 840 \times 170 = 214\,000 \text{ kg.}$$

Safety factor

$$s = \frac{214\,000}{26\,860} = 8.0 > 2.5 \times 0.9 = 2.25$$

(d) *Load-carrying capacity by the simplified method* (*section 7.5.7*)

The coefficient $\varphi(e)$ from formula [7.5.48] is given by:

$$\varphi\,(e) = 1 - 2\frac{e}{h} = 1 - 2 \times 0.11 = 0.78.$$

The coefficient $\varphi(\overline{\lambda})$ in formula [7.5.56], gives the design height l_0 (formula [7.5.61]) as:

$$l_0 = \frac{l}{1 + \dfrac{l}{4b}} = 127 \text{ cm}$$

411

$$\bar{\lambda} = \frac{127}{14\sqrt{1750}} = 0.22$$

$$\bar{\varphi}_0 = \frac{0.823}{2} = \frac{0.823}{0.22^2} = 17.0$$

$$\varphi\,(\bar{\lambda}) = \frac{\bar{\varphi}_0}{a + \bar{\varphi}_0} = \frac{17.0}{1 + 17.0} \approx 0.95.$$

The coefficient k is obtained from formula [7.5.60] as:

$$k = 1 - \frac{e}{h}\,(0.06\,\lambda - 0.2) = 1 - 0.11\left(0.06 \times \frac{127}{14} - 0.2\right) = 0.97.$$

The load-carrying capacity of the two piers is:

$$N_n = 0.78 \times 0.95 \times 0.97 \times 2 \times 840 \times 170 = 206\,000\ \text{kg}.$$

The safety factor is:

$$s = \frac{206\,000}{26\,860} = 7.7 > 2.5.$$

7.8.3. Solid Internal Wall Panel—W 16

Width of the panel $b = 4.65$ m, thickness $h = 14$ cm.

The ratio l_0/h is applicable in determining m_{d1} from Table 7.5.1, where l_0 is obtained from formula [7.5.6]

$$l_0 = \frac{l}{1 + \dfrac{l}{b}} = \frac{271}{1 + \dfrac{271}{465}} = 171\ \text{cm}$$

$$\frac{l_0}{h} = \frac{171}{14} = 12.2 > 8.$$

The long-term loading must therefore be increased.

Values R and a are as for the external wall panels,

$$R = 170\ \text{kg/cm}^2$$

$$a = 1750$$

$$\lambda = 0.464.$$

The panel works as a plate stiffened along both vertical edges. Cross-sectional area:

$$F_b = 14 \times 465 = 6500\ \text{cm}^2.$$

The value N_n' which limits the load-carrying capacity of the wall, is determined by taking into account the floor support condition (section 7.5.8):

$$m_0 = 0.70\ \text{(plates freely supported at the perimeter)}$$

whence

$$N_n' = 0.70 \times 6500 \times 170 = 772\,000\ \text{kg}.$$

Design of the 1st storey panel:

412

(a) *Loading*

The share of the floor loading transferred to the internal walls is distributed trapezoidally. From formula [7.5.7], this load may be changed into a uniformly distributed load of magnitude:

$$q = 0.7 \sqrt{\frac{4.66}{3.46}} \, q_{st} = 0.811 \, q_{st}.$$

The axial loading is given by:

	long-term	short-term

loft floor

$2 \times 0.811 \times \dfrac{3.46}{2} \times 4.66 \times 290 =$ 3800 kg

$2 \times 0.811 \times \dfrac{3.46}{2} \times 4.66 \times 50 =$ 655 kg

other floors

$2 \times 4 \times 0.811 \times \dfrac{3.46}{2} \times 4.66 \times 375 =$ 19650 kg

$2 \times 4 \times 0.811 \times \dfrac{3.46}{2} \times 4.66 \times 150 =$ 7860 kg

wall panels $4.5 \times 4650 =$ 20900 kg

$N_{d1} =$ 44350 kg   8515 kg

The reduction in the superimposed loading is

$(0.2 + 0.4 + 0.5) \times 2 \times 0.811 \times \dfrac{3.46}{2} \times 4.66 \times 150 =$ $- 2150$ kg

$N_{kr} =$ 6365 kg

The sum of the forces acting on the panel is

$$N_{d1} + N_{kr} = 44350 + 6365 = 50715 \text{ kg}.$$

For unreinforced panels made of ordinary concrete, with $l_0/h = 12.2$, we find from Table 7.5.1

$$m_{d1} = 1.15$$

whence

$$N_0 = 44350 \times 1.15 + 6365 = 57065 \text{ kg}.$$

(b) *Initial eccentricity*

Technical eccentricity:

— e_{t1}, as for ordinary concrete components, but reduced by half, because of the ratio $l/b < 1$,

$$e_{t1} = 0.5 \times 0.03 \times 14 = 0.2 \text{ cm}$$

— e_{t2}, as for the external wall

$$e_{t2} = 0.7 \text{ cm}$$

— total technical eccentricity

$$e = e_{t1} + e_{t2} = 0.2 + 0.7 = 0.9 \text{ cm}.$$

413

Constructional eccentricity:

The wall is symmetrically loaded relative to its centre line, and so

$$e_k = 0.$$

Total eccentricity

$$e = e_k + e_t = 0 + 0.9 = 0.9 \text{ cm}$$

$$\frac{e}{h} = \frac{0.9}{14} = 0.06.$$

(c) *Determination of the load-carrying capacity of the wall by means of graphs prepared by the basic method (section 7.5.6)*

For walls stiffened along both vertical edges, from formula [7.5.45]

$$\bar{\lambda}_\gamma = \frac{\bar{\lambda}}{1 + \gamma^2}$$

The reduced slenderness of the wall is

$$\bar{\lambda} = \frac{l}{h \sqrt{a}} = \frac{271}{14 \sqrt{1750}} = 0.464$$

The value γ is

$$\gamma = \frac{l}{b} = \frac{2.71}{4.66} = 0.582$$

whence

$$\bar{\lambda}_\gamma = \frac{0.464}{1 + 0.582^2} = 0.347.$$

From the graph in Fig. 7.5.31, for $\bar{\lambda}_\gamma = 0.347$ and $e/h = 0.06$ we read

$$\varphi = 0.70.$$

The load-carrying capacity is given by:

$$N_n = 0.70 \times 6500 \times 170 = 772\,000 \text{ kg.}$$

The safety factor

$$s = \frac{772\,000}{57\,065} = 13.5 > 2.5 \times 0.9 = 2.25.$$

(d) *Determination of the load-carrying capacity by the simplified method (section 7.5.7)*

The coefficient $\varphi(e)$ is given in formula [7.5.50] as:

$$\varphi(e) = 1 - 2 \times \frac{e}{h} = 1 - 2 \times 0.06 = 0.88.$$

The coefficient $\varphi(\bar{\lambda})$ given in formula [7.5.56], for a design height of $l_0 = 171$ cm is:

$$\bar{\lambda} = \frac{171}{14 \sqrt{1750}} = 0.296$$

$$\bar{\varphi}_0 = \frac{0.823}{\bar{\lambda}^2} = \frac{0.823}{0.296^2} = 9.4$$

$$\varphi(\bar{\lambda}) = \frac{\bar{\varphi}_0}{1 + \bar{\varphi}_0} = \frac{9.4}{1 + 9.4} = 0.91.$$

414

The coefficient k given in formula [7.5.60] is:

$$k = 1 - \frac{e}{h}\left(0.06\,\frac{l_0}{h} - 0.2\right) = 1 - 0.06\left(0.06 \times \frac{171}{14} - 0.2\right) = 0.97.$$

The product of the coefficients is

$$0.88 \times 0.91 \times 0.97 = 0.77$$

and the load-carrying capacity is then:

$$N_n = 0.77 \times 6500 \times 170 = 850\,000 \text{ kg.}$$

Since $N_n > N'_n$, the safety factor is:

$$s = \frac{N'_n}{N_o} = \frac{772\,000}{57\,065} = 13.5 > 2.5.$$

7.8.4. Door Panel W 16d — Internal Walls

Width of the panel 465 cm, width of the door opening 80 cm (Fig. 7.8.3).

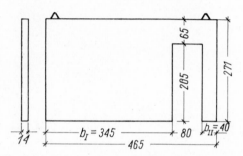

Fig. 7.8.3. Internal door panel W 16d-dimensions

The load is carried by part I — unreinforced, of width $b_I = 345$ cm, and part II (r.c. post) — $b_{II} = 40$ cm.

Part I: According to section 7.5.1, part I should be regarded as a plate stiffened along its vertical edge. But, since $b > l$, the effect of the stiffening is neglected in the calculations, and the load-carrying capacity is determined as for a wall unstiffened along its vertical edges.

The ratio l_0/h is

$$\frac{l_0}{h} = \frac{271}{14} = 19.4,$$

and the long-term load must consequently be multiplied by m_{d1}.
The cross-sectional area is

$$F_b = 345 \times 14 = 4820 \text{ cm}^2.$$

The load-carrying capacity is limited by the condition

$$N_n \leqslant N'_n = 0.70 \times F_b \times R = 0.70 \times 4820 \times 170 = 574\,000 \text{ kg.}$$

Part II: Because of the small width of the post, which gives:

$$\gamma = \frac{l}{b} = \frac{271}{40} = 6.8 > 5$$

the stiffening along one vertical edge is sufficient to offset the effect of slenderness on the load-carrying capacity.

The cross-sectional area of the post is

$$F_b = 40 \times 14 = 560 \text{ cm}^2.$$

The load-carrying capacity of the post is limited by

$$N_n \leqslant N'_n = 0.70 \times F \times R = 0.70 \times 560 \times 170 = 66\,600 \text{ kg}.$$

Design of the 1st storey panel.

(a) *Loading*

The panel carries floor loads identical to those carried by the panel W 16 (section 7.8.3).

Part I of the panel takes

$$N_I = N \times \frac{345 \times 0.5 \times 80}{465} = 0.83 \ N$$

and part II of the panel

$$N_{II} = N - N_I = 0.17 \ N,$$

where N is the total load on the panel.

	long-term	short-term
Axial loading		
Floors, as panel W 16		
3800 + 19650 =	23450 kg	
655 + 7860 − 2150 =		6365 kg
Wall panels 4.5 × 4045 =	18200 kg	
$N_{dl} =$	41650 kg	$N_{kr} = 6365$ kg

(b) *Initial eccentricity*

Total eccentricity—as for panel W 16,

$$e = 0.9 \text{ cm} \qquad \frac{e}{h} = 0.06.$$

(c) *Part I*

The long-term loading is multiplied by factor m_{d1}, taken from Table 7.5.1, for a ratio $l_0/h = 19.4$:

$$m_{d1} = 1.31.$$

Thus, the load N_0 is

$$N_0^I = (1.13 \times 41650 + 6365) \times 0.83 = 50500 \text{ kg}.$$

Determination of the load-carrying capacity of the wall by means of graphs prepared by the basic method (section 7.5.6).

The reduced slenderness is, as for W 16, given by

$$\bar{\lambda} = 0.464.$$

From the graph in Fig. 7.5.26 we obtain:

$$\varphi = 0.62$$

and the load-carrying capacity is then:

$$N_n = \varphi \cdot F_b \cdot R = 0.62 \times 4820 \times 170 = 507\,000 \text{ kg}.$$

The safety factor is:

$$s = \frac{507\,000}{50\,500} = 10.0 > 2.5 \times 0.9 = 2.25.$$

416

Determination of the l.c. capacity by the simplified method (section 7.5.7).
The coefficient $\varphi(e)$ is as for panel W 16

$$\varphi(e) = 0.88.$$

The coefficient $\varphi(\bar{\lambda})$ is obtained from formula [7.5.56], as:

$$\varphi(\bar{\lambda}) = \frac{\bar{\varphi}_0}{1 + \bar{\varphi}_0}$$

$$\bar{\varphi}_0 = \frac{0.823}{0.464^2} = 3.84$$

$$\varphi(\bar{\lambda}) = \frac{3.84}{1 + 3.84} = 0.80.$$

The coefficient k is given by formula [7.5.60]

$$k = 1 - \frac{e}{h}\left(0.06\frac{l}{h} - 0.2\right) = 1 - 0.06\left(0.06 \times \frac{271}{14} - 0.2\right) = 0.94.$$

The product of the coefficients is:

$$0.88 \times 0.80 \times 0.94 = 0.66.$$

The load-carrying capacity of the wall is then:

$$N_n = 0.66 \times 4820 \times 170 = 540\,000 \text{ kg.}$$

Safety factor

$$s = \frac{540\,000}{50\,500} = 10.7 > 2.5$$

(d) *Part II*
   For part II, the force N_0 is

$$N_0^{II} = (41650 + 6365) \times 0.17 = 8150 \text{ kg.}$$

Determination of the load-carrying capacity:
— by means of the graphs prepared by the basic method:

for $\dfrac{e}{h} = 0.06$ (with $\bar{\lambda} = 0$), we obtain from the graph in Fig. 7.5.20

$$\varphi = 0.83 > 0.70$$

— by the simplified method:
The coefficient $\varphi(e)$ is as for the panel W 16, i.e.

$$\varphi(e) = 0.88 > 0.70.$$

Since $\varphi > 0.70$, the safety factor is based on the value of N_n' and is

$$s = \frac{N_n'}{N_0} = \frac{66\,600}{8150} = 8.2 > 2.5.$$

417

Chapter 8

PROBLEMS OF THERMAL AND ACOUSTIC
INSULATION AND OF FIRE PROTECTION

8.1. THERMAL INSULATION

8.1.1. General Observations

The thermal insulation of the external walls is designed in accordance with the general rules of physics. However, constructional and technological conditions present some specific problems which must be more closely examined. There are:
— the need to provide good thermal resistance, even with materials of low storage capacity and without internal absorbent lagging;
— the considerable effect of dampness on the resistivity of the component materials, and therefore, the need to analyse the humidity conditions and to determine the true values of the conductivity, λ, of the materials used;
— the prevention of excessive temperature drops at the internal surfaces of the walls, in the corners, and where thermal bridges occur.

The problem of thermal bridges is extremely important. In calculating the thermal conductivity of a wall, allowance must be made for heat losses through any existing thermal bridges. When investigating humidity and moisture movement in the walls, one must also ascertain the internal surface temperatures at the points of maximum heat loss, and assess the chances of condensation taking place.

Correct ventilation is also essential, if comfortable internal conditions are to be maintained. In prefabricated buildings ventilation is particularly important, as concrete has a high resistance to the penetration of vapour and is, practically speaking, non-absorbent.

8.1.2. The required Values of the Thermal Conductivity U

The "U-value", as the coefficient of thermal conductivity of a wall is known, should be sufficiently low to ensure that in extreme external conditions the temperature of the inside face of the wall remains above the dew point.

The dew point is the temperature t_r at which air with a specified absolute humidity reaches saturation point. If the temperature falls below the dew point, water will condense out.

Considering the temperature t_{ws} of the inside face of the wall, the required conductivity of the wall may be expressed by the equation:

$$U_{max} = \frac{(t_w - t_{ws})\, a_n}{t_w - t_z} \qquad [8.1.1]$$

where t_w is the ambient temperature, normally taken as 18°C (65 °F), $t_{ws} > t_r$ is the temperature of the inside face of the wall which must be above the dew point t_r, and a_n is the rate of heat transfer from the atmosphere to the inside face of the wall; usually, $a_n = 7$ kcal/m²h °C, and t_z is the temperature of the outside air.

As is evident from equation [8.1.1], with set values of t_w and a_n, the quantity U_{max} is a function of t_{ws} and t_z.

The temperature t_{ws} depends on the relative humidity of the interior φ, which also governs the dew point t_r; the temperature t_z depends on the climatic zone in which the building is situated.

The values of U_{max} in various standard specifications pertain to traditional massive wall constructions, weighing at least 300 kg/m². Such walls have a relatively large thermal inertia, and because of this, when establishing U_{max}, the average temperature of the three consecutive coldest days in a one-year period was taken to represent t_z.

In the case of lighter walls, a significant lowering of the temperature of the inside face of the wall occurs sooner than three days after the onset of cold weather. Thus, when deciding the maximum value of conductivity U_{max} for such walls, t_z should be taken to be lower than the mean temperature of the three consecutive coldest days.

Traditional brick walls were normally given internal finishing coats of lime or gypsum rendering, which played the very important role of storing surplus moisture. When, because of a localised drop in the temperature of the inside face of the wall, or because of a sudden increase of the interior air humidity, water vapour condensed on the wall, the rendering absorbed the moisture and held it until the internal conditions improved. Part of this moisture moved into the brickwork which is characterised by a rather high absorption capacity.

Ordinary concrete is practically non-absorbent. Because of this, on unrendered concrete walls, even very slight condensation of water immediately becomes visible as damp patches or even running water.

The values of U_{max} quoted in the Polish standards were based on the assumption that the relative humidity of the interior $\varphi = 60\%$, and that the temperature of the inside face of the wall t_{ws} relative to the assumed external temperature t_z, will be 2.5 °C higher than the dew point.

Practical experience and laboratory research have proved that these assumptions usually give ample protection against the appearance of damp patches on the inside faces of walls with an internal absorbent coat of rendering. Condensation has often been noticed, however, on unrendered concrete walls designed on the basis of similar assumptions. This leads to the conclusion that, when deciding U_{max} for such walls, the relative humidity should be taken as $\varphi > 60\%$.

419

A graph of the values of U_{max} calculated from [8.1.1] for $t_w = 18\,°C$ and $a_n = 7\ \text{kcal/m}^2\text{h}\,°C$, with varying external temperatures t_z and internal relative humidities φ, is shown in Fig. 8.1.1. This graph can be used to determine the required value of U_{max} for walls with low thermal inertias (a lower t_z is taken), and for walls without any absorbent internal rendering (a higher relative humidity, $\varphi > 60\,\%$).

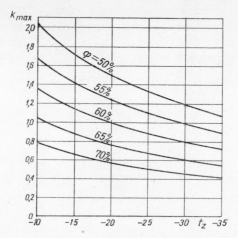

Fig. 8.1.1. Graph of the variation of U_{max} with outside temperature and the humidity (φ) of the interior, obtained from formula [8.1.1], with $t_w = 18\,°C$

In addition to the above considerations, the economics of thermal insulation should also be borne in mind. The lower the thermal conductivity of the wall U, the lower will be the cost of heating the building.

In traditional building, where the walls are of relatively heavy masonry, increased thermal resistance of the external walls is coupled with a considerable increase in the weight of the structure, and is often economically impracticable. In industrialised building, however, with the use of materials as light and as thermally effective as expanded polystyrene and mineral wool, an increase of the thermal resistance of the wall does not alter the weight of the building and only slightly affects the costs.

When the external walls possess a low thermal conductivity, a rather high inside temperature may be maintained for a relatively small outlay on fuel. This is favourable to proper ventilation and the maintenance of comfortable internal conditions.

The assumptions and the values of the parameters used in deciding the thermal conductivity U of a wall are still subject to discussion. Of particular importance are the local conditions, mainly the temperature differences during the winter months, the length of time during which heating is necessary, and the construction of the wall.

Firstly, to satisfy the condition $t_{ws} > t_r$, the author is of the opinion that, in the Polish climate, the following should be adopted:
— external design temperature t_z — as in Table 8.1.1;
— design relative humidity φ_{max} of the living quarters, when the walls have no absorbent internal rendering — $\varphi_{max} = 70\,\%$.

TABLE 8.1.1.

Weight of wall kg/m³	Polish climatic zones					
	I	II	III	IV	V	VI
300	−14	−16	−18	−20	−22	−24
200		−20		−24		−30
150		−24		−30		−35

Values of U_{max} calculated for these conditions are given in Table 8.1.2.

TABLE 8.1.2.

MAXIMUM PERMISSIBLE VALUES OF THERMAL CONDUCTIVITY OF THE
EXTERNAL WALLS
(U-values, in kcal/m²h°C)

Weight and type of wall		Polish climatic zones		
		I, II	III–V	VI
up to 300 kg/m²	with absorbent rendering	1.15	1.00	0.90
	without rendering	0.65	0.55	0.50
200 kg/m²	with absorbent rendering	1.00	0.90	0.80
	without rendering	0.75	0.50	0.45
below 150 kg/m²	with absorbent rendering	0.90	0.80	0.70
	without rendering	0.50	0.45	0.40

These stricter requirements for unrendered walls are particularly necessary in high density housing, where, in addition, not all apartments are properly ventilated.

For economical reasons, the values of U_{max} for walls with an absorbent rendering should be further lowered by some 10–15%.

In school and office buildings, which are occupied for only a part of the day, the values of U_{max} may be a little higher than in Table 8.1.2.

External walls lighter than 150 kg/m² are as a rule constructed from materials other than concrete, with an absorbent internal skin. The U-value for such walls is normally taken as follows:
for walls weighing approx.

$$100 \text{ kg/m}^2 \qquad U_{max} = 0.70-0.55 \text{ kcal/m}^2\text{h °C}$$

$$50 \text{ kg/m}^2 \qquad U_{max} = 0.45-0.40 \text{ kcal/m}^2\text{h °C}$$

$$20 \text{ kg/m}^2 \qquad U_{max} = 0.37-0.30 \text{ kcal/m}^2\text{h °C}.$$

421

The higher of the above values pertains to the climatic zones I and II, the lower, to those in zones III—VI.

For roofs, the Polish standards specify $U_{max} = 0.75$ kcal/m²h °C. This value was thought necessary to prevent the melting of snow and subsequent freezing of water on the roof in temperatures near 0 °C.

For ventilated roofs, the required conductivity is calculated from the equation

$$U = \frac{t_w - t_s}{t_w - t_z} \cdot U_d \qquad [8.1.2]$$

where t_s is the air temperature in the ventilated space, U_d the thermal conductivity of the lower structure.

The temperature t_s is 3–5 °C higher than the outside temperature t_z (for ordinary concrete planks $t_s = t_z + 3$, for timber boarding, $t_s = t_z + 5$). Thus $U_d \leqslant 0.80$ kcal/m² h °C normally satisfies the standard requirements. For fuel economy, however, it is advisable to aim at a value of U_d not higher than 0.70 kcal/m²h °C.

8.1.3. Moisture in Materials and their Thermal Conductivity

8.1.3.1. *General observations*. The dampness of the wall material may be the result of the production process, or it may be caused by moisture in the atmosphere and by condensation on the inner face of the wall. To calculate the thermal conductivity of the wall U, we must see the values of the thermal conductivities λ of the component materials pertaining to the state of balanced moisture content. As a rule, this moisture content is higher than in the air-dry state, i.e. when the moisture content of the materials used is governed only by the relative humidity of the air and the absorbtive properties of the materials.

In order to utilise the insulating properties of the materials fully, the external walls should be so designed that their balanced moisture content is as low as possible. If some occasional increase in the moisture content is unavoidable, one should try to create conditions favourable to subsequent drying out.

The ease of drying out is particularly important when dealing with the lighter varieties of lightweight concrete. These materials dry out very slowly, even in conditions favourable to evaporation, and, in addition, their initial moisture content is in excess of 20 %. For this reason, the use of, say, light gas concrete as an insulating layer in a sandwhich panel, where it would be contained between two relatively thick layers of ordinary concrete, is not recommended. On the other hand, these materials can be rationally used in homogeneous panels, rendered externally, or in composite prefabricates in which the external leaf is separated from the thermal insulation by a ventilated air space.

Condensation of water vapour on the inside face of the wall is always undesirable, but it does not always disqualify the wall from being used. The amount of water absorbed by the wall during the winter and returned to the atmosphere during the summer can be established by calculation.

If the rise in thermal conductivity of the wall caused by the condensation is not more than 10 % of the conductivity of the air-dry wall, and if the construction allows for complete evaporation of this moisture during the summer, the wall is considered to be properly designed.

The effect of the moisture content w on the conductivity of the material λ depends on the structure and the density of the material. Mean values of the increases of conductivity with respect to its air-dry value, calculated for 1 % volumetric increases of moisture content, are given in Table 8.1.3 for light aggregate concretes and cellular concretes.

TABLE 8.1.3.

INCREASE IN THE THERMAL CONDUCTIVITY λ WITH INCREASED MOISTURE CONTENT OF THE MATERIALS

Type of concrete	Increase of λ in % per 1 % volumetric increase in moisture content depending on the dry density (T/m^3) of the material												
	0.3	0.4	0.5	0.6	0.7	0.8	1.0	1.1	1.2	1.3	1.4	1.6	1.8
Cellular concretes	8.2	8.0	7.2	7.0	6.3	5.5	4.0	3.0	2.8	—	—	—	—
Light weight aggregate concretes	—	—	—	—	—	7.6	6.6	5.9	5.3	4.8	4.4	4.1	3.8

The moisture content of the wall depends mainly on the type of wall construction and on the relative humidity of the interior. In this respect, three types of walls may be distinguished:

— walls with a low moisture content, in buildings such as office blocks, where the relative humidity of the interior φ is less than 50 %;

— walls with an average moisture content, which include the walls of blocks of flats (relative humidity $\varphi = 50-65\%$), and all ventilated roofs;

— walls with a high moisture content, which include all solid roofs, walls in which the arrangement of the component layers prevents evaporation, and all walls of buildings with a high internal humidity (baths, laundries, farm buildings, etc.). The values of the coefficients of thermal conductivity of the materials used must be related to the type of wall which is being designed, if they are to yield accurate results in calculations.

8.1.3.2. *Light aggregate concretes.* Of all the light aggregate concretes, the most commonly used in Poland are the furnace clinker and the blast-furnace slag concretes. The production of expanded clay and expanded shale aggregates is now also gathering momentum.

The densities and strengths of furnace clinker concretes and foamed slag concretes are comparable, but the thermo-insulating properties of the foamed slag concrete are more advantageous.

TABLE 8.1.4.

Type of aggregate	Moisture content by weight in % depending on relative humidity of air in %				
	32	54	75	95	98
Furnace clinker	1.34	2.91	3.43	6.75	12.08
Blast-furnace slag	0.57	0.85	1.21	2.38	4.05

The main reason for the difference is the lower rate of moisture absorption from the air by foamed slag concrete (Table 8.1.4), which also causes it to have a lower balanced moisture content. The capillary properties of the two concretes are very similar.

An important factor in deciding the value of the thermal conductivity λ is the quantity of mineral sand added to increase the strength of the concrete. The crystalline structure of the mineral sand leads to a larger increase in the conductivity of concrete than could be expected from its increased density.

This effect is illustrated in Fig. 8.1.2.

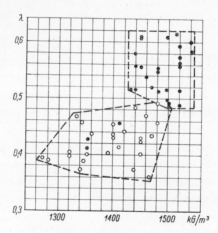

Fig. 8.1.2. Effect of the addition of sand on the value of the coefficient λ:
● — clinker concrete with river sand, o — clinker concrete with clinker fine aggregate

The large scatter of the results in Fig. 8.1.2 is caused, among other things, by the varied quantities of water used in production (from 160 kg/m³ for high conductivity concrete to 230 kg/m³ for low conductivity concrete). With increasing amounts of water used in production, the porosity of the cement matrix also increases, and in consequence, the conductivity decreases.

The grading of the aggregates also affects the thermal properties of the finished material. The results of investigations into the thermal properties of clinker concrete

TABLE 8.1.5.

Sample No.	Percentage by volume of size groups mm				Density	
	20–10	10–5	5–1.2	1.2	T/m³	λ
1	32.6	32.6	16.2	18.6	1.50	0.415
2	26	39.2	16.2	18.6	1.47	0.395
3	19.7	45.5	16.2	18.6	1.44	0.386
4	13	52.2	16.2	18.6	1.51	0.294

(1 : 2.5; 4.5 by volume) are shown in Table 8.1.5. When the proportion of 10–20 mm particles was decreased in favour of 5–10 mm particles, the coefficient λ was reduced by 40 %.

The equilibrium moisture content is reached, in walls made of light aggregate concretes, after 2–3 years.

Mean values of the equilibrium moisture content and the corresponding coefficients of thermal conductivity are compiled in Table 8.1.6.

8.1.3.3. *Cellular concretes.* Cellular concretes are, from the insulation point of view, more uniform than light aggregate concretes. The relationship between the density and the conductivity λ is here much more definite, although distinct differences exist between various types of concrete.

Lime-bound cellular concretes reach the state of balanced moisture content sooner than the cement-bound varieties, and their balanced moisture content is somewhat lover as a rule.

The structure of the material has an essential effect on its thermal properties. The cells of gas-concrete are isolated, whereas those of foam-concrete are often interconnected. As a result, the absorption of water by the foam-concrete is normally higher than that of gas concrete of the same density, Table 8.1.7.

Cellular concretes are characterised by very weak capillary suction. Very light varieties, e.g. gas-concrete weighing 350 kg/m³, absorb more water by direct contact than the heavier varieties, but compared with brickwork, this process is very slow.

The weak capillary suction is advantageous, as little water is absorbed during short rainfalls, but it is coupled with a most unwelcome characteristic—a very slow rate of drying.

When leaving the autoclave, the moisture content of the blocks is 30–40 % by weight. During storage in well ventilated sheds this content is somewhat lowered, but at the end of three months it is normally still above 25 %.

Block laying, or assembly of composite prefabricates by wet processes, further increases the moisture content of cellular concretes.

TABLE 8.1.6.

THERM AL CONDUCTIVITY λ OF LIGHTWEIGHT AGGREGATE CONCRETES IN kcal/m h °C

Type of aggregate		Density of dry concrete kg/m³	$R_{\square 16}$	Conductivity λ when dry	Moisture content by weight in low moisture walls %	Moisture content by weight in average moisture walls %	Moisture content by weight in high moisture walls %	Conductivity λ depending on moisture content in %				
								4	6	8	10	12
Clinker furnace	without mineral sand	1400	30–70	0.42	6	8	12	—	0.57	0.62	—	0.72
	with mineral sand	1500	70–40	0.47	6	8	12	—	0.65	0.71	—	0.83
Blast — furnace slag	without mineral sand	1250	30	0.30	4	6	10	0.38	0.43	—	0.51	
		1350	30–70	0.37	4	6	10	0.46	0.51	—	0.60	—
	with mineral sand	1450	70–140	0.44	4	6	10	0.55	0.60	—	0.72	—
expanded clay ("Mszczo-nów")		800	30–50	0.16	6	8	12	—	0.22	0.24	—	0.28
		1000	50–90	0.22	6	8	12	—	0.31	0.34	—	0.40
		1200	50–140	0.27	4	6	10	0.34	0.37	—	0.44	—
		1600	140–200	0.45				0.57	0.63	—	0.75	—
expanded shale ("Knurów")		1200		0.26	4	6	10	0.33	0.36	—	0.42	—
		1400		0.36	4	6	10	0.45	0.50	—	0.60	—

TABLE 8.1.7.

WATER ABSORPTION OF CELLULAR CONCRETES

Type of concrete	Moisture content in % by weight, against the relative humidity of air in %				
	32	54	75	95	98
Gas concrete 035	1.92	3.14	3.30	5.56	14.00
Gas concrete 07	1.50	2.15	2.60	5.00	8.65
Foam-concrete 035	2.35	3.34	4.91	9.45	19.50
Foam-concrete 08	4.11	6.28	8.45	12.80	14.90

The balanced moisture contents of cellular concretes in various types of walls and their corresponding conductivities are shown in Table 8.1.8.

TABLE 8.1.8.

THERMAL CONDUCTIVITY λ OF CELLULAR CONCRETES IN kcal/m h °C

Dry density T/m³	Conductivity λ when dry	Moisture content by volume in low moisture walls %	Moisture content by volume in average moisture walls %	Moisture content by volume in high moisture walls %	Conductivity λ depending on moisture content by volume		
					6	8	10
0.35	0.07	6	8	10	0.115	0.130	0.145
0.50	0.10	6	8	10	0.145	0.160	0.175
0.60	0.12	6	8	10	0.173	0.190	0.207
0.70	0.14	6	8	10	0.193	0.210	0.227
0.80	0.17	6	8	10	0.223	0.240	0.257
1.00	0.23	6	8	10	0.283	0.300	0.317
1.20	0.30	6	8	10	0.353	0.370	0.387

8.1.3.4. *Thermo-insulating materials.* Materials used as thermal insulation in sandwich prefabricates may be products of organic (vegetable) origin, mineral wools, foamed glass and expanded plastics.

A general characteristic of organic materials (except some of the heavier types, which are bonded with synthetic resins), is a rather high rate of water absorption and an equally quick rate of drying. These are very advantageous properties from the thermal point of view. On the other hand, such materials rot easily when subjected to prolonged damp, and are therefore used only in walls with low or medium moisture contents, i.e. under conditions in which easy drying out is assured (walls with ventilated cavities, internal finishes).

Mineral wools are widely used in sandwich walls, particularly in the U.S.S.R. and in the Scandinavian countries. The moisture content of the mineral wool in external walls stabilises at a very low level, and for all thermal calculations the air-dry value of the conductivity λ may be used.

An essential detail for the successful working of an external wall with mineral wool insulation is the protection of the wool against air penetration. It has been found that, without such protection, the conductivity λ may rise in windy conditions by as much as 300 %.

Foamed glass has very good insulating properties. The use of it in sandwich prefabricates is rather restricted, however, because of the considerable amount of labour required. Careless laying of insulating blocks results in gaps between them (Fig. 8.1.3), which, when filled with the concrete of the next layer, considerably reduce the insulating efficiency of the wall.

The example shown in Fig. 8.1.3 is rather extreme, but it proves that when the insulating material is used in the form of previously prepared small blocks, some increase in the effective conductivity of the material must be allowed for in the calculations.

Fig. 8.1.3. Careless assembly of foamed glass pads resulting in reduced thermal insulating properties of the wall

A further increase in the conductivity may take place as a result of some penetration of concrete into the porous surface of the insulation, which reduces the effective thickness of the insulating layer.

In one of the large-panel buildings in Warsaw, the measured U value of the wall was over 30 % higher than the theoretical value. This was caused by the concrete penetrating into the gaps between blocks of foamed glass insulation and by the consequent reduction of the effective thickness of the insulating layer.

Of a large group of synthetic materials, expanded polystyrene has the best thermo-insulating properties. This material is well known under several trade names. The wide use of expanded polystyrene in sandwich walls and as a barrier for thermal bridges is justified by its low conductivity, very low density, good resistance to water vapour penetration and complete stability in damp conditions.

8.1.4. Temperature of the Wall Surfaces at Thermal Bridges and in Corners

The temperature of the internal surface of the wall can be calculated fairly accurately, using the method of temperature fields, based on Laplace's equation for assumed two-directional flow of heat. These calculations, however, are very laborious, and in practice, approximate methods, normally based on the exact solution, are used.

The temperature t_m of the internal surface of the wall at the thermal bridge can be obtained approximately from the formula:

$$t_m = t_w = \frac{R_m + \eta\,(R_s - R_m)}{R_m R_s} \cdot \frac{(t_w - t_z)}{a_n} \qquad [8.1.3]$$

where t_w, t_z are respectively the temperatures inside and outside the building, R_s is the thermal resistance of the wall away from the thermal bridge, R_m the thermal resistance of the wall at the thermal bridge, and η a coefficient, defining the effect of the thermal bridge on the lowering of t_m, depending on the geometry of the bridge.

Values of η for several types of thermal bridges are given in Table 8.1.9.

The agreement of the results calculated from formula [8.1.3] with actual measurements by J. Berthier is illustrated by the examples shown in Figs. 8.1.4 and 8.1.5.

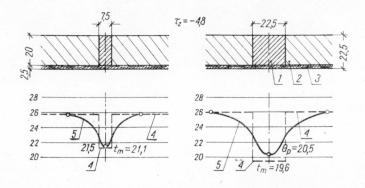

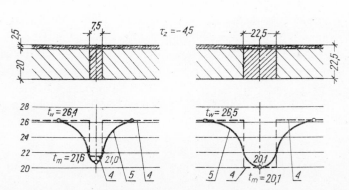

Fig. 8.1.4. Temperature on the inside face of a homogeneous wall near the thermal bridge: (1) ordinary concrete, (2) cellular concrete, (3) gypsum plaster, (4) temperature calculated from formula [8.1.3.], (5) temperature measured by J. Berthier

429

Shape of thermal bridge		0.05	0.10
		0.24	0.38
		0.15	0.26
	$h_m : h_s = 0.2$	0.05	0.09
	$h_m : h_s = 0.5$	0.10	0.17
	$h_m : h_s = 0.7$	0.14	0.23
	$h_m : h_s = 0.2$	1.50	2.70
	$h_m : h_s = 0.5$	0.70	1.35
	$h_m : h_s = 0.7$	0.40	0.85
	$h_m : h_s = 0.2$	0.60	0.88
	$h_m : h_s = 0.5$	0.40	0.62
	$h_m : h_s = 0.7$	0.25	0.48
	$h_m : h_s = 0.2$	0.03	0.07
	$h_m : h_s = 0.5$	0.16	0.24
	$h_m : h_s = 0.7$	0.20	0.29

8.1.9

				Ratio a/h_s									
0.20	0.30	0.40	0.50	0.60	0.70	0.80	0.90	1.00	1.10	1.20	1.30	1.40	1.50
0.55	0.67	0.74	0.79	0.82	0.85	0.87	0.88	0.90	0.92	0.94	0.95	0.96	0.98
0.42	0.54	0.63	0.69	0.74	0.77	0.81	0.84	0.86	0.88	0.90	0.91	0.92	0.94
0.18	0.27	0.34	0.41	0.46	0.51	0.54	0.58	0.62	0.65	0.68	0.71	0.73	0.74
0.32	0.43	0.50	0.57	0.62	0.67	0.71	0.74	0.77	0.80	0.83	0.85	0.87	0.89
0.39	0.49	0.56	0.63	0.68	0.72	0.75	0.78	0.81	0.84	0.86	0.88	0.89	0.91
2.87	2.71	2.54	2.38	2.20	2.05	1.91	1.80	1.70	1.62	1.52	1.47	1.43	1.41
1.77	1.80	1.78	1.74	1.70	1.67	1.63	1.58	1.54	1.50	1.47	1.44	1.41	1.40
1.30	1.36	1.38	1.37	1.35	1.32	1.30	1.28	1.26	1.24	1.21	1.18	1.17	1.15
1.23	1.36	1.42	1.43	1.40	1.36	1.33	1.29	1.26	1.23	1.18	1.15	1.11	1.00
1.04	1.18	1.23	1.25	1.26	1.26	1.26	1.25	1.24	1.22	1.21	1.21	1.19	1.17
0.70	0.84	0.92	0.97	1.01	1.04	1.05	1.07	1.08	1.08	1.07	1.07	1.07	1.06
0.14	0.20	0.26	0.31	0.36	0.41	0.46	0.50	0.55	0.59	0.63	0.67	0.72	0.76
0.39	0.49	0.57	0.63	0.68	0.73	0.77	0.81	0.84	0.87	0.89	0.92	0.94	0.96
0.44	0.55	0.64	0.71	0.75	0.79	0.82	0.85	0.87	0.90	0.92	0.94	0.96	0.98

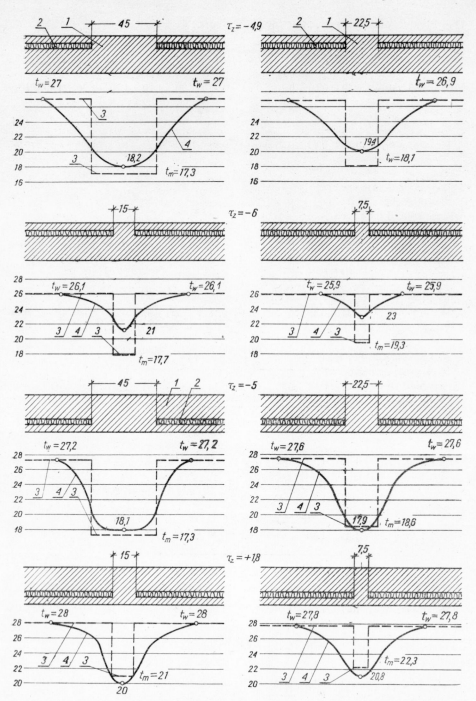

Fig. 8.1.5. Temperature on the inside face of a sandwich wall near the thermal bridge:
(1) ordinary concrete, (2) expanded polystyrene, (3) temperature calculated from formula [8.1.3.],
(4) temperature measured by J. Berthier

	Type of wall		Average sound attenuat- ion factor dB	Characteristic of the sound attenuation factor for various frequencies (I— the characte- ristic required by Polish standards)	Source
Item	Description	Section			
7	Double wall consisting of plastered woodwool slabs 5 cm thick, fixed to separate timber frames. In the air gap between the panels is a glass wool blanket 5 cm thick	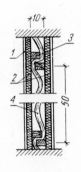	51	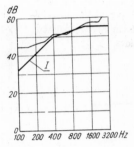	Gösele
8	Cavity wall, with 9 cm thick gypsum panels, unrendered, separated by 6 cm air gap. Total thickness 24 cm	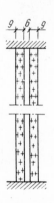	50	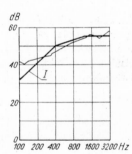	Sadowski
9	Cavity wall, with plastered gypsum panels 7 cm thick, 6 cm apart. Total thickness 20 cm	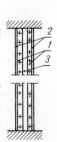	50	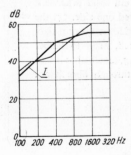	Sadowski

TABLE 8.2.1. (continued)

Item	Type of wall		Average sound attenuation factor dB	Characteristic of the sound attenuation factor for various frequencies (I—the characteristic required by Polish standards)	Source
	Description	Section			
10	Cavity wall, with gas concrete 09 panels 6 and 12 cm thick 6 cm apart, plastered both sides	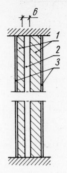	47	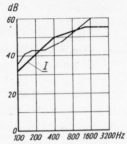	Sadowski
11	Sandwich wall consisting of 9 cm gypsum panel, plastered, covered with glass wool blanket 3 cm thick, with plaster on wire mesh		47	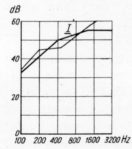	Gardaszjan
12	Sandwich wall, consisting of 12 cm solid brickwork plastered one side. On the other side wood-wool slab, plastered, fixed to timber framing, attached to brickwork through fibre board pads	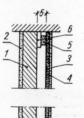	49	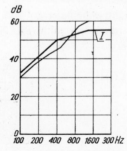	"

446

There are no prefabricated floors which would meet all the requirements without additional, sound-damping layers.

Additional acoustic insulation is designed according to the given type of floor.

In the first group of floors, acoustic insulation is normally limited to the provision of "soft floor" finishes, Fig. 8.2.9.

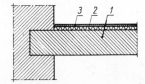

Fig. 8.2.9. The principle of "soft floor" construction:
(1) structural floor, (2) resilient material, (3) floor finish

The structural floor in this case is first covered with a layer of a resilient material, e.g. softboard, on which the flooring material is laid. If the flooring material is sufficiently soft, say thick linoleum or latex-backed floor covering, the intermediate resilient layer becomes unnecessary.

It may also be omitted, if the planned occupancy of the building calls for the provision of fitted carpets or felt covering (e.g. hotels or sanatoria).

The function of the insulating layers laid on floors of the second group is not only to damp the impact sounds, but also to improve their sound attenuation factors against air-borne noises. The arrangement is usually that of a "floating" floor, Fig. 8.2.10.

The principle of a floating floor is that the finishes are laid on a floating slab, which is separated from the structural floor and walls by a layer of resilient material.

Materials used in the resilient layer may be: glass-silk blankets, 2.5 cm thick (measured before pressing), several layers of reed wattling, total thickness 1 cm, 3 cm pressed reed panels, insulating board 1.25 cm thick, 2.5 cm thick panels of expanded urea resins, a 2 cm layer of granulated rubber, etc. The floating slab, normally about 4 cm thick, may be made of ordinary concrete, clinker concrete, sawdust concrete or gypsum screed.

In this case, the floor finishes have but a slight effect on the acoustic properties of the floor. An exception are soft finishes, such as rubber tiles or PVC tiles, which improve the damping of impact noises.

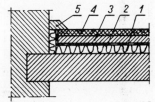

Fig. 8.2.10. The principle of "floating floor" construction:
(1) resilient layer, (2) waterproof course, (3) floating slab (e.g. concrete), (4) floor finishes, (5) skirting

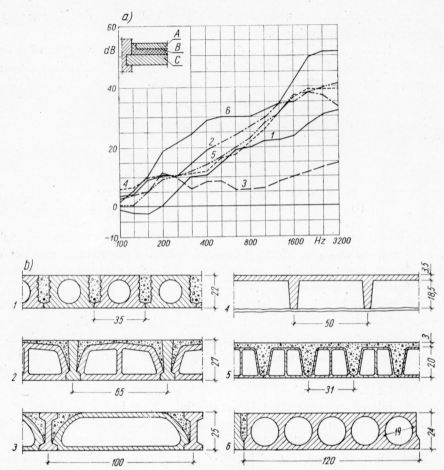

Fig. 8.2.11. Reduction in the effective average tapping level in relation to the construction of the structural floor:

(a) graph of the reduction in the effective average tapping level, (b) types of floor construction; (A) concrete floating slab 4 cm thick, (B) two reed mats, (C) structural floor

(1) hollow gypsum block floor, (2) DMS floors, clinker concrete pots, (3) KMM floors, gypsum hollow pots, (4) "waffle" floor, (5) ceramic hollow tiles, (6) cored panel floor

The floating slab may be laid in-situ, or may consist of precast panels with carefully filled joints.

To avoid passing moisture to the resilient layer, which would affect its elastic properties, it must be laid on a dry structural floor, and be given a damp-proof coating which will protect it from any moisture in the floating slab.

It is extremely important to bring the resilient layer to the level of the floor finish near the walls (Fig. 8.2.10). The skirting-board should be so shaped as to cover this emerging resilient layer. The skirting should be fixed to the floor only in this case, thus ensuring a loose fit at the wall face.

448

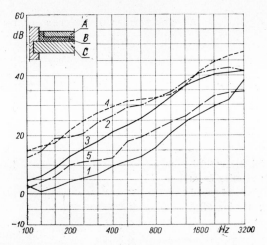

Fig. 8.2.12. Effect of the type of material in the resilient blanket on the reduction in the effective tapping level:
(A) 4 cm concrete slab, (B) resilient blanket, as described further, (C) 12 cm r.c. floor slab
(1) 12.5 mm porous fibreboard, (2) glass wool 3 cm thick, (3) 2.5 cm thick expanded urea resin slab, (4) glass wool 5 cm thick, (5) two reed mats

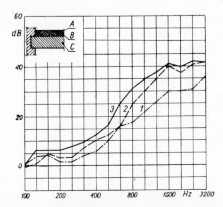

Fig. 8.2.13. Effect of the thickness of the resilient layer on the reduction of the effective tapping level:
(A) hardboard, (B) corrugated sheet, (C) 12 cm thick reinforced concrete slab
(1) corrugated PVC sheet 15 mm thick, (2) corrugated PVC sheet 30 mm thick, (3) corrugated PVC sheet 45 mm thick

The improvement in insulation, shown in a reduction of the effective tapping level under the floor, which is achieved by a floating floor is related to the structural characteristics of the floor (Fig. 8.2.11), the type and thickness of the resilient layer (Figs. 8.2.12 and 8.2.13) and the material in the floating slab (Fig. 8.2.14).

Several examples of acoustic floor insulation satisfying the standard requirements are given in Table 8.2.2.

Calculation of the damping effect of a floor on impact noises is very complex.

449

| Item | Type of floor | | Average sound attenuation factor dB |
	Description	Sketch	
1	Reinforced concrete slab 9 cm thick (1); Floating floor: fibre board (2), cement screed 4 cm thick (3), flooring (4)		1.—structure only 40 2.—with floating floor 45
2	Inverted tray panel with 8 cm table (1); Floating floor: (a) as item 1 (b) instead of fibre board, there is a glass wool blanket 3 cm thick (2)	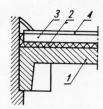	1.—structure only 40 2.—with floating floor (a) 47 (b) 48
3	12 cm reinforced concrete slab (1). Soft finish: 1.5 cm insulation board (2) and 0.5 cm hardboard (3)		1.—structure only 46 2.—with finishes 47

Characteristic of the sound attenuation factor for various frequencies (I-characteristic required by Polish standards)	Characteristic of the effective tapping level under the floor (I-characteristic required by Polish standards)	Source

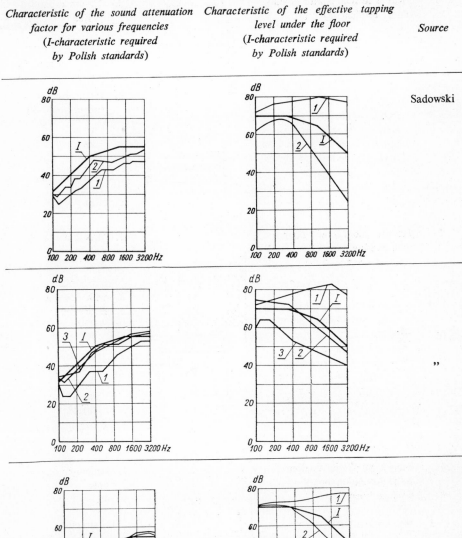

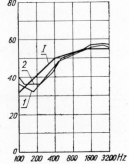

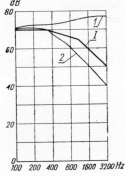

Sadowski

"

"

TABLE 8.2.2. (continued)

4	Slab as in item 3 with floating floor: resilient layer (a)		2.—1.5 cm expanded polystyrene—50

3.—corrugated PVC sheet, 1.5 cm—50

4.—2 cm layer of rubber shot—50

5	Hollow slab (Żerań) floor with floating floor. Glass wool resilient layer		1.—structure only 42

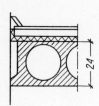

2.—with floating floor 50

6	Ribbed panel with floating floor. Insulation board resilient layer		1.—structure only 40

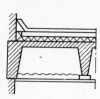

2.—with floating floor 48

Sadowski

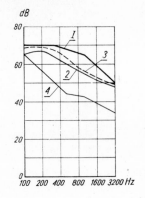

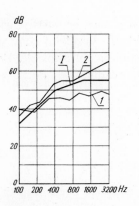

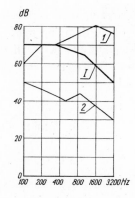

"

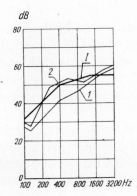

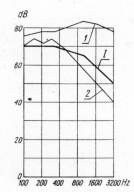

"

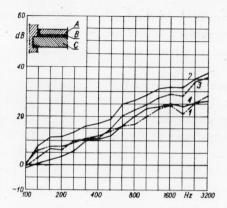

Fig. 8.2.14. Effect of the material of the floating slab on the reduction of the effective tapping level: (A) floating slab, (B) corrugated PVC sheet 15 mm thick, (C) reinforced concrete slab 12 cm thick, (1) floating concrete slab 4 cm thick, (2) floating clinker concrete slab 4 cm thick, (3) floating gypsum slab 4 cm thick, (4) 4 cm floating slab of gypsum screeding

In addition to the large amount of work required, one must be familiar with the physical properties of all damping materials and with the details of construction. As a rule, when designing the floor, all this information is not available. For this reason, acoustic protection against impact noises is normally based on the proved results of similar solutions.

8.3. FIRE PROTECTION

8.3.1. General Requirements

The requirements regarding fire resistance and fire protection depend on the heat generating capacity of the building, i.e. the amount of heat which would be produced during a fire by the materials present inside the building. This is usually expressed in Mcal/m². The following values are taken for dwellings and public buildings:
— for hospitals (wards and private rooms, staff rooms, operating theatres, consulting and waiting rooms), schools (lecture rooms, laboratories, staff rooms, gymnasia) and in shops in which incombustible materials only are sold — 100 Mcal/m²;
— for houses and flats with incombustible structural floors, offices (without archives), small libraries (up to 2000 volumes), entertainment halls and garages (without fuel storage) — 150 Mcal/m²;
— for houses and flats with combustible or semi-combustible floors (e.g. timber floors, block floors on screed), archives, large libraries, chemist shops, stores in hospitals, hotels and schools, and cellar stores in blocks of flats — 250 Mcal/m².
According to the designated heat generating capacity, the required fire resistance of the building falls into several classes:
— with a heat generating capacity of 100 Mcal/m² — class E

454

— with a heat generating capacity of 150 Mcal/m² — class D

—. with a heat generating capacity of 250 Mcal/m² — class C.

The fire resistance of a building as a whole is classified according to that of its components.

The fire resistance of a component is described by the length of time during which, in a fire, it will continue to carry out its function in the building, i.e. will not be destroyed or grossly deformed, will prevent the spread of flames and smoke, will not attain a temperature on the surface away from the fire, in excess of 150 °C.

Class A resistance of a unit means a 4-hour resistance, class B — 2 hour, class C — 1 hour, class D — 30 minute, and class E — 15 minute resistance.

The fire resistance requirements for various components of buildings are compiled in Table 8.3.1.

TABLE 8.3.1

REQUIRED CLASS OF FIRE RESISTANCE OF BUILDING COMPONENTS IN RELATION TO THE FIRE RESISTANCE OF THE BUILDING ITSELF

Fire resistance of the building	Fire resistance of the components					
	structural walls	columns and beams	floors	curtain walls	roof structure	roof covering
A	A	A	B	B	B	incombustible
B	B	B	B	C	C	incombustible
C 11-storey, or more	B	C	C	C	C	incombustible
C 6 to 10 storey	C	C	C	C	D	semi-combustible
up to 5-storey	C	C	C	D	D	semi-combustible
D	C	C	C	D	D	semi-combustible
E	E	E	E	E	E	semi-combustible

Thus, prefabricated floors and structural walls in housing and in public buildings must have at least a 1-hour fire resistance (class C), and curtain walls — 30 minutes (class D).

When a part of the building has a greater heat generating capacity than the rest of the building, all walls and floors within and enveloping this part must be of a suitably higher fire resistance.

Incombustible roofing materials are clay or concrete tiles, asbestos-cement sheeting, metal sheeting, glass, and impregnated roofing felt on a concrete backing. Semi-combustible materials include impregnated roofing felt on timber or similar materials.

If a low building is erected immediately next to a taller one, the lower building must be roofed with incombustible materials.

8.3.2. Fire Resistance of Building Components

The fire resistance of building components is determined by testing them in conditions similar, in respect of loading and temperature, to those which would exist in a real building during a real fire. The test could be carried out in a laboratory in specially constructed furnaces, or by creating a natural fire in a specially prepared building.

The test curve of temperature prescribed by Polish standards, which is practically identical to that agreed by the International Bureau of Standards, is shown in Fig. 8.3.1. This illustration also shows the rise in temperature during the test at several points of the tested component. The temperature inside the tested component is appropriately lower than its surface temperature.

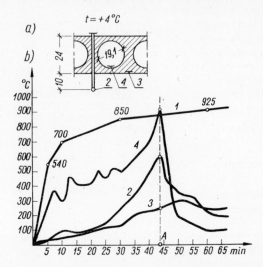

Fig. 8.3.1. Temperature inside cored panels, measured during a fire in the building:
(a) positioning of the thermocouples, 2, 3, and 4, (b) temperature changes during the fire
(1) assumed surface temperature during the fire, taken from Polish standards, (2), (3), and (4) readings of the thermocouples, (A) the start of quenching

The fire resistance of concrete components is mainly decided by their thickness (and, when dealing with hollow components, the thickness of their internal walls). In the case of reinforced concrete components, the thickness of the concrete cover of the reinforcing bars is also very important, as at a temperature of 500 °C the yield point of steel is at about half its normal value, and at higher temperatures considerable thermal deformation of steel will cause spalling off of the outside layer of concrete (Fig. 8.3.2).

The currently valid Polish figures governing the fire resistance of basic concrete and reinforced concrete structural components are given in Table 8.3.2.

When solid slab and ribbed slab floors are designed to be continuous or partly fixed at the supports (items 11 and 12 in Table 8.3.2), the cover to the bottom reinforcement may be reduced to 1.0 cm — for a 1-hour resistance — provided that

TABLE 8.3.2

FIRE RESISTANCE REQUIREMENTS FOR CONCRETE
AND REINFORCED CONCRETE COMPONENTS

Item	Type of component		minimum dimensions in cm for relevant class of resistance			
			A	B	C	D
1	(a) Structural walls solid concrete	thickness	19	12	8	6
2	hollow walls, with duct area not more than 50 % of gross c/s area, ordinary concrete or blast-furnace slag concrete, with plaster both sides, 1.5 cm min.	thickness	—	29	22	12
3	as above, but furnace clinker concrete	thickness	14	10	7	6
4	cellular concrete	thickness	32	25	12	6.5
5	reinforced concrete	thickness cover	14 4	10 3	7 2	6 1.5
6	(b) Columns, beams, trusses reinforced concrete	least c/s dimension cover	40 4	25 2.5	20 2	
7	cast iron or steel tubes, filled with concrete	column diameter least tube wall thickness	— —	— —	30 0.8	20 0.7
8	reinforced concrete beams, simply supported, any cross-section	cover to main reinforcing bars	—	5	3.5	
9	reinforced concrete beams, continuous or partly fixed at the supports, any cross-section	cover to main reinforcing bars	—	4	2	
10	prefabricated roof trusses	least dimension cover to main bars	— —	10 2.5	8 1.5	6 1.5
11	(c) Floors solid slabs	thickness (including incombustible screed) cover	— —	12 2.5	8 2.0	6 1.5
12	ribbed, tray, waffle	thickness including screed bottom cover to rib bars cover to bottom bars in topping		12 3.0 2.5	8 2.0 2.0	

TABLE 8.3.2 (continued)

13	multiduct, or hollow pot floors	thickness of topping or upper slab	—	5	
		cover to bottom bars	—	3	2
14	(d) *Stairs*, prefabricated, beams or slabs	cover to bottom reinforcement in stringers or landing beams	—	3	2
		cover to reinf. in landing slabs	—	2.5	2
		cover to reinf. in flights	—	2	1.5
15	(e) *Roof constructions*, ribbed r.c. slabs, not thinner than 3 cm, incl. screed	cover to rib reinforcement	—	2	1.5
		cover to slab reinforcement	—	1	1
16	(f) *Curtain walls* reinforced concrete	thickness of plate	—	3	3
		cover to reinforcement	—	—	1	1

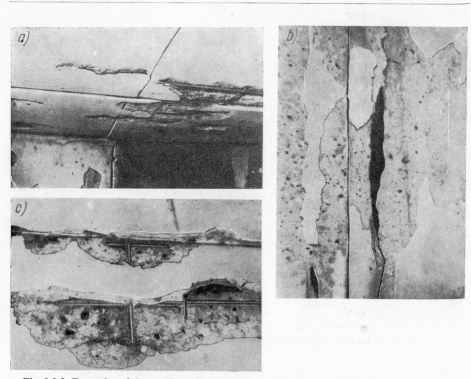

Fig. 8.3.2. Examples of the spalling of the concrete cover due to considerable thermal shock: (a) on the ceiling, (b) in the corner of the walls, (c) on the wall

the c/s area of the negative reinforcement provided at each support is at least one third of the span reinforcement.

Compared with floor slabs, slightly smaller covers to reinforcement are allowed in stair landing slabs and flights, because of the lower heat-governing capacity of the staircases.

In blocks of flats and public buildings, the main beams in items 8 and 9 of Table 8.3.2 are beams carrying loads from areas larger than 20 m².

In rectangular main beams, at least 20 cm wide and 30 cm deep, the cover to the bottom reinforcement can be:

class B units — 4.0 cm

class C units — 2.0 cm.

Plaster or rendering finish can be included in the required thickness of the reinforcement-covering layer.

The resistance of concrete components also depends on the type of aggregate used.

According to N. Davey and L. A. Ashton, the fire resistance of cross-reinforced slabs 8.7 cm thick and with 1.3 cm bottom cover was:

with quartz aggregate — 31 min.

with basalt aggregate — 65 min.

with brick aggregate — 120 min.

A list of fire resistance requirements, obtained from research at the British Building Research Station in Garston, are given in Table 8.3.3. In most cases these requirements are stricter than those in Table 8.3.2.

Fire resistance requirements usually conflict with the tendency to economise on the cross-sections of members. In traditional building, the fire resistance of reinforced concrete components was to a large extent boosted by a coat of plaster. In building with prefabricates, plastering is dispensed with, and in many cases,

TABLE 8.3.3

FIRE RESISTANCE OF REINFORCED CONCRETE SLABS AND BEAMS FROM RESEARCH AT THE BUILDING RESEARCH STATION, GARSTON

Type of component		Fire resistance in hours			
		4	2	1	1/2
Beams:					
	minimum width	15	13	10	9
	cover to top reinforcement	2.5	2.5	—	—
	cover to bottom reinforcement	2.5	2.5	1.3	1.3
Floor slabs:					
	minimum thickness	15	13	10	9
Multiduct hollow floors and hollow pot floors:					
	minimum reduced thickness	13	9	7.5	6.0
	cover to reinforcement	2.5	2.0	2.0	1.3

459

the thickness of the reinforcement-covering layers must be greater than in traditional building.

The fire resistances of some Polish mass-produced prefabricates are shown in Table 8.3.4.

TABLE 8.3.4

FIRE RESISTANCE OF STANDARD PREFABRICATES USED
IN THE POLISH BUILDING INDUSTRY

Prefabricate		Class of fire resistance
Description	Material	
Multiduct block, normal	Ordinary concrete Mk. 170–250	C
Multiduct block, strengthened (smaller number of ducts)	Ordinary concrete Mk. 200	B
Meter block	Ordinary concrete Mk. 200, reinf. steel $Q_r = 2500$ kg/cm²	C
Door block	Ordinary concrete Mk. 200, reinf. steel $Q_r = 2500$ kg/cm²	C
Multiduct floor panel	Ordinary concrete Mk. 200, reinf. steel $Q_r = 3600$ kg/cm²	C
Tray roof panel, used as simply supported, with side joints filled with cement mortar	Ordinary concrete Mk. 200, welded reinf. $Q_r = 2500$ kg/cm²	C
Tray flight panel	Ordinary concrete Mk. 200, main reinforcement $Q_r = 3600$ kg/cm²	C
Tray landing panel	Ordinary concrete Mk. 170, main reinforcement $Q_r = 3600$ kg/cm²	C

Thin-walled multiduct prefabricates (walls thinner than 4 cm) are characterised by a relatively low fire resistance. Large differences between the temperatures at various points of the cross-section cause the formation of vertical cracks in the internal walls, which considerably lower the load-carrying capacity of the prefabricates.

Filling the ducts with concrete lowers the temperature differences, and ordinary multiduct hollow blocks, when filled with concrete, show a fire resistance better than 2 hours.